Alexander Dyce

The works of William Shakespeare

King John, The Winter's tale and several others

Alexander Dyce

The works of William Shakespeare
King John, The Winter's tale and several others

ISBN/EAN: 9783742846600

Manufactured in Europe, USA, Canada, Australia, Japa

Cover: Foto ©Andreas Hilbeck / pixelio.de

Manufactured and distributed by brebook publishing software (www.brebook.com)

Alexander Dyce

The works of William Shakespeare

COLLECTION
OF
BRITISH AUTHORS.
VOL. XLI.

THE WORKS OF WILLIAM SHAKESPEARE.

IN SEVEN VOLUMES.

VOL. II.

THE WORKS

OF

WILLIAM SHAKESPEARE

FROM THE TEXT OF THE

REV. ALEXANDER DYCE'S

SECOND EDITION.

COMPLETE IN SEVEN VOLUMES:

VOL. II.

LEIPZIG

BERNHARD TAUCHNITZ

1868.

CONTENTS

OF VOLUME II.

	PAGE.
THE TAMING OF THE SHREW	1
ALL'S WELL THAT ENDS WELL	79
TWELFTH-NIGHT; OR, WHAT YOU WILL	163
THE WINTER'S TALE	235
KING JOHN	329
KING RICHARD II.	407

THE TAMING OF THE SHREW.

DRAMATIS PERSONÆ.

A Lord.
CHRISTOPHER SLY, a tinker.
Hostess, Page, Players, Huntsmen, and Servants.
} Persons in the Induction.

BAPTISTA, a gentleman of Padua.
VINCENTIO, a merchant of Pisa.
LUCENTIO, son to Vincentio.
PETRUCHIO, a gentleman of Verona.

GREMIO, HORTENSIO, } suitors to Bianca.
TRANIO, BIONDELLO, } servants to Lucentio.
GRUMIO, CURTIS, &c. } servants to Petruchio.
Pedant.

KATHARINA, BIANCA, } daughters to Baptista.
Widow.

Tailor, Haberdasher, and Servants.

SCENE — *sometimes in Padua, and sometimes in Petruchio's house in the country.*

INDUCTION.

SCENE I. *Before an alehouse on a heath.*

Enter Hostess *and* SLY.

Sly. I'll pheeze you, in faith.

Host. A pair of stocks, you rogue!

Sly. Y'are a baggage: the Slys are no rogues; look in the Chronicles; we came in with Richard Conqueror. Therefore, *paucas pallabris;* let the world slide: sessa!

Host. You will not pay for the glasses you have burst?

Sly. No, not a denier. Go by, Jeronimy, — go to thy cold bed, and warm thee.

Host. I know my remedy; I must go fetch the third-borough. [*Exit.*

Sly. Third, or fourth, or fifth borough, I'll answer him by law: I'll not budge an inch, boy: let him come, and kindly.
[*Lies down on the ground and falls asleep.*

Horns winded. Enter a Lord *from hunting, with* Huntsmen *and* Servants.

Lord. Huntsman, I charge thee, tender well my hounds:
Trash Merriman, — the poor cur is emboss'd;
And couple Clowder with the deep-mouth'd brach.
Saw'st thou not, boy, how Silver made it good
At the hedge-corner, in the coldest fault?
I would not lose the dog for twenty pound.

First Hun. Why, Belman is as good as he, my lord;
He cried upon it at the merest loss,
And twice to-day pick'd out the dullest scent:
Trust me, I take him for the better dog.

Lord. Thou art a fool: if Echo were as fleet,
I would esteem him worth a dozen such.
But sup them well, and look unto them all:
To-morrow I intend to hunt again.

First Hun. I will, my lord.

Lord. What's here? one dead, or drunk? See, doth he breathe?

Sec. Hun. He breathes, my lord. Were he not warm'd with ale,
This were a bed but cold to sleep so soundly.

Lord. O monstrous beast! how like a swine he lies! —
Grim death, how foul and loathsome is thine image! —
Sirs, I will practise on this drunken man.
What think you, if he were convey'd to bed,
Wrapp'd in sweet clothes, rings put upon his fingers,
A most delicious banquet by his bed,
And brave attendants near him when he wakes, —
Would not the beggar then forget himself?

First Hun. Believe me, lord, I think he cannot choose.

Sec. Hun. It would seem strange unto him when he wak'd.

Lord. Even as a flattering dream or worthless fancy.
Then take him up, and manage well the jest:—
Carry him gently to my fairest chamber,
And hang it round with all my wanton pictures:
Balm his foul head in warm distilled waters,
And burn sweet wood to make the lodging sweet:
Procure me music ready, when he wakes,
To make a dulcet and a heavenly sound;
And if he chance to speak, be ready straight,
And, with a low submissive reverence,
Say, "What is it your honour will command?"
Let one attend him with a silver basin
Full of rose-water, and bestrew'd with flowers;
Another bear the ewer, the third a diaper,
And say, "Will't please your lordship cool your hands?"
Some one be ready with a costly suit,
And ask him what apparel he will wear;
Another tell him of his hounds and horse,
And that his lady mourns at his disease:
Persuade him that he hath been lunatic;
And when he says he is —, say that he dreams,
For he is nothing but a mighty lord.
This do, and do it kindly, gentle sirs:
It will be pastime passing excellent,
If it be husbanded with modesty.

First Hun. My lord, I warrant you, we'll play our part,
As he shall think, by our true diligence,
He is no less than what we say he is.

Lord. Take him up gently, and to bed with him;
And each one to his office when he wakes.
                    [*Sly is borne out. A trumpet sounds.*
Sirrah, go see what trumpet 'tis that sounds:—[*Exit Servant.*
Belike, some noble gentleman, that means,
Travelling some journey, to repose him here. —
                  Re-enter Servant.
How now! who is it?

Serv. An it please your honour,
Players that offer service to your lordship.
Lord. Bid them come near.

Enter Players.

Now, fellows, you are welcome.
Players. We thank your honour.
Lord. Do you intend to stay with me to-night?
Sec. Play. So please your lordship to accept our duty.
Lord. With all my heart. — This fellow I remember,
Since once he play'd a farmer's eldest son: —
'Twas where you woo'd the gentlewoman so well:
I have forgot your name; but, sure, that part
Was aptly fit, and naturally perform'd.
First Play. I think 'twas Soto that your honour means.
Lord. 'Tis very true: thou didst it excellent. —
Well, you are come to me in happy time;
The rather for I have some sport in hand,
Wherein your cunning can assist me much.
There is a lord will hear you play to-night:
But I am doubtful of your modesties;
Lest, over-eying of his odd behaviour, —
For yet his honour never heard a play, —
You break into some merry passion,
And so offend him; for, I tell you, sirs,
If you should smile, he grows impatient.
First Play. Fear not, my lord: we can contain ourselves,
Were he the veriest antic in the world.
Lord. Go, sirrah, take them to the buttery,
And give them friendly welcome every one:
Let them want nothing that my house affords.

[*Exeunt Servant and Players.*
Sirrah, go you to Barthol'mew my page, [*To another Servant.*
And see him dress'd in all suits like a lady:
That done, conduct him to the drunkard's chamber;
And call him madam, do him all obeisance.
Tell him from me, — as he will win my love, —

He bear himself with honourable action,
Such as he hath observ'd in noble ladies
Unto their lords by them accomplishèd:
Such duty to the drunkard let him do,
With soft low tongue and lowly courtesy;
And say, "What is't your honour will command,
Wherein your lady and your humble wife
May show her duty and make known her love?"
And then, — with kind embracements, tempting kisses,
And with declining head into his bosom, —
Bid him shed tears, as being overjoy'd
To see her noble lord restor'd to health,
Who for this seven years hath esteemèd him
No better than a poor and loathsome beggar:
And if the boy have not a woman's gift
To rain a shower of commanded tears,
An onion will do well for such a shift;
Which in a napkin being close convey'd,
Shall in despite enforce a watery eye.
See this dispatch'd with all the haste thou canst: —
Anon I'll give thee more instructions. [*Exit Servant.*
I know the boy will well usurp the grace,
Voice, gait, and action of a gentlewoman:
I long to hear him call the drunkard husband;
And how my men will stay themselves from laughter
When they do homage to this simple peasant.
I'll in to counsel them; haply my presence
May well abate the over-merry spleen,
Which otherwise would grow into extremes. [*Exeunt.*

Scene II. *A bedchamber in the Lord's house.*

Sly *is discovered in a rich nightgown, with* Attendants; *some with apparel, others with basin, ewer, and other appurtenances.*
 Enter Lord, *dressed like a servant.*

 Sly. For God's sake, a pot of small ale.
 First Serv. Will't please your lordship drink a cup of sack?

Sec. Serv. Will't please your honour taste of these conserves?

Third Serv. What raiment will your honour wear to-day?

Sly. I am Christophero Sly; call not me honour nor lordship: I ne'er drank sack in my life; and if you give me any conserves, give me conserves of beef: ne'er ask me what raiment I'll wear; for I have no more doublets than backs, no more stockings than legs, nor no more shoes than feet, — nay, sometime more feet than shoes, or such shoes as my toes look through the overleather.

Lord. Heaven cease this idle humour in your honour!
O, that a mighty man, of such descent,
Of such possessions, and so high esteem,
Should be infused with so foul a spirit!

Sly. What, would you make me mad? Am not I Christopher Sly, old Sly's son of Burton-heath; by birth a pedler, by education a card-maker, by transmutation a bear-herd, and now by present profession a tinker? Ask Marian Hacket, the fat ale-wife of Wincot, if she know me not: if she say I am not fourteen pence on the score for sheer ale, score me up for the lyingest knave in Christendom. What! I am not bestraught: here's —

First Serv. O, this it is that makes your lady mourn!

Sec. Serv. O, this it is that makes your servants droop!

Lord. Hence comes it that your kindred shun your house,
As beaten hence by your strange lunacy.
O noble lord, bethink thee of thy birth;
Call home thy ancient thoughts from banishment,
And banish hence these abject lowly dreams.
Look how thy servants do attend on thee,
Each in his office ready at thy beck.
Wilt thou have music? hark! Apollo plays,   [*Music.*
And twenty cagèd nightingales do sing:
Or wilt thou sleep? we'll have thee to a couch
Softer and sweeter than the lustful bed
On purpose trimm'd up for Semiramis.
Say thou wilt walk; we will bestrew the ground:

Or wilt thou ride? thy horses shall be trapp'd,
Their harness studded all with gold and pearl.
Dost thou love hawking? thou hast hawks will soar
Above the morning lark: or wilt thou hunt?
Thy hounds shall make the welkin answer them,
And fetch shrill echoes from the hollow earth.
  First Serv. Say thou wilt course; thy greyhounds are as
                    swift
As breathèd stags, ay, fleeter than the roe.
  Sec. Serv. Dost thou love pictures? we will fetch thee
                    straight
Adonis painted by a running brook,
And Cytherea all in sedges hid,
Which seem to move and wanton with her breath,
Even as the waving sedges play with wind.
  Lord. We'll show thee Io as she was a maid,
And how she was beguilèd and surpris'd,
As lively painted as the deed was done.
  Third Serv. Or Daphne roaming through a thorny wood,
Scratching her legs, that one shall swear she bleeds;
And at that sight shall sad Apollo weep,
So workmanly the blood and tears are drawn.
  Lord. Thou art a lord, and nothing but a lord:
Thou hast a lady far more beautiful
Than any woman in this waning age.
  First Serv. And, till the tears that she hath shed for thee,
Like envious floods, o'er-run her lovely face,
She was the fairest creature in the world;
And yet she is inferior to none.
  Sly. Am I a lord? and have I such a lady?
Or do I dream? or have I dream'd till now?
I do not sleep: I see, I hear, I speak;
I smell sweet savours, and I feel soft things:
Upon my life, I am a lord indeed;
And not a tinker, nor Christophero Sly. —
Well, bring our lady hither to our sight;
And once again, a pot o' the smallest ale.

Sec. Serv. Will't please your mightiness to wash your
            hands? [*Servants present a ewer, basin, and napkin.*
O, how we joy to see your wits restor'd!
O, that once more you knew but what you are!
These fifteen years you have been in a dream;
Or when you wak'd, so wak'd as if you slept.

Sly. These fifteen years! by my fay, a goodly nap.
But did I never speak of all that time?

First Serv. O, yes, my lord; but very idle words:
For though you lay here in this goodly chamber,
Yet would you say, ye were beaten out of door;
And rail upon the hostess of the house;
And say, you would present her at the leet,
Because she brought stone jugs and no seal'd quarts:
Sometimes you would call out for Cicely Hacket.

Sly. Ay, the woman's maid of the house.

Third Serv. Why, sir, you know no house, nor no such
            maid;
Nor no such men as you have reckon'd up, —
As Stephen Sly, and old John Naps of Greece,
And Peter Turf, and Henry Pimpernell;
And twenty more such names and men as these,
Which never were, nor no man ever saw.

Sly. Now, Lord be thankèd for my good amends!
All. Amen.
Sly. I thank thee: thou shalt not lose by it.

Enter the Page *as a lady, with* Attendants.

Page. How fares my noble lord?

Sly. Marry, I fare well; for here is cheer enough.
Where is my wife?

Page. Here, noble lord: what is thy will with her?

Sly. Are you my wife, and will not call me husband?
My men should call me lord: I am your goodman.

Page. My husband and my lord, my lord and husband;
I am your wife in all obedience.

Sly. I know it well. — What must I call her?

Lord. Madam.
Sly. Al'ce madam, or Joan madam?
Lord. Madam, and nothing else: so lords call ladies.
Sly. Madam wife, they say that I have dream'd,
And slept about some fifteen year or more.
Page. Ay, and the time seems thirty unto me,
Being all this time abandon'd from your bed.
Sly. 'Tis much. — Servants, leave me and her alone. —
Madam, undress you, and come now to bed.
Page. Thrice-noble lord, let me entreat of you
To pardon me yet for a night or two;
Or, if not so, until the sun be set:
For your physicians have expressly charg'd,
In peril t' incur your former malady,
That I should yet absent me from your bed:
I hope this reason stands for my excuse.
Sly. Ay, it stands so, that I may hardly tarry so long.
But I would be loth to fall into my dreams again: I will therefore tarry, in despite of the flesh and the blood.

Enter a Servant.

Serv. Your honour's players, hearing your amendment,
Are come to play a pleasant comedy;
For so your doctors hold it very meet,
Seeing too much sadness hath congeal'd your blood,
And melancholy is the nurse of frenzy:
Therefore they thought it good you hear a play,
And frame your mind to mirth and merriment,
Which bars a thousand harms and lengthens life.
Sly. Marry, I will; let them play it. Is not a commonty a Christmas gambol or a tumbling-trick?
Page. No, my good lord; it is more pleasing stuff.
Sly. What, household stuff?
Page. It is a kind of history.
Sly. Well, we'll see't. —
Come, madam wife, sit by my side,
And let the world slip: we shall ne'er be younger. [*They sit down.*

ACT I.

SCENE I. *Padua. A public place.*

Enter LUCENTIO *and* TRANIO.

Luc. Tranio, since, for the great desire I had
To see fair Padua, nursery of arts,
I am arriv'd in fruitful Lombardy,
The pleasant garden of great Italy;
And, by my father's love and leave, am arm'd
With his good will, and thy good company,
My trusty servant, well approv'd in all;
Here let us breathe, and haply institute
A course of learning and ingenious studies.
Pisa, renowned for grave citizens,
Gave me my being, and my father first,
A merchant of great traffic through the world,
Vincentio, come of the Bentivolii.
Lucentio his son, brought up in Florence,
It shall become, to serve all hopes conceiv'd,
To deck his fortune with his virtuous deeds:
And therefore, Tranio, for the time I study,
Virtue, and that part of philosophy
Will I apply, that treats of happiness
By virtue specially to be achiev'd.
Tell me thy mind; for I have Pisa left,
And am to Padua come, as he that leaves
A shallow plash, to plunge him in the deep,
And with satiety seeks to quench his thirst.

Tra. Mi perdonate, gentle master mine,
I am in all affected as yourself;
Glad that you thus continue your resolve
To suck the sweets of sweet philosophy.
Only, good master, while we do admire
This virtue and this moral discipline,
Let's be no stoics nor no stocks, I pray;
Or so devote to Aristotle's ethics,
As Ovid be an outcast quite abjur'd:

Balk logic with acquaintance that you have,
And practise rhetoric in your common talk;
Music and poesy use to quicken you;
The mathematics and the metaphysics,
Fall to them, as you find your stomach serves you;
No profit grows, where is no pleasure ta'en:
In brief, sir, study what you most affect.

    Luc. Gramercies, Tranio, well dost thou advise.
If Biondello now were come ashore,
We could at once put us in readiness;
And take a lodging, fit to entertain
Such friends as time in Padua shall beget.
But stay awhile: what company is this?

    Tra. Master, some show, to welcome us to town.

Enter BAPTISTA, KATHARINA, BIANCA, GREMIO, *and* HORTENSIO.
    LUCENTIO *and* TRANIO *stand aside.*

    Bap. Gentlemen, impórtune me no further,
For how I firmly am resolv'd you know;
That is, not to bestow my youngest daughter
Before I have a husband for the elder:
If either of you both love Katharina,
Because I know you well, and love you well,
Leave shall you have to court her at your pleasure.

    Gre. To cart her rather: she's too rough for me. —
There, there, Hortensio, will you any wife?

    Kath. [*to Bap.*] I pray you, sir, is it your will
To make a stale of me amongst these mates?

    Hor. Mates, maid! how mean you that? no mates for you,
Unless you were of gentler, milder mood.

    Kath. I' faith, sir, you shall never need to fear:
I wis it is not half way to her heart;
But if it were, doubt not her care should be
To comb your noddle with a three-legg'd stool,
And paint your face, and use you like a fool.

    Hor. From all such devils, good Lord, deliver us!
    Gre. And me too, good Lord!

Tra. [*aside to Luc.*] Hush, master! here is some good
                                        pastime toward:
That wench is stark mad, or wonderful froward.
    Luc. [*aside to Tra.*] But in the other's silence do I see
Maid's mild behaviour and sobriety.
Peace, Tranio!
    Tra. [*aside to Luc.*] Well said, master; mum! and gaze
                                        your fill.
    Bap. Gentlemen, that I may soon make good
What I have said, — Bianca, get you in:
And let it not displease thee, good Bianca;
For I will love thee ne'er the less, my girl.
    Kath. A pretty peat! it is best —
Put finger in the eye,
An she knew why.
    Bian. Sister, content you in my discontent. —
Sir, to your pleasure humbly I subscribe:
My books and instruments shall be my company,
On them to look, and practise by myself.
    Luc. [*aside to Tra.*] Hark, Tranio! thou mayst hear Mi-
                                        nerva speak.
    Hor. Signior Baptista, will you be so strange?
Sorry am I that our good will effects
Bianca's grief.
    Gre.   Why, will you mew her up,
Signior Baptista, for this fiend of hell,
And make her bear the penance of her tongue?
    Bap. Gentlemen, content ye; I am resolv'd: —
Go in, Bianca: [*Exit Bianca.*
And for I know she taketh most delight
In music, instruments, and poetry,
Schoolmasters will I keep within my house,
Fit to instruct her youth. — If you, Hortensio, —
Or Signior Gremio, you, — know any such,
Prefer them hither; for to cunning men
I will be very kind, and liberal
To mine own children in good bringing-up:

And so, farewell. — Katharina, you may stay;
For I have more to commune with Bianca. [*Exit.*

Kath. Why, and I trust I may go too, may I not?
What, shall I be appointed hours; as though, belike,
I knew not what to take, and what to leave, ha? [*Exit.*

Gre. You may go to the devil's dam: your gifts are so good, here's none will hold you. — Our love is not so great, Hortensio, but we may blow our nails together, and fast it fairly out: our cake's dough on both sides. Farewell: — yet, for the love I bear my sweet Bianca, if I can by any means light on a fit man to teach her that wherein she delights, I will wish him to her father.

Hor. So will I, Signior Gremio: but a word, I pray. Though the nature of our quarrel yet never brooked parle, know now, upon advice, it toucheth us both, — that we may yet again have access to our fair mistress, and be happy rivals in Bianca's love, — to labour and effect one thing specially.

Gre. What's that, I pray?

Hor. Marry, sir, to get a husband for her sister.

Gre. A husband! a devil.

Hor. I say, a husband.

Gre. I say, a devil. Thinkest thou, Hortensio, though her father be very rich, any man is so very a fool to be married to hell?

Hor. Tush, Gremio, though it pass your patience and mine to endure her loud alarums, why, man, there be good fellows in the world, an a man could light on them, would take her with all faults and money enough.

Gre. I cannot tell; but I had as lief take her dowry with this condition, — to be whipped at the high-cross every morning.

Hor. Faith, as you say, there's small choice in rotten apples. But, come; since this bar in law makes us friends, it shall be so far forth friendly maintained, till by helping Baptista's eldest daughter to a husband, we set his youngest free for a husband, and then have to't afresh. — Sweet Bianca!

—Happy man be his dole! He that runs fastest gets the ring. How say you, Signior Gremio?

Gre. I am agreed: and would I had given him the best horse in Padua to begin his wooing, that would thoroughly woo her, wed her, and bed her, and rid the house of her! Come on. [*Exeunt Gremio and Hortensio.*

Tra. I pray, sir, tell me, — is it possible
That love should of a sudden take such hold?

Luc. O Tranio, till I found it to be true,
I never thought it possible or likely;
But, see! while idly I stood looking on,
I found th' effect of love in idleness:
And now in plainness do confess to thee, —
That art to me as secret and as dear
As Anna to the Queen of Carthage was, —
Tranio, I burn, I pine; I perish, Tranio,
If I achieve not this young modest girl.
Counsel me, Tranio, for I know thou canst;
Assist me, Tranio, for I know thou wilt.

Tra. Master, it is no time to chide you now;
Affection is not rated from the heart:
If love have touch'd you, naught remains but so, —
Redime te captum quam queas minimo.

Luc. Gramercies, lad; go forward; this contents:
The rest will comfort, for thy counsel's sound.

Tra. Master, you look'd so longly on the maid,
Perhaps you mark'd not what's the pith of all.

Luc. O, yes, I saw sweet beauty in her face,
Such as the daughter of Agenor had,
That made great Jove to humble him to her hand,
When with his knees he kiss'd the Cretan strand.

Tra. Saw you no more? mark'd you not how her sister
Began to scold, and raise up such a storm,
That mortal ears might hardly endure the din?

Luc. Tranio, I saw her coral lips to move,
And with her breath she did perfume the air:
Sacred and sweet was all I saw in her.

Tra. Nay, then, 'tis time to stir him from his trance. —
I pray, awake, sir: if you love the maid,
Bend thoughts and wits t' achieve her. Thus it stands: —
Her elder sister is so curst and shrewd,
That, till the father rid his hands of her,
Master, your love must live a maid at home
And therefore has he closely mew'd her up,
Because he will not be annoy'd with suitors.
   Luc. Ah, Tranio, what a cruel father's he!
But art thou not advis'd, he took some care
To get her cunning schoolmasters t' instruct her?
   Tra. Ay, marry, am I, sir; and now 'tis plotted.
   Luc. I have it, Tranio.
   Tra.   Master, for my hand,
Both our inventions meet and jump in one.
   Luc. Tell me thine first.
   Tra.   You will be schoolmaster,
And undertake the teaching of the maid:
That's your device.
   Luc.   It is: may it be done?
   Tra. Not possible; for who shall bear your part,
And be in Padua here Vincentio's son;
Keep house, and ply his book; welcome his friends;
Visit his countrymen, and banquet them?
   Luc. Basta; content thee; for I have it full.
We have not yet been seen in any house;
Nor can we be distinguish'd by our faces
For man or master: then it follows thus; —
Thou shalt be master, Tranio, in my stead,
Keep house, and port, and servants, as I should:
I will some other be; some Florentine,
Some Neapolitan, or mean man of Pisa.
'Tis hatch'd, and shall be so: — Tranio, at once
Uncase thee; take my colour'd hat and cloak:
When Biondello comes, he waits on thee;
But I will charm him first to keep his tongue.
   Tra. So had you need.   [*They exchange habits.*

In brief, sir, sithence it your pleasure is,
And I am tied to be obedient, —
For so your father charg'd me at our parting;
"Be serviceable to my son," quoth he,
Although I think 'twas in another sense, —
I am content to be Lucentio,
Because so well I love Lucentio.

   Luc. Tranio, be so, because Lucentio loves:
And let me be a slave, t' achieve that maid
Whose sudden sight hath thrall'd my wounded eye. —
Here comes the rogue.

               Enter BIONDELLO.

                    Sirrah, where have you been?
   Bion. Where have I been! Nay, how now! where are you?
Master, has my fellow Tranio stol'n your clothes?
Or you stol'n his? or both? pray, what's the news?

   Luc. Sirrah, come hither: 'tis no time to jest,
And therefore frame your manners to the time.
Your fellow Tranio here, to save my life,
'Puts my apparel and my countenance on,
And I for my escape have put on his;
For in a quarrel, since I came ashore,
I kill'd a man, and fear I was descried:
Wait you on him, I charge you, as becomes,
While I make way from hence to save my life:
You understand me?

   Bion.   Ay, sir. — [*Aside*] Ne'er a whit.
   Luc. And not a jot of Tranio in your mouth:
Tranio is chang'd into Lucentio.

   Bion. The better for him: would I were so too!

   Tra. So would I, faith, boy, to have the next wish after,
That Lucentio indeed had Baptista's youngest daughter.
But, sirrah, — not for my sake, but your master's, — I advise
You use your manners discreetly in all kind of companies:
When I am alone, why, then I am Tranio;
But in all places else, your master Lucentio.

[Scene II.] THE TAMING OF THE SHREW.

Luc. Tranio, let's go: —
One thing more rests, that thyself execute, —
To make one among these wooers: if thou ask me why, —
Sufficeth, my reasons are both good and weighty. [*Exeunt.*

First Serv. My lord, you nod; you do not mind the play.
Sly. Yes, by Saint Anne, do I. A good matter, surely: comes there any more of it?
Page. My lord, 'tis but begun.
Sly. 'Tis a very excellent piece of work, madam lady: would 'twere done!

SCENE II. *The same. Before* HORTENSIO'S *house.*
Enter PETRUCHIO *and* GRUMIO.

Pet. Verona for awhile I take my leave,
To see my friends in Padua; but, of all,
My best belovèd and approvèd friend,
Hortensio; and I trow this is his house. —
Here, sirrah Grumio; knock, I say.
Gru. Knock, sir! whom should I knock? is there any man has rebused your worship?
Pet. Villain, I say, knock me here soundly.
Gru. Knock you here, sir! why, sir, what am I, sir, that I should knock you here, sir?
Pet. Villain, I say, knock me at this gate,
And rap me well, or I'll knock your knave's pate.
Gru. My master is grown quarrelsome. — I should knock you first,
And then I know after who comes by the worst.
Pet. Will it not be?
Faith, sirrah, an you'll not knock, I'll wring it;
I'll try how you can *sol, fa,* and sing it.
[*Wrings Grumio by the ears; who falls.*
Gru. Help, masters, help! my master is mad.
Pet. Now, knock when I bid you, sirrah villain!
Enter HORTENSIO.
Hor. How now! what's the matter?—My old friend Grumio! and my good friend Petruchio! — How do you all at Verona?

Pet. Signior Hortensio, come you to part the fray?
Con tutto il core bene trovato, may I say.
  Hor. Alla nostra casa bene venuto, molto honorato signor mio Petruchio. —
Rise, Grumio, rise: we will compound this quarrel.
  Gru. [*rising*] Nay, 'tis no matter, sir, what he 'leges in Latin. — If this be not a lawful cause for me to leave his service, — look you, sir, — he bid me knock him and rap him soundly, sir: well, was it fit for a servant to use his master so; being perhaps, for aught I see, two-and-thirty, — a pip out? Whom would to God I had well knock'd at first,
Then had not Grumio come by the worst.
  Pet. A senseless villain! — Good Hortensio,
I bade the rascal knock upon your gate,
And could not get him for my heart to do it.
  Gru. Knock at the gate! — O heavens! Spake you not these words plain, — "Sirrah, knock me here, rap me here, knock me well, and knock me soundly"? And come you now with — knocking at the gate?
  Pet. Sirrah, be gone, or talk not, I advise you.
  Hor. Petruchio, patience; I am Grumio's pledge:
Why, this' a heavy chance 'twixt him and you,
Your ancient, trusty, pleasant servant Grumio.
And tell me now, sweet friend, what happy gale
Blows you to Padua here, from old Verona?
  Pet. Such wind as scatters young men through the world,
To seek their fortunes further than at home,
Where small experience grows. But, in a few,
Signior Hortensio, thus it stands with me: —
Antonio, my father, is deceas'd;
And I have thrust myself into this maze,
Haply to wive and thrive as best I may:
Crowns in my purse I have, and goods at home,
And so am come abroad to see the world.
  Hor. Petruchio, shall I, then, come roundly to thee,
And wish thee to a shrewd ill-favour'd wife?
Thou'dst thank me but a little for my counsel:

And yet I'll promise thee she shall be rich,
And very rich: — but thou'rt too much my friend,
And I'll not wish thee to her.

Pet. Signior Hortensio, 'twixt such friends as we
Few words suffice; and therefore, if thou know
One rich enough to be Petruchio's wife, —
As wealth is burden of my wooing dance, —
Be she as foul as was Florentius' love,
As old as Sibyl, and as curst and shrewd
As Socrates' Xantippe, or a worse,
She moves me not, or not removes, at least,
Affection's edge in me, — were she as rough
As are the swelling Adriatic seas:
I come to wive it wealthily in Padua;
If wealthily, then happily in Padua.

Gru. Nay, look you, sir, he tells you flatly what his mind
is: why, give him gold enough and marry him to a puppet or
an aglet-baby; or an old trot with ne'er a tooth in her head,
though she have as many diseases as two and fifty horses:
why, nothing comes amiss, so money comes withal.

Hor. Petruchio, since we are stepp'd thus far in,
I will continue that I broach'd in jest.
I can, Petruchio, help thee to a wife
With wealth enough, and young and beauteous;
Brought up as best becomes a gentlewoman:
Her only fault — and that is faults enough —
Is, that she is intolerable curst,
And shrewd, and froward; so beyond all measure,
That, were my state far worser than it is,
I would not wed her for a mine of gold.

Pet. Hortensio, peace! thou know'st not gold's effect: —
Tell me her father's name, and 'tis enough;
For I will board her, though she chide as loud
As thunder, when the clouds in autumn crack.

Hor. Her father is Baptista Minola,
An affable and courteous gentleman:

Her name is Katharina Minola,
Renown'd in Padua for her scolding tongue.

Pet. I know her father, though I know not her;
And he knew my deceasèd father well.
I will not sleep, Hortensio, till I see her;
And therefore let me be thus bold with you,
To give you over at this first encounter,
Unless you will accompany me thither.

Gru. I pray you, sir, let him go while the humour lasts. O' my word, an she knew him as well as I do, she would think scolding would do little good upon him: she may, perhaps, call him half a score knaves, or so: why, that's nothing; an he begin once, he'll rail in his rope-tricks. I'll tell you what, sir,—an she stand him but a little, he will throw a figure in her face, and so disfigure her with it, that she shall have no more eyes to see withal than a cat. You know him not, sir.

Hor. Tarry, Petruchio, I must go with thee;
For in Baptista's keep my treasure is:
He hath the jewel of my life in hold,
His youngest daughter, beautiful Bianca;
And her withholds from me, and other more,
Suitors to her and rivals in my love;
Supposing it a thing impossible,—
For those defects I have before rehears'd,—
That ever Katharina will be woo'd;
Therefore this order hath Baptista ta'en,
That none shall have access unto Bianca
Till Katharine the curst have got a husband.

Gru. Katharine the curst!
A title for a maid, of all titles the worst.

Hor. Now shall my friend Petruchio do me grace;
And offer me, disguis'd in sober robes,
To old Baptista as a schoolmaster
Well seen in music, to instruct Bianca;
That so I may, by this device, at least
Have leave and leisure to make love to her,
And unsuspected court her by herself.

That gives not half so great a blow to th' ear
As will a chestnut in a farmer's fire?
Tush, tush! fear boys with bugs.
    Gru. [*aside*]   For he fears none.
    Gre. Hortensio, hark:
This gentleman is happily arriv'd,
My mind presumes, for his own good and ours.
    Hor. I promis'd we would be contributors,
And bear his charge of wooing, whatsoe'er.
    Gre. And so we will, — provided that he win her.
    Gru. [*aside*] I would I were as sure of a good dinner.

    Enter TRANIO *bravely apparelled, and* BIONDELLO.

    Tra. Gentlemen, God save you! If I may be bold,
Tell me, I beseech you, which is the readiest way
To the house of Signior Baptista Minola?
    Gre. He that has the two fair daughters, — is't he you
        mean?
    Tra. Even he. — Biondello, —
    Gre. Hark you, sir; you mean not her to —
    Tra. Perhaps, him and her, sir: what have you to do?
    Pet. Not her that chides, sir, at any hand, I pray.
    Tra. I love no chiders, sir. — Biondello, let's away.
    Luc. [*aside*] Well begun, Tranio.
    Hor. Sir, a word ere you go; —
Are you a suitor to the maid you talk of, yea or no?
    Tra. An if I be, sir, is it any offence?
    Gre. No; if without more words you will get you hence.
    Tra. Why, sir, I pray, are not the streets as free
For me as for you?
    Gre.   But so is not she.
    Tra. For what reason, I beseech you?
    Gre. For this reason, if you'll know, —
That she's the choice love of Signior Gremio.
    Hor. That she's the chosen of Signior Hortensio.
    Tra. Softly, my masters! if you be gentlemen,
Do me this right, — hear me with patience.

Baptista is a noble gentleman,
To whom my father is not all unknown;
And, were his daughter fairer than she is,
She may more suitors have, and me for one.
Fair Leda's daughter had a thousand wooers;
Then well one more may fair Bianca have:
And so she shall; Lucentio shall make one,
Though Paris came in hope to speed alone.
    Gre. What, what, this gentleman will out-talk us all!
    Luc. Sir, give him head: I know he'll prove a jade.
    Pet. Hortensio, to what end are all these words?
    Hor. Sir, let me be so bold as ask you this,
Did you yet ever see Baptista's daughter?
    Tra. No, sir; but hear I do that he hath two;
The one as famous for a scolding tongue,
As is the other for beauteous modesty.
    Pet. Sir, sir, the first's for me; let her go by.
    Gre. Yea, leave that labour to great Hercules;
And let it be more than Alcides' twelve.
    Pet. Sir, understand you this of me, in sooth:
The youngest daughter, whom you hearken for,
Her father keeps from all access of suitors;
And will not promise her to any man
Until the elder sister first be wed:
The younger then is free, and not before.
    Tra. If it be so, sir, that you are the man
Must stead us all, and me amongst the rest;
And if you break the ice, and do this feat,
Achieve the elder, set the younger free
For our access, — whose hap shall be to have her
Will not so graceless be to be ingrate.
    Hor. Sir, you say well, and well you do conceive;
And since you do profess to be a suitor,
You must, as we do, gratify this gentleman,
To whom we all rest generally beholding.
    Tra. Sir, I shall not be slack: in sign whereof,
Please ye we may contrive this afternoon,

And quaff carouses to our mistress' health;
And do as adversaries do in law, —
Strive mightily, but eat and drink as friends.
    Gru., Bion. O excellent motion! Fellows, let's be gone.
    Hor. The motion's good indeed, and be it so: —
Petruchio, I shall be your *ben venuto*.   [*Exeunt.*

ACT II.

SCENE I. *Padua. A room in* BAPTISTA's *house.*

Enter KATHARINA, *and* BIANCA *with her hands bound.*

    Bian. Good sister, wrong me not, nor wrong yourself,
To make a bondmaid and a slave of me;
That I disdain: but for these other gauds,
Unbind my hands, I'll pull them off myself,
Yea, all my raiment, to my petticoat;
Or, what you will command me, will I do,
So well I know my duty to my elders.
    Kath. Of all thy suitors, here I charge thee, tell
Whom thou lov'st best: see thou dissemble not.
    Bian. Believe me, sister, of all men alive,
I never yet beheld that special face
Which I could fancy more than any other.
    Kath. Minion, thou liest: is't not Hortensio?
    Bian. If you affect him, sister, here I swear
I'll plead for you myself, but you shall have him.
    Kath. O, then, belike you fancy riches more:
You will have Gremio to keep you fair.
    Bian. Is it for him you do envy me so?
Nay, then, you jest; and now I well perceive
You have but jested with me all this while:
I prithee, sister Kate, untie my hands.
    Kath. If that be jest, then all the rest was so [*Strikes her.*

Enter BAPTISTA.

    Bap. Why, how now, dame! whence grows this inso-
        lence? —

Bianca, stand aside: — poor girl! she weeps. —
Go ply thy needle; meddle not with her. —
For shame, thou hilding of a devilish spirit,
Why dost thou wrong her that did ne'er wrong thee?
When did she cross thee with a bitter word?
 Kath. Her silence flouts me, and I'll be reveng'd.
            [*Flies after Bianca.*
 Bap. [*holding her back*] What, in my sight? — Bianca,
  get thee in.   [*Exit Bianca.*
 Kath. Will you not suffer me? Nay, now I see
She is your treasure, she must have a husband;
I must dance barefoot on her wedding-day,
And, for your love to her, lead apes in hell.
Talk not to me: I will go sit and weep,
Till I can find occasion of revenge.   [*Exit.*
 Bap. Was ever gentleman thus griev'd as I?
But who comes here?

Enter GREMIO, *with* LUCENTIO, *in the habit of a mean man;* PETRUCHIO, *with* HORTENSIO *as a musician; and* TRANIO, *with* BIONDELLO *bearing a lute and books.*

 Gre. Good morrow, neighbour Baptista.
 Bap. Good morrow, neighbour Gremio. — God save you, gentlemen!
 Pet. And you, good sir! Pray, have you not a daughter Call'd Katharina, fair and virtuous?
 Bap. I have a daughter, sir, call'd Katharina.
 Gre. You are too blunt: go to it orderly.
 Pet. You wrong me, Signior Gremio: give me leave. —
I am a gentleman of Verona, sir,
That, — hearing of her beauty and her wit,
Her affability and bashful modesty,
Her wondrous qualities and mild behaviour, —
Am bold to show myself a forward guest
Within your house, to make mine eye the witness
Of that report which I so oft have heard.
And, for an entrance to my entertainment,

I do present you with a man of mine, [*Presenting Hortensio.*
Cunning in music and the mathematics,
T' instruct her fully in those sciences,
Whereof I know she is not ignorant:
Accept of him, or else you do me wrong:
His name is Licio, born in Mantua.

 Bap. You're welcome, sir; and he, for your good sake.
But for my daughter Katharine, — this I know,
She is not for your turn, the more my grief.

 Pet. I see you do not mean to part with her;
Or else you like not of my company.

 Bap. Mistake me not; I speak but as I find.
Whence are you, sir? what may I call your name?

 Pet. Petruchio is my name; Antonio's son,
A man well known throughout all Italy.

 Bap. I knew him well: you're welcome for his sake.

 Gre. Saving your tale, Petruchio, I pray,
Let us, that are poor petitioners, speak too:
Baccare! you are marvellous forward.

 Pet. O, pardon me, Signior Gremio; I would fain be
   doing.

 Gre. I doubt it not, sir; but you will curse your wooing.
— Neighbour, this is a gift very grateful, I am sure of it. To
express the like kindness myself, that have been more kindly
beholding to you than any, I freely give unto you this young
scholar [*presenting Lucentio*], that hath been long studying at
Rheims; as cunning in Greek, Latin, and other languages,
as the other in music and mathematics: his name is Cambio;
pray, accept his service.

 Bap. A thousand thanks, Signior Gremio. — Welcome,
good Cambio. — But, gentle sir [*to Tranio*], methinks you
walk like a stranger: may I be so bold to know the cause of
your coming?

 Tra. Pardon me, sir, the boldness is mine own;
That, being a stranger in this city here,
Do make myself a suitor to your daughter,
Unto Bianca, fair and virtuous.

Nor is your firm resolve unknown to me,
In the preferment of the eldest sister.
This liberty is all that I request, —
That, upon knowledge of my parentage,
I may have welcome 'mongst the rest that woo,
And free access and favour as the rest:
And, toward the education of your daughters,
I here bestow a simple instrument,
And this small packet of Greek and Latin books:
If you accept them, then their worth is great.

   Bap. Lucentio is your name — of whence, I pray?
   Tra. Of Pisa, sir; son to Vincentio.
   Bap. A mighty man of Pisa; by report
I know him well: you're very welcome, sir. —
Take you [*to Hor.*] the lute, and you [*to Luc.*] the set of books;
You shall go see your pupils presently. —
Holla, within!

Enter a Servant.

   Sirrah, lead these gentlemen
To my two daughters; and tell them both,
These are their tutors: bid them use them well.

   [*Exit Servant, with Hortensio, Lucentio, and Biondello.*
We will go walk a little in the orchard,
And then to dinner. You are passing welcome,
And so I pray you all to think yourselves.
   Pet. Signior Baptista, my business asketh haste,
And every day I cannot come to woo.
You knew my father well; and in him, me,
Left solely heir to all his lands and goods,
Which I have better'd rather than decreas'd:
Then tell me, — if I get your daughter's love,
What dowry shall I have with her to wife?
   Bap. After my death, the one half of my lands;
And, in possession, twenty thousand crowns.
   Pet. And, for that dowry, I'll assure her of
Her widowhood, — be it that she survive me, —
In all my lands and leases whatsoever:

Let specialties be therefore drawn between us,
That covenants may be kept on either hand.

Bap. Ay, when the special thing is well obtain'd,
That is, her love; for that is all in all.

Pet. Why, that is nothing; for I tell you, father,
I am as peremptory as she proud-minded;
And where two raging fires meet together,
They do consume the thing that feeds their fury:
Though little fire grows great with little wind,
Yet extreme gusts will blow out fire and all:
So I to her, and so she yields to me;
For I am rough, and woo not like a babe.

Bap. Well mayst thou woo, and happy be thy speed!
But be thou arm'd for some unhappy words.

Pet. Ay, to the proof; as mountains are for winds,
That shake not, though they blow perpetually.

Re-enter HORTENSIO, *with his head broken.*

Bap. How now, my friend! why dost thou look so pale?
Hor. For fear, I promise you, if I look pale.
Bap. What, will my daughter prove a good musician?
Hor. I think she'll sooner prove a soldier:
Iron may hold with her, but never lutes.

Bap. Why, then thou canst not break her to the lute?
Hor. Why, no; for she hath broke the lute to me.
I did but tell her she mistook her frets,
And bow'd her hand to teach her fingering;
When, with a most impatient devilish spirit,
"Frets call you these?" quoth she; "I'll fume with them:"
And, with that word, she struck me on the head,
And through the instrument my pate made way;
And there I stood amazèd for a while,
As on a pillory, looking through the lute;
While she did call me rascal fiddler
And twangling Jack, with twenty such vile terms,
As she had studied to misuse me so.

Pet. Now, by the world, it is a lusty wench;

I love her ten times more than e'er I did:
O, how I long to have some chat with her!

 Bap. Well, go with me, and be not so discomfited:
Proceed in practice with my younger daughter;
She's apt to learn, and thankful for good turns. —
Signior Petruchio, will you go with us,
Or shall I send my daughter Kate to you?

 Pet. I pray you do; I will attend her here, —
    [*Exeunt Baptista, Gremio, Tranio, and Hortensio.*
And woo her with some spirit when she comes.
Say that she rail; why, then, I'll tell her plain,
She sings as sweetly as a nightingale:
Say that she frown; I'll say, she looks as clear
As morning roses newly wash'd with dew:
Say she be mute and will not speak a word;
Then I'll commend her volubility,
And say she uttereth piercing eloquence:
If she do bid me pack, I'll give her thanks,
As though she bid me stay by her a week:
If she deny to wed, I'll crave the day
When I shall ask the banns, and when be married. —
But here she comes; and now, Petruchio, speak.

    Enter KATHARINA.

Good morrow, Kate; for that's your name, I hear.

 Kath. Well have you heard, but something hard of hearing:
They call me Katharine that do talk of me.

 Pet. You lie, in faith; for you are call'd plain Kate,
And bonny Kate, and sometimes Kate the curst;
But, Kate, the prettiest Kate in Christendom,
Kate of Kate-Hall, my super-dainty Kate,
For dainties are all cates, — and therefore, Kate,
Take this of me, Kate of my consolation; —
Hearing thy mildness prais'd in every town,
Thy virtues spoke of, and thy beauty sounded,
Yet not so deeply as to thee belongs, —
Myself am mov'd to woo thee for my wife.

Kath. Mov'd! in good time: let him that mov'd you hither
Remove you hence: I knew you at the first,
You were a moveable.
 Pet.   Why, what's a moveable?
 Kath. A joint-stool.
 Pet.   Thou hast hit it: come, sit on me.
 Kath. Asses are made to bear, and so are you.
 Pet. Women are made to bear, and so are you.
 Kath. No such jade as bear you, if me you mean.
 Pet. Alas, good Kate, I will not burden thee!
For, knowing thee to be but young and light —
 Kath. Too light for such a swain as you to catch;
And yet as heavy as my weight should be.
 Pet. Should be! should buzz.
 Kath.   Well ta'en, and like a buzzard.
 Pet. O slow-wing'd turtle! shall a buzzard take thee?
 Kath. Ay, for a turtle, — as he takes a buzzard.
 Pet. Come, come, you wasp; i' faith, you are too angry.
 Kath. If I be waspish, best beware my sting.
 Pet. My remedy is then, to pluck it out.
 Kath. Ay, if the fool could find out where it lies.
 Pet. Who knows not where a wasp does wear his sting?
In his tail.
 Kath. In his tongue.
 Pet.   Whose tongue?
 Kath. Yours, if you talk of tails: and so farewell.
 Pet. What, with my tongue in your tail? nay, come again,
Good Kate; I am a gentleman. [*Detaining her.*
 Kath.   That I'll try. [*Striking him.*
 Pet. I swear I'll cuff you, if you strike again.
 Kath. So may you lose your arms:
If you strike me, you are no gentleman;
And if no gentleman, why, then no arms.
 Pet. A herald, Kate? O, put me in thy books!
 Kath. What is your crest? a coxcomb?
 Pet. A combless cock, so Kate will be my hen.
 Kath. No cock of mine; you crow too like a craven.

Pet. Nay, come, Kate, come; you must not look so sour.
Kath. It is my fashion when I see a crab.
Pet. Why, here's no crab; and therefore look not sour.
Kath. There is, there is.
Pet. Then show it me.
Kath.   Had I a glass, I would.
Pet. What, you mean my face?
Kath.   Well aim'd of such a young one.
Pet. Now, by Saint George, I am too young for you.
Kath. Yet you are wither'd.
Pet.   "Tis with cares.
Kath.   I care not.
Pet. Nay, hear you, Kate: in sooth, you scape not so.
Kath. I chafe you, if I tarry: let me go.
Pet. No, not a whit: I find you passing gentle.
'Twas told me you were rough, and coy, and sullen,
And now I find report a very liar;
For thou art pleasant, gamesome, passing courteous;
But slow in speech, yet sweet as spring-time flowers:
Thou canst not frown, thou canst not look askance,
Nor bite the lip, as angry wenches will;
Nor hast thou pleasure to be cross in talk;
But thou with mildness entertain'st thy wooers,
With gentle conference, soft and affable.
Why does the world report that Kate doth limp?
O slanderous world! Kate, like the hazel-twig,
Is straight and slender; and as brown in hue
As hazel-nuts, and sweeter than the kernels.
O, let me see thee walk: thou dost not halt.
Kath. Go, fool, and whom thou keep'st command.
Pet. Did ever Dian so become a grove,
As Kate this chamber with her princely gait?
O, be thou Dian, and let her be Kate;
And then let Kate be chaste, and Dian sportful!
Kath. Where did you study all this goodly speech?
Pet. It is extempore, from my mother-wit.
Kath. A witty mother! witless else her son.

Pet. Am I not wise?
Kath.   Yes; keep you warm.
Pet. Marry, so I mean, sweet Katharine, in thy bed:
And therefore, setting all this chat aside,
Thus in plain terms: — your father hath consented
That you shall be my wife; your dowry greed on;
And, will you, nill you, I will marry you.
Now, Kate, I am a husband for your turn;
For, by this light, whereby I see thy beauty, —
Thy beauty, that doth make me like thee well, —
Thou must be married to no man but me;
For I am he am born to tame you, Kate,
And bring you from a wild Kate to a Kate
Conformable, as other household Kates.
Here comes your father: never make denial;
I must and will have Katharine to my wife.

Re-enter BAPTISTA, GREMIO, *and* TRANIO.

Bap. Now, Signior Petruchio, how speed you with
My daughter?
Pet.   How but well, sir? how but well?
It were impossible I should speed amiss.
Bap. Why, how now, daughter Katharine! in your dumps?
Kath. Call you me daughter? now, I promise you,
You've show'd a tender fatherly regard,
To wish me wed to one half lunatic;
A mad-cap ruffian and a swearing Jack,
That thinks with oaths to face the matter out.
Pet. Father, 'tis thus: — yourself and all the world,
That talk'd of her, have talk'd amiss of her:
If she be curst, it is for policy,
For she's not froward, but modest as the dove;
She is not hot, but temperate as the morn;
For patience she will prove a second Grissel,
And Roman Lucrece for her chastity:
And to conclude, — we've greed so well together,
That upon Sunday is the wedding-day.

Kath. I'll see thee hang'd on Sunday first.
Gre. Hark, Petruchio; she says, she'll see thee hang'd first.
Tra. Is this your speeding? nay, then, good night our pact!
Pet. Be patient, gentlemen; I choose her for myself:
If she and I be pleas'd, what's that to you?
'Tis bargain'd 'twixt us twain, being alone,
That she shall still be curst in company.
I tell you, 'tis incredible to believe
How much she loves me: O, the kindest Kate! —
She hung about my neck; and kiss on kiss
She vied so fast, protesting oath on oath,
That in a twink she won me to her love.
O, you are novices! 'tis a world to see,
How tame, when men and women are alone,
A meacock wretch can make the curstest shrew. —
Give me thy hand, Kate: I will unto Venice,
To buy apparel 'gainst the wedding-day. —
Provide the feast, father, and bid the guests;
I will be sure my Katharine shall be fine.
Bap. I know not what to say: but give me your hands;
God send you joy, Petruchio! 'tis a match.
Gre. Tra. Amen, say we: we will be witnesses.
Pet. Father, and wife, and gentlemen, adieu;
I will to Venice; Sunday comes apace: —
We will have rings, and things, and fine array;
And kiss me, Kate; we will be married o' Sunday.
[*Exeunt Petruchio and Katharina severally.*
Gre. Was ever match clapp'd up so suddenly?
Bap. Faith, gentlemen, now I play a merchant's part,
And venture madly on a desperate mart.
Tra. 'Twas a commodity lay fretting by you:
'Twill bring you gain, or perish on the seas.
Bap. The gain I seek is, quiet in the match.
Gre. No doubt but he hath got a quiet catch.
But now, Baptista, to your younger daughter:
Now is the day we long have looked for:
I am your neighbour, and was suitor first.

Tra.   And I am one that love Bianca more
Than words can witness, or your thoughts can guess.
   Gre.   Youngling, thou canst not love so dear as I.
   Tra.   Greybeard, thy love doth freeze.
   Gre.   But thine doth fry.
Skipper, stand back: 'tis age that nourisheth.
   Tra.   But youth in ladies' eyes that flourisheth.
   Bap.   Content you, gentlemen: I'll compound this strife:
'Tis deeds must win the prize; and he, of both,
That can assure my daughter greatest dower
Shall have Bianca's love. —
Say, Signior Gremio, what can you assure her?
   Gre.   First, as you know, my house within the city
Is richly furnishèd with plate and gold;
Basins and ewers, to lave her dainty hands;
My hangings all of Tyrian tapestry;
In ivory coffers I have stuff'd my crowns;
In cypress chests my arras-counterpoints,
Costly apparel, tents, and canopies,
Fine linen, Turkey cushions boss'd with pearl,
Valance of Venice gold in needlework;
Pewter and brass, and all things that belong
To house or housekeeping: then, at my farm
I have a hundred milch-kine to the pail,
Sixscore fat oxen standing in my stalls;
And all things answerable to this portion.
Myself am struck in years, I must confess;
And if I die to-morrow, this is hers,
If whilst I live she will be only mine.
   Tra.   That "only" came well in. — Sir, list to me:
I am my father's heir and only son:
If I may have your daughter to my wife,
I'll leave her houses three or four as good,
Within rich Pisa walls, as any one
Old Signior Gremio has in Padua;
Besides two thousand ducats by the year

3*

Of fruitful land, all which shall be her jointure. —
What, have I pinch'd you, Signior Gremio?

Gre. Two thousand ducats by the year of land!
My land amounts but to so much in all:
That she shall have; besides an argosy
That now is lying in Marseilles' road. —
What, have I chok'd you with an argosy?

Tra. Gremio, 'tis known my father hath no less
Than three great argosies; besides two galliasses,
And twelve tight galleys: these I will assure her,
And twice as much, whate'er thou offer'st next.

Gre. Nay, I have offer'd all, — I have no more;
And she can have no more than all I have: —
If you like me, she shall have me and mine.

Tra. Why, then, the maid is mine from all the world,
By your firm promise: Gremio is out-vied.

Bap. I must confess your offer is the best;
And, let your father make her the assurance,
She is your own; else, you must pardon me:
If you should die before him, where's her dower?

Tra. That's but a cavil: he is old, I young.

Gre. And may not young men die, as well as old?

Bap. Well, gentlemen,
I'm thus resolv'd: — on Sunday next you know
My daughter Katharine is to be married:
Now, on the Sunday following, shall Bianca
Be bride to you, if you make this assurance;
If not, to Signior Gremio:
And so, I take my leave, and thank you both.

Gre. Adieu, good neighbour. [*Exit Baptista.*
Now I fear thee not:
Sirrah young gamester, your father were a fool
To give thee all, and in his waning age
Set foot under thy table: tut, a toy!
An old Italian fox is not so kind, my boy. [*Exit.*

Tra. A vengeance on your crafty wither'd hide!
Yet I have fac'd it with a card of ten.

'Tis in my head to do my master good: —
I see no reason but suppos'd Lucentio
Must get a father, call'd — suppos'd Vincentio;
And that's a wonder: fathers commonly
Do get their children; but in this case of wooing,
A child shall get a sire, if I fail not of my cunning. [*Exit.*

ACT III.

Scene I. *Padua. A room in* Baptista's *house.*

Enter Lucentio, Hortensio, *and* Bianca.

Luc. Fiddler, forbear; you grow too forward, sir:
Have you so soon forgot the entertainment
Her sister Katharine welcom'd you withal?

Hor. But, wrangling pedant, this is
The patroness of heavenly harmony:
Then give me leave to have prerogative;
And when in music we have spent an hour,
Your lecture shall have leisure for as much.

Luc. Preposterous ass, that never read so far
To know the cause why music was ordain'd!
Was it not to refresh the mind of man
After his studies or his usual pain?
Then give me leave to read philosophy,
And while I pause, serve in your harmony.

Hor. Sirrah, I will not bear these braves of thine.

Bian. Why, gentlemen, you do me double wrong,
To strive for that which resteth in my choice:
I am no breeching scholar in the schools;
I'll not be tied to hours nor 'pointed times,
But learn my lessons as I please myself.
And, to cut off all strife, here sit we down: —
Take you your instrument, play you the whiles;
His lecture will be done ere you have tun'd.

Hor. You'll leave his lecture when I am in tune?
[*To Bianca. Hortensio retires.*

Luc. That will be never: — tune your instrument.

Bian. Where left we last?
Luc. Here, madam: — [*Reads.*
  Hac ibat Simois; hic est Sigeia tellus;
  Hic steterat Priami regia celsa senis.
Bian. Construe them.
Luc. Hac ibat, as I told you before, — *Simois*, I am Lucentio, — *hic est*, son unto Vincentio of Pisa, — *Sigeia tellus*, disguised thus to get your love; — *Hic steterat*, and that Lucentio that comes a-wooing, — *Priami*, is my man Tranio, — *regia*, bearing my port, — *celsa senis*, that we might beguile the old pantaloon.
Hor. [*coming forward*] Madam, my instrument's in tune.
Bian.   Let's hear. [*Hortensio plays.*
O, fie! the treble jars.
Luc.   Spit in the hole, man,
And tune again.
Bian. Now let me see if I can construe it: —
Hac ibat Simois, I know you not, — *hic est Sigeia tellus*, I trust you not; — *Hic steterat Priami*, take heed he hear us not, — *regia*, presume not, — *celsa senis*, despair not.
Hor. Madam, 'tis now in tune.
Luc.   All but the base.
Hor. The base is right; 'tis the base knave that jars. —
[*Aside*] How fiery and forward is our pedant!
Now, for my life, the knave doth court my love:
Pedascule, I'll watch you better yet.
Bian. In time I may believe, yet I mistrust.
Luc. Mistrust it not; for, sure, Æacides
Was Ajax, — call'd so from his grandfather.
Bian. I must believe my master; else, I promise you,
I should be arguing still upon that doubt:
But let it rest. — Now, Licio, to you: —
Good masters, take it not unkindly, pray,
That I have been thus pleasant with you both.
Hor. [*to Lucentio*] You may go walk, and give me leave
     awhile:
My lessons make no music in three parts.

Luc. [*aside*] Are you so formal, sir? well, I must wait,
And watch withal; for, but I be deceiv'd,
Our fine musician groweth amorous.
　Hor.　Madam, before you touch the instrument,
To learn the order of my fingering,
I must begin with rudiments of art;
To teach you gamut in a briefer sort,
More pleasant, pithy, and effectual,
Than hath been taught by any of my trade:
And there it is in writing, fairly drawn.
　Bian.　Why, I am past my gamut long ago.
　Hor.　Yet read the gamut of Hortensio.
　Bian. [*reads*]
　　"*Gamut* I am, the ground of all accord,
　　　A re, to plead Hortensio's passion;
　　　B mi, Bianca, take him for thy lord,
　　　C fa ut, that loves with all affection:
　　　D sol re, one cliff, two notes have I:
　　　E la mi, show pity, or I die."
Call you this gamut? tut, I like it not:
Old fashions please me best; I'm not so nice,
To change true rules for odd inventions.

Enter a Servant.

　Serv.　Mistress, your father prays you leave your books,
And help to dress your sister's chamber up:
You know to-morrow is the wedding-day.
　Bian.　Farewell, sweet masters, both; I must be gone.
　　　　　　　　　　　[*Exeunt Bianca and Servant.*
　Luc.　Faith, mistress, then I have no cause to stay. [*Exit.*
　Hor.　But I have cause to pry into this pedant:
Methinks he looks as though he were in love: —
Yet if thy thoughts, Bianca, be so humble,
To cast thy wandering eyes on every stale,
Seize thee that list: if once I find thee ranging,
Hortensio will be quit with thee by changing.　　　[*Exit.*

Scene II. *The same. Before* Baptista's *house.*

Enter Baptista, Tranio, Katharina, Bianca, Lucentio, *and others, with* Attendants.

    Bap. [*to Tranio*] Signior Lucentio, this is the 'pointed day
That Katharine and Petruchio should be married,
And yet we hear not of our son-in-law.
What will be said? what mockery will it be,
To want the bridegroom when the priest attends
To speak the ceremonial rites of marriage!
What says Lucentio to this shame of ours?
    Kath. No shame but mine: I must, forsooth, be forc'd
To give my hand, oppos'd against my heart,
Unto a mad-brain'd rudesby, full of spleen;
Who woo'd in haste, and means to wed at leisure.
I told you, I, he was a frantic fool,
Hiding his bitter jests in blunt behaviour:
And, to be noted for a merry man,
He'll woo a thousand, 'point the day of marriage,
Make feasts, invite friends, and proclaim the banns;
Yet never means to wed where he hath woo'd.
Now must the world point at poor Katharine,
And say, "Lo, there is mad Petruchio's wife,
If it would please him come and marry her!"
    Tra. Patience, good Katharine, and Baptista too.
Upon my life, Petruchio means but well,
Whatever fortune stays him from his word:
Though he be blunt, I know him passing wise;
Though he be merry, yet withal he's honest.
    Kath. Would Katharine had never seen him though!
            [*Exit weeping, followed by Bianca and others.*
    Bap. Go, girl; I cannot blame thee now to weep;
For such an injury would vex a saint,
Much more a shrew of thy impatient humour.

            Enter Biondello.

    Bion. Master, master! news, and such old news as you never heard of!

Bap. Is it new and old too? how may that be?
Bion. Why, is it not news, to hear of Petruchio's coming?
Bap. Is he come?
Bion. Why, no, sir.
Bap. What then?
Bion. He is coming.
Bap. When will he be here?
Bion. When he stands where I am, and sees you there.
Tra. But, say, what to thine old news?
Bion. Why, Petruchio is coming, in a new hat and an old jerkin; a pair of old breeches thrice turned; a pair of boots that have been candle-cases, one buckled, another laced; an old rusty sword ta'en out of the town-armoury, with a broken hilt, and chapeless; with two broken points: his horse hipped with an old mothy saddle, and stirrups of no kindred; besides, possessed with the glanders, and like to mose in the chine; troubled with the lampass, infected with the fashions, full of windgalls, sped with spavins, rayed with the yellows, past cure of the fives, stark spoiled with the staggers, begnawn with the bots; swayed in the back, and shoulder-shotten; ne'er-legged before, and with a half-cheeked bit, and a headstall of sheep's leather, which, being restrained to keep him from stumbling, hath been often burst, and new-repaired with knots; one girth six times pieced, and a woman's crupper of velure, which hath two letters for her name fairly set down in studs, and here and there pieced with packthread.
Bap. Who comes with him?
Bion. O, sir, his lackey, for all the world caparisoned like the horse; with a linen stock on one leg, and a kersey boot-hose on the other, gartered with a red and blue list; an old hat, and *The Humour of Forty Fancies* pricked in't for a feather: a monster, a very monster in apparel; and not like a Christian footboy or a gentleman's lackey.
Tra. 'Tis some odd humour pricks him to this fashion;
Yet oftentimes he goes but mean-apparell'd.
Bap. I am glad he's come, howsoe'er he comes.
Bion. Why, sir, he comes not.

Bap. Didst thou not say he comes?
Bion. Who? that Petruchio came?
Bap. Ay, that Petruchio came.
Bion. No, sir; I say his horse comes, with him on his back.
Bap. Why, that's all one.
Bion. Nay, by Saint Jamy,
    I hold you a penny,
     A horse and a man
     Is more than one,
    And yet not many.

Enter PETRUCHIO *and* GRUMIO, *both of them meanly and fantastically dressed.*

Pet. Come, where be these gallants? who's at home?
Bap. You're welcome, sir.
Pet.   And yet I come not well.
Bap. And yet you halt not.
Tra.   Not so well apparell'd
As I wish you were.
Pet. Were it better, I should rush in thus.
But where is Kate? where is my lovely bride? —
How does my father? — Gentles, methinks you frown:
And wherefore gaze this goodly company,
As if they saw some wondrous monument,
Some comet or unusual prodigy?
Bap. Why, sir, you know this is your wedding-day:
First were we sad, fearing you would not come;
Now sadder, that you come so unprovided.
Fie, doff this habit, shame to your estate,
An eye-sore to our solemn festival!
Tra. And tell us, what occasion of import
Hath all so long detain'd you from your wife,
And sent you hither so unlike yourself?
Pet. Tedious it were to tell, and harsh to hear:
Sufficeth, I am come to keep my word,
Though in some part enforced to digress;
Which, at more leisure, I will so excuse

As you shall well be satisfied withal.
But where is Kate? I stay too long from her:
The morning wears, 'tis time we were at church.

   Tra. See not your bride in these unreverent robes:
Go to my chamber; put on clothes of mine.

   Pet. Not I, believe me: thus I'll visit her.

   Bap. But thus, I trust, you will not marry her.

   Pet. Good sooth, even thus; therefore ha' done with words:
To me she's married, not unto my clothes:
Could I repair what she will wear in me,
As I can change these poor accoutrements,
'Twere well for Kate, and better for myself.
But what a fool am I to chat with you,
When I should bid good morrow to my bride,
And seal the title with a lovely kiss!
                              [*Exeunt Petruchio and Grumio.*

   Tra. He hath some meaning in his mad attire:
We will persuade him, be it possible,
To put on better ere he go to church.

   Bap. I'll after him, and see th' event of this.
                                                [*Exit.*

   Tra. But to her love concerneth us to add
Her father's liking: which to bring to pass,
As I before imparted to your worship,
I am to get a man, — whate'er he be,
It skills not much, we'll fit him to our turn, —
And he shall be Vincentio of Pisa;
And make assurance, here in Padua,
Of greater sums than I have promisèd.
So shall you quietly enjoy your hope,
And marry sweet Bianca with consent.

   Luc. Were it not that my fellow-schoolmaster
Doth watch Bianca's steps so narrowly,
'Twere good, methinks, to steal our marriage;
Which once perform'd, let all the world say no,
I'll keep mine own, despite of all the world.

   Tra. That by degrees we mean to look into,

And watch our vantage in this business:
We'll over-reach the greybeard, Gremio,
The narrow-prying father, Minola,
The quaint musician, amorous Licio;
All for my master's sake, Lucentio.

Enter GREMIO.

Signior Gremio, — came you from the church?

    Gre. As willingly as e'er I came from school.

    Tra. And is the bride and bridegroom coming home?

    Gre. A bridegroom say you? 'tis a groom indeed,
A grumbling groom, and that the girl shall find.

    Tra. Curster than she? why, 'tis impossible.

    Gre. Why, he's a devil, a devil, a very fiend.

    Tra. Why, she's a devil, a devil, the devil's dam.

    Gre. Tut, she's a lamb, a dove, a fool to him.
I'll tell you, Sir Lucentio: when the priest
Should ask, if Katharine should be his wife,
"Ay, by gogs-wouns," quoth he; and swore so loud,
That, all amaz'd, the priest let fall the book;
And, as he stoop'd again to take it up,
The mad-brain'd bridegroom took him such a cuff,
That down fell priest and book, and book and priest:
"Now take them up," quoth he, "if any list."

    Tra. What said the wench when he arose again?

    Gre. Trembled and shook; for why he stamp'd and swore,
As if the vicar meant to cozen him.
But after many ceremonies done,
He calls for wine: "A health!" quoth he; as if
He had been aboard, carousing to his mates
After a storm; quaff'd off the muscadel,
And threw the sops all in the sexton's face;
Having no other reason
But that his beard grew thin and hungerly,
And seem'd to ask him sops as he was drinking.
This done, he took the bride about the neck,
And kiss'd her lips with such a clamorous smack,
That, at the parting, all the church did echo:

And I, seeing this, came thence for very shame;
And after me, I know, the rout is coming.
Such a mad marriage never was before: —
Hark, hark! I hear the minstrels play. [*Music.*

Re-enter PETRUCHIO, KATHARINA, BIANCA. BAPTISTA, GRUMIO;
with HORTENSIO *and Train.*

   Pet. Gentlemen and friends, I thank you for your pains:
I know you think to dine with me to-day,
And have prepar'd great store of wedding cheer;
But so it is, my haste doth call me hence,
And therefore here I mean to take my leave.
   Bap. Is't possible you will away to-night?
   Pet. I must away to-day, before night come:
Make it no wonder; if you knew my business,
You would entreat me rather go than stay.
And, honest company, I thank you all,
That have beheld me give away myself
To this most patient, sweet, and virtuous wife:
Dine with my father, drink a health to me;
For I must hence; and farewell to you all.
   Tra. Let us entreat you stay till after dinner.
   Pet. It may not be.
   Gre.   Let me entreat you.
   Pet. It cannot be.
   Kath.   Let me entreat you.
   Pet. I am content.
   Kath.   Are you content to stay?
   Pet. I am content you shall entreat me stay;
But yet not stay, entreat me how you can.
   Kath. Now, if you love me, stay.
   Pet.   Grumio, my horse'.
   Gru. Ay, sir, they be ready: the oats have eaten the
      horses.
   Kath. Nay, then,
Do what thou canst, I will not go to-day;
No, nor to-morrow, nor till please myself.

The door is open, sir; there lies your way;
You may be jogging whiles your boots are green;
For me, I'll not be gone till please myself:
'Tis like you'll prove a jolly surly groom,
That take it on you at the first so roundly.

   Pet. O, Kate, content thee; prithee, be not angry.
   Kath. I will be angry: what hast thou to do? —
Father, be quiet: he shall stay my leisure.
   Gre. Ay, marry, sir, now it begins to work.
   Kath. Gentlemen, forward to the bridal dinner:
I see a woman may be made a fool,
If she had not a spirit to resist.
   Pet. They shall go forward, Kate, at thy command. —
Obey the bride, you that attend on her;
Go to the feast, revel and domineer,
Carouse full measure to her maidenhead,
Be mad and merry, — or go hang yourselves:
But for my bonny Kate, she must with me.
Nay, look not big, nor stamp, nor stare, nor fret;
I will be master of what is mine own:
She is my goods, my chattels; she's my house,
My household-stuff, my field, my barn,
My horse, my ox, my ass, my anything;
And here she stands, touch her whoever dare;
I'll bring mine action on the proudest he
That stops my way in Padua. — Grumio,
Draw forth thy weapon, we're beset with thieves;
Rescue thy mistress, if thou be a man. —
Fear not, sweet wench, they shall not touch thee, Kate:
I'll buckler thee against a million.
               [*Exeunt Petruchio, Katharina, and Grumio.*
   Bap. Nay, let them go, a couple of quiet ones.
   Gre. Went they not quickly, I should die with laughing.
   Tra. Of all mad matches never was the like.
   Luc. Mistress, what's your opinion of your sister?
   Bian. That, being mad herself, she's madly mated.
   Gre. I warrant him, Petruchio is Kated.

Bap. Neighbours and friends, though bride and bride-
groom want
For to supply the places at the table,
You know there want no junkets at the feast. —
Lucentio, you shall supply the bridegroom's place;
And let Bianca take her sister's room.
  Tra. Shall sweet Bianca practise how to bride it?
  Bap. She shall, Lucentio. — Come, gentlemen, let's go.
                                          [*Exeunt.*

ACT IV.

SCENE I. *A hall in* PETRUCHIO's *country house.*

Enter GRUMIO.

  Gru. Fie, fie on all tired jades, on all mad masters, and all foul ways! Was ever man so beaten? was ever man so rayed? was ever man so weary? I am sent before to make a fire, and they are coming after to warm them. Now, were not I a little pot, and soon hot, my very lips might freeze to my teeth, my tongue to the roof of my mouth, my heart in my belly, ere I should come by a fire to thaw me: — but I, with blowing the fire, shall warm myself; for, considering the weather, a taller man than I will take cold. — Holla, ho! Curtis!

Enter CURTIS.

  Curt. Who is that calls so coldly?
  Gru. A piece of ice: if thou doubt it, thou mayst slide from my shoulder to my heel with no greater a run but my head and my neck. A fire, good Curtis.
  Curt. Is my master and his wife coming, Grumio?
  Gru. O, ay, Curtis, ay: and therefore fire, fire; cast on no water.
  Curt. Is she so hot a shrew as she's reported?
  Gru. She was, good Curtis, before this frost: but, thou knowest, winter tames man, woman, and beast; for it hath tamed my old master, and my new mistress, and myself, fellow Curtis.

Curt. Away, you three-inch fool! I am no beast.

Gru. Am I but three inches? why, thy horn is a foot; and so long am I at the least. But wilt thou make a fire, or shall I complain on thee to our mistress, whose hand — she being now at hand — thou shalt soon feel, to thy cold comfort, for being slow in thy hot office?

Curt. I prithee, good Grumio, tell me, how goes the world?

Gru. A cold world, Curtis, in every office but thine; and therefore fire: do thy duty, and have thy duty; for my master and mistress are almost frozen to death.

Curt. There's fire ready; and therefore, good Grumio, the news?

Gru. Why, "Jack, boy! ho, boy!" and as much news as thou wilt.

Curt. Come, you are so full of cony-catching! —

Gru. Why, therefore fire; for I have caught extreme cold. Where's the cook? is supper ready, the house trimmed, rushes strewed, cobwebs swept, the serving-men in their new fustian, their white stockings, and every officer his wedding-garment on? Be the jacks fair within, the jills fair without, the carpets laid, and every thing in order?

Curt. All ready; and therefore, I pray thee, news?

Gru. First, know, my horse is tired; my master and mistress fallen out.

Curt. How?

Gru. Out of their saddles into the dirt; and thereby hangs a tale.

Curt. Let's ha't, good Grumio.

Gru. Lend thine ear.

Curt. Here.

Gru. There. [*Striking him.*

Curt. This is to feel a tale, not to hear a tale.

Gru. And therefore 'tis called a sensible tale: and this cuff was but to knock at your ear, and beseech listening. Now I begin: *Imprimis,* we came down a foul hill, my master riding behind my mistress: —

Curt. Both of one horse?
Gru. What's that to thee?
Curt. Why, a horse.
Gru. Tell thou the tale: — but hadst thou not crossed me, thou shouldst have heard how her horse fell, and she under her horse; thou shouldst have heard, in how miry a place; how she was bemoiled; how he left her with the horse upon her; how he beat me because her horse stumbled; how she waded through the dirt to pluck him off me; how he swore; how she prayed — that never prayed before; how I cried; how the horses ran away; how her bridle was burst; how I lost my crupper; — with many things of worthy memory, which now shall die in oblivion, and thou return unexperienced to thy grave.
Curt. By this reckoning, he is more shrew than she.
Gru. Ay; and that thou and the proudest of you all shall find when he comes home. But what talk I of this? — Call forth Nathaniel, Joseph, Nicholas, Philip, Walter, Sugarsop, and the rest: let their heads be sleekly combed, their blue coats brushed, and their garters of an indifferent knit: let them curtsy with their left legs; and not presume to touch a hair of my master's horse-tail till they kiss their hands. Are they all ready?
Curt. They are.
Gru. Call them forth.
Curt. Do you hear, ho? you must meet my master, to countenance my mistress!
Gru. Why, she hath a face of her own.
Curt. Who knows not that?
Gru. Thou, it seems, that callest for company to countenance her.
Curt. I call them forth to credit her.
Gru. Why, she comes to borrow nothing of them.

Enter NATHANIEL, PHILIP, JOSEPH, NICHOLAS, *and other* Servants.

Nath. Welcome home, Grumio!
Phil. How now, Grumio!

Jos. What, Grumio!

Nich. Fellow Grumio!

Nath. How now, old lad!

Gru. Welcome, you! — how now, you! — what, you! — fellow, you! — and thus much for greeting. Now, my spruce companions, is all ready, and all things neat?

Nath. All things is ready. How near is our master?

Gru. E'en at hand, alighted by this; and therefore be not — Cock's passion, silence! — I hear my master.

Enter PETRUCHIO *and* KATHARINA.

Pet. Where be these knaves? What, no man at the door
To hold my stirrup nor to take my horse!
Where is Nathaniel, Gregory, Philip? —

All Serv. Here, here, sir; here, sir.

Pet. Here, sir! here, sir! here, sir! here, sir! —
You logger-headed and unpolish'd grooms!
What, no attendance? no regard? no duty? —
Where is the foolish knave I sent before?

Gru. Here, sir; as foolish as I was before.

Pet. You peasant swain! you whoreson malt-horse drudge!
Did I not bid thee meet me in the park,
And bring along these rascal knaves with thee?

Gru. Nathaniel's coat, sir, was not fully made,
And Gabriel's pumps were all unpink'd i' th' heel;
There was no link to colour Peter's hat,
And Walter's dagger was not come from sheathing:
There were none fine but Adam, Ralph, and Gregory;
The rest were ragged, old, and beggarly;
Yet, as they are, here are they come to meet you.

Pet. Go, rascals, go, and fetch my supper in. —
[*Exeunt some of the Servants.* Sings.
Where is the life that late I led —
Where are those — Sit down, Kate, and welcome. —
Soud, soud, soud, soud!

Re-enter Servants *with supper.*

Why, when, I say? — Nay, good sweet Kate, be merry. —
Off with my boots, you rogues! you villains, when?   [*Sings.*
      It was the friar of orders grey,
      As he forth walkèd on his way: —
Out, out, you rogue! you pluck my foot awry:
Take that, and mend the plucking off the other. —
                                [*Strikes him.*
Be merry, Kate. — Some water, here; what, ho! —
Where's my spaniel Troilus? — Sirrah, get you hence,
And bid my cousin Ferdinand come hither: — [*Exit Servant.*
One, Kate, that you must kiss, and be acquainted with. —
Where are my slippers? — Shall I have some water?

Enter a Servant *with a basin and ewer.*

Come, Kate, and wash, and welcome heartily. —
                            [*Servant lets the ewer fall.*
You whoreson villain! will you let it fall?   [*Strikes him.*
  Kath. Patience, I pray you; 'twas a fault unwilling.
  Pet. A whoreson, beetle-headed, flap-ear'd knave! —
Come, Kate, sit down; I know you have a stomach.
Will you give thanks, sweet Kate; or else shall I? —
What's this? mutton?
  First Serv.   Ay.
  Pet.   Who brought it?
  First Serv.   I.
  Pet. 'Tis burnt; and so is all the meat.
What dogs are these! — Where is the rascal cook?
How durst you, villains, bring it from the dresser,
And serve it thus to me that love it not?
There, take it to you, trenchers, cups, and all:
                        [*Throws the meat, &c. at them.*
You heedless joltheads and unmanner'd slaves!
What, do you grumble? I'll be with you straight.
                               [*Exeunt Servants.*
  Kath. I pray you, husband, be not so disquiet:
The meat was well, if you were so contented.

Pet. I tell thee, Kate, 'twas burnt and dried away;
And I expressly am forbid to touch it,
For it engenders choler, planteth anger;
And better 'twere that both of us did fast, —
Since, of ourselves, ourselves are choleric, —
Than feed it with such over-roasted flesh.
Be patient; to-morrow 't shall be mended,
And, for this night, we'll fast for company: —
Come, I will bring thee to thy bridal chamber. [*Exeunt.*

SCENE II. *Another room in the same.*

Enter, severally, NATHANIEL, PETER, *and* GRUMIO.

Nath. Peter, didst ever see the like?
Pet. He kills her
In her own humour.

Enter CURTIS.

Gru. Where is he?
Curt. In her chamber,
Making a sermon of continency to her;
And rails, and swears, and rates, that she, poor soul,
Knows not which way to stand, to look, to speak,
And sits as one new-risen from a dream. —
Away, away! for he is coming hither. [*Exeunt.*

Enter PETRUCHIO.

Pet. Thus have I politicly begun my reign,
And 'tis my hope to end successfully.
My falcon now is sharp, and passing empty;
And, till she stoop, she must not be full-gorg'd,
For then she never looks upon her lure.
Another way I have to man my haggard,
To make her come, and know her keeper's call,
That is, to watch her, as we watch these kites
That bate, and beat, and will not be obedient.
She eat no meat to-day, nor none shall eat;
Last night she slept not, nor to-night she shall not;

As with the meat, some undeservèd fault
I'll find about the making of the bed;
And here I'll fling the pillow, there the bolster,
This way the coverlet, another way the sheets: —
Ay, and amid this hurly, I intend
That all is done in reverent care of her;
And, in conclusion, she shall watch all night:
And, if she chance to nod, I'll rail and brawl,
And with the clamour keep her still awake.
This is a way to kill a wife with kindness;
And thus I'll curb her mad and headstrong humour. —
He that knows better how to tame a shrew,
Now let him speak: 'tis charity to show. [*Exit.*

SCENE III. *Padua. Before* BAPTISTA'S *house.*

Enter TRANIO *and* HORTENSIO.

Tra. Is't possible, friend Licio, that Mistress Bianca
Doth fancy any other but Lucentio?
I tell you, sir, she bears me fair in hand.
 Hor. Sir, to satisfy you in what I have said,
Stand by, and mark the manner of his teaching.
[*They stand aside.*

Enter BIANCA *and* LUCENTIO.

 Luc. Now, mistress, profit you in what you read?
 Bian. What, master, read you? first resolve me that.
 Luc. I read that I profess, the Art to Love.
 Bian. And may you prove, sir, master of your art!
 Luc. While you, sweet dear, prove mistress of my heart!
[*They retire.*
 Hor. Quick proceeders, marry! Now, tell me, I pray,
You that durst swear that your mistress Bianca
Lov'd none in the world so well as Lucentio, —
 Tra. O despiteful love! unconstant womankind! —
I tell thee, Licio, this is wonderful.
 Hor. Mistake no more: I am not Licio,
Nor a musician, as I seem to be;

But one that scorn to live in this disguise,
For such a one as leaves a gentleman,
And makes a god of such a cullion:
Know, sir, that I am call'd Hortensio.

   Tra. Signior Hortensio, I have often heard
Of your entire affection to Bianca;
And since mine eyes are witness of her lightness,
I will with you, — if you be so contented, —
Forswear Bianca and her love for ever.

   Hor. See, how they kiss and court! — Signior Lucentio,
Here is my hand, and here I firmly vow
Never to woo her more; but do forswear her,
As one unworthy all the former favours
That I have fondly flatter'd her withal.

   Tra. And here I take the like unfeignèd oath,
Never to marry wi' her though she'd entreat:
Fie on her! see, how beastly she doth court him!

   Hor. Would all the world but he had quite forsworn her!
For me, that I may surely keep mine oath,
I will be married to a wealthy widow,
Ere three days pass, which hath as long lov'd me
As I have lov'd this proud disdainful haggard.
And so farewell, Signior Lucentio. —
Kindness in women, not their beauteous looks,
Shall win my love: — and so, I take my leave,
In resolution as I swore before.

         [*Exit Hortensio. Lucentio and Bianca advance.*

   Tra. Mistress Bianca, bless you with such grace
As 'longeth to a lover's blessèd case!
Nay, I have ta'en you napping, gentle love;
And have forsworn you, with Hortensio.

   Bian. Tranio, you jest: but have you both forsworn me?
   Tra. Mistress, we have.
   Luc.   Then we are rid of Licio.
   Tra. I' faith, he'll have a lusty widow now,
That shall be woo'd and wedded in a day.
   Bian. God give him joy!

Tra. Ay, and he'll tame her.
Bian. He says so, Tranio.
Tra. Faith, he is gone unto the taming-school.
Bian. The taming-school! what, is there such a place?
Tra. Ay, mistress, and Petruchio is the master;
That teacheth tricks eleven and twenty long,
To tame a shrew, and charm her chattering tongue.

Enter BIONDELLO.

Bion. O master, master, I have watch'd so long
That I'm dog-weary! but at last I spied
An ancient angel coming down the hill,
Will serve the turn.
Tra. What is he, Biondello?
Bion. Master, a mercatantè, or a pedant,
I know not what; but formal in apparel,
In gait and countenance surely like a father.
Luc. And what of him, Tranio?
Tra. If he be credulous and trust my tale,
I'll make him glad to seem Vincentio;
And give assurance to Baptista Minola,
As if he were the right Vincentio.
Take in your love, and then let me alone.
[*Exeunt Lucentio and Bianca.*

Enter a Pedant.

Ped. God save you, sir!
Tra. And you, sir! you are welcome.
Travel you far on, or are you at the furthest?
Ped. Sir, at the furthest for a week or two:
But then up further, and as far as Rome;
And so to Tripoli, if God lend me life.
Tra. What countryman, I pray?
Ped. Of Mantua.
Tra. Of Mantua, sir? — marry, God forbid!
And come to Padua, careless of your life?
Ped. My life, sir! how, I pray? for that goes hard.
Tra. 'Tis death for any one in Mantua

To come to Padua. Know you not the cause?
Your ships are stay'd at Venice; and the duke —
For private quarrel 'twixt your duke and him —
Hath publish'd and proclaim'd it openly:
'Tis marvel, but that you're but newly come,
You might have heard it else proclaim'd about.

Ped. Alas, sir, it is worse for me than so!
For I have bills for money by exchange
From Florence, and must here deliver them.

Tra. Well, sir, to do you courtesy,
This will I do, and this I will advise you: —
First, tell me, have you ever been at Pisa?

Ped. Ay, sir, in Pisa have I often been;
Pisa renownèd for grave citizens.

Tra. Among them know you one Vincentio?

Ped. I know him not, but I have heard of him;
A merchant of incomparable wealth.

Tra. He is my father, sir; and, sooth to say,
In countenance somewhat doth resemble you.

Bion. [*aside*] As much as an apple doth an oyster, and all one.

Tra. To save your life in this extremity,
This favour will I do you for his sake;
And think it not the worst of all your fortunes
That you are like to Sir Vincentio.
His name and credit shall you undertake,
And in my house you shall be friendly lodg'd: —
Look that you take upon you as you should;
You understand me, sir: — so shall you stay
Till you have done your business in the city:
If this be courtesy, sir, accept of it.

Ped. O, sir, I do; and will repute you ever
The patron of my life and liberty.

Tra. Then go with me, to make the matter good.
This, by the way, I let you understand; —
My father is here look'd for every day,
To pass assurance of a dower in marriage

'Twixt me and one Baptista's daughter here:
In all these circumstances I'll instruct you:
Go with me, sir, to clothe you as becomes you. [*Exeunt.*

SCENE IV. *A room in* PETRUCHIO'S *house.*

Enter KATHARINA *and* GRUMIO.

Gru. No, no, forsooth; I dare not, for my life.
Kath. The more my wrong, the more his spite appears:
What, did he marry me to famish me?
Beggars, that come unto my father's door,
Upon entreaty have a present alms;
If not, elsewhere they meet with charity:
But I, — who never knew how to entreat,
Nor never needed that I should entreat, —
Am starv'd for meat, giddy for lack of sleep;
With oaths kept waking, and with brawling fed:
And that which spites me more than all these wants,
He does it under name of perfect love;
As who should say, if I should sleep or eat,
'Twere deadly sickness or else present death. —
I prithee go, and get me some repast;
I care not what, so it be wholesome food.
Gru. What say you to a neat's foot?
Kath. 'Tis passing good: I prithee let me have it.
Gru. I fear it is too choleric a meat.
How say you to a fat tripe finely broil'd?
Kath. I like it well: good Grumio, fetch it me.
Gru. I cannot tell; I fear 'tis choleric.
What say you to a piece of beef and mustard?
Kath. A dish that I do love to feed upon.
Gru. Ay, but the mustard is too hot a little.
Kath. Why, then the beef, and let the mustard rest.
Gru. Nay, then I will not: you shall have the mustard,
Or else you get no beef of Grumio.
Kath. Then both, or one, or any thing thou wilt.
Gru. Why, then the mustard without the beef.

Kath. Go, get thee gone, thou false deluding slave,
[*Beats him.*
That feed'st me with the very name of meat:
Sorrow on thee, and all the pack of you,
That triumph thus upon my misery!
Go, get thee gone, I say.

Enter PETRUCHIO *with a dish of meat; and* HORTENSIO.

Pet. How fares my Kate? What, sweeting, all amort?
Hor. Mistress, what cheer?
Kath. Faith, as cold as can be.
Pet. Pluck up thy spirits, look cheerfully upon me.
Here, love; thou see'st how diligent I am
To dress thy meat myself, and bring it thee:
[*Sets the dish on a table.*
I'm sure, sweet Kate, this kindness merits thanks.
What, not a word? Nay, then thou lov'st it not;
And all my pains is sorted to no proof. —
Here, take away this dish.
Kath. I pray you, let it stand.
Pet. The poorest service is repaid with thanks;
And so shall mine, before you touch the meat.
Kath. 'I thank you, sir.
Hor. Signior Petruchio, fie! you are to blame. —
Come, Mistress Kate, I'll bear you company.
Pet. [*aside to Hor.*] Eat it up all, Hortensio, if thou lov'st
me. —
[*To Kath.*] Much good do it unto thy gentle heart!
Kate, eat apace: — and now, my honey love,
Will we return unto thy father's house,
And revel it as bravely as the best,
With silken coats, and caps, and golden rings,
With ruffs, and cuffs, and farthingales, and things;
With scarfs, and fans, and double change of bravery,
With amber bracelets, beads, and all this knavery.
What, hast thou din'd? The tailor stays thy leisure,
To deck thy body with his ruffling treasure.

Enter Tailor.

Come, tailor, let us see these ornaments;
Lay forth the gown.

Enter Haberdasher.

What news with you, sir?
Hab. Here is the cap your worship did bespeak.
Pet. Why, this was moulded on a porringer;
A velvet dish: — fie, fie! 'tis lewd and filthy:
Why, 'tis a cockle or a walnut-shell,
A knack, a toy, a trick, a baby's cap:
Away with it! come, let me have a bigger.
Kath. I'll have no bigger: this doth fit the time,
And gentlewomen wear such caps as these.
Pet. When you are gentle, you shall have one too,
And not till then.
Hor. [*aside*] That will not be in haste.
Kath. Why, sir, I trust I may have leave to speak;
And speak I will; I am no child, no babe:
Your betters have endur'd me say my mind;
And if you cannot, best you stop your ears.
My tongue will tell the anger of my heart;
Or else my heart, concealing it, will break:
And rather than it shall, I will be free
Even to the uttermost, as I please, in words.
Pet. Why thou say'st true; it is a paltry cap,
A custard-coffin, a bauble, a silken pie:
I love thee well, in that thou lik'st it not.
Kath. Love me or love me not, I like the cap;
And it I will have, or I will have none.
Pet. Thy gown? why, ay: — come, tailor, let us see't.
O, mercy, God! what masquing stuff is here?
What's this? a sleeve? 'tis like a demi-cannon:
What, up and down, carv'd like an apple-tart?
Here's snip, and nip, and cut, and slish, and slash,
Like to a censer in a barber's shop: —
Why, what, o' devil's name, tailor, call'st thou this?

Hor. [*aside*] I see she's like t' have neither cap nor gown.
Tai. You bid me make it orderly and well,
According to the fashion and the time.
Pet. Marry, and did; but if you be remember'd,
I did not bid you mar it to the time.
Go, hop me over every kennel home,
For you shall hop without my custom, sir:
I'll none of it: hence! make your best of it.
Kath. I never saw a better-fashion'd gown,
More quaint, more pleasing, nor more commendable:
Belike you mean to make a puppet of me.
Pet. Why, true; he means to make a puppet of thee.
Tai. She says your worship means to make a puppet of her.
Pet. O monstrous arrogance! Thou liest, thou thread,
Thou thimble,
Thou yard, three-quarters, half-yard, quarter, nail!
Thou flea, thou nit, thou winter-cricket thou! —
Brav'd in mine own house with a skein of thread?
Away, thou rag, thou quantity, thou remnant;
Or I shall so be-mete thee with thy yard,
As thou shalt think on prating whilst thou liv'st!
I tell thee, I, that thou hast marr'd her gown.
Tai. Your worship is deceiv'd; the gown is made
Just as my master had direction:
Grumio gave order how it should be done.
Gru. I gave him no order; I gave him the stuff.
Tai. But how did you desire it should be made?
Gru. Marry, sir, with needle and thread.
Tai. But did you not request to have it cut?
Gru. Thou hast faced many things; —
Tai. I have.
Gru. Face not me: thou hast braved many men; brave not me: I will neither be faced nor braved. I say unto thee, I bid thy master cut out the gown; but I did not bid him cut it to pieces: *ergo*, thou liest.
Tai. Why, here is the note of the fashion to testify.
Pet. Read it.

Gru. The note lies in 's throat, if he say I said so.

Tai. [*reads*] "*Imprimis*, a loose-bodied gown:" —

Gru. Master, if ever I said loose-bodied gown, sew me in the skirts of it, and beat me to death with a bottom of brown thread: I said a gown.

Pet. Proceed.

Tai. [*reads*] "With a small compassed cape:" —

Gru. I confess the cape.

Tai. [*reads*] "With a trunk sleeve:" —

Gru. I confess two sleeves.

Tai. [*reads*] "The sleeves curiously cut."

Pet. Ay, there's the villany.

Gru. Error i' the bill, sir; error i' the bill. — I commanded the sleeves should be cut out, and sewed up again; and that I'll prove upon thee, though thy little finger be armed in a thimble.

Tai. This is true that I say; an I had thee in place where, thou shouldst know it.

Gru. I am for thee straight: take thou the bill, give me thy mete-yard, and spare not me.

Hor. God-a-mercy, Grumio! then he shall have no odds.

Pet. Well, sir, in brief, the gown is not for me.

Gru. You are i' the right, sir: 'tis for my mistress.

Pet. Go take it up unto thy master's use.

Gru. Villain, not for thy life: take up my mistress' gown for thy master's use!

Pet. Why, sir, what's your conceit in that?

Gru. O, sir, the conceit is deeper than you think for: Take up my mistress' gown to his master's use!
O, fie, fie, fie!

Pet. [*aside to Hor.*] Hortensio, say thou'lt see the tailor paid. —

[*To Tai.*] Go take it hence; be gone, and say no more.

Hor. Tailor, I'll pay thee for thy gown to-morrow:
Take no unkindness of his hasty words:
Away! I say; commend me to thy master.

[*Exeunt Tailor and Haberdasher.*

Pet. Well, come, my Kate; we will unto your father's,
Even in these honest mean habiliments:
Our purses shall be proud, our garments poor;
For 'tis the mind that makes the body rich;
And as the sun breaks through the darkest clouds,
So honour peereth in the meanest habit.
What is the jay more precious than the lark,
Because his feathers are more beautiful?
Or is the adder better than the eel,
Because his painted skin contents the eye?
O, no, good Kate; neither art thou the worse
For this poor furniture and mean array.
If thou account'st it shame, lay it on me;
And therefore frolic: we will hence forthwith,
To feast and sport us at thy father's house. —
Go call my men, and let us straight to him;
And bring our horses unto Long-lane end;
There will we mount, and thither walk on foot. —
Let's see; I think 'tis now some seven o'clock,
And well we may come there by dinner-time.

Kath. I dare assure you, sir, 'tis almost two;
And 'twill be supper-time ere you come there.

Pet. It shall be seven ere I go to horse:
Look, what I speak, or do, or think to do,
You are still crossing it. — Sirs, let 't alone:
I will not go to-day; and ere I do,
It shall be what o'clock I say it is.

Hor. Why, so! this gallant will command the sun!
[*Exeunt.*

SCENE V. *Padua. Before* BAPTISTA'S *house.*

Enter TRANIO, *and the* Pedant *dressed like* VINCENTIO.

Tra. Sir, this is the house: please it you that I call?
Ped. Ay, ay, what else? and, but I be deceiv'd,
Signior Baptista may remember me,
Near twenty years ago, in Genoa,
Where we were lodgers at the Pegasus.

THE TAMING OF THE SHREW.

Tra. 'Tis well; and hold your own, in any case,
With such austerity as 'longeth to a father.
Ped. I warrant you. But, sir, here comes your boy;
'Twere good he were school'd.

Enter BIONDELLO.

Tra. Fear you not him. — Sirrah Biondello,
Now do your duty throughly, I advise you:
Imagine 'twere the right Vincentio.
Bion. Tut, fear not me.
Tra. But hast thou done thy errand to Baptista?
Bion. I told him that your father was at Venice;
And that you look'd for him this day in Padua.
Tra. Thou'rt a tall fellow: hold thee that to drink.
Here comes Baptista: — set your countenance, sir.

Enter BAPTISTA *and* LUCENTIO.

Signior Baptista, you are happily met. —
[*To the Pedant*] Sir,
This is the gentleman I told you of:
I pray you, stand good father to me now,
Give me Bianca for my patrimony.
Ped. Soft, son! —
Sir, by your leave: having come to Padua
To gather in some debts, my son Lucentio
Made me acquainted with a weighty cause
Of love between your daughter and himself:
And, — for the good report I hear of you;
And for the love he beareth to your daughter,
And she to him, — to stay him not too long,
I am content, in a good father's care,
To have him match'd; and, — if you please to like
No worse than I, sir, — upon some agreement,
Me shall you find most ready and most willing
With one consent to have her so bestow'd;
For curious I cannot be with you,
Signior Baptista, of whom I hear so well.

Bap. Sir, pardon me in what I have to say:
Your plainness and your shortness please me well.
Right true it is, your son Lucentio here
Doth love my daughter, and she loveth him,
Or both dissemble deeply their affections:
And therefore, if you say no more than this,
That like a father you will deal with him,
And pass my daughter a sufficient dower,
The match is fully made, and all is done:
Your son shall have my daughter with consent.
   Tra. I thank you, sir. Where, then, do you hold best
We be affied, and such assurance ta'en
As shall with either part's agreement stand?
   Bap. Not in my house, Lucentio; for, you know,
Pitchers have ears, and I have many servants:
Besides, old Gremio is hearkening still;
And happily we might be interrupted.
   Tra. Then at my lodging, an it like you, sir:
There doth my father lie; and there, this night,
We'll pass the business privately and well.
Send for your daughter by your servant here;
My boy shall fetch the scrivener presently.
The worst is this, — that, at so slender warning,
You're like to have a thin and slender pittance.
   Bap. It likes me well. — Cambio, hie you home,
And bid Bianca make her ready straight;
And, if you will, tell what hath happened, —
Lucentio's father is arriv'd in Padua,
And how she's like to be Lucentio's wife.
   Luc. I pray the gods she may with all my heart!
   Tra. Dally not with the gods, but get thee gone. —
Signior Baptista, shall I lead the way? [*Lucentio retires*
Welcome! one mess is like to be your cheer:
Come, sir; we will better it in Pisa.
   Bap. I follow you. [*Exeunt Tranio, Pedant, and Baptista.*
   Bion. Cambio, —
   Luc. What sayest thou, Biondello?

Bion. You saw my master wink and laugh upon you?
Luc. Biondello, what of that?
Bion. Faith, nothing; but 'has left me here behind, to expound the meaning or moral of his signs and tokens.
Luc. I pray thee, moralise them.
Bion. Then thus. Baptista is safe, talking with the deceiving father of a deceitful son.
Luc. And what of him?
Bion. His daughter is to be brought by you to the supper.
Luc. And then? —
Bion. The old priest at Saint Luke's church is at your command at all hours.
Luc. And what of all this?
Bion. I cannot tell, except, while they are busied about a counterfeit assurance, take you assurance of her, *cum privilegio ad imprimendum solum:* to the church; — take the priest, clerk, and some sufficient-honest witnesses:
If this be not that you look for, I have no more to say,
But bid Bianca farewell for ever and a day.   [*Going.*
Luc. Hearest thou, Biondello?
Bion. I cannot tarry: I knew a wench married in an afternoon as she went to the garden for parsley to stuff a rabbit; and so may you, sir: and so, adieu, sir. My master hath appointed me to go to Saint Luke's, to bid the priest be ready to come against you come with your appendix. [*Exit.*
Luc. I may, and will, if she be so contented:
She will be pleas'd; then wherefore should I doubt?
Hap what hap may, I'll roundly go about her:
It shall go hard if Cambio go without her.   [*Exit.*

Scene VI. *A public road.*

Enter Petruchio, Katharina, *and* Hortensio.

Pet. Come on, o' God's name; once more toward our
            father's.
Good Lord, how bright and goodly shines the moon!
Kath. The moon! the sun: it is not moonlight now.
Pet. I say it is the moon that shines so bright.

Kath. I know it is the sun that shines so bright.
Pet. Now, by my mother's son, and that's myself,
It shall be moon, or star, or what I list,
Or e'er I journey to your father's house. —
Go one, and fetch our horses back again. —
Evermore cross'd and cross'd; nothing but cross'd!
Hor. [*aside to Kath.*] Say as he says, or we shall never go.
Kath. Forward, I pray, since we have come so far,
And be it moon, or sun, or what you please:
An if you please to call it a rush-candle,
Henceforth I vow it shall be so for me.
Pet. I say it is the moon.
Kath.   I know it is the moon.
Pet. Nay, then, you lie: it is the blessèd sun.
Kath. Then, God be bless'd, it is the blessèd sun: —
But sun it is not, when you say it is not;
And the moon changes, even as your mind.
What you will have it nam'd, even that it is;
And so it shall be still for Katharine.
Hor. [*aside*] Petruchio, go thy ways; the field is won.
Pet. Well, forward, forward! thus the bowl should run,
And not unluckily against the bias. —
But, soft! what company is coming here?

Enter VINCENTIO.

[*To Vincentio*] Good morrow, gentle mistress: where away? —
Tell me, sweet Kate, and tell me truly too,
Hast thou beheld a fresher gentlewoman?
Such war of white and red within her cheeks!
What stars do spangle heaven with such beauty,
As those two eyes become that heavenly face? —
Fair lovely maid, once more good day to thee. —
Sweet Kate, embrace her for her beauty's sake.
Hor. [*aside*] 'A will make the man mad, to make a woman
        of him.
Kath. Young budding virgin, fair and fresh and sweet,
Whither away; or where is thy abode?

Happy the parents of so fair a child;
Happier the man whom favourable stars
Allot thee for his lovely bedfellow!

Pet. Why, how now, Kate! I hope thou art not mad:
This is a man, old, wrinkled, faded, wither'd;
And not a maiden, as thou say'st he is.

Kath. Pardon, old father, my mistaking eyes,
That have been so bedazzled with the sun,
That every thing I look on seemeth green:
Now I perceive thou art a reverend father;
Pardon, I pray thee, for my mad mistaking.

Pet. Do, good old grandsire; and withal make known
Which way thou travell'st: if along with us,
We shall be joyful of thy company.

Vin. Fair sir, and you my merry mistress,
That with your strange encounter much amaz'd me,
My name is call'd Vincentio; my dwelling Pisa;
And bound I am to Padua; there to visit
A son of mine, which long I have not seen.

Pet. What is his name?

Vin. Lucentio, gentle sir.

Pet. Happily met; the happier for thy son.
And now by law, as well as reverend age,
I may entitle thee my loving father:
The sister to my wife, this gentlewoman,
Thy son by this hath married. Wonder not,
Nor be not griev'd: she is of good esteem,
Her dowry wealthy, and of worthy birth;
Beside, so qualified as may beseem
The spouse of any noble gentleman.
Let me embrace with old Vincentio:
And wander we to see thy honest son,
Who will of thy arrival be full joyous.

Vin. But is this true? or is it else your pleasure,
Like pleasant travellers, to break a jest
Upon the company you overtake?

Hor. I do assure thee, father, so it is.

Pet. Come, go along, and see the truth hereof;
For our first merriment hath made thee jealous.
                    [*Exeunt Petruchio, Katharina, and Vincentio.*
    Hor. Well, Petruchio, this has put me in heart.
Have to my widow! and if she be froward,
Then hast thou taught Hortensio to be untoward.   [*Exit.*

ACT V.

SCENE I. *Padua. Before* LUCENTIO's *house.*

Enter on one side BIONDELLO, LUCENTIO, *and* BIANCA; GREMIO *walking on the other side.*

Bion. Softly and swiftly, sir; for the priest is ready.
    Luc. I fly, Biondello: but they may chance to need thee at home; therefore leave us.
    Bion. Nay, faith, I'll see the church o' your back; and then come back to my master as soon as I can.
                    [*Exeunt Lucentio, Bianca, and Biondello.*
    Gre. I marvel Cambio comes not all this while.

Enter PETRUCHIO, KATHARINA, VINCENTIO, GRUMIO, *and Attendants.*

Pet. Sir, here's the door, this is Lucentio's house:
My father's bears more toward the market-place;
Thither must I; and here I leave you, sir.
    Vin. You shall not choose but drink before you go:
I think I shall command your welcome here,
And, by all likelihood, some cheer is toward.   [*Knocks.*
    Gre. They're busy within; you were best knock louder.

Enter Pedant *above, at a window.*

Ped. What's he that knocks as he would beat down the gate?
    Vin. Is Signior Lucentio within, sir?
    Ped. He's within, sir, but not to be spoken withal.
    Vin. What if a man bring him a hundred pound or two, to make merry withal?

Ped. Keep your hundred pounds to yourself: he shall need none, so long as I live.

Pet. Nay, I told you your son was well beloved in Padua. — Do you hear, sir? — to leave frivolous circumstances, — I pray you, tell Signior Lucentio, that his father is come from Pisa, and is here at the door to speak with him.

Ped. Thou liest: his father is come from Pisa, and is here looking out at the window.

Vin. Art thou his father?

Ped. Ay, sir; so his mother says, if I may believe her.

Pet. [*to Vincentio*] Why, how now, gentleman! why, this is flat knavery, to take upon you another man's name.

Ped. Lay hands on the villain: I believe 'a means to cozen somebody in this city under my countenance.

Re-enter BIONDELLO.

Bion. I have seen them in the church together: God send 'em good shipping! — But who is here? mine old master, Vincentio! now we are undone, and brought to nothing.

Vin. Come hither, crack-hemp. [*Seeing Biondello.*

Bion. I hope I may choose, sir.

Vin. Come hither, you rogue. What, have you forgot me?

Bion. Forgot you! no, sir: I could not forget you, for I never saw you before in all my life.

Vin. What, you notorious villain, didst thou never see thy master's father, Vincentio?

Bion. What, my worshipful old master? yes, marry, sir: see where he looks out of the window.

Vin. Is't so, indeed? [*Beats Biondello.*

Bion. Help, help, help! here's a madman will murder me. [*Exit.*

Ped. Help, son! help, Signior Baptista! [*Exit from the window.*

Pet. Prithee, Kate, let's stand aside, and see the end of this controversy. [*They retire.*

Enter Pedant *below;* BAPTISTA, TRANIO, *and* Servants.

Tra. Sir, what are you that offer to beat my servant?

Vin. What am I, sir! nay, what are you, sir? — O immortal gods! O fine villain! A silken doublet! a velvet hose! a scarlet cloak! and a copatain hat! — O, I am undone! I am undone! while I play the good husband at home, my son and my servant spend all at the university.

Tra. How now! what's the matter?

Bap. What, is the man lunatic?

Tra. Sir, you seem a sober ancient gentleman by your habit, but your words show you a madman. Why, sir, what 'cerns it you if I wear pearl and gold? I thank my good father, I am able to maintain it.

Vin. Thy father! O villain! he is a sail-maker in Bergamo.

Bap. You mistake, sir, you mistake, sir. Pray, what do you think is his name?

Vin. His name! as if I knew not his name: I have brought him up ever since he was three years old, and his name is Tranio.

Ped. Away, away, mad ass! his name is Lucentio; and he is mine only son, and heir to the lands of me, Signior Vincentio.

Vin. Lucentio! O, he hath murdered his master! — Lay hold on him, I charge you, in the duke's name. — O, my son, my son! — Tell me, thou villain, where is my son Lucentio?

Tra. Call forth an officer.

Servant brings in an Officer.

Carry this mad knave to the gaol.—Father Baptista, I charge you see that he be forthcoming.

Vin. Carry me to the gaol!

Gre. Stay, officer: he shall not go to prison.

Bap. Talk not, Signior Gremio: I say he shall go to prison.

Gre. Take heed, Signior Baptista, lest you be cony-catched in this business: I dare swear this is the right Vincentio.

Ped. Swear, if thou darest.

Gre. Nay, I dare not swear it.

Tra. Then thou wert best say, that I am not Lucentio.
Gre. Yes, I know thee to be Signior Lucentio.
Bap. Away with the dotard! to the gaol with him!
Vin. Thus strangers may be halèd and abus'd: —
O monstrous villany!

Re-enter BIONDELLO, *with* LUCENTIO *and* BIANCA.

Bion. O, we are spoiled! and yonder he is: deny him, forswear him, or else we are all undone.
Luc. Pardon, sweet father. [*Kneeling.*
Vin. Lives my sweet son?
[*Biondello, Tranio, and Pedant run out.*
Bian. Pardon, dear father. [*Kneeling.*
Bap. How hast thou offended? —
Where is Lucentio?
Luc. Here's Lucentio,
Right son unto the right Vincentio;
That have by marriage made thy daughter mine,
While counterfeit supposes blear'd thine eyne.
Gre. Here's packing, with a witness, to deceive us all!
Vin. Where is that damnèd villain Tranio,
That fac'd and brav'd me in this matter so?
Bap. Why, tell me, is not this my Cambio?
Bian. Cambio is chang'd into Lucentio.
Luc. Love wrought these miracles. Bianca's love
Made me exchange my state with Tranio,
While he did bear my countenance in the town;
And happily I have arriv'd at last
Unto the wishèd haven of my bliss.
What Tranio did, myself enforc'd him to;
Then pardon him, sweet father, for my sake.
Vin. I'll slit the villain's nose, that would have sent me to the gaol.
Bap. [*to Lucentio*] But do you hear, sir? have you married my daughter without asking my good-will?
Vin. Fear not, Baptista; we will content you, go to: but I will in, to be revenged for this villany. [*Exit.*

Bap. And I, to sound the depth of this knavery. [*Exit.*
Luc. Look not pale, Bianca; thy father will not frown.
[*Exeunt Lucentio and Bianca.*
Gre. My cake is dough: but I'll in among the rest;
Out of hope of all, but my share of the feast. [*Exit.*

PETRUCHIO *and* KATHARINA *come forward.*

Kath. Husband, let's follow, to see the end of this ado.
Pet. First kiss me, Kate, and we will.
Kath. What, in the midst of the street?
Pet. What, art thou ashamed of me?
Kath. No, sir, God forbid; but ashamed to kiss.
Pet. Why, then, let's home again: come, sirrah, let's away.
Kath. Nay, I will give thee a kiss [*kisses him*]: now, pray thee, love, stay.
Pet. Is not this well? — Come, my sweet Kate:
Better once than never, for never too late. [*Exeunt.*

SCENE II. *A room in* LUCENTIO's *house.*

A banquet set out; enter BAPTISTA, VINCENTIO, GREMIO, *the* Pedant, LUCENTIO, BIANCA, PETRUCHIO, KATHARINA, HORTENSIO, *and* Widow; TRANIO, BIONDELLO, GRUMIO, *and others, attending.*

Luc. At last, though long, our jarring notes agree:
And time it is, when raging war is done,
To smile at scapes and perils overblown. —
My fair Bianca, bid my father welcome,
While I with selfsame kindness welcome thine. —
Brother Petruchio, — sister Katharina, —
And thou, Hortensio, with thy loving widow, —
Feast with the best, and welcome to my house:
My banquet is to close our stomachs up,
After our great good cheer. Pray you, sit down;
For now we sit to chat, as well as eat. [*They sit at table.*
Pet. Nothing but sit and sit, and eat and eat!
Bap. Padua affords this kindness, son Petruchio.
Pet. Padua affords nothing but what is kind.

Hor. For both our sakes, I would that word were true.
Pet. Now, for my life, Hortensio fears his widow.
Wid. Then never trust me, if I be afeard.
Pet. You're sensible, and yet you miss my sense:
I mean, Hortensio is afeard of you.
Wid. He that is giddy thinks the world turns round.
Pet. Roundly replied.
Kath.   Mistress, how mean you that?
Wid. Thus I conceive by him.
Pet. Conceives by me! — How likes Hortensio that?
Hor. My widow says, thus she conceives her tale.
Pet. Very well mended. — Kiss him for that, good widow.
Kath. He that is giddy thinks the world turns round: —
I pray you, tell me what you meant by that.
Wid. Your husband, being troubled with a shrew,
Measures my husband's sorrow by his woe:
And now you know my meaning.
Kath. A very mean meaning.
Wid.   Right, I mean you.
Kath. And I am mean, indeed, respecting you.
Pet. To her, Kate!
Hor. To her, widow!
Pet. A hundred marks, my Kate does put her down.
Hor. That's my office.
Pet. Spoke like an officer: — ha' to thee, lad.
                              [*Drinks to Hortensio.*
Bap. How likes Gremio these quick-witted folks?
Gre. Believe me, sir, they butt together well.
Bian. Head and butt! an hasty-witted body
Would say your head and butt were head and horn.
Vin. Ay, mistress bride, hath that awaken'd you?
Bian. Ay, but not frighted me; therefore I'll sleep again.
Pet. Nay, that you shall not: since you have begun,
Have at you for a bitter jest or two!
Bian. Am I your bird? I mean to shift my bush;
And then pursue me as you draw your bow. —
You are welcome all. [*Exeunt Bianca, Katharina, and Widow.*

Pet. She hath prevented me. — Here, Signior Tranio,
This bird you aim'd at, though you hit her not;
Therefore a health to all that shot and miss'd.
  Tra. O, sir, Lucentio slipp'd me like his greyhound,
Which runs himself, and catches for his master.
  Pet. A good swift simile, but something currish.
  Tra. 'Tis well, sir, that you hunted for yourself:
'Tis thought your deer does hold you at a bay.
  Bap. O, ho, Petruchio! Tranio hits you now.
  Luc. I thank thee for that gird, good Tranio.
  Hor. Confess, confess, hath he not hit you here?
  Pet. 'A has a little gall'd me, I confess;
And, as the jest did glance away from me,
'Tis ten to one it maim'd you two outright.
  Bap. Now, in good sadness, son Petruchio,
I think thou hast the veriest shrew of all.
  Pet. Well, I say no: and therefore, for assurance,
Let's each one send unto his wife;
And he whose wife is most obedient
To come at first when he doth send for her,
Shall win the wager which we will propose.
  Hor. Content. What is the wager?
  Luc.   Twenty crowns.
  Pet. Twenty crowns!
I'll venture so much of my hawk or hound,
But twenty times so much upon my wife.
  Luc. A hundred, then.
  Hor.   Content.
  Pet.   A match! 'tis done.
  Hor. Who shall begin?
  Luc. That will I. —
Go, Biondello, bid your mistress come to me.
  Bion. I go.   [*Exit.*
  Bap. Son, I will be your half, Bianca comes.
  Luc. I'll have no halves; I'll bear it all myself.

        Re-enter BIONDELLO.
How now! what news?

Bion. Sir, my mistress sends you word
That she is busy, and she cannot come.
Pet. How! she is busy, and she cannot come!
Is that an answer?
Gre. Ay, and a kind one too:
Pray God, sir, your wife send you not a worse.
Pet. I hope, a better.
Hor. Sirrah Biondello, go and entreat my wife
To come to me forthwith. [*Exit Biondello.*
Pet. O, ho! entreat her!
Nay, then she must needs come.
Hor. I am afraid, sir,
Do what you can, yours will not be entreated.

Re-enter BIONDELLO.

Now, where's my wife?
Bion. She says you have some goodly jest in hand:
She will not come; she bids you come to her.
Pet. Worse and worse; she will not come! O vile,
Intolerable, not to be endur'd! —
Sirrah Grumio, go to your mistress;
Say, I command her come to me. [*Exit Grumio.*
Hor. I know her answer.
Pet. What?
Hor. She will not.
Pet. The fouler fortune mine, and there an end.
Bap. Now, by my halidom, here comes Katharina!

Re-enter KATHARINA.

Kath. What is your will, sir, that you send for me?
Pet. Where is your sister, and Hortensio's wife?
Kath. They sit conferring by the parlour fire.
Pet. Go fetch them hither: if they deny to come,
Swinge me them soundly forth unto their husbands:
Away, I say, and bring them hither straight. [*Exit Kath.*
Luc. Here is a wonder, if you talk of wonder.
Hor. And so it is: I wonder what it bodes.

Pet. Marry, peace it bodes, and love, and quiet life,
And awful rule, and right supremacy,
And, to be short, what not that's sweet and happy?
    Bap. Now, fair befal thee, good Petruchio!
The wager thou hast won; and I will add
Unto their losses twenty thousand crowns;
Another dowry to another daughter,
For she is chang'd, as she had never been.
    Pet. Nay, I will win my wager better yet,
And show more sign of her obedience,
Her new-built virtue and obedience.
See, where she comes, and brings your froward wives
As prisoners to her womanly persuasion.

    Re-enter KATHARINA, *with* BIANCA *and* Widow.

Katharine, that cap of yours becomes you not:
Off with that bauble, throw it under foot.
              [*Katharina pulls off her cap and throws it down.*
    Wid. Lord, let me never have a cause to sigh,
Till I be brought to such a silly pass!
    Bian. Fie, what a foolish duty call you this?
    Luc. I would your duty were as foolish too:
The wisdom of your duty, fair Bianca,
Hath cost me a hundred crowns since supper-time.
    Bian. The more fool you, for laying on my duty.
    Pet. Katharine, I charge thee, tell these headstrong
          women
What duty they do owe their lords and husbands.
    Wid. Come, come, you're mocking: we will have no
          telling.
    Pet. Come on, I say; and first begin with her.
    Wid. She shall not.
    Pet. I say she shall: — and first begin with her.
    Kath. Fie, fie! unknit that threatening unkind brow;
And dart not scornful glances from those eyes,
To wound thy lord, thy king, thy governor:
It blots thy beauty, as frosts bite the meads;

Confounds thy fame, as whirlwinds shake fair buds;
And in no sense is meet or amiable.
A woman mov'd is like a fountain troubled,
Muddy, ill-seeming, thick, bereft of beauty;
And while it is so, none so dry or thirsty
Will deign to sip, or touch one drop of it.
Thy husband is thy lord, thy life, thy keeper,
Thy head, thy sovereign; one that cares for thee
And for thy maintenance; commits his body
To painful labour both by sea and land,
To watch the night in storms, the day in cold,
Whilst thou liest warm at home, secure and safe;
And craves no other tribute at thy hands
But love, fair looks, and true obedience, —
Too little payment for so great a debt.
Such duty as the subject owes the prince,
Even such a woman oweth to her husband;
And when she's froward, peevish, sullen, sour,
And not obedient to his honest will,
What is she but a foul contending rebel,
And graceless traitor to her loving lord? —
I am asham'd that women are so simple
To offer war, where they should kneel for peace;
Or seek for rule, supremacy, and sway,
When they are bound to serve, love, and obey.
Why are our bodies soft and weak and smooth,
Unapt to toil and trouble in the world,
But that our soft conditions and our hearts
Should well agree with our external parts?
Come, come, you froward and unable worms!
My mind hath been as big as one of yours,
My heart as great; my reason, haply, more,
To bandy word for word and frown for frown:
But now I see our lances are but straws;
Our strength as weak, our weakness past compare, —
That seeming to be most, which we indeed least are.
Then vail your stomachs, for it is no boot,

And place your hands below your husband's foot:
In token of which duty, if he please,
My hand is ready, may it do him ease.
    Pet. Why, there's a wench! — Come on, and kiss me, Kate.
    Luc. Well, go thy ways, old lad; for thou shalt ha't.
    Vin. 'Tis a good hearing when children are toward.
    Luc. But a harsh hearing when women are froward.
    Pet. Come, Kate, we'll to bed. —
We three are married, but you two are sped.
'Twas I won the wager, though you hit the white;
                                  [*To Lucentio.*
And, being a winner, God give you good night!
                    [*Exeunt Petruchio and Katharina.*
    Hor. Now, go thy ways; thou hast tam'd a curst shrow.
    Luc. 'Tis a wonder, by your leave, she will be tam'd so.
                                            [*Exeunt.*

ALL'S WELL THAT ENDS WELL.

DRAMATIS PERSONÆ.

King of France.
Duke of Florence.
BERTRAM, Count of Rousillon.
LAFEU, an old lord.
PAROLLES, a follower of Bertram.
Several young French Lords, who serve with Bertram in the Florentine war.
Steward, } servants to the Countess
Clown,   }   of Rousillon.
A Page.

Countess of Rousillon, mother to Bertram.
HELENA, a gentlewoman protected by the Countess.
A Widow of Florence.
DIANA, her daughter.
VIOLENTA, } neighbours and
MARIANA, } friends to the Widow.

Lords attending on the King; Officers, Soldiers, &c., French and Florentine.

SCENE — *partly in France, and partly in Tuscany.*

ACT I.

SCENE I. *Rousillon. A hall in the house of the* Countess.

Enter BERTRAM, *the* Countess of Rousillon, HELENA, *and* LAFEU, *all in black.*

Count. In delivering my son from me, I bury a second husband.

Ber. And I, in going, madam, weep o'er my father's death anew: but I must attend his majesty's command, to whom I am now in ward, evermore in subjection.

Laf. You shall find of the king a husband, madam; — you, sir, a father: he that so generally is at all times good, must of necessity hold his virtue to you; whose worthiness would stir it up where it wanted, rather than lack it where there is such abundance.

Count. What hope is there of his majesty's amendment?

Laf. He hath abandoned his physicians, madam; under whose practices he hath persecuted time with hope; and finds no other advantage in the process but only the losing of hope by time.

Count. This young gentlewoman had a father, — O, that "had"! how sad a passage 'tis! — whose skill was almost as great as his honesty; had it stretched so far, 't would have made nature immortal, and death should have play for lack of work. Would, for the king's sake, he were living! I think it would be the death of the king's disease.

Laf. How called you the man you speak of, madam?

Count. He was famous, sir, in his profession, and it was his great right to be so, — Gerard de Narbon.

Laf. He was excellent indeed, madam: the king very lately spoke of him admiringly and mourningly: he was skilful enough to have lived still, if knowledge could be set up against mortality.

Ber. What is it, my good lord, the king languishes of?

Laf. A fistula, my lord.

Ber. I heard not of it before.

Laf. I would it were not notorious. — Was this gentlewoman the daughter of Gerard de Narbon?

Count. His sole child, my lord; and bequeathed to my overlooking. I have those hopes of her good that her education promises: her dispositions she inherits, which makes fair gifts fairer; for where an unclean mind carries virtuous qualities, there commendations go with pity,—they are virtues and traitors too: in her they are the better for their simpleness; she derives her honesty, and achieves her goodness.

Laf. Your commendations, madam, get from her tears.

Count. 'Tis the best brine a maiden can season her praise in. The remembrance of her father never approaches her heart but the tyranny of her sorrows takes all livelihood from her cheek. — No more of this, Helena, — go to, no more; lest it be rather thought you affect a sorrow than to have it.

Hel. I do affect a sorrow, indeed; but I have it too.

Laf. Moderate lamentation is the right of the dead; excessive grief the enemy to the living.

Hel. If the living be enemy to the grief, the excess makes it soon mortal.

Ber. Madam, I desire your holy wishes.

Laf. How understand we that?

Count. Be thou blest, Bertram! and succeed thy father
In manners, as in shape! thy blood and virtue
Contend for empire in thee, and thy goodness
Share with thy birthright! Love all, trust a few,
Do wrong to none; be able for thine enemy
Rather in power than use, and keep thy friend
Under thy own life's key; be check'd for silence,
But never tax'd for speech. What heaven more will,
That thee may furnish, and my prayers pluck down,
Fall on thy head! — Farewell, my lord: 'tis an
Unseason'd courtier; good my lord, advise him.

Laf. He cannot want the best that shall attend
His love.

Count. Heaven bless him! — Farewell, Bertram. [*Exit.*

Ber. [*to Helena*] The best wishes that can be forged in your thoughts be servants to you! Be comfortable to my mother, your mistress, and make much of her.

Laf. Farewell, pretty lady: you must hold the credit of your father. [*Exeunt Bertram and Lafeu.*

Hel. O, were that all! — I think not on my father;
And these great tears grace his remembrance more
Than those I shed for him. What was he like?
I have forgot him: my imagination
Carries no favour in 't but Bertram's.
I am undone: there is no living, none,
If Bertram be away. It were all one,
That I should love a bright particular star,
And think to wed it, he is so above me:

In his bright radiance and collateral light
Must I be comforted, not in his sphere.
Th' ambition in my love thus plagues itself:
The hind that would be mated by the lion
Must die for love. 'Twas pretty, though a plague,
To see him every hour; to sit and draw
His archèd brows, his hawking eye, his curls,
In our heart's table, — heart too capable
Of every line and trick of his sweet favour:
But now he's gone, and my idolatrous fancy
Must sanctify his relics. — Who comes here?
One that goes with him: I love him for his sake;
And yet I know him a notorious liar,
Think him a great way fool, solely a coward;
Yet these fix'd evils sit so fit in him,
That they take place, when virtue's steely bones
Look bleak i' the cold wind: withal, full oft we see
Cold wisdom waiting on superfluous folly.

Enter PAROLLES.

Par. Save you, fair queen!
Hel. And you, monarch!
Par. No.
Hel. And no.
Par. Are you meditating on virginity?
Hel. Ay. You have some stain of soldier in you: let me ask you a question. Man is enemy to virginity; how may we barricado it against him?
Par. Keep him out.
Hel. But he assails; and our virginity, though valiant in the defence, yet is weak: unfold to us some warlike resistance.
Par. There is none: man, sitting down before you, will undermine you, and blow you up.
Hel. Bless our poor virginity from underminers and blowers-up! — Is there no military policy, how virgins might blow up men?
Par. Virginity being blown down, man will quicklier be

blown up: marry, in blowing him down again, with the breach
yourselves made, you lose your city. It is not politic in the
commonwealth of nature to preserve virginity. Loss of virginity is rational increase; and there was never virgin got
till virginity was first lost. That you were made of, is metal
to make virgins. Virginity, by being once lost, may be ten
times found; by being ever kept, it is ever lost: 'tis too cold
a companion; away with 't!

Hel. I will stand for 't a little, though therefore I die a
virgin.

Par. There's little can be said in 't; 'tis against the rule
of nature. To speak on the part of virginity, is to accuse
your mothers; which is most infallible disobedience. He that
hangs himself is a virgin: virginity murders itself; and should
be buried in highways, out of all sanctified limit, as a desperate offendress against nature. Virginity breeds mites,
much like a cheese; consumes itself to the very paring, and
so dies with feeding his own stomach. Besides, virginity is
peevish, proud, idle, made of self-love, which is the most in-
hibited sin in the canon. Keep it not; you cannot choose but
lose by 't: out with 't! within one year it will make itself two,
which is a goodly increase; and the principal itself not much
the worse: away with 't!

Hel. How might one do, sir, to lose it to her own liking?

Par. Let me see: marry, ill, to like him that ne'er it likes.
'Tis a commodity will lose the gloss with lying; the longer
kept, the less worth: off with 't while 'tis vendible; answer the
time of request. Virginity, like an old courtier, wears her cap
out of fashion; richly suited, but unsuitable: just like the
brooch and the toothpick, which wear not now. Your date is
better in your pie and your porridge than in your cheek: and
your virginity, your old virginity, is like one of our French
withered pears, — it looks ill, it eats dryly; marry, 'tis a
withered pear; it was formerly better; marry, yet, 'tis a
withered pear: will you any thing with it?

Hel. Not my virginity yet.
There shall your master have a thousand loves,

A mother, and a mistress, and a friend,
A phœnix, captain, and an enemy,
A guide, a goddess, and a sovereign,
A counsellor, a traitress, and a dear;
His humble ambition, proud humility,
His jarring concord, and his discord dulcet,
His faith, his sweet disaster; with a world
Of pretty, fond-adoptious christendoms,
That blinking Cupid gossips. Now shall he —
I know not what he shall: — God send him well! —
The court's a learning-place; — and he is one —
    Par. What one, i' faith?
    Hel. That I wish well. — 'Tis pity —
    Par. What's pity?
    Hel. That wishing well had not a body in 't,
Which might be felt; that we, the poorer born,
Whose baser stars do shut us up in wishes,
Might with effects of them follow our friends,
And show what we alone must think; which never
Returns us thanks.

Enter a Page.

    Page. Monsieur Parolles, my lord calls for you.   [*Exit.*
    Par. Little Helen, farewell: if I can remember thee, I will think of thee at court.
    Hel. Monsieur Parolles, you were born under a charitable star.
    Par. Under Mars, I.
    Hel. I especially think, under Mars.
    Par. Why under Mars?
    Hel. The wars have so kept you under, that you must needs be born under Mars.
    Par. When he was predominant.
    Hel. When he was retrograde, I think, rather.
    Par. Why think you so?
    Hel. You go so much backward when you fight.
    Par. That's for advantage.

Hel. So is running away, when fear proposes the safety: but the composition, that your valour and fear make in you is a virtue of a good wing, and I like the wear well.

Par. I am so full of businesses, I cannot answer thee acutely. I will return perfect courtier; in the which, my instruction shall serve to naturalize thee, so thou wilt be capable of a courtier's counsel, and understand what advice shall thrust upon thee; else thou diest in thine unthankfulness, and thine ignorance makes thee away: farewell. When thou hast leisure, say thy prayers; when thou hast none, remember thy friends: get thee a good husband, and use him as he uses thee: so, farewell. [*Exit.*

Hel. Our remedies oft in ourselves do lie,
Which we ascribe to heaven: the fated sky
Gives us free scope; only doth backward pull
Our slow designs when we ourselves are dull.
What power is it which mounts my love so high;
That makes me see, and cannot feed mine eye?
The mightiest space in fortune nature brings
To join like likes, and kiss like native things.
Impossible be strange attempts to those
That weigh their pains in sense; and do suppose
What hath not been can't be: who ever strove
To show her merit, that did miss her love?
The king's disease, — my project may deceive me,
But my intents are fix'd, and will not leave me. [*Exit.*

SCENE II. *Paris. A room in the King's palace.*

Flourish of cornets. Enter the King *of France with letters; Lords and others attending.*

King. The Florentines and Senoys are by th' ears;
Have fought with equal fortune, and continue
A braving war.

First Lord. So 'tis reported, sir.

King. Nay, 'tis most credible; we here receive it
A certainty, vouch'd from our cousin Austria,

With caution, that the Florentine will move us
For speedy aid; wherein our dearest friend
Prejudicates the business, and would seem
To have us make denial.
  First Lord.   His love and wisdom,
Approv'd so to your majesty, may plead
For amplest credence.
  King.   He hath arm'd our answer,
And Florence is denied before he comes:
Yet, for our gentlemen that mean to see
The Tuscan service, freely have they leave
To stand on either part.
  Sec. Lord.   It well may serve
A nursery to our gentry, who are sick
For breathing and exploit.
  King.   What's he comes here?

    Enter BERTRAM, LAFEU, *and* PAROLLES.

  First Lord. It is the Count Rousillon, my good lord,
Young Bertram.
  King. Youth, thou bear'st thy father's face;
Frank nature, rather curious than in haste,
Hath well compos'd thee. Thy father's moral parts
Mayst thou inherit too! Welcome to Paris.
  Ber. My thanks and duty are your majesty's.
  King. I would I had that corporal soundness now
As when thy father and myself in friendship
First tried our soldiership! He did look far
Into the service of the time, and was
Discipled of the bravest: he lasted long;
But on us both did haggish age steal on,
And wore us out of act. It much repairs me
To talk of your good father. In his youth
He had the wit, which I can well observe
To-day in our young lords; but they may jest,
Till their own scorn return to them unnoted,
Ere they can hide their levity in honour
So like a courtier: contempt nor bitterness

Were in his pride or sharpness; if they were,
His equal had awak'd them; and his honour,
Clock to itself, knew the true minute when
Exception bid him speak, and at this time
His tongue obey'd his hand: who were below him
He us'd as creatures of another place;
And bow'd his eminent top to their low ranks,
Making them proud of his humility,
In their poor praise he humbled. Such a man
Might be a copy to these younger times;
Which, follow'd well, would démonstrate them now
But goers backward.

  Ber.   His good remembrance, sir,
Lies richer in your thoughts than on his tomb;
So in approof lives not his epitaph
As in your royal speech.

  King. Would I were with him! He would always say,—
Methinks I hear him now; his plausive words
He scatter'd not in ears, but grafted them,
To grow there, and to bear,—"Let me not live,"—
Thus his good melancholy oft began,
On the catastrophe and heel of pastime,
When it was out,—"Let me not live," quoth he,
"After my flame lacks oil, to be the snuff
Of younger spirits, whose apprehensive senses
All but new things disdain; whose judgments are
Mere fathers of their garments; whose constancies
Expire before their fashions:"—this he wish'd:
I, after him, do after him wish too,
Since I nor wax nor honey can bring home,
I quickly were dissolvèd from my hive,
To give some labourer room.

  Sec. Lord.   You're lovèd, sir;
They that least lend it you shall lack you first.

  King. I fill a place, I know 't.— How long is 't, count,
Since the physician at your father's died?
He was much fam'd.

Ber. Some six months since, my lord.
King. If he were living, I would try him yet; —
Lend me an arm; — the rest have worn me out
With several applications: — nature and sickness
Debate it at their leisure. Welcome, count;
My son's no dearer.
Ber. Thank your majesty. [*Exeunt. Flourish.*

SCENE III. *Rousillon. A room in the house of the* Countess.

Enter Countess, Steward, *and* Clown.

Count. I will now hear: what say you of this gentlewoman?

Stew. Madam, the care I have had to even your content, I wish might be found in the calendar of my past endeavours; for then we wound our modesty, and make foul the clearness of our deservings, when of ourselves we publish them.

Count. What does this knave here? Get you gone, sirrah: the complaints I have heard of you I do not all believe: 'tis my slowness that I do not; for I know you lack not folly to commit them, and have ability enough to make such knaveries yours.

Clo. 'Tis not unknown to you, madam, I am a poor fellow.

Count. Well, sir.

Clo. No, madam, 'tis not so well that I am poor; though many of the rich are damned: but, if I may have your ladyship's good-will to go to the world, Isbel your woman and I will do as we may.

Count. Wilt thou needs be a beggar?

Clo. I do beg your good-will in this case.

Count. In what case?

Clo. In Isbel's case and mine own. Service is no heritage: and I think I shall never have the blessing of God till I have issue o' my body; for they say barns are blessings.

Count. Tell me thy reason why thou wilt marry.

Clo. My poor body, madam, requires it: I am driven on by the flesh; and he must needs go that the devil drives.

Count. Is this all your worship's reason?

Clo. Faith, madam, I have other holy reasons, such as they are.

Count. May the world know them?

Clo. I have been, madam, a wicked creature, as you and all flesh and blood are; and, indeed, I do marry that I may repent.

Count. Thy marriage, — sooner than thy wickedness.

Clo. I am out o' friends, madam; and I hope to have friends for my wife's sake.

Count. Such friends are thine enemies, knave.

Clo. You're shallow, madam; e'en great friends; for the knaves come to do that for me, which I am a-weary of. He that ears my land spares my team, and gives me leave to inn the crop; if I be his cuckold, he's my drudge: he that comforts my wife is the cherisher of my flesh and blood; he that cherishes my flesh and blood loves my flesh and blood; he that loves my flesh and blood is my friend: *ergo*, he that kisses my wife is my friend. If men could be contented to be what they are, there were no fear in marriage; for young Chairbonne the puritan and old Poisson the papist, howsome'er their hearts are severed in religion, their heads are both one, — they may jole horns together, like any deer i' the herd.

Count. Wilt thou ever be a foul-mouthed and calumnious knave?

Clo. A prophet I, madam; and I speak the truth the next way:

> For I the ballad will repeat,
> Which men full true shall find;
> Your marriage comes by destiny,
> Your cuckoo sings by kind.

Count. Get you gone, sir; I'll talk with you more anon.

Stew. May it please you, madam, that he bid Helen come to you: of her I am to speak.

Count. Sirrah, tell my gentlewoman I would speak with her; Helen I mean.

Clo. Was this fair face the cause, quoth she,
   Why the Grecians sacked Troy?
Fond done, done fond,
   Was this King Priam's joy?
With that she sighed as she stood,
With that she sighed as she stood,
   And gave this sentence then;
Among nine bad if one be good,
Among nine bad if one be good,
   There's yet one good in ten.

Count. What, one good in ten? you corrupt the song, sirrah.

Clo. One good woman in ten, madam; which is a purifying o' the song: would God would serve the world so all the year! we 'd find no fault with the tithe-woman, if I were the parson: one in ten, quoth a'! an we might have a good woman born but for every blazing star, or at an earthquake, 'twould mend the lottery well: a man may draw his heart out, ere 'a pluck one.

Count. You'll be gone, sir knave, and do as I command you?

Clo. That man should be at woman's command, and yet no hurt done! — Though honesty be no puritan, yet it will do no hurt; it will wear the surplice of humility over the black gown of a big heart. — I am going, forsooth: the business is for Helen to come hither. [*Exit.*

Count. Well, now.

Stew. I know, madam, you love your gentlewoman entirely.

Count. Faith, I do: her father bequeathed her to me; and she herself, without other advantage, may lawfully make title to as much love as she finds: there is more owing her than is paid; and more shall be paid her than she'll demand.

Stew. Madam, I was very late more near her than I think she wished me: alone she was, and did communicate to herself her own words to her own ears; she thought, I dare vow for her, they touched not any stranger sense. Her matter was, she loved your son: Fortune, she said, was no goddess, that had put such difference betwixt their two estates; Love no god, that would not extend his might, only where qualities were level; Diana no queen of virgins, that would suffer her poor knight surprised, without rescue in the first assault, or ransom afterward. This she delivered in the most bitter touch of sorrow that e'er I heard virgin exclaim in: which I held my duty speedily to acquaint you withal; sithence, in the loss that may happen, it concerns you something to know it.

Count. You have discharged this honestly; keep it to yourself: many likelihoods informed me of this before, which hung so tottering in the balance, that I could neither believe nor misdoubt. Pray you, leave me: stall this in your bosom; and I thank you for your honest care: I will speak with you further anon. [*Exit Steward.*
Even so it was with me when I was young:
  If we are nature's, these are ours; this thorn
Doth to our rose of youth rightly belong;
  Our blood to us, this to our blood is born;
It is the show and seal of nature's truth,
Where love's strong passion is impress'd in youth:
By our remembrances of days foregone,
Such were our faults, though then we thought them none.

Enter HELENA.

Her eye is sick on't: I observe her now.
  Hel. What is your pleasure, madam?
  Count. You know, Helen,
I am a mother to you.
  Hel. Mine honourable mistress.
  Count. Nay, a mother:
Why not a mother? When I said a mother,
Methought you saw a serpent: what's in "mother,"
That you start at it? I say, I am your mother;
And put you in the catalogue of those
That were enwombèd mine: 'tis often seen

Adoption strives with nature; and choice breeds
A native slip to us from foreign seeds:
You ne'er oppress'd me with a mother's groan,
Yet I express to you a mother's care: —
God's mercy, maiden! does it curd thy blood,
To say, I am thy mother? What's the matter,
That this distemper'd messenger of wet,
The many-colour'd Iris, rounds thine eye?
Why, — that you are my daughter?
    Hel.   That I am not.
    Count. I say, I am your mother.
    Hel.   Pardon, madam,
The Count Rousillon cannot be my brother:
I am from humble, he from honour'd name;
No note upon my parents, his all noble:
My master, my dear lord he is; and I
His servant live, and will his vassal die:
He must not be my brother.
    Count.   Nor I your mother?
    Hel. You are my mother, madam; would you were —
So that my lord your son were not my brother —
Indeed my mother! — or were you both our mothers,
I care no more for than I do for heaven,
So I were not his sister. Can't no other,
But I your daughter, he must be my brother?
    Count. Yes, Helen, you might be my daughter-in-law:
God shield, you mean it not! "daughter" and "mother"
So strive upon your pulse. What, pale again?
My fear hath catch'd your fondness: now I see
The mystery of your loneliness, and find
Your salt tears' head: now to all sense 'tis gross
You love my son; invention is asham'd,
Against the proclamation of thy passion,
To say thou dost not: therefore tell me true;
But tell me then, 'tis so; — for, look, thy cheeks
Confess it, th' one to th' other; and thine eyes
See it so grossly shown in thy behaviours,

That in their kind they speak it: only sin
And hellish obstinacy tie thy tongue,
That truth should be suspected. Speak, is't so?
If it be so, you've wound a goodly clew;
If it be not, forswear 't: howe'er, I charge thee,
As heaven shall work in me for thine avail,
To tell me truly.
  Hel.   Good madam, pardon me!
  Count. Do you love my son?
  Hel.   Your pardon, noble mistress!
  Count. Love you my son?
  Hel.   Do not you love him, madam?
  Count. Go not about; my love hath in 't a bond,
Whereof the world takes note: come, come, disclose
The state of your affection; for your passions
Have to the full appeach'd.
  Hel.   Then, I confess,
Here on my knee, before high heaven and you,
That before you, and next unto high heaven,
I love your son:—
My friends were poor, but honest; so's my love:
Be not offended; for it hurts not him,
That he is lov'd of me: I follow him not
By any token of presumptuous suit;
Nor would I have him till I do deserve him;
Yet never know how that desert should be.
I know I love in vain, strive against hope;
Yet in this captious and intenible sieve
I still pour in the waters of my love,
And lack not to lose still: thus, Indian-like,
Religious in mine error, I adore
The sun, that looks upon his worshipper,
But knows of him no more. My dearest madam,
Let not your hate encounter with my love,
For loving where you do: but, if yourself,
Whose agèd honour cites a virtuous youth,
Did ever, in so true a flame of liking,

Wish chastely, and love dearly, that your Dian
Was both herself and Love; O, then, give pity
To her, whose state is such, that cannot choose
But lend and give, where she is sure to lose;
That seeks not to find that her search implies,
But, riddle-like, lives sweetly where she dies!

Count. Had you not lately an intent, — speak truly, —
To go to Paris?

Hel.   Madam, I had.

Count.   Wherefóre?
Tell true.

Hel. I will tell truth; by grace itself, I swear.
You know my father left me some prescriptions
Of rare and prov'd effects, such as his reading
And manifold experience had collected
For general sovereignty; and that he will'd me
In heedfull'st reservation to bestow them,
As notes, whose faculties inclusive were,
More than they were in note: amongst the rest,
There is a remedy, approv'd, set down,
To cure the desperate languishings whereof
The king is render'd lost.

Count.   This was your motive
For Paris, was it? speak.

Hel. My lord your son made me to think of this;
Else Paris, and the medicine, and the king,
Had from the conversation of my thoughts
Haply been absent then.

Count.   But think you, Helen,
If you should tender your supposèd aid,
He would receive it? he and his physicians
Are of a mind; he, that they cannot help him;
They, that they cannot help: how shall they credit
A poor unlearnèd virgin, when the schools,
Embowell'd of their doctrine, have left off
The danger to itself?

Hel.   There's something hints,

More than my father's skill, which was the greatest
Of his profession, that his good receipt
Shall, for my legacy, be sanctified
By the luckiest stars in heaven: and, would your honour
But give me leave to try success, I'd venture
This well-lost life of mine on's grace's cure
By such a day and hour.
  Count.   Dost thou believe 't?
  Hel. Ay, madam, knowingly.
  Count. Why, Helen, thou shalt have my leave, and love,
Means, and attendants, and my loving greetings
To those of mine in court: I'll stay at home,
And pray God's blessing into thy attempt:
Be gone to-morrow; and be sure of this,
What I can help thee to, thou shalt not miss. [*Exeunt.*

ACT II.

Scene I. *Paris. A room in the King's palace.*

Flourish. Enter King, *with divers young* Lords *taking leave for the Florentine war;* Bertram, Parolles, *and* Attendants.

  King. Farewell, young lord; these warlike principles
Do not throw from you: — and you, my lord, farewell: —
Share the advice betwixt you; if both gain all,
The gift doth stretch itself as 'tis receiv'd,
And is enough for both.
  First Lord.   It is our hope, sir,
After well-enter'd soldiers, to return
And find your grace in health.
  King. No, no, it cannot be; and yet my heart
Will not confess he owes the malady
That doth my life besiege. Farewell, young lords;
Whether I live or die, be you the sons
Of worthy Frenchmen: let higher Italy —
Those bated that inherit but the fall
Of the last monarchy — see that you come
Not to woo honour, but to wed it; when

The bravest questant shrinks, find what you seek,
That fame may cry you loud: I say, farewell.
   Sec. Lord. Health, at your bidding, serve your majesty!
   King. Those girls of Italy, take heed of them:
They say, our French lack language to deny,
If they demand: beware of being captives,
Before you serve.
   Both Lords.   Our hearts receive your warnings.
   King. Farewell. — Come hither to me.
                           [*Exit, led out by Attendants.*
   First Lord. O my sweet lord, that you will stay behind us!
   Par. 'Tis not his fault, the spark.
   Sec. Lord.   O, 'tis brave wars!
   Par. Most admirable: I have seen those wars.
   Ber. I am commanded here, and kept a coil with, —
"Too young," and "the next year," and "'tis too early."
   Par. An thy mind stand to't, boy, steal away bravely.
   Ber. I shall stay here the forehorse to a smock,
Creaking my shoes on the plain masonry,
'Till honour be bought up, and no sword worn
But one to dance with! By heaven, I'll steal away.
   First Lord. There's honour in the theft.
   Par.   Commit it, count.
   Sec. Lord. I am your accessary; and so, farewell.
   Ber. I grow to you, and our parting is a tortured body.
   First Lord. Farewell, captain.
   Sec. Lord. Sweet Monsieur Parolles!
   Par. Noble heroes, my sword and yours are kin. Good sparks and lustrous, a word, good metals: — you shall find in the regiment of the Spinii one Captain Spurio, with his cicatrice, an emblem of war, here on his sinister cheek; it was this very sword entrenched it: say to him, I live; and observe his reports for me.
   Sec. Lord. We shall, noble captain.
   Par. Mars dote on you for his novices! [*Exeunt Lords.*]
What will ye do?
   Ber. Stay; the king!

Re-enter the King, *led back to his chair by* Attendants.

Par. Use a more spacious ceremony to the noble lords; you have restrained yourself within the list of too cold an adieu: be more expressive to them: for they wear themselves in the cap of the time, there do muster true gait, eat, speak, and move under the influence of the most received star; and though the devil lead the measure, such are to be followed: after them, and take a more dilated farewell.

Ber. And I will do so.

Par. Worthy fellows; and like to prove most sinewy sword-men. [*Exeunt Bertram and Parolles.*

Enter LAFEU.

Laf. [*kneeling*] Pardon, my lord, for me and for my tidings.

King. I'll fee thee to stand up.

Laf. [*rising*] Then here's a man stands that has bought his pardon.
I would you had kneel'd, my lord, to ask me mercy:
And that, at my bidding, you could so stand up.

King. I would I had; so I had broke thy pate,
And ask'd thee mercy for't.

Laf. Good faith, across: but, my good lord, 'tis thus;
Will you be cur'd of your infirmity?

King. No.

Laf. O, will you eat no grapes, my royal fox?
Yes, but you will my noble grapes, an if
My royal fox could reach them: I've seen a medicine
That's able to breathe life into a stone,
Quicken a rock, and make you dance canary
With sprightly fire and motion; whose simple touch
Is powerful to araise King Pepin, nay,
To give great Charlemain a pen in's hand,
And write to her a love-line.

King. What "her" is this?

Laf. Why, doctor she: my lord, there's one arriv'd
If you will see her: — now, by my faith and honour,

If seriously I may convey my thoughts
In this my light deliverance, I have spoke
With one that, in her sex, her years, profession,
Wisdom, and constancy, hath amaz'd me more
Than I dare blame my weakness: will you see her,—
For that is her demand,— and know her business?
That done, laugh well at me.
  King.   Now, good Lafeu,
Bring in the admiration; that we with thee
May spend our wonder too, or take off thine
By wondering how thou took'st it.
  Laf.   Nay, I'll fit you,
And not be all day neither.   [*Exit.*
  King. Thus he his special nothing ever prologues.

    Re-enter LAFEU, *with* HELENA.

  Laf. Nay, come your ways.
  King.   This haste hath wings indeed.
  Laf. Nay, come your ways;
This is his majesty, say your mind to him:
A traitor you do look like; but such traitors
His majesty seldom fears: I'm Cressid's uncle,
That dare leave two together; fare you well. [*Exit.*
  King. Now, fair one, does your business follow us?
  Hel. Ay, my good lord.
Gerard de Narbon was my father; one,
In what he did profess, well found.
  King.   I knew him.
  Hel. The rather will I spare my praises towards him;
Knowing him is enough. On 's bed of death
Many receipts he gave me; chiefly one,
Which, as the dearest issue of his practice,
And of his old experience th' only darling,
He bade me store up, as a triple eye,
Safer than mine own two, more dear: I have so:
And, hearing your high majesty is touch'd
With that malignant cause, wherein the honour

Of my dear father's gift stands chief in power,
I come to tender it, and my appliance,
With all bound humbleness.
  King.   We thank you, maiden;
But may not be so credulous of cure,
When our most learnèd doctors leave us, and
The congregated college have concluded
That labouring art can never ransom nature
From her inaidable state, — I say we must not
So stain our judgment, or corrupt our hope,
To prostitute our past-cure malady
To empirics; or to dissever so
Our great self and our credit, to esteem
A senseless help, when help past sense we deem.
 Hel. My duty, then, shall pay me for my pains:
I will no more enforce mine office on you;
Humbly entreating from your royal thoughts
A modest one, to bear me back again.
 King. I cannot give thee less, to be call'd grateful:
Thou thought'st to help me; and such thanks I give
As one near death to those that wish him live:
But, what at full I know, thou know'st no part;
I knowing all my peril, thou no art.
 Hel. What I can do can do no hurt to try,
Since you set up your rest 'gainst remedy.
He that of greatest works is finisher,
Oft does them by the weakest minister:
So holy writ in babes hath judgment shown,
When judges have been babes; great floods have flown
From simple sources; and great seas have dried,
When miracles have by the greatest been denied.
Oft expectation fails, and most oft there
Where most it promises; and oft it hits
Where hope is coldest, and despair most fits.
 King. I must not hear thee; fare thee well, kind maid;
Thy pains, not us'd, must by thyself be paid:
Proffers not took reap thanks for their reward.

Hel.   Inspirèd merit so by breath is barr'd:
It is not so with Him that all things knows,
As 'tis with us that square our guess by shows;
But most it is presumption in us when
The help of heaven we count the act of men.
Dear sir, to my endeavours give consent;
Of heaven, not me, make an experiment.
I am not an impostor, that proclaim
Myself against the level of mine aim;
But know I think, and think I know most sure,
My art is not past power, nor you past cure.

King.   Art thou so confident? within what space
Hop'st thou my cure?

Hel.   The great'st grace lending grace,
Ere twice the horses of the sun shall bring
Their fiery torcher his diurnal ring;
Ere twice in murk and occidental damp
Moist Hesperus hath quench'd his sleepy lamp;
Or four and twenty times the pilot's glass
Hath told the thievish minutes how they pass;
What is infirm from your sound parts shall fly,
Health shall live free, and sickness freely die.

King.   Upon thy certainty and confidence
What dar'st thou venture?

Hel.   Tax of impudence, —
A strumpet's boldness, a divulgèd shame, —
Traduc'd by odious ballads; my maid's name
Sear'd otherwise; the worst of worst extended, —
With vilest torture let my life be ended.

King.   Methinks in thee some blessèd spirit doth speak,
His powerful sound within an organ weak:
And what impossibility would slay
In common sense, sense saves another way.
Thy life is dear; for all, that life can rate
Worth name of life, in thee hath estimate, —
Youth, beauty, wisdom, courage, virtue, all
That happiness and prime can happy call:

Thou this to hazard, needs must intimate
Skill infinite or monstrous desperate.
Sweet practiser, thy physic I will try,
That ministers thine own death, if I die.

   Hel. If I break time, or flinch in property
Of what I spoke, unpitied let me die;
And well deserv'd: not helping, death's my fee;
But, if I help, what do you promise me?

   King. Make thy demand.

   Hel.   But will you make it even?

   King. Ay, by my sceptre and my hopes of heaven.

   Hel. Then shalt thou give me with thy kingly hand
What husband in thy power I will command:
Exempted be from me the arrogance
To choose from forth the royal blood of France,
My low and humble name to propagate
With any branch or image of thy state;
But such a one, thy vassal, whom I know
Is free for me to ask, thee to bestow.

   King. Here is my hand; the premises observ'd,
Thy will by my performance shall be serv'd:
So make the choice of thy own time; for I,
Thy résolv'd patient, on thee still rely.
More should I question thee, and more I must, —
Though more to know could not be more to trust, —
From whence thou cam'st, how tended on: but rest
Unquestion'd welcome, and undoubted blest. —
Give me some help here, ho! — If thou proceed
As high as word, my deed shall match thy deed.

                                      [*Flourish. Exeunt.*

   Scene II. *Rousillon. A room in the house of the* Countess.

                   Enter Countess *and* Clown.

   Count. Come on, sir; I shall now put you to the height of your breeding.

   Clo. I will show myself highly fed and lowly taught: I know my business is but to the court.

Count. To the court! why, what place make you special, when you put off that with such contempt? But to the court!

Clo. Truly, madam, if God have lent a man any manners, he may easily put it off at court: he that cannot make a leg, put off's cap, kiss his hand, and say nothing, has neither leg, hands, lip, nor cap; and, indeed, such a fellow, to say precisely, were not for the court: but, for me, I have an answer will serve all men.

Count. Marry, that's a bountiful answer that fits all questions.

Clo. It is like a barber's chair, that fits all buttocks,— the pin-buttock, the quatch-buttock, the brawn-buttock, or any buttock.

Count. Will your answer serve fit to all questions?

Clo. As fit as ten groats is for the hand of an attorney, as your French crown for your taffeta punk, as Tib's rush for Tom's forefinger, as a pancake for Shrove-Tuesday, a morris for May-day, as the nail to his hole, the cuckold to his horn, as a scolding quean to a wrangling knave, as the nun's lip to the friar's mouth, nay, as the pudding to his skin.

Count. Have you, I say, an answer of such fitness for all questions?

Clo. From below your duke to beneath your constable, it will fit any question.

Count. It must be an answer of most monstrous size that must fit all demands.

Clo. But a trifle neither, in good faith, if the learned should speak truth of it: here it is, and all that belongs to 't. Ask me if I am a courtier: it shall do you no harm to learn.

Count. To be young again, if we could:—I will be a fool in question, hoping to be the wiser by your answer. I pray you, sir, are you a courtier?

Clo. "O Lord, sir!"— there's a simple putting off.— More, more, a hundred of them.

Count. Sir, I am a poor friend of yours that loves you.

Clo. "O Lord, sir!"— Thick, thick, spare not me.

Count. I think, sir, you can eat none of this homely meat.

Clo. "O Lord, sir!" — Nay, put me to 't, I warrant you.
Count. You were lately whipped, sir, as I think.
Clo. "O Lord, sir!" — Spare not me.
Count. Do you cry, "O Lord, sir!" at your whipping, and "Spare not me"? Indeed, your "O Lord, sir!" is very sequent to your whipping: you would answer very well to a whipping, if you were but bound to 't.
Clo. I ne'er had worse luck in my life in my "O Lord, sir!" I see things may serve long, but not serve ever.
Count. I play the noble housewife with the time,
To entertain 't so merrily with a fool.
Clo. "O Lord, sir!" — why, there 't serves well again.
Count. An end, sir: to your business. Give Helen this,
And urge her to a present answer back:
Commend me to my kinsmen and my son:
This is not much.
Clo. Not much commendation to them.
Count. Not much employment for you: you understand me?
Clo. Most fruitfully: I am there before my legs.
Count. Haste you again. [*Exeunt severally.*

SCENE III. *Paris. A room in the* King's *palace.*

Enter LAFEU *and* PAROLLES.

Laf. They say miracles are past; and we have our philosophical persons, to make modern and familiar, things supernatural and causeless. Hence is it that we make trifles of terrors; ensconcing ourselves into seeming knowledge, when we should submit ourselves to an unknown fear. Why, 'tis the rarest argument of wonder that hath shot out in our latter times.
Par. And so 'tis.
Laf. To be relinquished of the artists, —
Par. So I say.
Laf. Both of Galen and Paracelsus, of all the learned and authentic fellows. —

Par. Right; so I say.
Laf. That gave him out incurable, —
Par. Why, there 'tis; so say I too.
Laf. Not to be helped, —
Par. Right; as 'twere, a man assured of a —
Laf. Uncertain life, and sure death.
Par. Just, you say well; so would I have said.
Laf. I may truly say, it is a novelty to the world.
Par. It is, indeed: if you will have it in showing, you shall read it in What do ye call there —
Laf. A showing of a heavenly effect in an earthly actor.
Par. That's it I would have said, the very same.
Laf. Why, your dolphin is not lustier: 'fore me, I speak in respect —
Par. Nay, 'tis strange, 'tis very strange, that is the brief and the tedious of it; and he's of a most facinorous spirit that will not acknowledge it to be the —
Laf. Very hand of heaven —
Par. Ay, so I say.
Laf. In a most weak and debile minister great power, great transcendence: which should, indeed, give us a further use to be made than alone the recovery of the king.
Par. As to be —
Laf. Generally thankful.
Par. I would have said it; you say well. — Here comes the king.

Enter King, HELENA, *and* Attendants.

Laf. Lustic, as the Dutchman says: I'll like a maid the better, whilst I have a tooth in my head: why, he's able to lead her a coranto.
Par. Mort du vinaigre! is not this Helen?
Laf. 'Fore God, I think so.
King. Go, call before me all the lords in court. —
[*Exit an Attendant.*
Sit, my preserver, by thy patient's side;
And with this healthful hand, whose banish'd sense
Thou hast repeal'd, a second time receive

The confirmation of my promis'd gift,
Which but attends thy naming.

Enter several Lords *and* BERTRAM.

Fair maid, send forth thine eye: this youthful parcel
Of noble bachelors stand at my bestowing,
O'er whom both sovereign power and father's voice
I have to use: thy frank election make;
Thou'st power to choose, and they none to forsake.

    Hel. To each of you one fair and virtuous mistress
Fall, when Love please! — marry, to each, but one!

    Laf. I'd give bay curtal and his furniture,
My mouth no more were broken than these boys',
And writ as little beard.

    King.   Peruse them well:
Not one of those but had a noble father.

    Hel. Gentlemen,
Heaven hath, through me, restor'd the king to health.

    All. We understand it, and thank heaven for you.

    Hel. I am a simple maid; and therein wealthiest,
That I protest I simply am a maid. —
Please it your majesty, I've done already:
The blushes in my cheeks thus whisper me,
"We blush that thou shouldst choose; but, be refus'd,
Let the white death sit on thy cheek for ever;
We'll ne'er come there again."

    King.   Make choice; and, see,
Who shuns thy love shuns all his love in me.

    Hel. Now, Dian, from thy altar do I fly;
And to imperial Love, that god most high,
Do my sighs stream. — [*To First Lord*] Sir, will you hear
        my suit?

    First Lord. And grant it.

    Hel.   Thanks, sir; all the rest is mute.

    Laf. I had rather be in this choice than throw ames-ace
for my life.

    Hel. [*to Sec. Lord*] The honour, sir, that flames in your
        fair eyes,

Before I speak, too threateningly replies:
Love make your fortunes twenty times above
Her that so wishes and her humble love!

Sec. Lord. No better, if you please.

Hel. My wish receive,
Which great Love grant! and so, I take my leave.

Laf. Do all they deny her? An they were sons of mine,
I'd have them whipped; or I would send them to the Turk, to
make eunuchs of.

Hel. [*to Third Lord*] Be not afraid that I your hand should take;
I'll never do you wrong for your own sake:
Blessing upon your vows! and in your bed
Find fairer fortune, if you ever wed!

Laf. These boys are boys of ice, they'll none of her:
sure, they are bastards to the English; the French ne'er
got 'em.

Hel. [*to Fourth Lord*] You are too young, too happy, and too good,
To make yourself a son out of my blood.

Fourth Lord. Fair one, I think not so.

Laf. There's one grape yet,—I am sure thy father drunk
wine:—but if thou be'st not an ass, I am a youth of fourteen;
I have known thee already.

Hel. [*to Bertram*] I dare not say I take you; but I give
Me and my service, ever whilst I live,
Into your guiding power. — This is the man.

King. Why, then, young Bertram, take her; she's thy wife.

Ber. My wife, my liege! I shall beseech your highness,
In such a business give me leave to use
The help of mine own eyes.

King. Know'st thou not, Bertram,
What she has done for me?

Ber. Yes, my good lord;
But never hope to know why I should marry her.

King. Thou know'st she has rais'd me from my sickly bed.

Ber. But follows it, my lord, to bring me down

Must answer for your raising? I know her well:
She had her breeding at my father's charge.
A poor physician's daughter my wife! — Disdain
Rather corrupt me ever!

   King. 'Tis only title thou disdain'st in her, the which
I can build up. Strange is it that our bloods,
Of colour, weight, and heat, pour'd all together,
Would quite confound distinction, yet stand off
In differences so mighty. If she be
All that is virtuous, — save what thou dislik'st,
A poor physician's daughter, — thou dislik'st
Of virtue for the name: but do not so:
From lowest place when virtuous things proceed,
The place is dignified by the doer's deed:
Where great additions swell's, and virtue none,
It is a dropsied honour: good alone
Is good without a name; vileness is so:
The property by what it is should go,
Not by the title. She is young, wise, fair;
In these to nature she's immediate heir;
And these breed honour: that is honour's scorn,
Which challenges itself as honour's born,
And is not like the sire: honours thrive,
When rather from our acts we them derive
Than our foregoers: the mere word's a slave,
Debauch'd on every tomb, on every grave
A lying trophy; and as oft is dumb
Where dust and damn'd oblivion is the tomb
Of honour'd bones indeed. What should be said?
If thou canst like this creature as a maid,
I can create the rest: virtue and she
Is her own dower; honour and wealth from me.

   Ber. I cannot love her, nor will strive to do't.

   King. Thou wrong'st thyself, if thou shouldst strive to choose.

   Hel. That you are well restor'd, my lord, I'm glad:
Let the rest go.

   King. My honour's at the stake; which to defend,

I must produce my power.   Here, take her hand,
Proud scornful boy, unworthy this good gift;
That dost in vile misprision shackle up
My love and her desert; that canst not dream,
We, poising us in her defective scale,
Shall weigh thee to the beam; that wilt not know,
It is in us to plant thine honour where
We please to have it grow.   Check thy contempt:
Obey our will, which travails in thy good:
Believe not thy disdain, but presently
Do thine own fortunes that obedient right
Which both thy duty owes and our power claims;
Or I will throw thee from my care for ever
Into the staggers and the cureless lapse
Of youth and ignorance; both my revenge and hate
Loosing upon thee, in the name of justice,
Without all terms of pity.   Speak; thine answer.

Ber.   Pardon, my gracious lord; for I submit
My fancy to your eyes: when I consider
What great creation and what dole of honour
Flies where you bid it, I find that she, which late
Was in my nobler thoughts most base, is now
The praisèd of the king; who, so ennobled,
Is, as 'twere, born so.

King.   Take her by the hand,
And tell her she is thine: to whom I promise
A counterpoise; if not to thy estate,
A balance more replete.

Ber.   I take her hand.

King.   Good fortune and the favour of the king
Smile upon this contráct; whose ceremony
Shall seem expedient on the new-born brief,
And be perform'd to-night: the solemn feast
Shall more attend upon the coming space,
Expecting absent friends.   As thou lov'st her,
Thy love's to me religious; else, does err.

[*Exeunt King, Bertram, Helena, Lords, and Attendants.*

Laf. Do you hear, monsieur? a word with you.
Par. Your pleasure, sir?
Laf. Your lord and master did well to make his recantation.
Par. Recantation! — My lord! my master!
Laf. Ay; is it not a language I speak?
Par. A most harsh one, and not to be understood without bloody succeeding. My master!
Laf. Are you companion to the Count Rousillon?
Par. To any count, — to all counts, — to what is man.
Laf. To what is count's man: count's master is of another style.
Par. You are too old, sir; let it satisfy you, you are too old.
Laf. I must tell thee, sirrah, I write man; to which title age cannot bring thee.
Par. What I dare too well do, I dare not do.
Laf. I did think thee, for two ordinaries, to be a pretty wise fellow; thou didst make tolerable vent of thy travel; it might pass: yet the scarfs and the bannerets about thee did manifoldly dissuade me from believing thee a vessel of too great a burden. I have now found thee; when I lose thee again, I care not: yet art thou good for nothing but taking up; and that thou 'rt scarce worth.
Par. Hadst thou not the privilege of antiquity upon thee, —
Laf. Do not plunge thyself too far in anger, lest thou hasten thy trial; which if — Lord have mercy on thee for a hen! So, my good window of lattice, fare thee well: thy casement I need not open, for I look through thee. Give me thy hand.
Par. My lord, you give me most egregious indignity.
Laf. Ay, with all my heart; and thou art worthy of it.
Par. I have not, my lord, deserved it.
Laf. Yes, good faith, every dram of it; and I will not bate thee a scruple.
Par. Well, I shall be wiser —

Laf. E'en as soon as thou canst, for thou hast to pull at a smack o' the contrary. If ever thou be'st bound in thy scarf and beaten, thou shalt find what it is to be proud of thy bondage. I have a desire to hold my acquaintance with thee, or rather my knowledge, that I may say, in the default, he is a man I know.

Par. My lord, you do me most insupportable vexation.

Laf. I would it were hell-pains for thy sake, and my poor doing eternal: for doing I am past; as I will by thee, in what motion age will give me leave. [*Exit.*

Par. Well, thou hast a son shall take this disgrace off me; scurvy, old, filthy, scurvy lord! — Well, I must be patient; there is no fettering of authority. I'll beat him, by my life, if I can meet him with any convenience, an he were double and double a lord. I'll have no more pity of his age than I would have of — I'll beat him, an if I could but meet him again.

Re-enter LAFEU.

Laf. Sirrah, your lord and master's married; there's news for you: you have a new mistress.

Par. I most unfeignedly beseech your lordship to make some reservation of your wrongs: he is my good lord; whom I serve above is my master.

Laf. Who? God?

Par. Ay, sir.

Laf. The devil it is that's thy master. Why dost thou garter up thy arms o' this fashion? dost make hose of thy sleeves? do other servants so? Thou wert best set thy lower part where thy nose stands. By mine honour, if I were but two hours younger, I'd beat thee: methinks 't, thou art a general offence, and every man should beat thee: I think thou wast created for men to breathe themselves upon thee.

Par. This is hard and undeserved measure, my lord.

Laf. Go to, sir; you were beaten in Italy for picking a kernel out of a pomegranate; you are a vagabond, and no true traveller: you are more saucy with lords and honourable personages than the heraldry of your birth and virtue gives

you commission. You are not worth another word, else I'd
call you knave. I leave you. [*Exit.*

Par. Good, very good; it is so then:— good, very good;
let it be concealed awhile.

Re-enter BERTRAM.

Ber. Undone, and forfeited to cares for ever!
Par. What's the matter, sweet-heart?
Ber. Although before the solemn priest I've sworn,
I will not bed her.
Par. What, what, sweet-heart?
Ber. O, my Parolles, they have married me!—
I'll to the Tuscan wars, and never bed her.
Par. France is a dog-hole, and it no more merits
The tread of a man's foot: to the wars!
Ber. There's letters from my mother: what th' impórt is,
I know not yet
Par. Ay,
That would be known. To the wars, my boy, to the wars!
He wears his honour in a box unseen,
That hugs his kicky-wicky here at home,
Spending his manly marrow in her arms,
Which should sustain the bound and high curvet
Of Mars's fiery steed. To other regions!
France is a stable; we that dwell in 't jades;
Therefore, to the wars!
Ber. It shall be so: I'll send her to my house,
Acquaint my mother with my hate to her,
And wherefore I am fled; write to the king
That which I durst not speak: his present gift
Shall furnish me to those Italian fields,
Where noble fellows strike: war is no strife
To the dark house and the detested wife.
Par. Will this capriccio hold in thee, art sure?
Ber. Go with me to my chamber, and advise me.
I'll send her straight away: to-morrow
I'll to the wars, she to her single sorrow.

Par.   Why, these balls bound; there's noise in it. — 'Tis
          hard:
A young man married is a man that's marr'd:
Therefore, away, and leave her; bravely go:
The king has done you wrong; but, hush, 'tis so.   [*Exeunt.*

   SCENE IV.   *The same.   Another room in the same.*

          Enter HELENA *and* Clown.

Hel.   My mother greets me kindly: is she well?
Clo.   She is not well; but yet she has her health: she's very merry; but yet she is not well: but thanks be given, she's very well, and wants nothing i' the world; but yet she is not well.
Hel.   If she be very well, what does she ail, that she's not very well?
Clo.   Truly, she's very well indeed, but for two things.
Hel.   What two things?
Clo.   One, that she's not in heaven, whither God send her quickly! the other, that she's in earth, from whence God send her quickly!

          Enter PAROLLES.

Par.   Bless you, my fortunate lady!
Hel.   I hope, sir, I have your good will to have mine own good fortunes.
Par.   You had my prayers to lead them on; and to keep them on, have them still. — O, my knave, — how does my old lady?
Clo.   So that you had her wrinkles, and I her money, I would she did as you say.
Par.   Why, I say nothing.
Clo.   Marry, you are the wiser man; for many a man's tongue shakes out his master's undoing: to say nothing, to do nothing, to know nothing, and to have nothing, is to be a great part of your title; which is within a very little of nothing.
Par.   Away! thou'rt a knave.
Clo.   You should have said, sir, before a knave thou'rt a

knave; that's, before me thou'rt a knave: this had been truth, sir.

Par. Go to, thou art a witty fool; I have found thee.

Clo. Did you find me in yourself, sir? or were you taught to find me? The search, sir, was profitable; and much fool may you find in you, even to the world's pleasure, and the increase of laughter.

Par. A good knave, i' faith, and well fed. — Madam, my lord will go away to-night;
A very serious business calls on him.
The great prerogative and rite of love,
Which, as your due, time claims, he does acknowledge;
But puts it off to a compell'd restraint;
Whose want, and whose delay, is strew'd with sweets,
Which they distil now in the curbèd time,
To make the coming hour o'erflow with joy,
And pleasure drown the brim.

Hel.   What's his will else?

Par. That you will take your instant leave o' the king,
And make this haste as your own good proceeding,
Strengthen'd with what apology you think
May make it probable need.

Hel.   What more commands he?

Par. That, having this obtain'd, you presently
Attend his further pleasure.

Hel. In every thing I wait upon his will.

Par. I shall report it so.

Hel.   I pray you. [*Exit Par.*] Come, sirrah.
              [*Exeunt.*

SCENE V. *Another room in the same.*

Enter LAFEU *and* BERTRAM.

Laf. But I hope your lordship thinks not him a soldier.

Ber. Yes, my lord, and of very valiant approof.

Laf. You have it from his own deliverance.

Ber. And by other warranted testimony.

Laf. Then my dial goes not true: I took this lark for a bunting.

Ber. I do assure you, my lord, he is very great in knowledge, and accordingly valiant.

Laf. I have, then, sinned against his experience, and transgressed against his valour; and my state that way is dangerous, since I cannot yet find in my heart to repent. Here he comes: I pray you, make us friends; I will pursue the amity.

Enter PAROLLES.

Par. [*to Bertram*] These things shall be done, sir.
Laf. Pray you, sir, who's his tailor?
Par. Sir?
Laf. O, I know him well, I, sir; he, sir, 's a good workman, a very good tailor.
Ber. [*aside to Par.*] Is she gone to the king?
Par. [*aside to Ber.*] She is.
Ber. [*aside to Par.*] Will she away to-night?
Par. [*aside to Ber.*] As you'll have her.
Ber. [*aside to Par.*] I've writ my letters, casketed my
    treasure,
Given order for our horses; and to-night,
When I should take possession of the bride,
End ere I do begin.

Laf. A good traveller is something at the latter end of a dinner; but one that lies three-thirds, and uses a known truth to pass a thousand nothings with, should be once heard, and thrice beaten. — God save you, captain.

Ber. Is there any unkindness between my lord and you, monsieur?

Par. I know not how I have deserved to run into my lord's displeasure.

Laf. You have made shift to run into 't, boots and spurs and all, like him that leaped into the custard; and out of it you'll run again, rather than suffer question for your residence.

Ber. It may be you have mistaken him, my lord.

Laf. And shall do so ever, though I took him at 's prayers.

Fare you well, my lord; and believe this of me, there can be no kernel in this light nut; the soul of this man is his clothes: trust him not in matter of heavy consequence; I have kept of them tame, and know their natures. — Farewell, monsieur: I have spoken better of you than you have or will deserve at my hand; but we must do good against evil. [*Exit.*

Par. An idle lord, I swear.
Ber.   I think not so.
Par. Why, do you know him?
Ber. Yes, I do know him well; and common speech Gives him a worthy pass. — Here comes my clog..

Enter HELENA.

Hel. I have, sir, as I was commanded from you,
Spoke with the king, and have procur'd his leave
For present parting; only, he desires
Some private speech with you.
Ber.   I shall obey his will.
You must not marvel, Helen, at my course,
Which holds not colour with the time, nor does
The ministration and required office
On my particular. Prepar'd I was not
For such a business; therefore am I found
So much unsettled: this drives me to entreat you,
That presently you take your way for home,
And rather muse than ask why I entreat you;
For my respects are better than they seem,
And my appointments have in them a need
Greater than shows itself, at the first view,
To you that know them not. This to my mother:
                              [*Giving a letter.*
'Twill be two days ere I shall see you; so,
I leave you to your wisdom.
Hel.   Sir, I can nothing say,
But that I am your most obedient servant.
Ber. Come, come, no more of that.
Hel.   And ever shall

With true observance seek to eke out that
Wherein toward me my homely stars have fail'd
To equal my great fortune.
 Ber.   Let that go:
My haste is very great: farewell; hie home.
 Hel. Pray, sir, your pardon.
 Ber.   Well, what would you say?
 Hel. I am not worthy of the wealth I owe;
Nor dare I say 'tis mine, — and yet it is;
But, like a timorous thief, most fain would steal
What law does vouch mine own.
 Ber.   What would you have?
 Hel. Something; and scarce so much: — nothing, indeed.—
I would not tell you what I would, my lord: —
Faith, yes; —
Strangers and foes do sunder, and not kiss.
 Ber. I pray you, stay not, but in haste to horse.
 Hel. I shall not break your bidding, good my lord.
 Ber. Where are my other men, monsieur? — Farewell.
            [*Exit Helena.*
Go thou toward home; where I will never come,
Whilst I can shake my sword, or hear the drum. —
Away, and for our flight.
 Par.   Bravely, coragio!   [*Exeunt.*

ACT III.

 S CENE I. *Florence. A room in the* Duke's *palace.*

Flourish. Enter the Duke *of Florence, attended; two French Lords and* Soldiers.

 Duke. So that, from point to point, now have you heard
The fundamental reasons of this war;
Whose great decision hath much blood let forth,
And more thirsts after.
 First Lord.   Holy seems the quarrel
Upon your grace's party; black and fearful
On the opposer's.

Duke. Therefore we marvel much our cousin France
Would, in so just a business, shut his bosom
Against our borrowing prayers.
  First Lord.   Good my lord,
The reasons of our state I cannot yield,
But like a common and an outward man,
That the great figure of a council frames
By self-unable motion: therefore dare not
Say what I think of it, since I have found
Myself in my incertain grounds to fail
As often as I guess'd.
  Duke.   Be it his pleasure.
  Sec. Lord. But I am sure the younger of our nation,
That surfeit on their ease, will day by day
Come here for physic.
  Duke.   Welcome shall they be;
And all the honours that can fly from us
Shall on them settle. You know your places well;
When better fall, for your avails they fell:
To-morrow to the field.   [*Flourish. Exeunt.*

Scene II. *Rousillon. A room in the house of the Countess.*

Enter Countess *and* Clown.

  Count. It hath happened all as I would have had it, save that he comes not along with her.

  Clo. By my troth, I take my young lord to be a very melancholy man.

  Count. By what observance, I pray you?

  Clo. Why, he will look upon his boot, and sing; mend the ruff, and sing; ask questions, and sing; pick his teeth, and sing. I knew a man that had this trick of melancholy sold a goodly manor for a song.

  Count. Let me see what he writes, and when he means to come.   [*Opening a letter.*

  Clo. I have no mind to Isbel, since I was at court: our old ling and our Isbels o' the country are nothing like your old ling and your Isbels o' the court: the brains of my Cupid's knocked out; and I begin to love, as an old man loves money, with no stomach.

Count. What have we here?

Clo. E'en that you have there. [*Exit.*

Count. [*reads*] "I have sent you a daughter-in-law: she hath recovered the king, and undone me. I have wedded her, not bedded her; and sworn to make the *not* eternal. You shall hear I am run away: know it before the report come. If there be breadth enough in the world, I will hold a long distance. My duty to you. Your unfortunate son,

BERTRAM."

This is not well, rash and unbridled boy,
To fly the favours of so good a king;
To pluck his indignation on thy head
By the misprizing of a maid too virtuous
For the contempt of empire.

Re-enter Clown.

Clo. O madam, yonder is heavy news within between two soldiers and my young lady!

Count. What is the matter?

Clo. Nay, there is some comfort in the news, some comfort; your son will not be killed so soon as I thought he would.

Count. Why should he be killed?

Clo. So say I, madam, if he run away, as I hear he does: the danger is in standing to't; that's the loss of men, though it be the getting of children. Here they come will tell you more: for my part, I only heard your son was run away. [*Exit.*

Enter HELENA *and two* Gentlemen.

First Gent. Save you, good madam.

Hel. Madam, my lord is gone, for ever gone.

Sec. Gent. Do not say so.

Count. Think upon patience. — Pray you, gentlemen, —
I've felt so many quirks of joy and grief,
That the first face of neither, on the start,
Can woman me unto 't: — where is my son, I pray you?

Sec. Gent. Madam, he's gone to serve the Duke of
            Florence:
We met him thitherward; for thence we came,
And, after some dispatch in hand at court,
Thither we bend again.
   Hel. Look on his letter, madam; here's my passport.
[*Reads*] "When thou canst get the ring upon my finger which
never shall come off, and show me a child begotten of thy
body that I am father to, then call me husband: but in such
a *then* I write a *never*."
This is a dreadful sentence.
   Count. Brought you this letter, gentlemen?
   First Gent.   Ay, madam;
And, for the contents' sake, are sorry for our pains.
   Count. I prithee, lady, have a better cheer;
If thou engrossest all the griefs as thine,
Thou robb'st me of a moiety: he was my son;
But I do wash his name out of my blood,
And thou art all my child. — Towards Florence is he?
   Sec. Gent. Ay, madam.
   Count.   And to be a soldier?
   Sec. Gent. Such is his noble purpose: and, believe 't,
The duke will lay upon him all the honour
That good convenience claims.
   Count.   Return you thither?
   First Gent. Ay, madam, with the swiftest wing of speed.
   Hel.[*reads*] "Till I have no wife, I have nothing in France."
'Tis bitter.
   Count. Find you that there?
   Hel.   Ay, madam.
   First Gent. 'Tis but the boldness of his hand, which, haply,
His heart was not consenting to.
   Count. Nothing in France, until he have no wife!
There's nothing here that is too good for him,
But only she; and she deserves a lord,
That twenty such rude boys might tend upon,
And call her hourly mistress. — Who was with him?

First Gent. A servant only, and a gentleman
Which I have some time known.
    Count.   Parolles, was't not?
    First Gent. Ay, my good lady, he.
    Count. A very tainted fellow, and full of wickedness.
My son corrupts a well-derivèd nature
With his inducement.
    First Gent.   Indeed, good lady,
The fellow has a deal of that too much,
Which holds him much to have.
    Count. Y' are welcome, gentlemen.
I will entreat you, when you see my son,
To tell him that his sword can never win
The honour that he loses: more I'll entreat you
Written to bear along.
    Sec. Gent.   We serve you, madam,
In that and all your worthiest affairs.
    Count. Not so, but as we change our courtesies.
Will you draw near?   [*Exeunt Countess and Gentlemen.*
    Hel. "Till I have no wife, I have nothing in France."
Nothing in France, until he has no wife!
Thou shalt have none, Rousillon, none in France;
Then hast thou all again. Poor lord! is 't I
That chase thee from thy country, and expose
Those tender limbs of thine to the event
Of the none-sparing war? and is it I
That drive thee from the sportive court, where thou
Wast shot at with fair eyes, to be the mark
Of smoky muskets? O you leaden messengers,
That ride upon the violent speed of fire,
Fly with false aim; move the still-piecing air,
That sings with piercing; do not touch my lord!
Whoever shoots at him, I set him there;
Whoever charges on his forward breast,
I am the caitiff that do hold him to 't;
And, though I kill him not, I am the cause
His death was so effected: better 'twere

I met the ravin lion when he roar'd
With sharp constraint of hunger; better 'twere
That all the miseries which nature owes
Were mine at once. No, come thou home, Rousillon,
Whence honour but of danger wins a scar,
As oft it loses all: I will be gone;
My being here it is that holds thee hence:
Shall I stay here to do 't? no, no, although
The air of paradise did fan the house,
And angels offic'd all: I will be gone,
That pitiful rumour may report my flight,
To consolate thine ear. Come, night; end, day!
For with the dark, poor thief, I'll steal away. [*Exit.*

SCENE III. *Florence. Before the Duke's palace.*

Flourish. Enter the Duke of Florence, BERTRAM, PAROLLES, *Lords, Officers, Soldiers, and others.*

Duke. The general of our horse thou art; and we,
Great in our hope, lay our best love and credence
Upon thy promising fortune.
    Ber.   Sir, it is
A charge too heavy for my strength; but yet
We'll strive to bear it, for your worthy sake,
To th' extreme edge of hazard.
    Duke.   Then go thou forth;
And Fortune play upon thy prosperous helm,
As thy auspicious mistress!
    Ber.   This very day,
Great Mars, I put myself into thy file:
Make me but like my thoughts, and I shall prove
A lover of thy drum, hater of love. [*Exeunt.*

SCENE IV. *Rousillon. A room in the house of the* Countess.

Enter Countess *and* Steward.

Count. Alas! and would you take the letter of her?
Might you not know she'd do as she has done,
By sending me a letter? Read it again.

Stew. [*reads*]
"I am Saint Jaques' pilgrim, thither gone:
   Ambitious love hath so in me offended,
That barefoot plod I the cold ground upon,
   With sainted vow my faults to have amended.
Write, write, that from the bloody course of war
   My dearest master, your dear son, may hie:
Bless him at home in peace, whilst I from far
   His name with zealous fervour sanctify:
His taken labours bid him me forgive;
   I, his despiteful Juno, sent him forth
From courtly friends, with camping foes to live,
   Where death and danger dog the heels of worth:
He is too good and fair for death and me;
   Whom I myself embrace, to set him free."
   Count. Ah, what sharp stings are in her mildest words!—
Rinaldo, you did never lack advice so much,
As letting her pass so: had I spoke with her,
I could have well diverted her intents,
Which thus she hath prevented.
   Stew.   Pardon me, madam:
If I had given you this at over-night,
She might have been o'erta'en; and yet she writes,
Pursuit would be but vain.
   Count.   What angel shall
Bless this unworthy husband? he cannot thrive,
Unless her prayers, whom heaven delights to hear,
And loves to grant, reprieve him from the wrath
Of greatest justice. — Write, write, Rinaldo,
To this unworthy husband of his wife;
Let every word weigh heavy of her worth,
That he does weigh too light: my greatest grief,
Though little he do feel it, set down sharply.
Dispatch the most convenient messenger: —
When haply he shall hear that she is gone,
He will return; and hope I may that she,
Hearing so much, will speed her foot again,

Led hither by pure love: which of them both
Is dearest to me, I've no skill in sense
To make distinction: — provide this messenger: —
My heart is heavy and mine age is weak:
Grief would have tears, and sorrow bids me speak. [*Exeunt.*

SCENE V. *Without the walls of Florence.*

Enter an old Widow *of Florence,* DIANA, VIOLENTA, MARIANA, *and other* Citizens.

Wid. Nay, come; for if they do approach the city, we shall lose all the sight.

Dia. They say the French count has done most honourable service.

Wid. It is reported that he has taken their greatest commander; and that with his own hand he slew the duke's brother. [*A tucket afar off.*] We have lost our labour; they are gone a contrary way: hark! you may know by their trumpets.

Mar. Come, let's return again, and suffice ourselves with the report of it. Well, Diana, take heed of this French earl: the honour of a maid is her name; and no legacy is so rich as honesty.

Wid. I have told my neighbour how you have been solicited by a gentleman his companion.

Mar. I know that knave; hang him! one Parolles: a filthy officer he is in those suggestions for the young earl.—Beware of them, Diana; their promises, enticements, oaths, tokens, and all these engines of lust, are not the things they go under: many a maid hath been seduced by them; and the misery is, example, that so terrible shows in the wreck of maidenhood, cannot for all that dissuade succession, but that they are limed with the twigs that threaten them. I hope I need not to advise you further; but I hope your own grace will keep you where you are, though there were no further danger known but the modesty which is so lost.

Dia. You shall not need to fear me.

Wid. I hope so. — Look, here comes a pilgrim: I know she will lie at my house; thither they send one another: I'll question her.

Enter HELENA, *in the dress of a pilgrim.*

God save you, pilgrim! whither are you bound?
 Hel. To Saint Jaques le Grand.
Where do the palmers lodge, I do beseech you?
 Wid. At the Saint Francis here, beside the port.
 Hel. Is this the way?
 Wid. Ay, marry, is 't. — Hark you! they come this way. —
           [*A march afar off.*
If you will tarry, holy pilgrim,
But till the troops come by,
I will conduct you where you shall be lodg'd;
The rather, for I think I know your hostess
As ample as myself.
 Hel.   Is it yourself?
 Wid. If you shall please so, pilgrim.
 Hel. I thank you, and will stay upon your leisure.
 Wid. You came, I think, from France?
 Hel.   I did so.
 Wid. Here you shall see a countryman of yours
That has done worthy service.
 Hel.   His name, I pray you.
 Dia. The Count Rousillon: know you such a one?
 Hel. But by the ear, that hears most nobly of him:
His face I know not.
 Dia.   Whatsoe'er he is,
He's bravely taken here. He stole from France,
As 'tis reported, for the king had married him
Against his liking: think you it is so?
 Hel. Ay, surely, mere the truth: I know his lady.
 Dia. There is a gentleman that serves the count
Reports but coarsely of her.
 Hel.   What's his name?
 Dia. Monsieur Parolles.

Hel. O, I believe with him,
In argument of praise, or to the worth
Of the great count himself, she is too mean
To have her name repeated: all her deserving
Is a reservèd honesty, and that
I have not heard examin'd.
    Dia. Alas, poor lady!
'Tis a hard bondage to become the wife
Of a detesting lord.
    Wid. I wot, good creature, wheresoe'er she is,
Her heart weighs sadly: this young maid might do her
A shrewd turn, if she pleas'd.
    Hel. How do you mean?
May be the amorous count solicits her
In the unlawful purpose.
    Wid. He does indeed;
And brokes with all that can in such a suit
Corrupt the tender honour of a maid:
But she is arm'd for him, and keeps her guard
In honestest defence.
    Mar. The gods forbid else!
    Wid. So, now they come:—

Enter BERTRAM, PAROLLES, *and the Florentine army with drum and colours.*

That is Antonio, the duke's eldest son;
That, Escalus.
    Hel. Which is the Frenchman?
    Dia. He;
That with the plume: 'tis a most gallant fellow.
I would he lov'd his wife: if he were honester,
He were much goodlier: is 't not a handsome gentleman?
    Hel. I like him well.
    Dia. 'Tis pity he's not honest: yond's that same knave
That leads him to these passes: were I his lady,
I'd poison that vile rascal.
    Hel. Which is he?

Dia. That jack-an-apes with scarfs: why is he melancholy?
Hel. Perchance he's hurt i' the battle.
Par. Lose our drum! well.
Mar. He's shrewdly vex'd at something: look, he has spied us.
Wid. Marry, hang you!
Mar. And your courtesy, for a ring-carrier!
[*Exeunt Bertram, Parolles, &c.*
Wid. The troop is past. Come, pilgrim, I will bring you
Where you shall host: of enjoin'd penitents
There's four or five, to Great Saint Jaques bound,
Already at my house.
Hel.   I humbly thank you:
Please it this matron and this gentle maid
To eat with us to-night, the charge and thanking
Shall be for me; and, to requite you further,
I will bestow some precepts of this virgin
Worthy the note.
Both.   We'll take your offer kindly.   [*Exeunt.*

SCENE VI. *Camp before Florence.*

Enter BERTRAM *and the two French* Lords.

First Lord. Nay, good my lord, put him to 't; let him have his way.
Sec. Lord. If your lordship find him not a hilding, hold me no more in your respect.
First Lord. On my life, my lord, a bubble.
Ber. Do you think I am so far deceived in him?
First Lord. Believe it, my lord, in mine own direct knowledge, without any malice, but to speak of him as my kinsman, he's a most notable coward, an infinite and endless liar, an hourly promise-breaker, the owner of no one good quality worthy your lordship's entertainment.
Sec. Lord. It were fit you knew him; lest, reposing too far in his virtue, which he hath not, he might at some great and trusty business, in a°main danger, fail you.'

Ber. I would I knew in what particular action to try him.

Sec. Lord. None better than to let him fetch off his drum, which you hear him so confidently undertake to do.

First Lord. I, with a troop of Florentines, will suddenly surprise him; such I will have, whom, I am sure, he knows not from the enemy: we will bind and hoodwink him so, that he shall suppose no other but that he is carried into the leaguer of the adversaries, when we bring him to our own tents. Be but your lordship present at his examination: if he do not, for the promise of his life, and in the highest compulsion of base fear, offer to betray you, and deliver all the intelligence in his power against you, and that with the divine forfeit of his soul upon oath, never trust my judgment in any thing.

Sec. Lord. O, for the love of laughter, let him fetch off his drum; he says he has a stratagem for 't: when your lordship sees the bottom of his success in 't, and to what metal this counterfeit lump of ore will be melted, if you give him not John Drum's entertainment, your inclining cannot be removed. — Here he comes.

First Lord. O, for the love of laughter, hinder not the humour of his design: let him fetch off his drum in any hand.

Enter PAROLLES.

Ber. How now, monsieur! this drum sticks sorely in your disposition.

Sec. Lord. A pox on 't, let it go; 'tis but a drum.

Par. But a drum! is 't but a drum? A drum so lost! — There was excellent command, — to charge in with our horse upon our own wings, and to rend our own soldiers!

Sec. Lord. That was not to be blamed in the command of the service: it was a disaster of war that Cæsar himself could not have prevented, if he had been there to command.

Ber. Well, we cannot greatly condemn our success: some dishonour we had in the loss of that drum; but it is not to be recovered.

Par. It might have been recovered.

Ber. It might; but it is not now.

Par. It is to be recovered: but that the merit of service is seldom attributed to the true and exact performer, I would have that drum or another, or *hic jacet*.

Ber. Why, if you have a stomach to 't, monsieur, if you think your mystery in stratagem can bring this instrument of honour again into his native quarter, be magnanimous in the enterprise, and go on; I will grace the attempt for a worthy exploit: if you speed well in it, the duke shall both speak of it, and extend to you what further becomes his greatness, even to the utmost syllable of your worthiness.

Par. By the hand of a soldier, I will undertake it.

Ber. But you must not now slumber in it.

Par. I'll about it this evening: and I will presently pen down my dilemmas, encourage myself in my certainty, put myself into my mortal preparation; and, by midnight, look to hear further from me.

Ber. May I be bold to acquaint his grace you are gone about it?

Par. I know not what the success will be, my lord; but the attempt I vow.

Ber. I know thou'rt valiant; and, to the possibility of thy soldiership, will subscribe for thee. Farewell.

Par. I love not many words. [*Exit.*

First Lord. No more than a fish loves water. — Is not this a strange fellow, my lord, that so confidently seems to undertake this business, which he knows is not to be done; damns himself to do, and dares better be damned than to do 't?

Sec. Lord. You do not know him, my lord, as we do: certain it is, that he will steal himself into a man's favour, and for a week escape a great deal of discoveries; but when you find him out, you have him ever after.

Ber. Why, do you think he will make no deed at all of this, that so seriously he does address himself unto?

First Lord. None in the world; but return with an invention, and clap upon you two or three probable lies: but we

have almost embossed him, — you shall see his fall to-night;
for indeed he is not for your lordship's respect.

Sec. Lord. We'll make you some sport with the fox, ere
we case him. He was first smoked by the old Lord Lafeu:
when his disguise and he is parted, tell me what a sprat you
shall find him; which you shall see this very night.

First Lord. I must go look my twigs: he shall be caught.

Ber. Your brother, he shall go along with me.

First Lord. As 't please your lordship: I'll leave you.
[*Exit.*

Ber. Now will I lead you to the house, and show you
The lass I spoke of.

Sec. Lord. But you say she's honest.

Ber. That's all the fault: I spoke with her but once,
And found her wondrous cold; but I sent to her,
By this same coxcomb that we have i' the wind,
Tokens and letters which she did re-send;
And this is all I've done. She's a fair creature:
Will you go see her?

Sec. Lord. With all my heart, my lord. [*Exeunt.*

Scene VII. *Florence. A room in the Widow's house.*

Enter Helena *and* Widow.

Hel. If you misdoubt me that I am not she,
I know not how I shall assure you further,
But I shall lose the grounds I work upon.

Wid. Though my estate be fall'n, I was well born,
Nothing acquainted with these businesses;
And would not put my reputation now
In any staining act.

Hel. Nor would I wish you.
First, give me trust, the county is my husband,
And what to your sworn counsel I have spoken
Is so from word to word; and then you cannot,
By the good aid that I of you shall borrow,
Err in bestowing it.

Wid. I should believe you;

For you have show'd me that which well approves
You're great in fortune.
 Hel.   Take this purse of gold,
And let me buy your friendly help thus far,
Which I will over-pay and pay again,
When I have found it. The county woos your daughter,
Lays down his wanton siege before her beauty,
Resolv'd to carry her: let her, in fine, consent,
As we'll direct her how 'tis best to bear it;
Now his important blood will naught deny
That she'll demand: a ring the county wears,
That downward hath succeeded in his house
From son to son, some four or five descents
Since the first father wore it: this ring he holds
In most rich choice; yet, in his idle fire,
To buy his will, it would not seem too dear,
Howe'er repented after.
 Wid.   Now I see
The bottom of your purpose.
 Hel. You see it lawful, then: it is no more,
But that your daughter, ere she seems as won,
Desires this ring; appoints him an encounter;
In fine, delivers me to fill the time,
Herself most chastely absent: after this,
To marry her, I'll add three thousand crowns
To what is past already.
 Wid.   I have yielded:
Instruct my daughter how she shall persévér,
That time and place with this deceit so lawful
May prove coherent. Every night he comes
With music of all sorts, and songs compos'd
To her unworthiness: it nothing steads us
To chide him from our eaves; for he persists,
As if his life lay on 't.
 Hel.   Why, then, to-night
* Let us assay our plot; which, if it speed,
Is wicked meaning in a lawful deed,

And lawful meaning in a wicked act;
Where both not sin, and yet a sinful fact:
But let's about it. [*Exeunt.*

ACT IV.

SCENE I. *Without the Florentine camp.*

Enter First French Lord, *with five or six* Soldiers *in ambush.*

First Lord. He can come no other way but by this hedge-corner. When you sally upon him, speak what terrible language you will, — though you understand it not yourselves, no matter; for we must not seem to understand him, unless some one among us, whom we must produce for an interpreter.

First Sold. Good captain, let me be the interpreter.

First Lord. Art not acquainted with him? knows he not thy voice?

First Sold. No, sir, I warrant you.

First Lord. But what linsey-woolsey hast thou to speak to us again?

First Sold. E'en such as you speak to me.

First Lord. He must think us some band of strangers i' the adversary's entertainment. Now, he hath a smack of all neighbouring languages; therefore we must every one be a man of his own fancy, not to know what we speak one to another; so we seem to know, is to know straight our purpose: choughs' language, gabble enough, and good enough. As for you, interpreter, you must seem very politic. — But couch, ho! here he comes, — to beguile two hours in a sleep, and then to return and swear the lies he forges.

Enter PAROLLES.

Par. Ten o'clock: within these three hours 'twill be time enough to go home. What shall I say I have done? It must be a very plausive invention that carries it: they begin to smoke me; and disgraces have of late knocked too often at my door. I find my tongue is too foolhardy; but my heart hath the fear of Mars before it and of his creatures, not daring the reports of my tongue.

First Lord. [*aside*] This is the first truth that e'er thine own tongue was guilty of.

Par. What the devil should move me to undertake the recovery of this drum, being not ignorant of the impossibility, and knowing I had no such purpose? I must give myself some hurts, and say I got them in exploit: yet slight ones will not carry it; they will say, "Came you off with so little?" and great ones I dare not give. Wherefore, what's the instance? Tongue, I must put you into a butter-woman's mouth, and buy myself another of Bajazet's mute, if you prattle me into these perils.

First Lord. [*aside*] Is it possible he should know what he is, and be that he is?

Par. I would the cutting of my garments would serve the turn, or the breaking of my Spanish sword.

First Lord. [*aside*] We cannot afford you so.

Par. Or the baring of my beard; and to say it was in stratagem.

First Lord. [*aside*] 'Twould not do.

Par. Or to drown my clothes, and say I was stripped —

First Lord. [*aside*] Hardly serve.

Par. Though I swore I leaped from the window of the citadel —

First Lord. [*aside*] How deep?

Par. Thirty fathom.

First Lord. [*aside*] Three great oaths would scarce make that be believed.

Par. I would I had any drum of the enemy's: I would swear I recovered it.

First Lord. [*aside*] You shall hear one anon.

[*Alarum within.*

Par. A drum now of the enemy's!

First Lord. *Throca movousus, cargo, cargo, cargo.*

All. *Cargo, cargo, cargo, villianda par corbo, cargo.*

Par. O, ransom, ransom! — do not hide mine eyes.

[*They seize and blindfold him.*

First Sold. *Boskos thromuldo boskos.*

Par. I know you are the Muskos' regiment;
And I shall lose my life for want of language:
If there be here German, or Dane, low Dutch,
Italian, or French, let him speak to me;
I will discover that which shall undo
The Florentine.

First Sold.   *Boskos vauvado:* —
I understand thee, and can speak thy tongue: —
Kerelybonto: — sir,
Betake thee to thy faith, for seventeen poniards
Are at thy bosom.

Par.   O!

First Sold.   O, pray, pray, pray! —
Manka revania dulche.

First Lord.   *Oscorbi dulchos volivorco.*

First Sold. The general is content to spare thee yet;
And, hoodwink'd as thou art, will lead thee on
To gather from thee: haply thou mayst inform
Something to save thy life.

Par.   O, let me live!
And all the secrets of our camp I'll show,
Their force, their purposes; nay, I'll speak that
Which you will wonder at.

First Sold.   But wilt thou faithfully?

Par. If I do not, damn me

First Sold.   *Acordo linta:* —
Come on; thou art granted space.

[*Exit, with Parolles guarded. A short alarum within.*

First Lord. Go, tell the Count Rousillon, and my brother,
We've caught the woodcock, and will keep him muffled
Till we do hear from them.

Sec. Sold.   Captain, I will.

First Lord. 'A will betray us all unto ourselves: —
Inform 'em that.

Sec. Sold. So I will, sir.

First Lord. Till then I'll keep him dark and safely lock'd.

[*Exeunt.*

SCENE II. *Florence. A room in the Widow's house.*

Enter BERTRAM *and* DIANA.

Ber. They told me that your name was Fontibell.
Dia. No, my good lord, Diana.
Ber. . Titled goddess;
And worth it, with addition! But, fair soul,
In your fine frame hath love no quality?
If the quick fire of youth light not' your mind,
You are no maiden, but a monument:
When you are dead, you should be such a one
As you are now, for you are cold and stern;
And now you should be as your mother was
When your sweet self was got.
Dia. She then was honest.
Ber. So should you be.
Dia. No:
My mother did but duty; such, my lord,
As you owe to your wife.
Ber. No more o' that, —
I prithee, do not strive against my vows:
I was compell'd to her; but I love thee
By love's own sweet constraint, and will for ever
Do thee all rights of service.
Dia. Ay, so you serve us
Till we serve you; but when you have our roses,
You barely leave our thorns to prick ourselves,
And mock us with our bareness.
Ber. How have I sworn!
Dia. 'Tis not the many oaths that make the truth,
But the plain single vow that is vow'd true.
What is not holy, that we swear not by,
But take the High'st to witness: then, pray you, tell me,
If I should swear by Jove's great attributes,
I lov'd you dearly, would you believe my oaths,
When I did love you ill? this has no holding,
To swear to him whom I protest to love,

That I will work against him. Therefore your oaths
Are words and poor conditions; but unseal'd, —
At least in my opinion.
  Ber.   Change it, change it;
Be not so holy-cruel: love is holy;
And my integrity ne'er knew the crafts
That you do charge men with. Stand no more off,
But give thyself unto my sick desires,
Who then recover: say thou'rt mine, and ever
My love as it begins shall so perséver.
  Dia. I see that men make hopes, in such a case,
That we'll forsake ourselves. Give me that ring.
  Ber. I'll lend it thee, my dear; but have no power
To give it from me.
  Dia   Will you not, my lord?
  Ber. It is an honour 'longing to our house,
Bequeathèd down from many ancestors;
Which were the greatest obloquy i' the world
In me to lose.
  Dia. Mine honour's such a ring:
My chastity's the jewel of our house,
Bequeathèd down from many ancestors;
Which were the greatest obloquy i' the world
In me to lose: thus your own proper wisdom
Brings in the champion honour on my part,
Against your vain assault.
  Ber.   Here, take my ring:
My house, mine honour, yea, my life, be thine,
And I'll be bid by thee.
  Dia. When midnight comes, knock at my chamber-window:
I'll order take my mother shall not hear.
Now will I charge you in the band of truth,
When you have conquer'd my yet-maiden bed,
Remain there but an hour, nor speak to me:
My reasons are most strong; and you shall know them
When back again this ring shall be deliver'd:
And on your finger, in the night, I'll put

Another ring, that what in time proceeds
May token to the future our past deeds.
Adieu, till then; then fail not. You have won
A wife of me, though there my hope be done.

Ber. A heaven on earth I've won by wooing thee. [*Exit.*
Dia. For which live long to thank both heaven and me!
You may so in the end. —
My mother told me just how he would woo,
As if she sat in 's heart; she says all men
Have the like oaths: he has sworn to marry me
When his wife's dead; therefore I'll lie with him
When I am buried. Since Frenchmen are so braid,
Marry that will, I live and die a maid:
Only, in this disguise, I think 't no sin
To cozen him that would unjustly win. [*Exit.*

Scene III. *The Florentine camp.*

Enter the two French Lords *and two or three* Soldiers.

First Lord. You have not given him his mother's letter?

Sec. Lord. I have delivered it an hour since: there is something in 't that stings his nature; for, on the reading it, he changed almost into another man.

First Lord. He has much worthy blame laid upon him for shaking off so good a wife and so sweet a lady.

Sec. Lord. Especially he hath incurred the everlasting displeasure of the king, who had even tuned his bounty to sing happiness to him. I will tell you a thing, but you shall let it dwell darkly with you.

First Lord. When you have spoken it, 'tis dead, and I am the grave of it.

Sec. Lord. He hath perverted a young gentlewoman here in Florence, of a most chaste renown; and this night he fleshes his will in the spoil of her honour: he hath given her his monumental ring, and thinks himself made in the unchaste composition.

First Lord. Now, God delay our rebellion! as we are ourselves, what things are we!

Sec. Lord. Merely our own traitors. And as in the common course of all treasons, we still see them reveal themselves, till they attain to their abhorred ends, so he that in this action contrives against his own nobility, in his proper stream o'erflows himself.

First Lord. Is it not most damnable in us, to be trumpeters of our unlawful intents? We shall not, then, have his company to-night?

Sec. Lord. Not till after midnight; for he is dieted to his hour.

First Lord. That approaches apace: I would gladly have him see his company anatomized, that he might take a measure of his own judgment, wherein so curiously he had set this counterfeit.

Sec. Lord. We will not meddle with him till he come; for his presence must be the whip of the other.

First Lord. In the mean time, what hear you of these wars?

Sec. Lord. I hear there is an overture of peace.

First Lord. Nay, I assure you, a peace concluded.

Sec. Lord. What will Count Rousillon do then? will he travel higher, or return again into France?

First Lord. I perceive, by this demand, you are not altogether of his council.

Sec. Lord. Let it be forbid, sir! so should I be a great deal of his act.

First Lord. Sir, his wife, some two months since, fled from his house; her pretence a pilgrimage to Saint Jaques le Grand; which holy undertaking, with most austere sanctimony, she accomplished; and, there residing, the tenderness of her nature became as a prey to her grief; in fine, made a groan of her last breath; and now she sings in heaven.

Sec. Lord. How is this justified?

First Lord. The stranger part of it by her own letters, which make her story true, even to the point of her death: her death itself, which could not be her office to say is come, was faithfully confirmed by the rector of the place.

Sec. Lord. Hath the count all this intelligence?

First Lord. Ay, and the particular confirmations, point from point, to the full arming of the verity.

Sec. Lord. I am heartily sorry that he'll be glad of this.

First Lord. How mightily sometimes we make us comforts of our losses!

Sec. Lord. And how mightily some other times we drown our gain in tears! The great dignity that his valour hath here acquired for him shall at home be encountered with a shame as ample.

First Lord. The web of our life is of a mingled yarn, good and ill together: our virtues would be proud, if our faults whipped them not; and our crimes would despair, if they were not cherished by our virtues.

Enter a Servant.

How now! where's your master?

Serv. He met the duke in the street, sir, of whom he hath taken a solemn leave: his lordship will next morning for France. The duke hath offered him letters of commendations to the king. [*Exit.*

Sec. Lord. They shall be no more than needful there, if they were more than they can commend.

First Lord. They cannot be too sweet for the king's tartness. Here's his lordship now.

Enter BERTRAM.

How now, my lord! is 't not after midnight?

Ber. I have to-night dispatched sixteen businesses, a month's length a-piece, by an abstract of success: I have conge'd with the duke, done my adieu with his nearest; buried a wife, mourned for her; writ to my lady mother I am returning; entertained my convoy; and between these main parcels of dispatch, effected many nicer needs: the last was the greatest, but that I have not ended yet.

Sec. Lord. If the business be of any difficulty, and this morning your departure hence, it requires haste of your lordship.

Ber. I mean, the business is not ended, as fearing to hear of it hereafter. But shall we have this dialogue between the fool and the soldier? — Come, bring forth this counterfeit model: 'has deceived me, like a double-meaning prophesier.

Sec. Lord. Bring him forth [*Exeunt Soldiers*]: — 'has sat i' the stocks all night, poor gallant knave.

Ber. No matter; his heels have deserved it, in usurping his spurs so long. How does he carry himself?

Sec. Lord. I have told your lordship already,—the stocks carry him. But, to answer you as you would be understood; he weeps like a wench that had shed her milk: he hath confessed himself to Morgan, whom he supposes to be a friar, from the time of his remembrance to this very instant disaster of his setting i' the stocks: and what think you he hath confessed?

Ber. Nothing of me, has 'a?

Sec. Lord. His confession is taken, and it shall be read to his face: if your lordship be in 't, as I believe you are, you must have the patience to hear it.

Re-enter Soldiers, *with* PAROLLES *muffled.*

Ber. A plague upon him! muffled! he can say nothing of me.

First Lord. Hush, hush! Hoodman comes! — *Porto tartarossa.*

First Sold. He calls for the tortures: what will you say without 'em?

Par. I will confess what I know without constraint: if ye pinch me like a pasty, I can say no more.

First Sold. Bosko chimurcho.

First Lord. Boblibindo chicurmurco.

First Sold. You are a merciful general. — Our general bids you answer to what I shall ask you out of a note.

Par. And truly, as I hope to live.

First Sold. [*reads*] "First demand of him how many horse' the duke is strong." What say you to that?

Par. Five or six thousand; but very weak and unserviceable: the troops are all scattered, and the commanders very poor rogues, upon my reputation and credit, and as I hope to live.

First Sold. Shall I set down your answer so?

Par. Do: I'll take the sacrament on't, how and which way you will.

Ber. All's one to him. What a past-saving slave is this!

First Lord. You're deceived, my lord: this is Monsieur Parolles, the gallant militarist,—that was his own phrase,—that had the whole theoric of war in the knot of his scarf, and the practice in the chape of his dagger.

Sec. Lord. I will never trust a man again for keeping his sword clean; nor believe he can have every thing in him by wearing his apparel neatly.

First Sold. Well, that's set down.

Par. Five or six thousand horse', I said,— I will say true,— or thereabouts, set down,— for I'll speak truth.

First Lord. He's very near the truth in this.

Ber. But I con him no thanks for't, in the nature he delivers it.

Par. Poor rogues, I pray you, say.

First Sold. Well, that's set down.

Par. I humbly thank you, sir.

First Lord. A truth's a truth,— the rogues are marvellous poor.

First Sold. [reads] "Demand of him, of what strength they are a-foot." What say you to that?

Par. By my troth, sir, if I were to die this present hour, I will tell true. Let me see: Spurio, a hundred and fifty; Sebastian, so many; Corambus, so many; Jaques, so many; Guiltian, Cosmo, Lodowick, and Gratii, two hundred fifty each; mine own company, Chitopher, Vaumond, Bentii, two hundred fifty each: so that the musterfile, rotten and sound, upon my life, amounts not to fifteen thousand poll; half of the which dare not shake the snow from off their cassocks, lest they shake themselves to pieces.

Ber. What shall be done to him?

First Lord. Nothing, but let him have thanks.—Demand of him my condition, and what credit I have with the duke.

First Sold. Well, that's set down. [*Reads*] "You shall demand of him, whether one Captain Dumain be i' the camp, a Frenchman; what his reputation is with the duke; what his valour, honesty, and expertness in wars; or whether he thinks it were not possible, with well-weighing sums of gold, to corrupt him to a revolt." What say you to this? what do you know of it?

Par. I beseech you, let me answer to the particular of the inter'gatories: demand them singly.

First Sold. Do you know this Captain Dumain?

Par. I know him: 'a was a botcher's 'prentice in Paris, from whence he was whipped for getting the shrieve's fool with child,—a dumb innocent, that could not say him nay.

[*First Lord lifts up his hand in anger.*

Ber. Nay, by your leave, hold your hands; though I know his brains are forfeit to the next tile that falls.

First Sold. Well, is this captain in the Duke of Florence's camp?

Par. Upon my knowledge, he is, and lousy.

First Lord. Nay, look not so upon me; we shall hear of your lordship anon.

First Sold. What is his reputation with the duke?

Par. The duke knows him for no other but a poor officer of mine; and writ to me this other day to turn him out o' the band: I think I have his letter in my pocket.

First Sold. Marry, we'll search.

Par. In good sadness, I do not know; either it is there, or it is upon a file, with the duke's other letters, in my tent.

First Sold. Here 'tis; here's a paper: shall I read it to you?

Par. I do not know if it be it or no.

Ber. Our interpreter does it well.

First Lord. Excellently.

First Sold. [*reads*]

"Dian, the count's a fool, and full of gold,"—

Par. That is not the duke's letter, sir; that is an advertisement to a proper maid in Florence, one Diana, to take heed of the allurement of one Count Rousillon, a foolish idle boy, but, for all that, very ruttish: I pray you, sir, put it up again.

First Sold. Nay, I'll read it first, by your favour.

Par. My meaning in 't, I protest, was very honest in the behalf of the maid; for I knew the young count to be a dangerous and lascivious boy, who is a whale to virginity, and devours up all the fry it finds.

Ber. Damnable, both-sides rogue!

First Sold. [*reads*]
"When he swears oaths, bid him drop gold, and take it;
   After he scores, he never pays the score:
Half won is match well made; match, and well make it;
   He ne'er pays after-debts, take it before;
And say a soldier, Dian, told thee this,
Men are to mell with, boys are but to kiss:
For count of this, the count's a fool, I know it,
Who pays before, but not when he does owe it.
    Thine, as he vowed to thee in thine ear,
                           Parolles."

Ber. He shall be whipped through the army, with this rhyme in 's forehead.

Sec. Lord. This is your devoted friend, sir, the manifold linguist, and the armipotent soldier.

Ber. I could endure any thing before but a cat, and now he's a cat to me.

First Sold. I perceive, sir, by our general's looks, we shall be fain to hang you.

Par. My life, sir, in any case: not that I am afraid to die; but that, my offences being many, I would repent out the remainder of nature: let me live, sir, in a dungeon, i' the stocks, or any where, so I may live.

First Sold. We'll see what may be done, so you confess freely; therefore, once more to this Captain Dumain: you have answered to his reputation with the duke, and to his valour: what is his honesty?

Par. He will steal, sir, an egg out of a cloister: for rapes and ravishments he parallels Nessus: he professes not keeping of oaths; in breaking 'em he is stronger than Hercules: he will lie, sir, with such volubility, that you would think truth were a fool: drunkenness is his best virtue, for he will be swine-drunk; and in his sleep he does little harm, save to his bed-clothes about him; but they know his conditions, and lay him in straw. I have but little more to say, sir, of his honesty: he has every thing that an honest man should not have; what an honest man should have, he has nothing.

First Lord. I begin to love him for this.

Ber. For this description of thine honesty? A pox upon him for me, he's more and more a cat.

First Sold. What say you to his expertness in war?

Par. Faith, sir, 'has led the drum before the English tragedians,—to belie him, I will not,—and more of his soldiership I know not; except, in that country he had the honour to be the officer at a place there called Mile-end, to instruct for the doubling of files: I would do the man what honour I can, but of this I am not certain.

First Lord. He hath out-villained villany so far, that the rarity redeems him.

Ber. A pox on him, he's a cat still.

First Sold. His qualities being at this poor price, I need not to ask you if gold will corrupt him to revolt.

Par. Sir, for a cardecu he will sell the fee-simple of his salvation, the inheritance of it; and cut the entail from all remainders, and a perpetual succession for it perpetually.

First Sold. What's his brother, the other Captain Dumain?

Sec. Lord. Why does he ask him of me?

First Sold. What's he?

Par. E'en a crow o' the same nest; not altogether so great as the first in goodness, but greater a great deal in evil:

he excels his brother for a coward, yet his brother is reputed one of the best that is: in a retreat he outruns any lackey; marry, in coming on he has the cramp.

First Sold. If your life be saved, will you undertake to betray the Florentine?

Par. Ay, and the captain of his horse, Count Rousillon.

First Sold. I'll whisper with the general, and know his pleasure.

Par. [*aside*] I'll no more drumming; a plague of all drums! Only to seem to deserve well, and to beguile the supposition of that lascivious young boy the count, have I run into this danger: yet who would have suspected an ambush where I was taken?

First Sold. There is no remedy, sir, but you must die: the general says, you that have so traitorously discovered the secrets of your army, and made such pestiferous reports of men very nobly held, can serve the world for no honest use; therefore you must die.—Come, headsman, off with his head.

Par. O Lord, sir, let me live, or let me see my death!

First Sold. That shall you, and take your leave of all your friends. [*Unmuffling him.*
So, look about you: know you any here?

Ber. Good morrow, noble captain.

Sec. Lord. God bless you, Captain Parolles.

First Lord. God save you, noble captain.

Sec. Lord. Captain, what greeting will you to my Lord Lafeu? I am for France.

First Lord. Good captain, will you give me a copy of the sonnet you writ to Diana in behalf of the Count Rousillon? an I were not a very coward, I'd compel it of you: but fare you well. [*Exeunt Bertram and Lords.*

First Sold. You are undone, captain; all but your scarf, that has a knot on 't yet.

Par. Who cannot be crushed with a plot?

First Sold. If you could find out a country where but women were that had received so much shame, you might

begin an impudent nation. Fare ye well, sir; I am for France
too: we shall speak of you there.   [*Exit with Soldiers.*

   Par.   Yet am I thankful: if my heart were great,
'Twould burst at this. Captain I'll be no more;
But I will eat and drink, and sleep as soft
As captain shall: simply the thing I am
Shall make me live. Who knows himself a braggart,
Let him fear this; for it will come to pass,
That every braggart shall be found an ass.
Rust, sword! cool, blushes! and, Parolles, live
Safest in shame! being fool'd, by foolery thrive!
There's place and means for every man alive.
I'll after them.   [*Exit.*

   SCENE IV.   *Florence.   A room in the* Widow's *house.*

          Enter HELENA, Widow, *and* DIANA.

   Hel. That you may well perceive I have not wrong'd you,
One of the greatest in the Christian world
Shall be my surety; 'fore whose throne 'tis needful,
Ere I can perfect mine intents, to kneel:
Time was, I did him a desirèd office,
Dear almost as his life; which gratitude
Through flinty Tartar's bosom would peep forth,
And answer, thanks: I duly am inform'd
His grace is at Marseilles; to which place
We have convenient convoy. You must know,
I am supposèd dead: the army breaking,
My husband hies him home; where, heaven aiding,
And by the leave of my good lord the king,
We'll be before our welcome.
   Wid.   Gentle madam,
You never had a servant to whose trust
Your business was more welcome.
   Hel.   Nor you, mistress,
Ever a friend whose thoughts more truly labour
To recompense your love: doubt not but heaven
Hath brought me up to be your daughter's dower,

. As it hath fated her to be my motive
And helper to a husband. But, O strange men!
That can such sweet use make of what they hate,
When saucy trusting of the cozen'd thoughts
Defiles the pitchy night! so lust doth play
With what it loathes, for that which is away:
But more of this hereafter. — You, Diana,
Under my poor instructions yet must suffer
Something in my behalf.
  Dia.   Let death and honesty
Go with your impositions, I am yours
Upon your will to suffer.
  Hel.   Yet, I pray you:
But, with the word, the time will bring on summer,
When briers shall have leaves as well as thorns,
And be as sweet as sharp. We must away;
Our wagon is prepar'd, and time revives us:
All's well that ends well: still the fine's the crown;
Whate'er the course, the end is the renown. [*Exeunt.*

 Scene V. *Rousillon. A room in the house of the* Countess.

  Enter Countess, Lafeu, *and* Clown.

 Laf. No, no, no, your son was misled with a snipt-taffeta fellow there, whose villanous saffron would have made all the unbaked and doughy youth of a nation in his colour: your daughter-in-law had been alive at this hour, and your son here at home, more advanced by the king than by that red-tailed humble-bee I speak of.

 Count. I would he had not known him! it was the death of the most virtuous gentlewoman that ever nature had praise for creating: if she had partaken of my flesh, and cost me the dearest groans of a mother, I could not have owed her a more rooted love.

 Laf. 'Twas a good lady, 'twas a good lady: we may pick a thousand salads ere we light on such another herb

 Clo. Indeed, sir, she was the sweet-marjoram of the salad, or rather, the herb of grace.

Laf. They are not salad-herbs, you knave; they are nose-herbs.

Clo. I am no great Nebuchadnezzar, sir; I have not much skill in grass.

Laf. Whether dost thou profess thyself, — a knave or a fool?

Clo. A fool, sir, at a woman's service, and a knave at a man's.

Laf. Your distinction?

Clo. I would cozen the man of his wife, and do his service.

Laf. So you were a knave at his service, indeed.

Clo. And I would give his wife my bauble, sir, to do her service.

Laf. I will subscribe for thee, thou art both knave and fool.

Clo. At your service.

Laf. No, no, no.

Clo. Why, sir, if I cannot serve you, I can serve as great a prince as you are.

Laf. Who's that? a Frenchman?

Clo. Faith, sir, 'a has an English name; but his phisnomy is more hotter in France than there.

Laf. What prince is that?

Clo. The black prince, sir; *alias*, the prince of darkness; *alias*, the devil.

Laf. Hold thee, there's my purse: I give thee not this to suggest thee from thy master thou talkest of; serve him still.

Clo. I am a woodland fellow, sir, that always loved a great fire; and the master I speak of ever keeps a good fire. But, since he is the prince of the world, let his nobility remain in's court. I am for the house with the narrow gate, which I take to be too little for pomp to enter: some that humble themselves may; but the many will be too chill and tender, and they'll be for the flowery way that leads to the broad gate and the great fire.

Laf. Go thy ways, I begin to be a-weary of thee; and I tell thee so before, because I would not fall out with thee.

Go thy ways: let my horses be well looked to, without any tricks.

Clo. If I put any tricks upon 'em, sir, they shall be jades' tricks; which are their own right by the law of nature. [*Exit.*

Laf. A shrewd knave and an unhappy.

Count. So he is. My lord that's gone made himself much sport out of him: by his authority he remains here, which he thinks is a patent for his sauciness; and, indeed, he has no place, but runs where he will.

Laf. I like him well; 'tis not amiss. And I was about to tell you, since I heard of the good lady's death, and that my lord your son was upon his return home, I moved the king my master to speak in the behalf of my daughter; which, in the minority of them both, his majesty, out of a self-gracious remembrance, did first propose: his highness hath promised me to do it: and, to stop up the displeasure he hath conceived against your son, there is no fitter matter. How does your ladyship like it?

Count. With very much content, my lord; and I wish it happily effected.

Laf. His highness comes post from Marseilles, of as able body as when he numbered thirty: he will be here to-morrow, or I am deceived by him that in such intelligence hath seldom failed.

Count. It rejoices me, that I hope I shall see him ere I die. I have letters that my son will be here to-night: I shall beseech your lordship to remain with me till they meet together.

Laf. Madam, I was thinking with what manners I might safely be admitted.

Count. You need but plead your honourable privilege.

Laf. Lady, of that I have made a bold charter; but, I thank my God, it holds yet.

Re-enter Clown.

Clo. O madam, yonder's my lord your son with a patch of velvet on's face: whether there be a scar under't or no, the velvet knows; but 'tis a goodly patch of velvet: his left cheek is a cheek of two pile and a half, but his right cheek is worn bare.

Count. A scar nobly got, or a noble scar, is a good livery of honour; so belike is that.

Clo. But it is your carbonadoed face.

Laf. Let us go see your son, I pray you: I long to talk with the young noble soldier.

Clo. Faith, there's a dozen of 'em, with delicate fine hats, and most courteous feathers, which bow the head and nod at every man. [*Exeunt.*

ACT V.

Scene I. *Marseilles. A street.*

Enter Helena, Widow, *and* Diana, *with two* Attendants.

Hel. But this exceeding posting day and night
Must wear your spirits low; we cannot help it:
But, since you've made the days and nights as one,
To wear your gentle limbs in my affairs,
Be bold you do so grow in my requital
As nothing can unroot you. — In happy time; —

Enter a Gentleman.

This man may help me to his majesty's ear,
If he would spend his power. — God save you, sir.

Gent. And you.

Hel. Sir, I have seen you in the court of France.

Gent. I have been sometimes there.

Hel. I do presume, sir, that you are not fall'n
From the report that goes upon your goodness;
And therefore, goaded with most sharp occasions,
Which lay nice manners by, I put you to
The use of your own virtues; for the which
I shall continue thankful.

Gent. What's your will?

Hel. That it will please you
To give this poor petition to the king;

And aid me with that store of power you have
To come into his presence.
    Gent. The king's not here.
    Hel.   Not here, sir!
    Gent.   Not, indeed:
He hence remov'd last night, and with more haste
Than is his use.
    Wid.   Lord, how we lose our pains!
    Hel. All's well that ends well yet,
Though time seem so adverse and means unfit. —
I do beseech you, whither is he gone?
    Gent. Marry, as I take it, to Rousillon;
Whither I am going.
    Hel.   I do beseech you, sir,
Since you are like to see the king before me,
Commend the paper to his gracious hand;
Which, I presume, shall render you no blame,
But rather make you thank your pains for it
I will come after you with what good speed
Our means will make us means.
    Gent.   This I'll do for you.
    Hel. And you shall find yourself to be well thank'd,
Whate'er falls more. — We must to horse again: —
Go, go, provide.   *[Exeunt.*

    SCENE II. *Rousillon. The inner court of the house of the
            Countess.*

Enter Clown *and* PAROLLES.

    Par. Good Monsieur Lavache, give my Lord Lafeu this letter: I have ere now, sir, been better known to you, when I have held familiarity with fresher clothes; but I am now, sir, mudded in Fortune's mood, and smell somewhat strong of her strong displeasure.
    Clo. Truly, Fortune's displeasure is but sluttish, if it smell so strongly as thou speakest of: I will henceforth eat no fish of Fortune's buttering. Prithee, allow the wind.

Par. Nay, you need not to stop your nose, sir; I spake but by a metaphor.

Clo. Indeed, sir, if your metaphor stink, I will stop my nose; or against any man's metaphor. Prithee, get thee further.

Par. Pray you, sir, deliver me this paper.

Clo. Foh, prithee, stand away: a paper from Fortune's close-stool to give to a nobleman! Look, here he comes himself.

Enter LAFEU.

Here is a pur of Fortune's, sir, or of Fortune's cat, — but not a musk-cat, — that has fallen into the unclean fishpond of her displeasure, and, as he says, is mudded withal: pray you, sir, use the carp as you may; for he looks like a poor, decayed, ingenious, foolish, rascally knave. I do pity his distress in my similes of comfort, and leave him to your lordship.

[*Exit.*

Par. My lord, I am a man whom Fortune hath cruelly scratched.

Laf. And what would you have me to do? 'tis too late to pare her nails now. Wherein have you played the knave with Fortune, that she should scratch you, who of herself is a good lady, and would not have knaves thrive long under her? There's a cardecu for you: let the justices make you and Fortune friends; I am for other business.

Par. I beseech your honour to hear me one single word.

Laf. You beg a single penny more: come, you shall ha't; save your word.

Par. My name, my good lord, is Parolles.

Laf. You beg more than one word, then. — Cox' my passion! give me your hand: — how does your drum?

Par. O my good lord, you were the first that found me!

Laf. Was I, in sooth? and I was the first that lost thee.

Par. It lies in you, my lord, to bring me in some grace, for you did bring me out.

Laf. Out upon thee, knave! dost thou put upon me at once both the office of God and the devil? one brings thee in

152   ALL'S WELL THAT ENDS WELL.   [ACT V.

grace, and the other brings thee out. [*Trumpets sound.*] The
king's coming; I know by his trumpets. — Sirrah, inquire
further after me; I had talk of you last night: though you
are a fool and a knave, you shall eat; go to, follow.

 Par. I praise God for you.   [*Exeunt.*

Scene III. *The same. A room in the house of the* Countess.

Flourish. Enter King, Countess, Lafeu, Lords, Gentlemen,
      Guards, &c.

 King. We lost a jewel of her; and our esteem
Was made much poorer by it: but your son,
As mad in folly, lack'd the sense to know
Her estimation home.
 Count.   'Tis past, my liege;
And I beseech your majesty to make it
Natural rebellion, done i' the blaze of youth;
When oil and fire, too strong for reason's force,
O'erbear it, and burn on.
 King.   My honour'd lady,
I have forgiven and forgotten all;
Though my revenges were high-bent upon him,
And watch'd the time to shoot.
 Laf.   This I must say, —
But first I beg my pardon, — the young lord
Did to his majesty, his mother, and his lady,
Offence of mighty note; but to himself
The greatest wrong of all: he lost a wife,
Whose beauty did astonish the survey
Of richest eyes; whose words all ears took captive;
Whose dear perfection hearts that scorn'd to serve
Humbly call'd mistress.
 King.   Praising what is lost
Makes the remembrance dear. — Well, call him hither; —
We're reconcil'd, and the first view shall kill
All repetition: — let him not ask our pardon;
The nature of his great offence is dead,
And deeper than oblivion we do bury

Th' incensing relics of it: let him approach,
A stranger, no offender; and inform him
So 'tis our will he should.
  First Gent.   I shall, my liege.   [*Exit.*
  King. What says he to your daughter? have you spoke?
  Laf. All that he is hath reference to your highness.
  King. Then shall we have a match. I've letters sent me
That set him high in fame.

    Enter BERTRAM, *with* First Gentleman.

  Laf.   He looks well on't.
  King. I am not a day of season,
For thou mayst see a sunshine and a hail
In me at once: but to the brightest beams
Distracted clouds give way; so stand thou forth,
The time is fair again.
  Ber.   My high-repented blames,
Dear sovereign, pardon to me.
  King.   All is whole;
Not one word more of the consumèd time.
Let's take the instant by the forward top;
For we are old, and on our quick'st decrees
Th' inaudible and noiseless foot of Time
Steals ere we can effect them You remember
The daughter of this lord?
  Ber. Admiringly, my liege: at first
I stuck my choice upon her, ere my heart
Durst make too bold a herald of my tongue:
Where the impression of mine eye infixing,
Contempt his scornful pérspective did lend me,
Which warp'd the line of every other favour;
Scorn'd a fair colour, or express'd it stol'n;
Extended or contracted all proportions
To a most hideous object: thence it came
That she whom all men prais'd, and whom myself,
Since I have lost, have lov'd, was in mine eye
The dust that did offend it.

King. Well excus'd:
That thou didst love her, strikes some scores away
From the great compt: but love that comes too late,
Like a remorseful pardon slowly carried,
To the great sender turns a sour offence,
Crying, "That's good that's gone." Our rasher faults
Make trivial price of serious things we have,
Not knowing them until we know their grave:
Oft our displeasures, to ourselves unjust,
Destroy our friends, and after weep their dust:
Our old love waking cries to see what's done,
While shameful hate sleeps out the afternoon.
Be this sweet Helen's knell, and now forget her.
Send forth your amorous token for fair Maudlin:
The main consents are had; and here we'll stay
To see our widower's second marriage-day.

Count. Which better than the first, O dear heaven, bless!
Or, ere they meet, in me, O nature, cesse!

Laf. Come on, my son, in whom my house's name
Must be digested, give a favour from you,
To sparkle in the spirits of my daughter,
That she may quickly come.— [*Bertram gives a ring to Lafeu.*
By my old beard,
And every hair that's on't, Helen, that's dead,
Was a sweet creature: such a ring as this,
The last time, ere she took her leave at court,
I saw upon her finger.

Ber. Hers it was not.

King. Now, pray you, let me see it; for mine eye,
While I was speaking, oft was fasten'd to 't. —
This ring was mine; and, when I gave it Helen,
I bade her, if her fortunes ever stood
Necessitied to help, that by this token
I would relieve her. Had you that craft, to reave her
Of what should stead her most?

Ber. My gracious sovereign,

Howe'er it pleases you to take it so,
The ring was never her's.
    Count.   Son, on my life,
I've seen her wear it; and she reckon'd it
At her life's rate.
    Laf.   I'm sure I saw her wear it.
    Ber. You are deceiv'd, my lord; she never saw it:
In Florence was it from a casement thrown me,
Wrapp'd in a paper, which contain'd the name
Of her that threw it: noble she was, and thought
I stood engag'd: but when I had subscrib'd
To mine own fortune, and inform'd her fully
I could not answer in that course of honour
As she had made the overture, she ceas'd
In heavy satisfaction, and would never
Receive the ring again.
    King.   Plutus himself,
That knows the tinct and multiplying medicine,
Hath not in nature's mystery more science
Than I have in this ring: 'twas mine, 'twas Helen's,
Whoever gave it you. Then, if you know
That you are well acquainted with yourself,
Confess 'twas hers, and by what rough enforcement
You got it from her: she call'd the saints to surety
That she would never put it from her finger,
Unless she gave it to yourself in bed, —
Where you have never come, — or sent it us
Upon her great disaster.
    Ber.   She never saw it.
    King. Thou speak'st it falsely, as I love mine honour;
And mak'st conjectural fears to come into me,
Which I would fain shut out. If it should prove
That thou art so inhuman, — 'twill not prove so; —
And yet I know not: — thou didst hate her deadly,
And she is dead; which nothing, but to close
Her eyes myself, could win me to believe,
More than to see this ring. — Take him away. —
                      [Guards seize Bertram.

My fore-past proofs, howe'er the matter fall,
Shall tax my fears of little vanity,
Having vainly fear'd too little. — Away with him! —
We'll sift this matter further.
  Ber.   If you shall prove
This ring was ever hers, you shall as easy
Prove that I husbanded her bed in Florence,
Where yet she never was.   *[Exit, guarded.*
  King. I am wrapp'd in dismal thinkings.

     Enter a Gentleman.
  Gent.   Gracious sovereign,
Whether I've been to blame or no, I know not:
Here's a petition from a Florentine,
Who hath for four or five removes come short
To tender it herself. I undertook it,
Vanquish'd thereto by the fair grace and speech
Of the poor suppliant, who by this, I know,
Is here attending: her business looks in her
With an importing visage; and she told me,
In a sweet verbal brief, it did concern
Your highness with herself.
  King. [*reads*] "Upon his many protestations to marry me when his wife was dead, I blush to say it, he won me. Now is the Count Rousillon a widower: his vows are forfeited to me, and my honour's paid to him. He stole from Florence, taking no leave, and I follow him to his country for justice: grant it me, O king! in you it best lies; otherwise a seducer flourishes, and a poor maid is undone.   DIANA CAPULET."
  Laf. I will buy me a son-in-law in a fair, and toll him: for this, I'll none of him.
  King. The heavens have thought well on thee, Lafeu,
To bring forth this discovery. — Seek these suitors: —
Go speedily and bring again the count.
      [Exeunt Gentleman and some Attendants.
I am afeard the life of Helen, lady,
Was foully snatch'd.
  Count.   Now, justice on the doers!

Re-enter BERTRAM, *guarded.*

King. I wonder, sir, sith wives are monsters to you,
And that you fly them as you swear them lordship,
Yet you desire to marry.

Re-enter Gentleman, *with* Widow *and* DIANA.
                            What woman's that?

Dia. I am, my lord, a wretched Florentine,
Derivèd from the ancient Capulet:
My suit, as I do understand, you know,
And therefore know how far I may be pitied.

Wid. I am her mother, sir, whose age and honour
Both suffer under this complaint we bring;
And both shall cease, without your remedy.

King. Come hither, county: do you know these women?

Ber. My lord, I neither can nor will deny
But that I know them: do they charge me further?

Dia. Why do you look so strange upon your wife?

Ber. She's none of mine, my lord.

Dia.   If you shall marry,
You give away this hand, and that is mine;
You give away heaven's vows, and those are mine;
You give away myself, which is known mine;
For I by vow am so embodied yours,
That she which marries you must marry me, —
Either both or none.

Laf. [*to Bertram*] Your reputation comes too short for my daughter; you are no husband for her.

Ber. My lord, this is a fond and desperate creature,
Whom sometime I have laugh'd with: let your highness
Lay a more noble thought upon mine honour
Than for to think that I would sink it here.

King. Sir, for my thoughts, you have them ill to friend
Till your deeds gain them: fairer prove your honour
Than in my thought it lies!

Dia.   Good my lord,
Ask him upon his oath, if he does think
He had not my virginity.

King. What say'st thou to her?
Ber.   She's impudent, my lord,
And was a common gamester to the camp.
    Dia. He does me wrong, my lord; if I were so,
He might have bought me at a common price:
Do not believe him: O, behold this ring,
Whose high respect and rich validity
Did lack a parallel; yet, for all that,
He gave it to a commoner o' the camp,
If I be one.
    Count.   He blushes, and 'tis his:
Of six preceding ancestors, that gem,
Conferr'd by testament to the sequent issue,
Hath it been ow'd and worn. This is his wife;
That ring's a thousand proofs.
    King.   Methought you said
You saw one here in court could witness it.
    Dia. I did, my lord, but loth am to produce
So bad an instrument: his name's Parolles.
    Laf. I saw the man to-day, if man he be.
    King. Find him, and bring him hither.
                            [*Exit an Attendant.*
    Ber.   What of him?
He's quoted for a most perfidious slave,
With all the spots o' the world tax'd and debauch'd;
Whose nature sickens but to speak a truth.
Am I or that or this for what he'll utter,
That will speak any thing?
    King.   She hath that ring of yours.
    Ber. I think she has: certain it is I lik'd her,
And boarded her i' the wanton way of youth:
She knew her distance, and did angle for me,
Madding my eagerness with her restraint,
As all impediments in fancy's course
Are motives of more fancy; and, in fine,
Her infinite cunning, with her modern grace,
Subdu'd me to her rate: she got the ring;

And I had that which an inferior might
At market-price have bought.
 Dia.   I must be patient:
You, that turn'd off a first so noble wife,
May justly diet me. I pray you yet, —
Since you lack virtue, I will lose a husband, —
Send for your ring, I will return it home,
And give me mine again.
 Ber.   I have it not.
 King. What ring was yours, I pray you?
 Dia.   Sir, much like
The same upon your finger.
 King. Know you this ring? this ring was his of late.
 Dia. And this was it I gave him, being a-bed.
 King. The story, then, goes false, you threw it him
Out of a casement.
 Dia.   I have spoke the truth.
 Ber. My lord, I do confess the ring was hers.
 King. You boggle shrewdly, every feather starts you. —

   Enter PAROLLES, *with* Attendant.

Is this the man you speak of?
 Dia.   Ay, my lord.
 King. Tell me, sirrah, — but tell me true, I charge you,
Not fearing the displeasure of your master,
Which, on your just proceeding, I'll keep off, —
By him and by this woman here what know you?
 Par. So please your majesty, my master hath been an honourable gentleman: tricks he hath had in him, which gentlemen have.
 King. Come, come, to the purpose: did he love this woman?
 Par. Faith, sir, he did love her; but how?
 King. How, I pray you?
 Par. He did love her, sir, as a gentleman loves a woman.
 King. How is that?
 Par. He loved her, sir, and loved her not.

King. As thou art a knave, and no knave. — What an equivocal companion is this!

Par. I am a poor man, and at your majesty's command.

Laf. He's a good drum, my lord, but a naughty orator.

Dia. Do you know he promised me marriage?

Par. Faith, I know more than I'll speak.

King. But wilt thou not speak all thou knowest?

Par. Yes, so please your majesty. I did go between them, as I said; but more than that, he loved her, — for, indeed, he was mad for her, and talked of Satan, and of Limbo, and of Furies, and I know not what: yet I was in that credit with them at that time, that I knew of their going to bed; and of other motions, as promising her marriage, and things which would derive me ill will to speak of; therefore I will not speak what I know.

King. Thou hast spoken all already, unless thou canst say they are married: but thou art too fine in thy evidence; therefore stand aside. —

This ring, you say, was yours?

Dia. Ay, my good lord.

King. Where did you buy it? or who gave it you?

Dia. It was not given me, nor I did not buy it.

King. Who lent it you?

Dia. It was not lent me neither.

King. Where did you find it, then?

Dia. I found it not.

King. If it were yours by none of all these ways,
How could you give it him?

Dia. I never gave't him.

Laf. This woman's an easy glove, my lord; she goes off and on at pleasure.

King. This ring was mine; I gave it his first wife.

Dia. It might be yours or hers, for aught I know.

King. Take her away; I do not like her now;
To prison with her: and away with him. —
Unless thou tell'st me where thou hadst this ring,
Thou diest within this hour.

Dia.   I'll never tell you.
King. Take her away.
Dia.   I'll put in bail, my liege.
King. I think thee now some common customer.
Dia. By Jove, if ever I knew man, 'twas you.
King. Wherefore hast thou accus'd him all this while?
Dia. Because he's guilty, and he is not guilty:
He knows I am no maid, and he'll swear to 't;
I'll swear I am a maid, and he knows not.
Great king, I am no strumpet, by my life;
I'm either maid, or else this old man's wife.
                              [*Pointing to Lafeu.*
King. She does abuse our ears: to prison with her.
Dia. Good mother, fetch my bail. — Stay, royal sir:
                              [*Exit Widow.*
The jeweller that owes the ring is sent for,
And he shall surety me. But for this lord,
Who hath abus'd me, as he knows himself,
Though yet he never harm'd me, here I quit him:
He knows himself my bed he hath defil'd;
And at that time he got his wife with child:
Dead though she be, she feels her young one kick:
So there's my riddle, — One that's dead is quick:
And now behold the meaning.

            Re-enter Widow, *with* HELENA.

King.   Is there no exorcist
Beguiles the truer office of mine eyes?
Is 't real that I see?
Hel.   No, my good lord;
'Tis but the shadow of a wife you see,
The name, and not the thing.
Ber.   Both, both: — O, pardon!
Hel. O my good lord, when I was like this maid,
I found you wondrous kind. There is your ring;
And, look you, here's your letter; this it says:
"When from my finger you can get this ring,

And are by me with child, &c." This is done:
Will you be mine, now you are doubly won?
    Ber. If she, my liege, can make me know this clearly,
I'll love her dearly, ever, ever dearly.
    Hel. If it appear not plain, and prove untrue,
Deadly divorce step between me and you! —
O my dear mother, do I see you living?
    Laf. Mine eyes smell onions; I shall weep anon: —
[*To Parolles*] Good Tom Drum, lend me a handkercher: so,
I thank thee: wait on me home, I'll make sport with thee:
let thy courtesies alone, they are scurvy ones.
    King. Let us from point to point this story know,
To make the even truth in pleasure flow. —
[*To Diana*] If thou be'st yet a fresh uncroppèd flower,
Choose thou thy husband, and I'll pay thy dower;
For I can guess that, by thy honest aid,
Thou kept'st a wife herself, thyself a maid. —
Of that, and all the progress, more and less,
Resolvedly more leisure shall express:
All yet seems well; and if it end so meet,
The bitter past, more welcome is the sweet.   [*Flourish.*

The king's a beggar, now the play is done:
All is well ended, if this suit be won,
That you express content; which we will pay,
With strife to please you, day exceeding day:
Ours be your patience then, and yours our parts;
Your gentle hands lend us, and take our hearts.   [*Exeunt.*

TWELFTH-NIGHT;

OR,

WHAT YOU WILL.

DRAMATIS PERSONÆ.

ORSINO, duke of Illyria.
SEBASTIAN, a young gentleman.
ANTONIO, a sea captain, friend to Sebastian.
A Sea Captain, friend to Viola.
VALENTINE,) gentlemen attend-
CURIO,   ) ing on the Duke.
SIR TOBY BELCH, uncle to Olivia.

SIR ANDREW AGUECHEEK.
MALVOLIO, steward to Olivia.
FABIAN,)
CLOWN,   ) servants to Olivia.

OLIVIA, a countess.
VIOLA, sister to Sebastian.
MARIA, Olivia's woman.

Lords, a Priest, Sailors, Officers, Musicians, and Attendants.

SCENE — *A city in Illyria, and the sea-coast near it.*

ACT I.

SCENE I. *An apartment in the Duke's palace.*

Enter Duke, Lords, *and* Curio; Musicians *attending.*

Duke. If music be the food of love, play on;
Give me excess of it, that, surfeiting,
The appetite may sicken, and so die. —
That strain again! — it had a dying fall:
O, it came o'er my ear like the sweet south,
That breathes upon a bank of violets,
Stealing and giving odour! — Enough; no more:
'Tis not so sweet now as it was before.
O spirit of love, how quick and fresh art thou!
That, notwithstanding thy capacity

Receiveth as the sea, naught enters there,
Of what validity and pitch soe'er,
But falls into abatement and low price,
Even in a minute! so full of shapes is fancy,
That it alone is high-fantastical.
  Cur. Will you go hunt, my lord?
  Duke.   What, Curio?
  Cur. The hart.
  Duke. Why, so I do, the noblest that I have:
O, when mine eyes did see Olivia first,
Methought she purg'd the air of pestilence!
That instant was I turn'd into a hart;
And my desires, like fell and cruel hounds,
E'er since pursue me.

Enter VALENTINE.

                    How now! what news from her?
  Val. So please my lord, I might not be admitted;
But from her handmaid do return this answer:
The element itself, till seven years hence,
Shall not behold her face at ample view;
But, like a cloistress, she will veilèd walk,
And water once a day her chamber round
With eye-offending brine: all this to season
A brother's dead love, which she would keep fresh
And lasting in her sad remembrance.
  Duke. O, she that hath a heart of that fine frame
To pay this debt of love but to a brother,
How will she love, when the rich golden shaft
Hath kill'd the flock of all affections else
That live in her; when liver, brain, and heart,
These sovereign thrones, are all supplied and fill'd —
Her sweet perfections — with one self king! —
Away before me to sweet beds of flowers:
Love-thoughts lie rich when canopied with bowers.
                                              [*Exeunt.*

SCENE II. *The sea-coast.*

Enter VIOLA, Captain, *and* Sailors.

Vio. What country, friends, is this?
Cap.   This is Illyria, lady.
Vio. And what should I do in Illyria?
My brother he is in Elysium.
Perchance he is not drown'd: — what think you, sailors?
    Cap. It is perchance that you yourself were sav'd.
    Vio. O my poor brother! and so perchance may he be.
    Cap. True, madam: and, to comfort you with chance,
Assure yourself, after our ship did split,
When you, and this poor number sav'd with you,
Hung on our driving boat, I saw your brother,
Most provident in peril, bind himself —
Courage and hope both teaching him the practice —
To a strong mast that liv'd upon the sea;
Where, like Arion on the dolphin's back,
I saw him hold acquaintance with the waves
So long as I could see.
    Vio.   For saying so, there's gold:
Mine own escape unfoldeth to my hope,
Whereto thy speech serves for authority,
The like of him. Know'st thou this country?
    Cap. Ay, madam, well; for I was bred and born
Not three hours' travel from this very place.
    Vio. Who governs here?
    Cap. A noble duke, in nature as in name.
    Vio. What is his name?
    Cap. Orsino.
    Vio. Orsino! I have heard my father name him:
He was a bachelor then.
    Cap. And so is now, or was so very late;
For but a month ago I went from hence,
And then 'twas fresh in murmur, — as, you know,
What great ones do, the less will prattle of, —
That he did seek the love of fair Olivia.

Vio. What's she?

Cap. A virtuous maid, the daughter of a count
That died some twelvemonth since; then leaving her
In the protection of his son, her brother,
Who shortly also died: for whose dear loss,
They say, she hath abjur'd the company
And sight of men.

Vio. O, that I serv'd that lady,
And might not be deliver'd to the world,
Till I had made mine own occasion mellow,
What my estate is!

Cap. That were hard to compass;
Because she will admit no kind of suit,
No, not the duke's.

Vio. There is a fair behaviour in thee, captain;
And though that nature with a beauteous wall
Doth oft close-in pollution, yet of thee
I will believe thou hast a mind that suits
With this thy fair and outward character.
I prithee, — and I'll pay thee bounteously, —
Conceal me what I am; and be my aid
For such disguise as haply shall become
The form of my intent. I'll serve this duke:
Thou shalt present me as an eunuch to him:
It may be worth thy pains; for I can sing,
And speak to him in many sorts of music,
That will allow me very worth his service.
What else may hap, to time I will commit;
Only shape thou thy silence to my wit.

Cap. Be you his eunuch, and your mute I'll be:
When my tongue blabs, then let mine eyes not see.

Vio. I thank thee: lead me on. [*Exeunt.*

SCENE III. *A room in OLIVIA's house.*

Enter Sir TOBY BELCH *and* MARIA.

Sir To. What a plague means my niece, to take the death of her brother thus? I am sure care's an enemy to life.

Mar. By my troth, Sir Toby, you must come in earlier o' nights: your cousin, my lady, takes great exceptions to your ill hours.

Sir To. Why, let her except before excepted.

Mar. Ay, but you must confine yourself within the modest limits of order.

Sir To. Confine! I'll confine myself no finer than I am: these clothes are good enough to drink in; and so be these boots too,—an they be not, let them hang themselves in their own straps.

Mar. That quaffing and drinking will undo you: I heard my lady talk of it yesterday; and of a foolish knight that you brought in one night here to be her wooer.

Sir To. Who, Sir Andrew Aguecheek?

Mar. Ay, he.

Sir To. He's as tall a man as any's in Illyria.

Mar. What's that to the purpose?

Sir To. Why, he has three thousand ducats a year.

Mar. Ay, but he'll have but a year in all these ducats: he's a very fool and a prodigal.

Sir To. Fie, that you'll say so! he plays o' the viol-de-gamboys, and speaks three or four languages word for word without book, and hath all the good gifts of nature.

Mar. He hath, indeed, all most natural: for, besides that he's a fool, he's a great quarreller; and, but that he hath the gift of a coward to allay the gust he hath in quarrelling, 'tis thought among the prudent he would quickly have the gift of a grave.

Sir To. By this hand, they are scoundrels and substractors that say so of him. Who are they?

Mar. They that add, moreover, he's drunk nightly in your company.

Sir To. With drinking healths to my niece: I'll drink to her as long as there is a passage in my throat and drink in Illyria: he's a coward and a coistrel that will not drink to my niece till his brains turn o' the toe like a parish-top. What, wench! *Castiliano volto;* for here comes Sir Andrew Agueface.

Enter Sir ANDREW AGUECHEEK.

Sir And. Sir Toby Belch, — how now, Sir Toby Belch!
Sir To. Sweet Sir Andrew!
Sir And. Bless you, fair shrew.
Mar. And you too, sir.
Sir To. Accost, Sir Andrew, accost.
Sir And. What's that?
Sir To. My niece's chambermaid.
Sir And. Good Mistress Accost, I desire better acquaintance.
Mar. My name is Mary, sir.
Sir And. Good Mistress Mary Accost, —
Sir To. You mistake, knight: "accost" is front her, board her, woo her, assail her.
Sir And. By my troth, I would not undertake her in this company. Is that the meaning of "accost"?
Mar. Fare you well, gentlemen.
Sir To. An thou let her part so, Sir Andrew, would thou mightst never draw sword again.
Sir And. An you part so, mistress, I would I might never draw sword again. Fair lady, do you think you have fools in hand?
Mar. Sir, I have not you by the hand.
Sir And. Marry, but you shall have; and here's my hand.
Mar. Now, sir, thought is free: I pray you, bring your hand to the buttery-bar, and let it drink.
Sir And. Wherefore, sweet-heart? what's your metaphor?
Mar. It's dry, sir.
Sir And. Why, I think so: I am not such an ass but I can keep my hand dry. But what's your jest?
Mar. A dry jest, sir.
Sir And. Are you full of them?
Mar. Ay, sir, I have them at my fingers' ends: marry, now I let go your hand, I am barren. [*Exit.*
Sir To. O knight, thou lackest a cup of canary: when did I see thee so put down?

Sir And. Never in your life, I think; unless you saw canary put me down. Methinks sometimes I have no more wit than a Christian or an ordinary man has: but I am a great eater of beef, and I believe that does harm to my wit.

Sir To. No question.

Sir And. An I thought that, I'd forswear it. I'll ride home to-morrow, Sir Toby.

Sir To. Pourquoi, my dear knight?

Sir And. What is *pourquoi?* do or not do? I would I had bestowed that time in the tongues that I have in fencing, dancing, and bear-baiting: O, had I but followed the arts!

Sir To. Then hadst thou had an excellent head of hair.

Sir And. Why, would that have mended my hair?

Sir To. Past question; for thou seest it will not curl by nature.

Sir And. But it becomes me well enough, does 't not?

Sir To. Excellent; it hangs like flax on a distaff; and I hope to see a housewife take thee between her legs and spin it off.

Sir And. Faith, I'll home to-morrow, Sir Toby: your niece will not be seen; or if she be, it's four to one she'll none of me: the count himself here hard by woos her.

Sir To. She'll none o' the count: she'll not match above her degree, neither in estate, years, nor wit; I have heard her swear't. Tut, there's life in't, man.

Sir And. I'll stay a month longer. I am a fellow o' the strangest mind i' the world; I delight in masques and revels sometimes altogether.

Sir To. Art thou good at these kickshaws, knight?

Sir And. As any man in Illyria, whatsoever he be, under the degree of my betters; and yet I will not compare with an old man.

Sir To. What is thy excellence in a galliard, knight?

Sir And. Faith, I can cut a caper.

Sir To. And I can cut the mutton to't.

Sir And. And I think I have the back-trick simply as strong as any man in Illyria.

Sir To. Wherefore are these things hid? wherefore have these gifts a curtain before 'em? are they like to take dust, like Mistress Mall's picture? why dost thou not go to church in a galliard, and come home in a coranto? My very walk should be a jig; I would not so much as make water but in a sink-a-pace. What dost thou mean? is it a world to hide virtues in? I did think, by the excellent constitution of thy leg, it was formed under the star of a galliard.

Sir And. Ay, 'tis strong, and it does indifferent well in a flame-coloured stock. Shall we set about some revels?

Sir To. What shall we do else? were we not born under Taurus?

Sir And. Taurus! that's sides and heart.

Sir To. No, sir; it is legs and thighs. Let me see thee caper [*Sir And. dances*]: ha! higher: ha, ha! — excellent!

[*Exeunt.*

SCENE IV. *An apartment in the Duke's palace.*

Enter VALENTINE, *and* VIOLA *in man's attire.*

Val. If the duke continue these favours towards you, Cesario, you are like to be much advanced: he hath known you but three days, and already you are no stranger.

Vio. You either fear his humour or my negligence, that you call in question the continuance of his love: is he inconstant, sir, in his favours?

Val. No, believe me.

Vio. I thank you. Here comes the count.

Enter Duke, CURIO, *and* Attendants.

Duke. Who saw Cesario, ho?

Vio. On your attendance, my lord; here.

Duke. Stand you awhile aloof. — Cesario,
Thou know'st no less but all; I have unclasp'd
To thee the book even of my secret soul:
Therefore, good youth, address thy gait unto her,
Be not denied access, stand at her doors,

And tell them, there thy fixèd foot shall grow
Till thou have audience.
  Vio.   Sure, my noble lord.
If she be so abandon'd to her sorrow
As it is spoke, she never will admit me.
  Duke. Be clamorous, and leap all civil bounds,
Rather than make unprofited return.
  Vio. Say I do speak with her, my lord, what then?
  Duke. O, then unfold the passion of my love,
Surprise her with discourse of my dear faith!
It shall become thee well to act my woes;
She will attend it better in thy youth
Than in a nuncio of more grave aspéct.
  Vio. I think not so, my lord.
  Duke.   Dear lad, believe it;
For they shall yet belie thy happy years,
That say thou art a man: Diana's lip
Is not more smooth and rubious; thy small pipe
Is as the maiden's organ, shrill in sound;
And all is semblative a woman's part.
I know thy constellation is right apt
For this affair: — some four or five attend him;
All, if you will; for I myself am best
When least in company: — prosper well in this,
And thou shalt live as freely as thy lord,
To call his fortunes thine.
  Vio.   I'll do my best
To woo your lady: — [*Aside*] yet, a barful strife!
Whoe'er I woo, myself would be his wife. [*Exeunt.*

   Scene V. *A room in* Olivia's *house.*

    Enter Maria *and* Clown.

  Mar. Nay, either tell me where thou hast been, or I will not open my lips so wide as a bristle may enter in way of thy excuse: my lady will hang thee for thy absence.

  Clo. Let her hang me: he that is well hanged in this world needs to fear no colours.

Mar. Make that good.

Clo. He shall see none to fear.

Mar. A good lenten answer: I can tell thee where that saying was born, of, — I fear no colours.

Clo. Where, good Mistress Mary?

Mar. In the wars; and that may you be bold to say in your foolery.

Clo. Well, God give them wisdom that have it; and those that are fools, let them use their talents.

Mar. Yet you will be hanged for being so long absent; or, to be turned away, — is not that as good as a hanging to you?

Clo. Many a good hanging prevents a bad marriage; and, for turning away, let summer bear it out.

Mar. You are resolute, then?

Clo. Not so, neither; but I am resolved on two points.

Mar. That if one break, the other will hold; or, if both break, your gaskins fall.

Clo. Apt, in good faith; very apt. Well, go thy way; if Sir Toby would leave drinking, thou wert as witty a piece of Eve's flesh as any in Illyria.

Mar. Peace, you rogue, no more o' that. Here comes my lady: make your excuse wisely, you were best. [*Exit.*

Clo. Wit, an't be thy will, put me into good fooling! Those wits, that think they have thee, do very oft prove fools; and I, that am sure I lack thee, may pass for a wise man: for what says Quinapalus? "Better a witty fool than a foolish wit."

Enter OLIVIA *and* MALVOLIO.

God bless thee, lady!

Oli. Take the fool away.

Clo. Do you not hear, fellows? Take away the lady.

Oli. Go to, you're a dry fool; I'll no more of you: besides, you grow dishonest.

Clo. Two faults, madonna, that drink and good counsel will amend: for give the dry fool drink, then is the fool not dry: bid the dishonest man mend himself; if he mend, he is

no longer dishonest; if he cannot, let the botcher mend him:
any thing that's mended is but patched: virtue that transgresses is but patched with sin; and sin that amends is but patched with virtue: if that this simple syllogism will serve, so; if it will not, what remedy? As there is no true cuckold but calamity, so beauty's a flower. — The lady bade take away the fool; therefore, I say again, take her away.

Oli. Sir, I bade them take away you.

Clo. Misprision in the highest degree! — Lady, *cucullus non facit monachum;* that's as much to say as, I wear not motley in my brain. Good madonna, give me leave to prove you a fool.

Oli. Can you do it?

Clo. Dexteriously, good madonna.

Oli. Make your proof.

Clo. I must catechize you for it, madonna: good my mouse of virtue, answer me.

Oli. Well, sir, for want of other idleness, I'll bide your proof.

Clo. Good madonna, why mournest thou?

Oli. Good fool, for my brother's death.

Clo. I think his soul is in hell, madonna.

Oli. I know his soul is in heaven, fool.

Clo. The more fool, madonna, to mourn for your brother's soul being in heaven. — Take away the fool, gentlemen.

Oli. What think you of this fool, Malvolio? doth he not mend?

Mal. Yes, and shall do till the pangs of death shake him: infirmity, that decays the wise, doth ever make the better fool.

Clo. God send you, sir, a speedy infirmity, for the better increasing your folly! Sir Toby will be sworn that I am no fox; but he will not pass his word for twopence that you are no fool.

Oli. How say you to that, Malvolio?

Mal. I marvel your ladyship takes delight in such a barren rascal: I saw him put down the other day with an ordinary fool, that has no more brain than a stone. Look you now, he's out of his guard already; unless you laugh and minister occasion to him, he is gagged. I protest, I take these wise men, that crow so at these set kind of fools, no better than the fools' zanies.

Oli. O, you are sick of self-love, Malvolio, and taste with a distempered appetite. To be generous, guiltless, and of free disposition, is to take those things for bird-bolts that you deem cannon-bullets: there is no slander in an allowed fool, though he do nothing but rail; nor no railing in a known discreet man, though he do nothing but reprove.

Clo. Now Mercury endue thee with leasing, for thou speakest well of fools!

Re-enter MARIA.

Mar. Madam, there is at the gate a young gentleman much desires to speak with you.

Oli. From the Count Orsino, is it?

Mar. I know not, madam: 'tis a fair young man, and well attended.

Oli. Who of my people hold him in delay?

Mar. Sir Toby, madam, your kinsman.

Oli. Fetch him off, I pray you; he speaks nothing but madman: fie on him! [*Exit Maria.*] Go you, Malvolio: if it be a suit from the count, I am sick, or not at home; what you will, to dismiss it. [*Exit Malvolio.*] Now you see, sir, how your fooling grows old, and people dislike it.

Clo. Thou hast spoke for us, madonna, as if thy eldest son should be a fool, — whose skull Jove cram with brains! for here comes one of thy kin has a most weak *pia mater.*

Enter Sir TOBY BELCH.

Oli. By mine honour, half drunk. — What is he at the gate, cousin?

Sir To. A gentleman.

Oli. A gentleman! what gentleman?

Sir To. 'Tis a gentleman here — a plague o' these pickle-herring'! — How now, sot!

Clo. Good Sir Toby! —

Oli. Cousin, cousin, how have you come so early by this lethargy?

Sir To. Lechery! I defy lechery. There's one at the gate.

Oli. Ay, marry, what is he?

Sir To. Let him be the devil, an he will, I care not: give me faith, say I. Well, it's all one. [*Exit.*

Oli. What's a drunken man like, fool?

Clo. Like a drowned man, a fool, and a madman: one draught above heat makes him a fool; the second mads him; and a third drowns him.

Oli. Go thou and seek the crowner, and let him sit o' my coz; for he's in the third degree of drink, — he's drowned: go, look after him.

Clo. He is but mad yet, madonna; and the fool shall look to the madman [*Exit.*

Re-enter MALVOLIO.

Mal. Madam, yond young fellow swears he will speak with you. I told him you were sick; he takes on him to understand so much, and therefore comes to speak with you: I told him you were asleep; he seems to have a foreknowledge of that too, and therefore comes to speak with you. What is to be said to him, lady? he's fortified against any denial.

Oli. Tell him he shall not speak with me.

Mal. 'Has been told so; and he says, he'll stand at your door like a sheriff's post, and be the supporter to a bench, but he'll speak with you.

Oli. What kind o' man is he?

Mal. Why, of man kind.

Oli. What manner of man?

Mal. Of very ill manner; he'll speak with you, will you or no.

Oli. Of what personage and years is he?

Mal. Not yet old enough for a man, nor young enough for a boy; as a squash is before 'tis a peascod, or a codling when 'tis almost an apple: 'tis with him e'en standing water, between boy and man. He is very well-favoured, and he speaks very shrewishly; one would think his mother's milk were scarce out of him.

Oli. Let him approach: call in my gentlewoman.

Mal. Gentlewoman, my lady calls. [*Exit.*

Re-enter MARIA.

Oli. Give me my veil: come, throw it o'er my face. We'll once more hear Orsino's embassy.

Enter VIOLA.

Vio. The honourable lady of the house, which is she?

Oli. Speak to me; I shall answer for her. Your will?

Vio. Most radiant, exquisite, and unmatchable beauty,— I pray you, tell me if this be the lady of the house, for I never saw her: I would be loth to cast away my speech; for, besides that it is excellently well penned, I have taken great pains to con it. Good beauties, let me sustain no scorn; I am very comptible, even to the least sinister usage.

Oli. Whence came you, sir?

Vio. I can say little more than I have studied, and that question's out of my part. Good gentle one, give me modest assurance if you be the lady of the house, that I may proceed in my speech.

Oli. Are you a comedian?

Vio. No, my profound heart: and yet, by the very fangs of malice I swear I am not that I play. Are you the lady of the house?

Oli. If I do not usurp myself, I am.

Vio. Most certain, if you are she, you do usurp yourself; for, what is yours to bestow is not yours to reserve. But this is from my commission: I will on with my speech in your praise, and then show you the heart of my message.

Oli. Come to what is important in't: I forgive you the praise.

Vio. Alas, I took great pains to study it, and 'tis poetical.

Oli. It is the more like to be feigned: I pray you, keep

it in. I heard you were saucy at my gates; and allowed your approach rather to wonder at you than to hear you. If you be mad, be gone; if you have reason, be brief: 'tis not that time of moon with me to make one in so skipping a dialogue.

Mar. Will you hoist sail, sir? here lies your way.

Vio. No, good swabber; I am to hull here a little longer. — Some mollification for your giant, sweet lady.

Oli. Tell me your mind.

Vio. I am a messenger.

Oli. Sure, you have some hideous matter to deliver, when the courtesy of it is so fearful. Speak your office.

Vio. It alone concerns your ear. I bring no overture of war, no taxation of homage: I hold the olive in my hand; my words are as full of peace as matter.

Oli. Yet you began rudely. What are you? what would you?

Vio. The rudeness that hath appeared in me have I learned from my entertainment. What I am, and what I would, are as secret as maidenhead: to your ears, divinity; to any other's, profanation.

Oli. Give us the place alone: we will hear this divinity. [*Exit Maria.*] Now, sir, what is your text?

Vio. Most sweet lady, —

Oli. A comfortable doctrine, and much may be said of it. Where lies your text?

Vio. In Orsino's bosom.

Oli. In his bosom! In what chapter of his bosom?

Vio. To answer by the method, in the first of his heart.

Oli. O, I have read it: it is heresy. Have you no more to say?

Vio. Good madam, let me see your face.

Oli. Have you any commission from your lord to negotiate with my face? You are now out of your text: but we will draw the curtain, and show you the picture. Look you, sir, such a one I was this present: is 't not well done?

[*Unveiling.*

Vio. Excellently done, if God did all.
Oli. 'Tis in grain, sir; 'twill endure wind and weather.
Vio. 'Tis beauty truly blent, whose red and white
Nature's own sweet and cunning hand laid on:
Lady, you are the cruell'st she alive,
If you will lead these graces to the grave,
And leave the world no copy.
Oli. O, sir, I will not be so hard-hearted; I will give out divers schedules of my beauty: it shall be inventoried, and every particle and utensil labelled to my will:—as, item, two lips, indifferent red; item, two gray eyes, with lids to them; item, one neck, one chin, and so forth. Were you sent hither to 'praise me?
Vio. I see you what you are,—you are too proud;
But, if you were the devil, you are fair.
My lord and master loves you: O, such love
Could be but recompens'd, though you were crown'd
The nonpareil of beauty!
Oli. How does he love me?
Vio. With adorations, with fertile tears,
With groans that thunder love, with sighs of fire.
Oli. Your lord does know my mind; I cannot love him:
Yet I suppose him virtuous, know him noble,
Of great estate, of fresh and stainless youth;
In voices well divulg'd, free, learn'd, and valiant;
And, in dimension and the shape of nature,
A gracious person: but yet I cannot love him;
He might have took his answer long ago.
Vio. If I did love you in my master's flame,
With such a suffering, such a deadly life,
In your denial I would find no sense;
I would not understand it.
Oli. Why, what would you?
Vio. Make me a willow cabin at your gate,
And call upon my soul within the house;
Write loyal cantons of contemnèd love,
And sing them loud even in the dead of night;

Holla your name to the reverberate hills,
And make the babbling gossip of the air
Cry out, "Olivia!" O, you should not rest
Between the elements of air and earth,
But you should pity me!

Oli. You might do much. What is your parentage?

Vio. Above my fortunes, yet my state is well:
I am a gentleman.

Oli.   Get you to your lord;
I cannot love him: let him send no more;
Unless, perchance, you come to me again,
To tell me how he takes it. Fare you well:
I thank you for your pains: spend this for me.

Vio. I am no fee'd post, lady; keep your purse:
My master, not myself, lacks recompense.
Love make his heart of flint, that you shall love;
And let your fervour, like my master's, be
Plac'd in contempt! Farewell, fair cruelty.   [*Exit.*

Oli. "What is your parentage?"
"Above my fortunes, yet my state is well:
I am a gentleman." I'll be sworn thou art;
Thy tongue, thy face, thy limbs, actions, and spirit,
Do give thee fivefold blazon: — not too fast; —
Soft, soft! —
Unless the master were the man. — How now!
Even so quickly may one catch the plague?
Methinks I feel this youth's perfections
With an invisible and subtle stealth
To creep in at mine eyes. Well, let it be. —
What, ho, Malvolio!

Re-enter MALVOLIO.

Mal.   Here, madam, at your service.

Oli. Run after that same peevish messenger,
The county's man: he left this ring behind him,
Would I or not: tell him I'll none of it.
Desire him not to flatter with his lord,

Nor hold him up with hopes; I am not for him:
If that the youth will come this way to-morrow,
I'll give him reasons for 't. Hie thee, Malvolio.
 Mal. Madam, I will.   [*Exit.*
 Oli. I do I know not what; and fear to find
Mine eye too great a flatterer for my mind.
Fate, show thy force: ourselves we do not owe;
What is decreed must be, — and be this so!   [*Exit.*

ACT II.

Scene I. *The sea-coast.*

Enter Antonio *and* Sebastian.

 Ant. Will you stay no longer? nor will you not that I go with you?

 Seb. By your patience, no. My stars shine darkly over me: the malignancy of my fate might perhaps distemper yours; therefore I shall crave of you your leave that I may bear my evils alone: it were a bad recompense for your love, to lay any of them on you.

 Ant. Let me yet know of you whither you are bound.

 Seb. No, sooth, sir: my determinate voyage is mere extravagancy. But I perceive in you so excellent a touch of modesty, that you will not extort from me what I am willing to keep in; therefore it charges me in manners the rather to express myself. You must know of me, then, Antonio, my name is Sebastian, which I called Roderigo. My father was that Sebastian of Messaline, whom I know you have heard of. He left behind him myself and a sister, both born in an hour: if the heavens had been pleased, would we had so ended! but you, sir, altered that; for some hour before you took me from the breach of the sea was my sister drowned.

 Ant. Alas the day!

 Seb. A lady, sir, though it was said she much resembled me, was yet of many accounted beautiful: but, though I could not, with such estimable wonder, overfar believe that, yet thus far I will boldly publish her,— she bore a mind that envy could not but call fair. She is drowned already, sir, with salt water, though I seem to drown her remembrance again with more.

Ant. Pardon me, sir, your bad entertainment.

Seb. O good Antonio, forgive me your trouble!

Ant. If you will not murder me for my love, let me be your servant.

Seb. If you will not undo what you have done, that is, kill him whom you have recovered, desire it not. Fare ye well, at once: my bosom is full of kindness; and I am yet so near the manners of my mother, that, upon the least occasion more, mine eyes will tell tales of me. I am bound to the Count Orsino's court: farewell. [*Exit.*

Ant. The gentleness of all the gods go with thee!
I have many enemies in Orsino's court,
Else would I very shortly see thee there:
But, come what may, I do adore thee so,
That danger shall seem sport, and I will go. [*Exit.*

SCENE II. *A street.*

Enter VIOLA, MALVOLIO *following.*

Mal. Were not you even now with the Countess Olivia?

Vio. Even now, sir; on a moderate pace I have since arrived but hither.

Mal. She returns this ring to you, sir: you might have saved me my pains, to have taken it away yourself. She adds, moreover, that you should put your lord into a desperate assurance she will none of him: and one thing more, that you be never so hardy to come again in his affairs, unless it be to report your lord's taking of this. Receive it so.

Vio. She took no ring of me; — I'll none of it.

Mal. Come, sir, you peevishly threw it to her; and her will is, it should be so returned: if it be worth stooping for, there it lies in your eye; if not, be it his that finds it. [*Exit.*

Vio. I left no ring with her: what means this lady?
Fortune forbid, my outside have not charm'd her!
She made good view of me; indeed, so much,

That, as methought, her eyes had lost her tongue,
For she did speak in starts distractedly.
She loves me, sure; the cunning of her passion
Invites me in this churlish messenger.
None of my lord's ring! why, he sent her none.
I am the man: — if it be so, — as 'tis, —
Poor lady, she were better love a dream.
Disguise, I see, thou art a wickedness,
Wherein the pregnant enemy does much.
How easy is it for the proper-false
In women's waxen hearts to set their forms!
Alas, our frailty is the cause, not we!
For such as we are made of, such we be.
How will this fadge? my master loves her dearly;
And I, poor monster, fond as much on him,
As she, mistaken, seems to dote on me.
What will become of this? As I am man,
My state is desperate for my master's love;
As I am woman, — now, alas the day! —
What thriftless sighs shall poor Olivia breathe!
O Time, thou must untangle this, not I;
It is too hard a knot for me t' untie! [*Exit.*

SCENE III. *A room in* OLIVIA's *house.*

Enter Sir TOBY BELCH *and* Sir ANDREW AGUECHEEK.

Sir To. Approach, Sir Andrew: not to be a-bed after midnight is to be up betimes; and *diluculo surgere*, thou knowest, —

Sir And. Nay, by my troth, I know not: but I know, to be up late is to be up late.

Sir To. A false conclusion: I hate it as an unfilled can. To be up after midnight, and to go to bed then, is early: so that, to go to bed after midnight, is to go to bed betimes. Does not our life consist of the four elements?

Sir And. Faith, so they say; but, I think, it rather consists of eating and drinking.

Sir To. Thou'rt a scholar: let us therefore eat and drink. — Maria, I say! a stoop of wine!

Sir And. Here comes the fool, i' faith.

Enter Clown.

Clo. How now, my hearts! did you never see the picture of We Three?

Sir To. Welcome, ass. Now let's have a catch.

Sir And. By my troth, the fool has an excellent breast. I had rather than forty shillings I had such a leg, and so sweet a breath to sing, as the fool has. In sooth, thou wast in very gracious fooling last night, when thou spokest of Pigrogromitus, of the Vapians passing the equinoctial of Queubus: 'twas very good, i' faith. I sent thee sixpence for thy leman: hadst it?

Clo. I did impeticos thy gratillity; for Malvolio's nose is no whipstock; my lady has a white hand, and the Myrmidons are no bottle-ale houses.

Sir And. Excellent! why, this is the best fooling, when all is done. Now, a song.

Sir To. Come on; there is sixpence for you: let's have a song.

Sir And. There's a testril of me too: if one knight give a—

Clo. Would you have a love-song, or a song of good life?

Sir To. A love-song, a love-song.

Sir And. Ay, ay: I care not for good life.

Song.

Clo. *O, mistress mine, where are you roaming?*
O, stay and hear; your true-love's coming,
  That can sing both high and low:
Trip no further, pretty sweeting;
Journeys end in lovers' meeting,
  Every wise man's son doth know.

Sir And. Excellent good, i' faith.

Sir To. Good, good.

Clo. *What is love? 'tis not hereafter;*
Present mirth hath present laughter;
  What's to come is still unsure:

In delay there lies no plenty;
Then come kiss me, sweet-and-twenty,
Youth's a stuff will not endure.

Sir And. A mellifluous voice, as I am true knight.

Sir To. A contagious breath.

Sir And. Very sweet and contagious, i' faith.

Sir To. To hear by the nose, it is dulcet in contagion. But shall we make the welkin dance indeed? shall we rouse the night-owl in a catch that will draw three souls out of one weaver? shall we do that?

Sir And. An you love me, let's do't: I am dog at a catch.

Clo. By'r lady, sir, and some dogs will catch well.

Sir And. Most certain. Let our catch be, "Thou knave."

Clo. "Hold thy peace, thou knave," knight? I shall be constrained in't to call thee knave, knight.

Sir And. 'Tis not the first time I have constrained one to call me knave. Begin, fool: it begins, "Hold thy peace."

Clo. I shall never begin, if I hold my peace.

Sir And. Good, i' faith. Come, begin.

[*They sing the catch.*

Enter MARIA.

Mar. What a caterwauling do you keep here! If my lady have not called up her steward Malvolio, and bid him turn you out of doors, never trust me.

Sir To. My lady's a Cataian, we are politicians; Malvolio's a Peg-a-Ramsey, and "Three merry men be we." Am not I consanguineous? am I not of her blood? Tilly-vally, lady! There dwelt a man in Babylon, lady, lady! [*Singing.*

Clo. Beshrew me, the knight's in admirable fooling.

Sir And. Ay, he does well enough if he be disposed, and so do I too: he does it with a better grace, but I do it more natural.

Sir To. O, the twelfth day of December, — [*Singing.*

Mar. For the love o' God, peace!

Enter MALVOLIO.

Mal. My masters, are you mad? or what are you? Have you no wit, manners, nor honesty, but to gabble like tinkers at this time of night? Do ye make an alehouse of my lady's house, that ye squeak out your cosiers' catches without any mitigation or remorse of voice? Is there no respect of place, persons, nor time, in you?

Sir To. We did keep time, sir, in our catches. Snick-up!

Mal. Sir Toby, I must be round with you. My lady bade me tell you, that, though she harbours you as her kinsman, she's nothing allied to your disorders. If you can separate yourself and your misdemeanours, you are welcome to the house; if not, an it would please you to take leave of her, she is very willing to bid you farewell.

Sir To. Farewell, dear heart, since I must needs be gone. [*Singing.*

Mar. Nay, good Sir Toby.

Clo. His eyes do show his days are almost done. [*Singing.*

Mal. Is 't even so?

Sir To. But I will never die. [*Singing.*

Clo. Sir Toby, there you lie.

Mal. This is much credit to you.

Sir To. Shall I bid him go? [*Singing.*

Clo. What an if you do? [*Singing.*

Sir To. Shall I bid him go, and spare not? [*Singing.*

Clo. O, no, no, no, no, you dare not. [*Singing.*

Sir To. Out o' time, sir? ye lie. — Art any more than a steward? Dost thou think, because thou art virtuous, there shall be no more cakes and ale?

Clo. Yes, by Saint Anne; and ginger shall be hot i' the mouth too.

Sir To. Thou'rt i' the right. — Go, sir, rub your chain with crumbs. — A stoop of wine, Maria!

Mal. Mistress Mary, if you prized my lady's favour at any thing more than contempt, you would not give means for this uncivil rule: she shall know of it, by this hand. [*Exit.*

Mar. Go shake your ears.

Sir And. 'Twere as good a deed as to drink when a man's a-hungry, to challenge him the field, and then to break promise with him, and make a fool of him.

Sir To. Do't, knight: I'll write thee a challenge; or I'll deliver thy indignation to him by word of mouth.

Mar. Sweet Sir Toby, be patient for to-night: since the youth of the count's was to-day with my lady, she is much out of quiet. For Monsieur Malvolio, let me alone with him: if I do not gull him into a nayword, and make him a common recreation, do not think I have wit enough to lie straight in my bed: I know I can do it.

Sir And. Possess us, possess us; tell us something of him

Mar. Marry, sir, sometimes he is a kind of puritan.

Sir And. O, if I thought that, I'd beat him like a dog!

Sir To. What, for being a puritan? thy exquisite reason, dear knight?

Sir And. I have no exquisite reason for't, but I have reason good enough.

Mar. The devil a puritan that he is, or any thing constantly, but a time-pleaser; an affectioned ass, that cons state without book, and utters it by great swaths: the best persuaded of himself, so crammed, as he thinks, with excellencies, that it is his grounds of faith, that all that look on him love him; and on that vice in him will my revenge find notable cause to work.

Sir To. What wilt thou do?

Mar. I will drop in his way some obscure epistles of love; wherein, by the colour of his beard, the shape of his leg, the manner of his gait, the expressure of his eye, forehead, and complexion, he shall find himself most feelingly personated: I can write very like my lady, your niece; on a forgotten matter we can hardly make distinction of our hands.

Sir To. Excellent! I smell a device.

Sir And. I have't in my nose too.

Sir To. He shall think, by the letters that thou wilt drop, that they come from my niece, and that she's in love with him.

Mar. My purpose is, indeed, a horse of that colour.

Sir To. And your horse now would make him an ass.
Mar. Ass, I doubt not.
Sir And. O, 'twill be admirable!
Mar. Sport royal, I warrant you: I know my physic will work with him. I will plant you two, and let the fool make a third, where he shall find the letter: observe his construction of it. For this night, to bed, and dream on the event. Farewell.
Sir To. Good night, Penthesilea.   [*Exit Maria.*
Sir And. Before me, she's a good wench.
Sir To. She's a beagle, true-bred, and one that adores me: what o' that?
Sir And. I was adored once too.
Sir To. Let's to bed, knight. — Thou hadst need send for more money.
Sir And. If I cannot recover your niece, I am a foul way out.
Sir To. Send for money, knight: if thou hast her not i' the end, call me cut.
Sir And. If I do not, never trust me, take it how you will.
Sir To. Come, come; I'll go burn some sack; 'tis too late to go to bed now: come, knight; come, knight.   [*Exeunt.*

SCENE IV. *An apartment in the Duke's palace.*

Enter Duke, VIOLA, CURIO, *and others.*

Duke. Give me some music: — now, good morrow, friends: —
Now, good Cesario, but that piece of song,
That old and antique song we heard last night:
Methought it did relieve my passion much,
More than light airs and recollected terms
Of these most brisk and giddy-pacèd times: —
Come, but one verse.

Cur. He is not here, so please your lordship, that should sing it.

Duke. Who was it?

Cur. Feste, the jester, my lord; a fool that the Lady Olivia's father took much delight in: he is about the house.

Duke. Seek him out: — and play the tune the while.
[*Exit Curio. Music.*
Come hither, boy: if ever thou shalt love,
In the sweet pangs of it remember me;
For such as I am all true lovers are, —
Unstaid and skittish in all motions else,
Save in the constant image of the creature
That is belov'd. — How dost thou like this tune?
   Vio. It gives a very echo to the seat
Where Love is thron'd.
   Duke.   Thou dost speak masterly:
My life upon't, young though thou art, thine eye
Hath stay'd upon some favour that it loves; —
Hath it not, boy?
   Vio.   A little, by your favour.
   Duke. What kind of woman is't?
   Vio.   Of your complexion.
   Duke. She is not worth thee, then. What years, i' faith?
   Vio. About your years, my lord.
   Duke. Too old, by heaven: let still the woman take
An elder than herself; so wears she to him,
So sways she level in her husband's heart:
For, boy, however we do praise ourselves,
Our fancies are more giddy and unfirm,
More longing, wavering, sooner lost and won,
Than women's are.
   Vio.   I think it well, my lord.
   Duke. Then let thy love be younger than thyself,
Or thy affection cannot hold the bent;
For women are as roses, whose fair flower
Being once display'd, doth fall that very hour.
   Vio. And so they are: alas, that they are so, —
To die, even when they to perfection grow!

            Re-enter CURIO *with* Clown.

   Duke. O, fellow, come, the song we had last night. —
Mark it, Cesario; it is old and plain:

The spinsters and the knitters in the sun,
And the free maids that weave their thread with bones,
Do use to chant it: it is silly sooth,
And dallies with the innocence of love,
Like the old age.
   Clo. Are you ready, sir?
   Duke. Ay; prithee, sing.   [*Music.*

Song.

   Clo. *Come away, come away, death,*
       And in sad cypress let me be laid;
   Fly away, fly away, breath;
       I am slain by a fair cruel maid.
   My shroud of white, stuck all with yew,
           O, prepare it!
   My part of death, no one so true
           Did share it.

   Not a flower, not a flower sweet,
       On my black coffin let there be strown;
   Not a friend, not a friend greet
       My poor corpse, where my bones shall be thrown:
   A thousand thousand sighs to save,
           Lay me, O, where
   Sad true-love never find my grave,
           To weep there!

   Duke. There's for thy pains.
   Clo. No pains, sir; I take pleasure in singing, sir.
   Duke. I'll pay thy pleasure, then.
   Clo. Truly, sir, and pleasure will be paid, one time or another.
   Duke. Give me now leave to leave thee.
   Clo. Now, the melancholy god protect thee; and the tailor make thy doublet of changeable taffeta, for thy mind is a very opal! — I would have men of such constancy put to sea, that their business might be every thing, and their intent every where; for that's it that always makes a good voyage of nothing. — Farewell.   [*Exit.*

Duke. Let all the rest give place.
 [*Exeunt Curio and Attendants.*
                      Once more, Cesario,
Get thee to yond same sovereign cruelty:
Tell her, my love, more noble than the world,
Prizes not quantity of dirty lands;
The parts that Fortune hath bestow'd upon her,
Tell her, I hold as giddily as Fortune;
But 'tis that miracle and queen of gems,
That nature pranks her in, attracts my soul.
  Vio. But if she cannot love you, sir?
  Duke. I cannot be so answer'd.
  Vio.   Sooth, but you must.
Say that some lady — as, perhaps, there is —
Hath for your love as great a pang of heart
As you have for Olivia: you cannot love her;
You tell her so; must she not, then, be answer'd?
  Duke. There is no woman's sides
Can bide the beating of so strong a passion
As love doth give my heart; no woman's heart
So big, to hold so much; they lack retention.
Alas, their love may be call'd appetite, —
No motion of the liver, but the palate, —
That suffers surfeit, cloyment, and revolt;
But mine is all as hungry as the sea,
And can digest as much: make no compare
Between that love a woman can bear me
And that I owe Olivia.
  Vio.   Ay, but I know, —
  Duke. What dost thou know?
  Vio. Too well what love women to men may owe:
In faith, they are as true of heart as we.
My father had a daughter lov'd a man,
As it might be, perhaps, were I a woman,
I should your lordship.
  Duke.   And what's her history?
  Vio. A blank, my lord. She never told her love,

But let concealment, like a worm i' the bud,
Feed on her damask cheek: she pin'd in thought;
And, with a green and yellow melancholy,
She sat like Patience on a monument,
Smiling at grief. Was not this love indeed?
We men may say more, swear more: but, indeed,
Our shows are more than will; for still we prove
Much in our vows, but little in our love.

Duke. But died thy sister of her love, my boy?

Vio. I am all the daughters of my father's house,
And all the brothers too; — and yet I know not. —
Sir, shall I to this lady?

Duke.   Ay, that's the theme.
To her in haste; give her this jewel; say,
My love can give no place, bide no denay.   [*Exeunt.*

Scene V. Olivia's *garden.*

Enter Sir Toby Belch, Sir Andrew Aguecheek, *and* Fabian.

Sir To. Come thy ways, Signior Fabian.

Fab. Nay, I'll come: if I lose a scruple of this sport, let me be boiled to death with melancholy.

Sir To. Wouldst thou not be glad to have the niggardly rascally sheep-biter come by some notable shame?

Fab. I would exult, man: you know he brought me out o' favour with my lady about a bear-baiting here.

Sir To. To anger him, we'll have the bear again; and we will fool him black and blue: — shall we not, Sir Andrew?

Sir And. An we do not, it is pity of our lives.

Sir To. Here comes the little villain.

Enter Maria.

How now, my metal of India!

Mar. Get ye all three into the box-tree: Malvolio's coming down this walk: he has been yonder i' the sun practising behaviour to his own shadow this half hour: observe him, for the love of mockery; for I know this letter will make a contemplative idiot of him. Close; in the name of jesting!

[*The others hide themselves.*] Lie thou there [*Throws down a letter*]; for here comes the trout that must be caught with tickling. [*Exit.*

Enter MALVOLIO.

Mal. 'Tis but fortune; all is fortune. Maria once told me she did affect me: and I have heard herself come thus near, that, should she fancy, it should be one of my complexion. Besides, she uses me with a more exalted respect than any one else that follows her. What should I think on't?

Sir To. Here's an overweening rogue!

Fab. O, peace! Contemplation makes a rare turkey-cock of him: how he jets under his advanced plumes!

Sir And. 'Slight, I could so beat the rogue!

Sir To. Peace, I say.

Mal. To be Count Malvolio, —

Sir To. Ah, rogue!

Sir And. Pistol him, pistol him.

Sir To. Peace, peace!

Mal. There is example for't; the lady of the Strachy married the yeoman of the wardrobe.

Sir And. Fie on him, Jezebel!

Fab. O, peace! now he's deeply in: look how imagination blows him.

Mal. Having been three months married to her, sitting in my state, —

Sir To. O, for a stone-bow, to hit him in the eye!

Mal. Calling my officers about me, in my branched velvet gown; having come from a day-bed, where I have left Olivia sleeping, —

Sir To. Fire and brimstone!

Fab. O, peace, peace!

Mal. And then to have the humour of state; and after a demure travel of regard, — telling them I know my place, as I would they should do theirs, — to ask for my kinsman Toby, —

Sir To. Bolts and shackles!

Fab. O, peace, peace, peace! now, now.

Mal. Seven of my people, with an obedient start, make out for him: I frown the while; and perchance wind up my watch, or play with some rich jewel. Toby approaches; court'sies there to me, —

Sir To. Shall this fellow live?

Fab. Though our silence be drawn from us by th' ears, yet peace.

Mal. I extend my hand to him thus, quenching my familiar smile with an austere regard of control, —

Sir To. And does not Toby take you a blow o' the lips, then?

Mal. Saying, "Cousin Toby, my fortunes having cast me on your niece, give me this prerogative of speech," —

Sir To. What, what?

Mal. "You must amend your drunkenness."

Sir To. Out, scab!

Fab. Nay, patience, or we break the sinews of our plot.

Mal. "Besides, you waste the treasure of your time with a foolish knight," —

Sir And. That's me, I warrant you.

Mal. "One Sir Andrew," —

Sir And. I knew 'twas I; for many do call me fool.

Mal. What employment have we here?

[*Taking up the letter.*

Fab. Now is the woodcock near the gin.

Sir To. O, peace! and the spirit of humours intimate reading aloud to him!

Mal. By my life, this is my lady's hand: these be her very C's, her U's, and her T's; and thus makes she her great P's. It is, in contempt of question, her hand.

Sir And. Her C's, her U's, and her T's: why that?

Mal. [*reads*] "To the unknown beloved, this, and my good wishes:" her very phrases! — By your leave, wax. — Soft! — and the impressure her Lucrece, with which she uses to seal: 'tis my lady. To whom should this be?

Fab. This wins him, liver and all.

Mal. [*reads*] "Jove knows I love:
                    But who?
                    Lips, do not move;
                    No man must know."

"No man must know." — What follows? the numbers altered! — "No man must know:" — if this should be thee, Malvolio?

Sir To. Marry, hang thee, brock!

Mal. [*reads*]
            "I may command where I adore;
              But silence, like a Lucrece' knife,
            With bloodless stroke my heart doth gore:
              M, O, A, I, doth sway my life."

Fab. A fustian riddle!

Sir To. Excellent wench, say I.

Mal. "M, O, A, I, doth sway my life." — Nay, but first, let me see, — let me see, — let me see.

Fab. What dish o' poison has she dressed him!

Sir To. And with what wing the staniel checks at it!

Mal. "I may command where I adore." Why, she may command me: I serve her; she is my lady. Why, this is evident to any formal capacity; there is no obstruction in this: — and the end, — what should that alphabetical position portend? if I could make that resemble something in me, — Softly! — M, O, A, I, —

Sir To. O, ay, make up that: — he is now at a cold scent.

Fab. Sowter will cry upon 't, for all this, though it be as rank as a fox.

Mal. M, — Malvolio; — M, — why, that begins my name.

Fab. Did not I say he would work it out? the cur is excellent at faults.

Mal. M, — but then there is no consonancy in the sequel; that suffers under probation: A should follow, but O does.

Fab. And O shall end, I hope.

Sir To. Ay, or I'll cudgel him, and make him cry O!

Mal. And then I comes behind

Fab. Ay, an you had any eye behind you, you might see more detraction at your heels than fortunes before you.

Mal. M, O, A, I; — this simulation is not as the former: — and yet, to crush this a little, it would bow to me, for every one of these letters are in my name. Soft! here follows prose. — [*Reads*] "If this fall into thy hand, revolve. In my stars I am above thee; but be not afraid of greatness: some are born great, some achieve greatness, and some have greatness thrust upon 'em. Thy Fates open their hands; let thy blood and spirit embrace them: and, to inure thyself to what thou art like to be, cast thy humble slough, and appear fresh. Be opposite with a kinsman, surly with servants; let thy tongue tang arguments of state; put thyself into the trick of singularity: she thus advises thee that sighs for thee. Remember who commended thy yellow stockings, and wished to see thee ever cross-gartered: I say, remember. Go to, thou art made, if thou desirest to be so; if not, let me see thee a steward still, the fellow of servants, and not worthy to touch Fortune's fingers. Farewell. She that would alter services with thee,

THE FORTUNATE-UNHAPPY."

Daylight and champain discover not more: this is open. I will be proud, I will read politic authors, I will baffle Sir Toby, I will wash off gross acquaintance, I will be point-devise the very man. I do not now fool myself, to let imagination jade me; for every reason excites to this, that my lady loves me. She did commend my yellow stockings of late, she did praise my leg being cross-gartered; and in this she manifests herself to my love, and, with a kind of injunction, drives me to these habits of her liking. I thank my stars, I am happy. I will be strange, stout, in yellow stockings, and cross-gartered, even with the swiftness of putting on. Jove and my stars be praised! — Here is yet a postscript. [*Reads*] "Thou canst not choose but know who I am. If thou entertainest my love, let it appear in thy smiling: thy smiles become thee well; therefore in my presence still smile, dear my sweet, I prithee." Jove, I thank thee. — I will smile; I will do every thing that thou wilt have me. [*Exit.*

Fab. I will not give my part of this sport for a pension of thousands to be paid from the Sophy.

Sir To. I could marry this wench for this device, —

Sir And. So could I too.

Sir To. And ask no other dowry with her but such another jest.

Sir And. Nor I neither.

Fab. Here comes my noble gull-catcher.

Re-enter MARIA.

Sir To. Wilt thou set thy foot o' my neck?

Sir And. Or o' mine either?

Sir To. Shall I play my freedom at tray-trip, and become thy bond-slave?

Sir And. I' faith, or I either?

Sir To. Why, thou hast put him in such a dream, that, when the image of it leaves him, he must run mad.

Mar. Nay, but say true; does it work upon him?

Sir To. Like aqua-vitæ with a midwife.

Mar. If you will, then, see the fruits of the sport, mark his first approach before my lady: he will come to her in yellow stockings, and 'tis a colour she abhors, and cross-gartered, a fashion she detests; and he will smile upon her, which will now be so unsuitable to her disposition, being addicted to a melancholy as she is, that it cannot but turn him into a notable contempt. If you will see it, follow me.

Sir To. To the gates of Tartar, thou most excellent devil of wit!

Sir And. I'll make one too. [*Exeunt.*

ACT III.

SCENE I. OLIVIA'S *garden.*

Enter VIOLA, *and* CLOWN *with a tabor.*

Vio. Save thee, friend, and thy music! dost thou live by thy tabor?

Clo. No, sir, I live by the church.

Vio. Art thou a churchman?

Clo. No such matter, sir: I do live by the church; for I do live at my house, and my house doth stand by the church.

Vio. So thou mayst say, the king lives by a beggar, if a beggar dwell near him; or, the church stands by thy tabor, if thy tabor stand by the church.

Clo. You have said, sir.—To see this age!—A sentence is but a cheveril glove to a good wit: how quickly the wrong side may be turned outward!

Vio. Nay, that's certain; they that dally nicely with words may quickly make them wanton.

Clo. I would, therefore, my sister had had no name, sir.

Vio. Why, man?

Clo. Why, sir, her name's a word; and to dally with that word might make my sister wanton. But, indeed, words are very rascals, since bonds disgraced them.

Vio. Thy reason, man?

Clo. Troth, sir, I can yield you none without words; and words are grown so false, I am loth to prove reason with them.

Vio. I warrant thou art a merry fellow, and carest for nothing.

Clo. Not so, sir; I do care for something; but in my conscience, sir, I do not care for you: if that be to care for nothing, sir, I would it would make you invisible.

Vio. Art not thou the Lady Olivia's fool?

Clo. No, indeed, sir; the Lady Olivia has no folly: she will keep no fool, sir, till she be married; and fools are as like husbands as pilchers are to herrings,—the husband's the bigger: I am, indeed, not her fool, but her corrupter of words.

Vio. I saw thee late at the Count Orsino's.

Clo. Foolery, sir, does walk about the orb; like the sun, it shines every where. I would be sorry, sir, but the fool should be as oft with your master as with my mistress: I think I saw your wisdom there.

Vio. Nay, an thou pass upon me, I'll no more with thee. Hold, there's expenses for thee. [*Gives a piece of money.*

Clo. Now Jove, in his next commodity of hair, send thee a beard!

Vio. By my troth, I'll tell thee, — I am almost sick for one; though I would not have it grow on my chin. Is thy lady within?

Clo. Would not a pair of these have bred, sir?

Vio. Yes, being kept together and put to use.

Clo. I would play Lord Pandarus of Phrygia, sir, to bring a Cressida to this Troilus.

Vio. I understand you, sir; 'tis well begged.

[*Gives another piece of money.*

Clo. The matter, I hope, is not great, sir, begging but a beggar: Cressida was a beggar. My lady is within, sir. I will construe to them whence you come; who you are, and what you would, are out of my welkin,—I might say element, but the word is over-worn. [*Exit.*

Vio. This fellow's wise enough to play the fool;
And to do that well craves a kind of wit:
He must observe their mood on whom he jests,
The quality of persons, and the time;
Not, like the haggard, check at every feather
That comes before his eye. This is a practice
As full of labour as a wise man's art:
For folly, that he wisely shows, is fit;
But wise men, folly-fall'n, quite taint their wit.

Enter Sir Toby Belch *and* Sir Andrew Aguecheek.

Sir To. Save you, gentleman!

Vio. And you, sir.

Sir And. Dieu vous garde, monsieur.

Vio. Et vous aussi; votre serviteur.

Sir And. I hope, sir, you are; and I am yours.

Sir To. Will you encounter the house? my niece is desirous you should enter, if your trade be to her.

Vio. I am bound to your niece, sir; I mean, she is the list of my voyage.

Sir To. Taste your legs, sir; put them to motion.

Vio. My legs do better understand me, sir, than I understand what you mean by bidding me taste my legs.

Sir To. I mean, to go, sir, to enter.

Vio. I will answer you with gait and entrance: — but we are prevented.

Enter OLIVIA *and* MARIA.

Most excellent-accomplished lady, the heavens rain odours on you!

Sir And. [*aside*] That youth's a rare courtier: "Rain odours:" — well.

Vio. My matter hath no voice, lady, but to your own most pregnant and vouchsafed ear.

Sir And. [*aside*] "Odours," "pregnant," and "vouchsafed:" — I'll get 'em all three ready.

Oli. Let the garden-door be shut, and leave me to my hearing. [*Exeunt Sir Toby, Sir Andrew, and Maria.*] Give me your hand, sir.

Vio. My duty, madam, and most humble service.

Oli. What is your name?

Vio. Cesario is your servant's name, fair princess.

Oli. My servant, sir! 'Twas never merry world
Since lowly feigning was call'd compliment:
You're servant to the Count Orsino, youth.

Vio. And he is yours, and his must needs be yours:
Your servant's servant is your servant, madam.

Oli. For him, I think not on him: for his thoughts,
Would they were blanks, rather than fill'd with me!

Vio. Madam, I come to whet your gentle thoughts
On his behalf: —

Oli. O, by your leave, I pray you, —
I bade you never speak again of him:
But, would you undertake another suit,
I had rather hear you to solicit that
Than music from the spheres.

Vio. Dear lady, —

Oli. Give me leave, I beseech you. I did send,
After the last enchantment you did here,
A ring in chase of you: so did I abuse
Myself, my servant, and, I fear me, you:
Under your hard construction must I sit,
To force that on you, in a shameful cunning,
Which you knew none of yours: what might you think?
Have you not set mine honour at the stake,
And baited it with all th' unmuzzled thoughts
That tyrannous heart can think? To one of your receiving
Enough is shown: a cyprus, not a bosom,
Hides my heart. So, let me hear you speak.
 Vio. I pity you.
 Oli.   That's a degree to love.
 Vio. No, not a grise; for 'tis a vulgar proof,
That very oft we pity enemies.
 Oli. Why, then, methinks 'tis time to smile again.
O world, how apt the poor are to be proud!
If one should be a prey, how much the better
To fall before the lion than the wolf!   [*Clock strikes.*
The clock upbraids me with the waste of time. —
Be not afraid, good youth, I will not have you:
And yet, when wit and youth is come to harvest,
Your wife is like to reap a proper man:
There lies your way, due west.
 Vio.   Then westward-ho! —
Grace and good disposition tend your ladyship!
You'll nothing, madam, to my lord by me?
 Oli. Stay:
I prithee, tell me what thou think'st of me.
  Vio. That you do think you are not what you are.
  Oli. If I think so, I think the same of you.
  Vio. Then think you right: I am not what I am.
  Oli. I would you were as I would have you be!
  Vio. Would it be better, madam, than I am,
I wish it might; for now I am your fool.
  Oli. O, what a deal of scorn looks beautiful

In the contempt and anger of his lip!
A murderous guilt shows not itself more soon
Than love that would seem hid: love's night is noon.
Cesario, by the roses of the spring,
By maidhood, honour, truth, and every thing,
I love thee so, that, maugre all thy pride,
Nor wit nor reason can my passion hide.
Do not extort thy reasons from this clause,
For that I woo, thou therefore hast no cause;
But, rather, reason thus with reason fetter, —
Love sought is good, but given unsought is better.

Vio. By innocence I swear, and by my youth,
I have one heart, one bosom, and one truth, —
And that no woman has; nor never none
Shall mistress be of it, save I alone.
And so adieu, good madam; never more
Will I my master's tears to you deplore.

Oli. Yet come again; for thou perhaps mayst move
That heart, which now abhors, to like his love. [*Exeunt.*

SCENE II. *A room in* OLIVIA'S *house.*

Enter Sir TOBY BELCH, Sir ANDREW AGUECHEEK, *and* FABIAN.

Sir And. No, faith, I'll not stay a jot longer.

Sir To. Thy reason, dear venom; give thy reason.

Fab. You must needs yield your reason, Sir Andrew.

Sir And. Marry, I saw your niece do more favours to the count's serving-man than ever she bestowed upon me; I saw 't i' the orchard.

Sir To. Did she see thee the while, old boy? tell me that.

Sir And. As plain as I see you now.

Fab. This was a great argument of love in her toward you.

Sir And. 'Slight, will you make an ass o' me?

Fab. I will prove it legitimate, sir, upon the oaths of judgment and reason.

Sir To. And they have been grand-jurymen since before Noah was a sailor.

Fab. She did show favour to the youth in your sight only to exasperate you, to awake your dormouse valour, to put fire in your heart, and brimstone in your liver. You should then have accosted her; and with some excellent jests, fire-new from the mint, you should have banged the youth into dumbness. This was looked for at your hand, and this was balked: the double gilt of this opportunity you let time wash off, and you are now sailed into the north of my lady's opinion; where you will hang like an icicle on a Dutchman's beard, unless you do redeem it by some laudable attempt either of valour or policy.

Sir And. An 't be any way, it must be with valour; for policy I hate: I had as lief be a Brownist as a politician.

Sir To. Why, then, build me thy fortunes upon the basis of valour. Challenge me the count's youth to fight with him; hurt him in eleven places: my niece shall take note of it; and assure thyself, there is no love-broker in the world can more prevail in man's commendation with woman than report of valour.

Fab. There is no way but this, Sir Andrew.

Sir And. Will either of you bear me a challenge to him?

Sir To. Go, write it in a martial hand; be curst and brief; it is no matter how witty, so it be eloquent and full of invention: taunt him with the license of ink: if thou "thou'st" him some thrice, it shall not be amiss; and as many lies as will lie in thy sheet of paper, although the sheet were big enough for the bed of Ware in England, set 'em down: go, about it. Let there be gall enough in thy ink; though thou write with a goose-pen, no matter: about it.

Sir And. Where shall I find you?

Sir To. We'll call thee at thy *cubiculo:* go.

[*Exit Sir Andrew.*

Fab. This is a dear manakin to you, Sir Toby.

Sir To. I have been dear to him, lad, — some two thousand strong, or so.

Fab. We shall have a rare letter from him: but you'll not deliver 't?

SCENE III.] WHAT YOU WILL. 203

Sir To. Never trust me, then; and by all means stir on the youth to an answer. I think oxen and wainropes cannot hale them together. For Andrew, if he were opened, and you find so much blood in his liver as will clog the foot of a flea, I'll eat the rest of the anatomy.

Fab. And his opposite, the youth, bears in his visage no great presage of cruelty.

Sir To. Look, where the youngest wren of nine comes.

Enter MARIA.

Mar. If you desire the spleen, and will laugh yourselves into stitches, follow me. Yond gull Malvolio is turned heathen, a very renegado; for there is no Christian, that means to be saved by believing rightly, can ever believe such impossible passages of grossness. He's in yellow stockings.

Sir To. And cross-gartered?

Mar. Most villanously; like a pedant that keeps a school i' the church. — I have dogged him, like his murderer. He does obey every point of the letter that I dropped to betray him: he does smile his face into more lines than are in the new map, with the augmentation of the Indies; you have not seen such a thing as 'tis; I can hardly forbear hurling things at him. I know my lady will strike him: if she do, he'll smile, and take 't for a great favour.

Sir To. Come, bring us, bring us where he is. [*Exeunt.*

SCENE III. *A street.*

Enter SEBASTIAN *and* ANTONIO.

Seb. I would not, by my will, have troubled you;
But, since you make your pleasure of your pains,
I will no further chide you.

Ant. I could not stay behind you: my desire,
More sharp than filèd steel, did spur me forth;
And not all love to see you, — though so much
As might have drawn me to a longer voyage, —
But jealousy what might befall your travel,
Being skilless in these parts; which to a stranger,

Unguided and unfriended, often prove
Rough and unhospitable: my willing love,
The rather by these arguments of fear,
Set forth in your pursuit.

 Seb.   My kind Antonio,
I can no other answer make, but thanks,
And thanks, still thanks; and very oft good turns
Are shuffled off with such uncurrent pay:
But, were my worth, as is my conscience, firm,
You should find better dealing. What's to do?
Shall we go see the relics of this town?

 Ant. To-morrow, sir; best first go see your lodging.

 Seb. I am not weary, and 'tis long to night:
I pray you, let us satisfy our eyes
With the memorials and the things of fame
That do renown this city.

 Ant.   Would you'd pardon me;
I do not without danger walk these streets:
Once, in a sea-fight, 'gainst the count his galleys
I did some service; of such note, indeed,
That, were I ta'en here, it would scarce be answer'd.

 Seb. Belike you slew great number of his people?

 Ant. Th' offence is not of such a bloody nature;
Albeit the quality of the time and quarrel
Might well have given us bloody argument.
It might have since been answer'd in repaying
What we took from them; which, for traffic's sake,
Most of our city did: only myself stood out;
For which, if I be lapsèd in this place,
I shall pay dear.

 Seb. Do not, then, walk too open.

 Ant. It doth not fit me. Hold, sir, here's my purse.
In the south suburbs, at the Elephant,
Is best to lodge: I will bespeak our diet,
Whiles you beguile the time and feed your knowledge
With viewing of the town: there shall you have me.

 Seb. Why 1 your purse?

Ant. Haply your eye shall light upon some toy
You have desire to purchase; and your store,
I think, is not for idle markets, sir.

Seb. I'll be your purse-bearer, and leave you for
An hour.

Ant. To th' Elephant.
Seb.   I do remember.   *[Exeunt.*

Scene IV. Olivia's *garden.*

Enter Olivia *and* Maria.

Oli. I have sent after him: he says he'll come; —
How shall I feast him? what bestow of him?
For youth is bought more oft than begg'd or borrow'd.
I speak too loud. —
Where is Malvolio? — he is sad and civil,
And suits well for a servant with my fortunes: —
Where is Malvolio?

Mar. He's coming, madam; but in very strange manner.
He is, sure, possessed, madam.

Oli. Why, what's the matter? does he rave?

Mar. No, madam, he does nothing but smile: your ladyship were best to have some guard about you, if he come; for, sure, the man is tainted in 's wits.

Oli. Go call him hither. [*Exit Maria.*] I'm as mad as he,
If sad and merry madness equal be.

Re-enter Maria, *with* Malvolio.

How now, Malvolio!

Mal. Sweet lady, ho, ho.   [*Smiles fantastically.*

Oli. Smil'st thou?
I sent for thee upon a sad occasion.

Mal. Sad, lady! I could be sad: this does make some obstruction in the blood, this cross-gartering; but what of that? if it please the eye of one, it is with me as the very true sonnet is, "Please one, and please all."

Oli. Why, how dost thou, man? what is the matter with thee?

Mal. Not black in my mind, though yellow in my legs. It did come to his hands, and commands shall be executed: I think we do know the sweet Roman hand.

Oli. Wilt thou go to bed, Malvolio?

Mal. To bed! ay, sweet-heart; and I'll come to thee.

Oli. God comfort thee! Why dost thou smile so, and kiss thy hand so oft?

Mar. How do you, Malvolio?

Mal. At your request! yes; nightingales answer daws.

Mar. Why appear you with this ridiculous boldness before my lady?

Mal. "Be not afraid of greatness:"— 'twas well writ.

Oli. What meanest thou by that, Malvolio?

Mal. "Some are born great,"—

Oli. Ha!

Mal. "Some achieve greatness,"—

Oli. What sayest thou?

Mal. "And some have greatness thrust upon them."

Oli. Heaven restore thee!

Mal. "Remember who commended thy yellow stockings,"—

Oli. My yellow stockings!

Mal. "And wished to see thee cross-gartered."

Oli. Cross-gartered!

Mal. "Go to, thou art made, if thou desirest to be so;"—

Oli. Am I made?

Mal. "If not, let me see thee a servant still."

Oli. Why, this is very midsummer madness.

Enter Servant.

Ser. Madam, the young gentleman of the Count Orsino's is returned: I could hardly entreat him back: he attends your ladyship's pleasure.

Oli. I'll come to him. [*Exit Servant.*] Good Maria, let this fellow be looked to. Where's my cousin Toby? Let some of my people have a special care of him: I would not have him miscarry for the half of my dowry. [*Exeunt Olivia and Maria.*

Mal. O, ho! do you come near me now? no worse man than Sir Toby to look to me? This concurs directly with the letter: she sends him on purpose, that I may appear stubborn to him; for she incites me to that in the letter. "Cast thy humble slough," says she; "be opposite with a kinsman, surly with servants; let thy tongue tang arguments of state; put thyself into the trick of singularity;"— and, consequently, sets down the manner how; as, a sad face, a reverent carriage, a slow tongue, in the habit of some air of note, and so forth. I have limed her; but it is Jove's doing, and Jove make me thankful! And, when she went away now, "Let this fellow be looked to:" fellow! not Malvolio, nor after my degree, but fellow. Why, every thing adheres together, that no dram of a scruple, no scruple of a scruple, no obstacle, no incredulous or unsafe circumstance — What can be said? Nothing, that can be, can come between me and the full prospect of my hopes. Well, Jove, not I, is the doer of this, and he is to be thanked.

Re-enter MARIA *with* Sir TOBY BELCH *and* FABIAN.

Sir To. Which way is he, in the name of sanctity? If all the devils of hell be drawn in little, and Legion himself possessed him, yet I'll speak to him.

Fab. Here he is, here he is. — How is 't with you, sir? how is 't with you, man?

Mal. Go off; I discard you: let me enjoy my private: go off.

Mar. Lo, how hollow the fiend speaks within him! did not I tell you? — Sir Toby, my lady prays you to have a care of him.

Mal. Ah, ha! does she so?

Sir To. Go to, go to; peace, peace; we must deal gently with him: let me alone. — How do you, Malvolio? how is 't with you? What, man! defy the devil: consider, he's an enemy to mankind.

Mal. Do you know what you say?

Mar. La you, an you speak ill of the devil, how he takes it at heart! Pray God, he be not bewitched!

Fab. Carry his water to the wise woman.

Mar. Marry, and it shall be done to-morrow morning, if I live. My lady would not lose him for more than I'll say.

Mal. How now, mistress!

Mar. O Lord!

Sir To. Prithee, hold thy peace; this is not the way: do you not see you move him? let me alone with him.

Fab. No way but gentleness; gently, gently: the fiend is rough, and will not be roughly used.

Sir To. Why, how now, my bawcock! how dost thou chuck?

Mal. Sir!

Sir To. Ay, Biddy, come with me. What, man! 'tis not for gravity to play at cherry-pit with Satan: hang him, foul collier!

Mar. Get him to say his prayers; good Sir Toby, get him to pray.

Mal. My prayers, minx!

Mar. No, I warrant you, he will not hear of godliness.

Mal. Go, hang yourselves all! you are idle shallow things: I am not of your element: you shall know more hereafter. [*Exit.*

Sir To. Is't possible?

Fab. If this were played upon a stage now, I could condemn it as an improbable fiction.

Sir To. His very genius hath taken the infection of the device, man.

Mar. Nay, pursue him now, lest the device take air, and taint.

Fab. Why, we shall make him mad indeed.

Mar. The house will be the quieter.

Sir To. Come, we'll have him in a dark room and bound. My niece is already in the belief that he's mad; we may carry it thus, for our pleasure and his penance, till our very pastime, tired out of breath, prompt us to have mercy on him: at which time we will bring the device to the bar, and crown thee for a finder of madmen. — But see, but see.

Fab. More matter for a May morning.

Enter Sir ANDREW AGUECHEEK.

Sir And. Here's the challenge, read it: I warrant there's vinegar and pepper in 't.

Fab. Is 't so saucy?

Sir And. Ay, is 't, I warrant him: do but read.

Sir To. Give me. [*Reads*] "Youth, whatsoever thou art, thou art but a scurvy fellow."

Fab. Good, and valiant.

Sir To. [*reads*] "Wonder not, nor admire not in thy mind, why I do call thee so, for I will show thee no reason for't."

Fab. A good note: that keeps you from the blow of the law.

Sir To. [*reads*] "Thou comest to the Lady Olivia, and in my sight she uses thee kindly: but thou liest in thy throat; that is not the matter I challenge thee for."

Fab. Very brief, and to exceeding good sense — less.

Sir To. [*reads*] "I will waylay thee going home; where if it be thy chance to kill me," —

Fab. Good.

Sir To. [*reads*] "Thou killest me like a rogue and a villain."

Fab. Still you keep o' the windy side of the law: good.

Sir To. [*reads*] "Fare thee well; and God have mercy upon one of our souls! He may have mercy upon mine; but my hope is better, and so look to thyself. Thy friend, as thou usest him, and thy sworn enemy, ANDREW AGUECHEEK." If this letter move him not, his legs cannot: I'll give 't him.

Mar. You may have very fit occasion for 't: he is now in some commerce with my lady, and will by and by depart.

Sir To. Go, Sir Andrew; scout me for him at the corner of the orchard, like a bum-baily: so soon as ever thou seest him, draw; and, as thou drawest, swear horrible; for it comes to pass oft, that a terrible oath, with a swaggering accent sharply twanged off, gives manhood more approbation than ever proof itself would have earned him. Away!

Sir And. Nay, let me alone for swearing. [*Exit.*

Sir To. Now will not I deliver his letter: for the behaviour of the young gentleman gives him out to be of good capacity and breeding; his employment between his lord and my niece confirms no less: therefore this letter, being so excellently ignorant, will breed no terror in the youth, — he will find it comes from a clodpole. But, sir, I will deliver his challenge by word of mouth; set upon Aguecheek a notable report of valour; and drive the gentleman — as I know his youth will aptly receive it — into a most hideous opinion of his rage, skill, fury, and impetuosity. This will so fright them both, that they will kill one another by the look, like cockatrices.

Fab. Here he comes with your niece: give them way till he take leave, and presently after him.

Sir To. I will meditate the while upon some horrid message for a challenge. [*Exeunt Sir Toby, Fabian, and Maria.*

Re-enter OLIVIA, *with* VIOLA.

Oli. I've said too much unto a heart of stone,
And laid mine honour too unchary out:
There's something in me that reproves my fault;
But such a headstrong potent fault it is,
That it but mocks reproof.

Vio. With the same 'haviour that your passion bears,
Goes on my master's grief.

Oli. Here, wear this jewel for me, — 'tis my picture:
Refuse it not; it hath no tongue to vex you:
And, I beseech you, come again to-morrow.
What shall you ask of me that I'll deny,
That honour, sav'd, may upon asking give?

Vio. Nothing but this, — your true love for my master.

Oli. How with mine honour may I give him that
Which I have given to you?

Vio. I will acquit you.

Oli. Well, come again to-morrow: fare thee well:
A fiend like thee might bear my soul to hell. [*Exit.*

Re-enter Sir TOBY BELCH *and* FABIAN.

Sir To. Gentleman, God save thee!

Vio. And you, sir.

Sir To. That defence thou hast, betake thee to 't: of what nature the wrongs are thou hast done him, I know not; but thy intercepter, full of despite, bloody as the hunter, attends thee at the orchard-end: dismount thy tuck, be yare in thy preparation; for thy assailant is quick, skilful, and deadly.

Vio. You mistake, sir; I am sure no man hath any quarrel to me: my remembrance is very free and clear from any image of offence done to any man.

Sir To. You'll find it otherwise, I assure you: therefore, if you hold your life at any price, betake you to your guard; for your opposite hath in him what youth, strength, skill, and wrath can furnish man withal.

Vio. I pray you, sir, what is he?

Sir To. He is knight, dubbed with unhacked rapier and on carpet consideration; but he is a devil in private brawl: souls and bodies hath he divorced three; and his incensement at this moment is so implacable, that satisfaction can be none but by pangs of death and sepulchre: hob-nob is his word; give 't or take 't.

Vio. I will return again into the house, and desire some conduct of the lady. I am no fighter. I have heard of some kind of men that put quarrels purposely on others, to taste their valour: belike this is a man of that quirk.

Sir To. Sir, no; his indignation derives itself out of a very competent injury: therefore, get you on, and give him his desire. Back you shall not to the house, unless you undertake that with me which with as much safety you might answer him: therefore, on, or strip your sword stark naked; for meddle you must, that's certain, or forswear to wear iron about you.

Vio. This is as uncivil as strange. I beseech you, do me this courteous office, as to know of the knight what my offence to him is: it is something of my negligence, nothing of my purpose.

Sir To. I will do so. — Signior Fabian, stay you by this gentleman till my return. [*Exit.*

Vio. Pray you, sir, do you know of this matter?

Fab. I know the knight is incensed against you, even to a mortal arbitrement; but nothing of the circumstance more.

Vio. I beseech you, what manner of man is he?

Fab. Nothing of that wonderful promise, to read him by his form, as you are like to find him in the proof of his valour. He is, indeed, sir, the most skilful, bloody, and fatal opposite that you could possibly have found in any part of Illyria. Will you walk towards him? I will make your peace with him, if I can.

Vio. I shall be much bound to you for 't: I am one that had rather go with sir priest than sir knight: I care not who knows so much of my mettle. [*Exeunt.*

SCENE V. *The street adjoining* OLIVIA'S *garden.*

Enter SIR TOBY BELCH *and* SIR ANDREW AGUECHEEK.

Sir To. Why, man, he's a very devil; I have not seen such a firago. I had a pass with him, rapier, scabbard, and all, and he gives me the stuck-in with such a mortal motion, that it is inevitable; and on the answer, he pays you as surely as your feet hit the ground they step on: they say he has been fencer to the Sophy.

Sir And. Pox on 't, I'll not meddle with him.

Sir To. Ay, but he will not now be pacified: Fabian can scarce hold him yonder.

Sir And. Plague on 't, an I thought he had been valiant and so cunning in fence, I'd have seen him damned ere I'd have challenged him. Let him let the matter slip, and I'll give him my horse, gray Capulet.

Sir To. I'll make the motion: stand here, make a good show on 't: this shall end without the perdition of souls. — [*Aside*] Marry, I'll ride your horse as well as I ride you.

Enter FABIAN *and* VIOLA.

[*To Fab.*] I have his horse to take up the quarrel: I have persuaded him the youth's a devil.

Fab. He is as horribly conceited of him; and pants and looks pale, as if a bear were at his heels.

Sir To. [*to Vio.*] There's no remedy, sir; he will fight with you for's oath-sake: marry, he hath better bethought him of his quarrel, and he finds that now scarce to be worth talking of: therefore draw, for the supportance of his vow; he protests he will not hurt you.

Vio. [*aside*] Pray God defend me! A little thing would make me tell them how much I lack of a man.

Fab. Give ground, if you see him furious.

Sir To. Come, Sir Andrew, there's no remedy; the gentleman will, for his honour's sake, have one bout with you; he cannot by the duello avoid it: but he has promised me, as he is a gentleman and a soldier, he will not hurt you. Come on; to 't.

Sir And. Pray God, he keep his oath! [*Draws.*
Vio. I do assure you, 'tis against my will. [*Draws.*

Enter ANTONIO.

Ant. Put up your sword. If this young gentleman
Have done offence, I take the fault on me:
If you offend him, I for him defy you.

Sir To. You, sir! why, what are you?

Ant. [*drawing*] One, sir, that for his love dares yet do more
Than you have heard him brag to you he will.

Sir To. Nay, if you be an undertaker, I am for you.
[*Draws.*

Fab. O good Sir Toby, hold! here come the officers.

Sir To. [*to Antonio*] I'll be with you anon.

Vio. [*to Sir Andrew*] Pray, sir, put your sword up, if you please.

Sir And. Marry, will I, sir; — and, for that I promised you, I'll be as good as my word: he will bear you easily, and reins well.

Enter Officers.

First Off. This is the man; do thy office.

Sec. Off. Antonio, I arrest thee at the suit
Of Count Orsino.

Ant. You do mistake me, sir.

First Off. No, sir, no jot; I know your favour well,
Though now you have no sea-cap on your head. —
Take him away: he knows I know him well.

Ant. I must obey.—[*To Vio.*] This comes with seeking you:
But there's no remedy; I shall answer it.
What will you do, now my necessity
Makes me to ask you for my purse? It grieves me
Much more for what I cannot do for you
Than what befalls myself. You stand amaz'd;
But be of comfort.

Sec. Off. Come, sir, away.

Ant. I must entreat of you some of that money.

Vio. What money, sir?
For the fair kindness you have show'd me here,
And, part, being prompted by your present trouble,
Out of my lean and low ability
I'll lend you something: my having is not much;
I'll make division of my present with you:
Hold, there's half my coffer.

Ant. Will you deny me now?
Is 't possible that my deserts to you
Can lack persuasion? Do not tempt my misery,
Lest that it make me so unsound a man
As to upbraid you with those kindnesses
That I have done for you.

Vio. I know of none;
Nor know I you by voice or any feature:
I hate ingratitude more in a man
Than lying, vainness, babbling, drunkenness,
Or any taint of vice whose strong corruption
Inhabits our frail blood.

Ant. O heavens themselves!

Sec. Off. Come, sir, I pray you, go.

Ant. Let me speak a little. This youth that you see here
I snatch'd one half out of the jaws of death;
Reliev'd him with such sanctity of love, —

And to his image, which methought did promise
Most venerable worth, did I devotion.
    First Off. What's that to us? The time goes by: away!
    Ant. But, O, how vile an idol proves this god! —
Thou hast, Sebastian, done good feature shame. —
In nature there's no blemish but the mind;
None can be call'd deform'd but the unkind:
Virtue is beauty; but the beauteous-evil
Are empty trunks, o'erflourish'd by the devil.
    First Off. The man grows mad: away with him!—Come,
        come, sir.
    Ant. Lead me on.   [*Exeunt Officers with Antonio.*
    Vio. Methinks his words do from such passion fly,
That he believes himself: so do not I.
Prove true, imagination, O, prove true,
That I, dear brother, be now ta'en for you!
    Sir To. Come hither, knight; come hither, Fabian: we'll
whisper o'er a couplet or two of most sage saws.
    Vio. He nam'd Sebastian: I my brother know
Yet living in my glass; even such, and so,
In favour was my brother; and he went
Still in this fashion, colour, ornament, —
For him I imitate: O, if it prove,
Tempests are kind, and salt waves fresh in love!   [*Exit.*
    Sir To. A very dishonest paltry boy, and more a coward
than a hare: his dishonesty appears in leaving his friend here
in necessity, and denying him; and for his cowardship, ask
Fabian.
    Fab. A coward, a most devout coward, religious in it.
    Sir And. 'Slid, I'll after him again, and beat him.
    Sir To. Do; cuff him soundly, but never draw thy sword.
    Sir And. An I do not, —   [*Exit.*
    Fab. Come, let's see the event.
    Sir To. I dare lay any money 'twill be nothing yet.
                                          [*Exeunt.*

ACT IV.

Scene I. *The street adjoining* Olivia's *garden.*

Enter Sebastian *and* Clown.

Clo. Will you make me believe that I am not sent for you?
Seb. Go to, go to, thou art a foolish fellow:
Let me be clear of thee.
Clo. Well held out, i' faith! No, I do not know you; nor I am not sent to you by my lady, to bid you come speak with her; nor your name is not Master Cesario; nor this is not my nose neither. Nothing that is so is so.
Seb. I prithee, vent thy folly somewhere else:
Thou know'st not me.
Clo. Vent my folly! he has heard that word of some great man, and now applies it to a fool: vent my folly! I am afraid this great lubber, the world, will prove a cockney. — I prithee, now, ungird thy strangeness, and tell me what I shall vent to my lady: shall I vent to her that thou art coming?
Seb. I prithee, foolish Greek, depart from me:
There's money for thee: if you tarry longer,
I shall give worse payment.
Clo. By my troth, thou hast an open hand. — These wise men, that give fools money, get themselves a good report after fourteen years' purchase.

Enter Sir Andrew Aguecheek.

Sir And. Now, sir, have I met you again? there's for you.
[*Striking Sebastian.*
Seb. Why, there's for thee, and there, and there, and there! [*Beating Sir Andrew.*
Are all the people mad?

Enter Sir Toby Belch *and* Fabian.

Sir To. Hold, sir, or I'll throw your dagger o'er the house.
Clo. This will I tell my lady straight: I would not be in some of your coats for twopence. [*Exit.*
Sir To. Come on, sir; hold.

Sir And. Nay, let him alone: I'll go another way to work with him; I'll have an action of battery against him, if there be any law in Illyria: though I struck him first, yet it's no matter for that.

Seb. Let go thy hand.

Sir To. Come, sir, I will not let you go. Come, my young soldier, put up your iron: you are well fleshed; come on.

Seb. I will be free from thee. [*Disengages himself.*] What
　　　　wouldst thou now?
If thou dar'st tempt me further, draw thy sword. [*Draws.*

Sir To. What, what? Nay, then I must have an ounce or two of this malapert blood from you. [*Draws.*

Enter OLIVIA.

Oli. Hold, Toby; on thy life, I charge thee, hold!

Sir To. Madam!

Oli. Will it be ever thus? Ungracious wretch,
Fit for the mountains and the barbarous caves,
Where manners ne'er were preach'd! out of my sight! —
Be not offended, dear Cesario. —
Rudesby, be gone! [*Exeunt Sir To., Sir And., and Fab.*
　　　　　　I prithee, gentle friend,
Let thy fair wisdom, not thy passion, sway
In this uncivil and unjust extent
Against thy peace. Go with me to my house;
And hear thou there how many fruitless pranks
This ruffian hath botch'd up, that thou thereby
Mayst smile at this: thou shalt not choose but go:
Do not deny. Beshrew his soul for me,
He started one poor heart of mine in thee.

Seb. What relish is in this? how runs the stream?
Or I am mad, or else this is a dream:
Let fancy still my sense in Lethe steep;
If it be thus to dream, still let me sleep!

Oli. Nay, come, I prithee: would thou'dst be rul'd by me!

Seb. Madam, I will.

Oli. 　　　　　　O, say so, and so be! [*Exeunt.*

SCENE II. *A room in* OLIVIA'S *house.*

Enter MARIA *and* Clown.

Mar. Nay, I prithee, put on this gown and this beard; make him believe thou art Sir Topas the curate: do it quickly; I'll call Sir Toby the whilst. [*Exit.*

Clo. Well, I'll put it on, and I will dissemble myself in 't; and I would I were the first that ever dissembled in such a gown. I am not tall enough to become the function well; nor lean enough to be thought a good student: but to be said an honest man and a good housekeeper, goes as fairly as to say a careful man and a great scholar. The competitors enter.

Enter Sir TOBY BELCH *and* MARIA.

Sir To. Jove bless thee, master parson.

Clo. *Bonos dies,* Sir Toby: for, as the old hermit of Prague, that never saw pen and ink, very wittily said to a niece of King Gorboduc, "That that is is;" so I, being master parson, am master parson; for, what is that but that, and is but is?

Sir To. To him, Sir Topas.

Clo. What, ho, I say, — peace in this prison!

Sir To. The knave counterfeits well; a good knave.

Mal. [*within*] Who calls there?

Clo. Sir Topas the curate, who comes to visit Malvolio the lunatic.

Mal. [*within*] Sir Topas, Sir Topas, good Sir Topas, go to my lady.

Clo. Out, hyperbolical fiend! how vexest thou this man! talkest thou nothing but of ladies?

Sir To. Well said, master parson.

Mal. [*within*] Sir Topas, never was man thus wronged: good Sir Topas, do not think I am mad: they have laid me here in hideous darkness.

Clo. Fie, thou dishonest Satan! I call thee by the most modest terms; for I am one of those gentle ones that will use the devil himself with courtesy: sayest thou that house is dark?

Mal. [*within*] As hell, Sir Topas.

Clo. Why, it hath bay-windows transparent as barricadoes, and the clear-stories toward the south-north are as lustrous as ebony; and yet complainest thou of obstruction?

Mal. [*within*] I am not mad, Sir Topas: I say to you, this house is dark.

Clo. Madman, thou errest: I say, there is no darkness but ignorance; in which thou art more puzzled than the Egyptians in their fog.

Mal. [*within*] I say, this house is as dark as ignorance, though ignorance were as dark as hell; and I say, there was never man thus abused. I am no more mad than you are: make the trial of it in any constant question.

Clo. What is the opinion of Pythagoras concerning wild-fowl?

Mal. [*within*] That the soul of our grandam might haply inhabit a bird.

Clo. What thinkest thou of his opinion?

Mal. [*within*] I think nobly of the soul, and no way approve his opinion.

Clo. Fare thee well. Remain thou still in darkness: thou shalt hold the opinion of Pythagoras ere I will allow of thy wits; and fear to kill a woodcock, lest thou dispossess the soul of thy grandam. Fare thee well.

Mal. [*within*] Sir Topas, Sir Topas, —

Sir To. My most exquisite Sir Topas!

Clo. Nay, I am for all waters.

Mar. Thou mightst have done this without thy beard and gown: he sees thee not.

Sir To. To him in thine own voice, and bring me word how thou findest him: I would we were well rid of this knavery. If he may be conveniently delivered, I would he were; for I am now so far in offence with my niece, that I cannot pursue with any safety this sport to the upshot. Come by and by to my chamber.   [*Exeunt Sir Toby and Maria.*

Clo. [*singing*] Hey, Robin, jolly Robin,
   Tell me how thy lady does.

Mal. [*within*] Fool, —
Clo. [*singing*] My lady is unkind, perdy.
Mal. [*within*] Fool, —
Clo. [*singing*] Alas, why is she so?
Mal. [*within*] Fool, I say, —
Clo. [*singing*] She loves another — Who calls, ha?
Mal. [*within*] Good fool, as ever thou wilt deserve well at my hand, help me to a candle, and pen, ink, and paper: as I am a gentleman, I will live to be thankful to thee for 't.
Clo. Master Malvolio!
Mal. [*within*] Ay, good fool.
Clo. Alas, sir, how fell you besides your five wits?
Mal. [*within*] Fool, there was never man so notoriously abused: I am as well in my wits, fool, as thou art.
Clo. But as well? then you are mad indeed, if you be no better in your wits than a fool.
Mal. [*within*] They have here propertied me; keep me in darkness, send ministers to me, asses, and do all they can to face me out of my wits.
Clo. Advise you what you say; the minister is here. — Malvolio, Malvolio, thy wits the heavens restore! endeavour thyself to sleep, and leave thy vain bibble-babble.
Mal. [*within*] Sir Topas, —
Clo. Maintain no words with him, good fellow. — Who, I, sir? not I, sir. God b' wi' you, good Sir Topas! — Marry, amen. — I will, sir, I will.
Mal. [*within*] Fool, fool, fool, I say, —
Clo. Alas, sir, be patient. What say you, sir? I am shent for speaking to you.
Mal. [*within*] Good fool, help me to some light and some paper: I tell thee, I am as well in my wits as any man in Illyria.
Clo. Well-a-day, that you were, sir!
Mal. [*within*] By this hand, I am. Good fool, some ink, paper, and light; and convey what I will set down to my lady: it shall advantage thee more than ever the bearing of letter did.

Clo. I will help you to 't. But tell me true, are you not mad indeed? or do you but counterfeit?

Mal. [*within*] Believe me, I am not; I tell thee true.

Clo. Nay, I'll ne'er believe a madman till I see his brains. I will fetch you light, and paper, and ink.

Mal. [*within*] Fool, I'll requite it in the highest degree: I prithee, be gone.

Clo. [*singing*] *I am gone, sir;*
  And anon, sir,
 I'll be with you again,
  In a trice,
  Like to the old Vice
 Your need to sustain;

 Who, with dagger of lath,
 In his rage and his wrath,
  Cries, ah, ha! to the devil:
 Like a mad lad,
 Pare thy nails, dad;
  Adieu, goodman drivel.   [*Exit.*

Scene III. Olivia's *garden.*

Enter Sebastian.

Seb. This is the air; that is the glorious sun;
This pearl she gave me, I do feel 't and see 't:
And though 'tis wonder that enwraps me thus,
Yet 'tis not madness. Where's Antonio, then?
I could not find him at the Elephant:
Yet there he was; and there I found this credit,
That he did range the town to seek me out.
His counsel now might do me golden service;
For though my soul disputes well with my sense,
That this may be some error, but no madness,
Yet doth this accident and flood of fortune
So far exceed all instance, all discourse,
That I am ready to distrust mine eyes,
And wrangle with my reason, that persuades me

To any other trust but that I'm mad, —
Or else the lady's mad; yet, if 'twere so,
She could not sway her house, command her followers,
Take and give back affairs, and their dispatch,
With such a smooth, discreet, and stable bearing,
As I perceive she does: there's something in 't
That is deceivable. But here the lady comes.

Enter OLIVIA *and a* Priest.

Oli. Blame not this haste of mine. If you mean well,
Now go with me and with this holy man
Into the chantry by: there, before him,
And underneath that consecrated roof,
Plight me the full assurance of your faith;
That my most jealous and too doubtful soul
May live at peace: he shall conceal it,
Whiles you are willing it shall come to note,
What time we will our celebration keep
According to my birth. — What do you say?

Seb. I'll follow this good man, and go with you;
And, having sworn truth, ever will be true.

Oli. Then lead the way, good father; — and heavens so shine,
That they may fairly note this act of mine! [*Exeunt.*

ACT V.

SCENE I. *The street before* OLIVIA's *house.*

Enter Clown *and* FABIAN.

Fab. Now, as thou lovest me, let me see his letter.
Clo. Good Master Fabian, grant me another request.
Fab. Any thing.
Clo. Do not desire to see this letter.
Fab. This is, to give a dog, and, in recompense, desire my dog again.

Enter Duke, VIOLA, CURIO, *and* Attendants.

Duke. Belong you to the Lady Olivia friends?
Clo. Ay, sir; we are some of her trappings.

Duke. I know thee well: how dost thou, my good fellow?

Clo. Truly, sir, the better for my foes, and the worse for my friends.

Duke. Just the contrary; the better for thy friends.

Clo. No, sir, the worse.

Duke. How can that be?

Clo. Marry, sir, they praise me, and make an ass of me; now my foes tell me plainly I am an ass: so that by my foes, sir, I profit in the knowledge of myself; and by my friends I am abused: so that, conclusions to be as kisses, if your four negatives make your two affirmatives, why, then, the worse for my friends, and the better for my foes.

Duke. Why, this is excellent.

Clo. By my troth, sir, no; though it please you to be one of my friends.

Duke. Thou shalt not be the worse for me: there's gold.
[*Gives money.*

Clo. But that it would be double-dealing, sir, I would you could make it another.

Duke. O, you give me ill counsel.

Clo. Put your grace in your pocket, sir, for this once, and let your flesh and blood obey it.

Duke. Well, I will be so much a sinner to be a double-dealer: there's another. [*Gives money.*

Clo. *Primo, secundo, tertio*, is a good play; and the old saying is, the third pays for all: the *triplex*, sir, is a good tripping measure; or the bells of Saint Bennet, sir, may put you in mind, — one, two, three.

Duke. You can fool no more money out of me at this throw: if you will let your lady know I am here to speak with her, and bring her along with you, it may awake my bounty further.

Clo. Marry, sir, lullaby to your bounty till I come again. I go, sir; but I would not have you to think that my desire of having is the sin of covetousness: but, as you say, sir, let your bounty take a nap, I will awake it anon. [*Exit.*

Vio. Here comes the man, sir, that did rescue me.

Enter Officers, *with* ANTONIO.

Duke. That face of his I do remember well;
Yet, when I saw it last, it was besmear'd
As black as Vulcan in the smoke of war:
A bawbling vessel was he captain of,
For shallow draught and bulk unprizable;
With which such scatheful grapple did he make
With the most noble bottom of our fleet,
That very envy and the tongue of loss
Cried fame and honour on him. — What's the matter?

First Off. Orsino, this is that Antonio
That took the Phœnix and her fraught from Candy;
And this is he that did the Tiger board,
When your young nephew Titus lost his leg:
Here in the streets, desperate of shame and state,
In private brabble did we apprehend him.

Vio. He did me kindness, sir; drew on my side;
But, in conclusion, put strange speech upon me, —
I know not what 'twas, but distraction.

Duke. Notable pirate! thou salt-water thief!
What foolish boldness brought thee to their mercies,
Whom thou, in terms so bloody and so dear,
Hast made thine enemies?

Ant. Orsino, noble sir,
Be pleas'd that I shake off these names you give me:
Antonio never yet was thief or pirate,
Though, I confess, on base and ground enough,
Orsino's enemy. A witchcraft drew me hither:
That most ingrateful boy there, by your side,
From the rude sea's enrag'd and foamy mouth
Did I redeem; a wreck past hope he was:
His life I gave him, and did thereto add
My love, without retention or restraint,
All his in dedication; for his sake
Did I expose myself, pure for his love,
Into the danger of this adverse town;
Drew to defend him when he was beset:

Where being apprehended, his false cunning —
Not meaning to partake with me in danger —
Taught him to face me out of his acquaintance,
And grew a twenty-years-removèd thing
While one would wink; denied me mine own purse,
Which I had recommended to his use
Not half an hour before.
    Vio.   How can this be?
    Duke. When came ye to this town?
    Ant. To-day, my lord: and for three months before —
No interim, not a minute's vacancy —
Both day and night did we keep company.
    Duke. Here comes the countess: now heaven walks on
               earth. —
But for thee, fellow, — fellow, thy words are madness:
Three months this youth hath tended upon me;
But more of that anon. — Take him aside.

            Enter OLIVIA *and* Attendants.

    Oli. What would my lord, but that he may not have,
Wherein Olivia may seem serviceable? —
Cesario, you do not keep promise with me.
    Vio. Madam!
    Duke. Gracious Olivia, —
    Oli. What do you say, Cesario? — Good my lord, —
    Vio. My lord would speak; my duty hushes me.
    Oli. If it be aught to the old tune, my lord,
It is as fat and fulsome to mine ear
As howling after music.
    Duke.   Still so cruel?
    Oli. Still so constant, lord.
    Duke. What, to perverseness? you uncivil lady,
To whose ingrate and unauspicious altars
My soul the faithfull'st offerings hath breath'd out
That e'er devotion tender'd! What shall I do?
    Oli. Even what it please my lord, that shall become him.
    Duke. Why should I not, had I the heart to do it,

Like to th' Egyptian thief at point of death,
Kill what I love? a savage jealousy
That sometime savours nobly. — But hear me this:
Since you to non-regardance cast my faith,
And that I partly know the instrument
That screws me from my true place in your favour,
Live you, the marble-breasted tyrant, still;
But this your minion, whom I know you love,
And whom, by heaven I swear, I tender dearly,
Him will I tear out of that cruel eye,
Where he sits crownèd in his master's spite. —
Come, boy, with me; my thoughts are ripe in mischief:
I'll sacrifice the lamb that I do love,
To spite a raven's heart within a dove. [*Going.*
   Vio. And I, most jocund, apt, and willingly,
To do you rest, a thousand deaths would die. [*Following.*
   Oli. Where goes Cesario?
   Vio.   After him I love
More than I love these eyes, more than my life,
More, by all mores, than e'er I shall love wife.
If I do feign, you witnesses above
Punish my life for tainting of my love!
   Oli. Ay me, detested! how am I beguil'd!
   Vio. Who does beguile you? who does do you wrong?
   Oli. Hast thou forgot thyself? is it so long? —
Call forth the holy father. [*Exit an Attendant.*
   Duke.   Come, away! [*To Viola.*
   Oli. Whither, my lord? — Cesario, husband, stay.
   Duke. Husband!
   Oli.   Ay, husband: can he that deny?
   Duke. Her husband, sirrah!
   Vio.   No, my lord, not I.
   Oli. Alas, it is the baseness of thy fear
That makes thee strangle thy propriety:
Fear not, Cesario; take thy fortunes up;
Be that thou know'st thou art, and then thou art
As great as that thou fear'st.

Re-enter Attendant, *with* Priest.

                    O, welcome, father!
Father, I charge thee, by thy reverence,
Here to unfold — though lately we intended
To keep in darkness what occasion now
Reveals before 'tis ripe — what thou dost know
Hath newly pass'd between this youth and me.

  Priest. A contract and eternal bond of love,
Confirm'd by mutual joinder of your hands,
Attested by the holy close of lips,
Strengthen'd by interchangement of your rings;
And all the ceremony of this compáct
Seal'd in my function, by my testimony:
Since when, my watch hath told me, toward my grave
I have travell'd but two hours.

  Duke. O thou dissembling cub! what wilt thou be
When time hath sow'd a grizzle on thy case?
Or will not else thy craft so quickly grow,
That thine own trip shall be thine overthrow?
Farewell, and take her; but direct thy feet
Where thou and I henceforth may never meet.

  Vio. My lord, I do protest, —
  Oli.   O, do not swear!
Hold little faith, though thou hast too much fear.

Enter Sir ANDREW AGUECHEEK *with his head broken.*

  Sir And. For the love of God, a surgeon! and send one presently to Sir Toby.

  Oli. What's the matter?

  Sir And. 'Has broke my head across, and 'has given Sir Toby a bloody coxcomb too: for the love of God, your help! I had rather than forty pound I were at home.

  Oli. Who has done this, Sir Andrew?

  Sir And. The count's gentleman, one Cesario: we took him for a coward, but he's the very devil incardinate.

  Duke. My gentleman Cesario?

  Sir And. 'Od's lifelings, here he is! — You broke my head

for nothing; and that that I did, I was set on to do 't by Sir Toby.

Vio. Why do you speak to me? I never hurt you:
You drew your sword upon me without cause;
But I bespake you fair, and hurt you not.

Sir And. If a bloody coxcomb be a hurt, you have hurt me: I think you set nothing by a bloody coxcomb. — Here comes Sir Toby halting, — you shall hear more: but if he had not been in drink, he would have tickled you othergates than he did.

Enter Sir TOBY BELCH, *led by the* Clown.

Duke. How now, gentleman! how is 't with you?

Sir To. That's all one: 'has hurt me, and there's the end on 't. — Sot, didst see Dick surgeon, sot?

Clo. O, he's drunk, Sir Toby, an hour agone; his eyes were set at eight i' the morning.

Sir To. Then he's a rogue and a passy-measures pavin: I hate a drunken rogue.

Oli. Away with him! Who hath made this havoc with them?

Sir And. I'll help you, Sir Toby, because we'll be dressed together.

Sir To. Will you help, — an ass-head and a coxcomb and a knave, — a thin-faced knave, a gull?

Oli. Get him to bed, and let his hurt be look'd to.

[*Exeunt Clown, Fabian, Sir Toby, and Sir Andrew.*

Enter SEBASTIAN.

Seb. I'm sorry, madam, I have hurt your kinsman;
But, had it been the brother of my blood,
I must have done no less with wit and safety.
You throw a strange regard upon me, and by that
I do perceive it hath offended you:
Pardon me, sweet one, even for the vows
We made each other but so late ago.

Duke. One face, one voice, one habit, and two persons,—
A natural perspective, that is and is not!

Seb. Antonio, O my dear Antonio!
How have the hours rack'd and tortur'd me,
Since I have lost thee!
   Ant. Sebastian are you?
   Seb.   Fear'st thou that, Antonio?
   Ant. How have you made division of yourself? —
An apple, cleft in two, is not more twin
Than these two creatures. Which is Sebastian?
   Oli. Most wonderful!
   Seb. Do I stand there? I never had a brother;
Nor can there be that deity in my nature,
Of here and every where. I had a sister,
Whom the blind waves and surges have devour'd. —
Of charity, what kin are you to me?   [*To Viola.*
What countryman? what name? what parentage?
   Vio. Of Messaline: Sebastian was my father;
Such a Sebastian was my brother too,
So went he suited to his watery tomb:
If spirits can assume both form and suit,
You come to fright us.
   Seb.   A spirit I am indeed;
But am in that dimension grossly clad,
Which from the womb I did participate.
Were you a woman, as the rest goes even,
I should my tears let fall upon your cheek,
And say, "Thrice-welcome, drownèd Viola!"
   Vio. My father had a mole upon his brow, —
   Seb. And so had mine.
   Vio. And died that day when Viola from her birth
Had number'd thirteen years.
   Seb. O, that record is lively in my soul!
He finishèd, indeed, his mortal act
That day that made my sister thirteen years.
   Vio. If nothing lets to make us happy both
But this my masculine usurp'd attire,
Do not embrace me till each circumstance
Of place, time, fortune, do cohere and jump,

That I am Viola: which to confirm,
I'll bring you to a captain's in this town,
Where lie my maid's weeds; by whose gentle help
I was preferr'd to serve this noble count.
All the occurrence of my fortune since
Hath been between this lady and this lord.

Seb. So comes it, lady, you have been mistook: [*To Olivia.*
But nature to her bias drew in that.
You would have been contracted to a maid;
Nor are you therein, by my life, deceiv'd, —
You are betroth'd both to a maid and man.

Duke. Be not amaz'd; right noble is his blood. —
If this be so, as yet the glass seems true,
I shall have share in this most happy wreck. —
Boy, thou hast said to me a thousand times [*To Viola.*
Thou never shouldst love woman like to me.

Vio. And all those sayings will I over-swear;
And all those swearings keep as true in soul
As doth that orbèd continent the fire
That severs day from night.

Duke. Give me thy hand;
And let me see thee in thy woman's weeds.

Vio. The captain that did bring me first on shore
Hath my maid's garments: he, upon some action,
Is now in durance, at Malvolio's suit,
A gentleman and follower of my lady's.

Oli. He shall enlarge him: — fetch Malvolio hither: —
And yet, alas, now I remember me,
They say, poor gentleman, he's much-distract.

Re-enter Clown *with a letter, and* Fabian.

A most extracting frenzy of mine own
From my remembrance clearly banish'd his —
How does he, sirrah?

Clo. Truly, madam, he holds Beelzebub at the stave's end as well as a man in his case may do: 'has here writ a letter to you; I should have given 't you to-day morning, — but as a madman's epistles are no gospels, so it skills not much when they are delivered.

Oli. Open 't, and read it.

Clo. Look, then, to be well edified when the fool delivers the madman. [*Reads*] "By the Lord, madam," —

Oli. How now! art thou mad?

Clo. No, madam, I do but read madness: an your ladyship will have it as it ought to be, you must allow *vox.*

Oli. Prithee, read i' thy right wits.

Clo. So I do, madonna; but to read his right wits is to read thus: therefore perpend, my princess, and give ear.

Oli. Read it you, sirrah. [*To Fabian.*

Fab. [*reads*] "By the Lord, madam, you wrong me, and the world shall know it: though you have put me into darkness, and given your drunken cousin rule over me, yet have I the benefit of my senses as well as your ladyship. I have your own letter that induced me to the semblance I put on; with the which I doubt not but to do myself much right, or you much shame. Think of me as you please. I leave my duty a little unthought of, and speak out of my injury.

THE MADLY-USED MALVOLIO."

Oli. Did he write this?

Clo. Ay, madam.

Duke. This savours not much of distraction.

Oli. See him deliver'd, Fabian; bring him hither.

[*Exit Fabian.*

My lord, so please you, these things further thought on,
To think me as well a sister as a wife,
One day shall crown th' alliance on's, so please you,
Here at my house, and at my proper cost

Duke. Madam, I am most apt t' embrace your offer. —
[*To Viola*] Your master quits you; and, for your service done him,
So much against the mettle of your sex,
So far beneath your soft and tender breeding,
And since you call'd me master for so long,

Here is my hand: you shall from this time be
Your master's mistress.
    Oli.   A sister! — you are she.

Re-enter FABIAN, *with* MALVOLIO.

    Duke.   Is this the madman?
    Oli.   Ay, my lord, this same. —
How now, Malvolio!
    Mal.   Madam, you've done me wrong,
Notorious wrong.
    Oli.   Have I, Malvolio? no.
    Mal.   Lady, you have. Pray you, peruse that letter:
You must not now deny it is your hand, —
Write from it, if you can, in hand or phrase;
Or say 'tis not your seal, not your invention:
You can say none of this: well, grant it, then,
And tell me, in the modesty of honour,
Why you have given me such clear lights of favour,
Bade me come smiling and cross-garter'd to you,
To put on yellow stockings, and to frown
Upon Sir Toby and the lighter people;
And, acting this in an obedient hope,
Why have you suffer'd me to be imprison'd,
Kept in a dark house, visited by the priest,
And made the most notorious geck and gull
That e'er invention play'd on? tell me why.
    Oli.   Alas, Malvolio, this is not my writing,
Though, I confess, much like the character:
But, out of question, 'tis Maria's hand.
And now I do bethink me, it was she
First told me thou wast mad: thou cam'st in smiling,
And in such forms which here were presuppos'd
Upon thee in the letter. Prithee, be content:
This practice hath most shrewdly pass'd upon thee;
But, when we know the grounds and authors of it,
Thou shalt be both the plaintiff and the judge
Of thine own cause.

Fab.   Good madam, hear me speak;
And let no quarrel nor no brawl to come
Taint the condition of this present hour,
Which I have wonder'd at. In hope it shall not,
Most freely I confess, myself and Toby
Set this device against Malvolio here,
Upon some stubborn and uncourteous parts
We had conceiv'd in him: Maria writ
The letter at Sir Toby's great importance;
In recompense whereof he hath married her.
How with a sportful malice it was follow'd,
May rather pluck on laughter than revenge;
If that the injuries be justly weigh'd
That have on both sides pass'd.

Oli. Alas, poor fool, how have they baffled thee!

Clo. Why, "some are born great, some achieve greatness, and some have greatness thrown upon them." I was one, sir, in this interlude,— one Sir Topas, sir; but that's all one.— "By the Lord, fool, I am not mad;"— but do you remember? "Madam, why laugh you at such a barren rascal? an you smile not, he's gagged:" and thus the whirligig of time brings in his revenges.

Mal. I'll be reveng'd on the whole pack of you.   [*Exit.*

Oli. He hath been most notoriously abus'd.

Duke. Pursue him, and entreat him to a peace:—
He hath not told us of the captain yet:
When that is known, and golden time convents,
A solemn combination shall be made
Of our dear souls. Meantime, sweet sister,
We will not part from hence.— Cesario, come;
For so you shall be, while you are a man;
But when in other habits you are seen,
Orsino's mistress and his fancy's queen.
                    [*Exeunt all, except Clown.*

Song.

Clo. *When that I was and a little tiny boy,*
    With hey, ho, the wind and the rain,

A foolish thing was but a toy,
  For the rain it raineth every day.

But when I came to man's estate,
  With hey, ho, the wind and the rain,
'Gainst knaves and thieves men shut their gate,
  For the rain it raineth every day.

But when I came, alas! to wive,
  With hey, ho, the wind and the rain,
By swaggering could I never thrive,
  For the rain it raineth every day.

But when I came unto my bed,
  With hey, ho, the wind and the rain,
With toss-pots still had drunken head,
  For the rain it raineth every day.

A great while ago the world begun,
  With hey, ho, the wind and the rain: —
But that's all one, our play is done,
  And we'll strive to please you every day.

[*Exit.*

THE WINTER'S TALE.

DRAMATIS PERSONÆ.

LEONTES, king of Sicilia.
MAMILLIUS, his son.
CAMILLO,
ANTIGONUS, } Sicilian Lords.
CLEOMENES,
DION,
Other Sicilian Lords.
Officers of a Court of Judicature.
Sicilian Gentlemen.
POLIXENES, king of Bohemia.
FLORIZEL, his son.
ARCHIDAMUS, a Bohemian Lord.
A Mariner.
Gaoler.

An old Shepherd.
Clown, his son.
Servant to the old Shepherd.
AUTOLYCUS, a rogue.

HERMIONE, queen to Leontes.
PERDITA, daughter to Leontes and Hermione.
PAULINA, wife to Antigonus.
EMILIA, a lady, } attending on
Other Ladies, } the Queen.
MOPSA, } Shepherdesses.
DORCAS, }

Attendants, Guards; Shepherds and Shepherdesses.
Time, as Chorus.
SCENE — *Sometimes in Sicilia, sometimes in Bohemia.*

ACT I.

SCENE I. *Sicilia. An antechamber in the palace of* LEONTES.

Enter CAMILLO *and* ARCHIDAMUS.

Arch. If you shall chance, Camillo, to visit Bohemia, on the like occasion whereon my services are now on foot, you shall see, as I have said, great difference betwixt our Bohemia and your Sicilia.

Cam. I think, this coming summer, the King of Sicilia means to pay Bohemia the visitation which he justly owes him.

Arch. Wherein our entertainment shall shame us we will be justified in our loves; for, indeed,—

Cam. Beseech you,—

Arch. Verily, I speak it in the freedom of my knowledge: we cannot with such magnificence — in so rare — I know not what to say.—We will give you sleepy drinks, that your senses, unintelligent of our insufficience, may, though they cannot praise us, as little accuse us.

Cam. You pay a great deal too dear for what's given freely.

Arch. Believe me, I speak as my understanding instructs me, and as mine honesty puts it to utterance.

Cam. Sicilia cannot show himself over-kind to Bohemia. They were trained together in their childhoods; and there rooted betwixt them then such an affection, which cannot choose but branch now. Since their more mature dignities and royal necessities made separation of their society, their encounters, though not personal, have been royally attorneyed with interchange of gifts, letters, loving embassies; that they have seemed to be together, though absent; shook hands, as over a vast; and embraced, as it were, from the ends of opposed winds. The heavens continue their love!

Arch. I think there is not in the world either malice or matter to alter it. You have an unspeakable comfort of your young prince Mamillius: it is a gentleman of the greatest promise that ever came into my note.

Cam. I very well agree with you in the hopes of him: it is a gallant child; one that, indeed, physics the subject, makes old hearts fresh: they that went on crutches ere he was born desire yet their life to see him a man.

Arch. Would they else be content to die?

Cam. Yes; if there were no other excuse why they should desire to live.

Arch. If the king had no son, they would desire to live on crutches till he had one.

[*Exeunt.*

Scene II. *The same. A room of state in the palace.*

Enter Leontes, Polixenes, Hermione, Mamillius, Camillo, *and* Attendants.

Pol. Nine changes of the watery star have been
The shepherd's note since we have left our throne
Without a burden: time as long again
Would be fill'd up, my brother, with our thanks;
And yet we should, for perpetuity,
Go hence in debt: and therefore, like a cipher,
Yet standing in rich place, I multiply
With one we-thank-you many thousands more
That go before it.
   Leon.   Stay your thanks awhile,
And pay them when you part.
   Pol.   Sir, that's to-morrow.
I'm question'd by my fears, of what may chance
Or breed upon our absence: that may blow
No sneaping winds at home, to make us say,
"This is put forth too truly!" Besides, I've stay'd
To tire your royalty.
   Leon.   We are tougher, brother,
Than you can put us to't.
   Pol.   No longer stay.
   Leon. One seven-night longer.
   Pol.   Very sooth, to-morrow.
   Leon. We'll part the time between's, then: and in that
I'll no gainsaying.
   Pol.   Press me not, beseech you, so.
There is no tongue that moves, none, none i' the world,
So soon as yours, could win me: so it should now,
Were there necessity in your request, although
'Twere needful I denied it. My affairs
Do even drag me homeward: which to hinder,
Were, in your love, a whip to me; my stay,
To you a charge and trouble: to save both,
Farewell, our brother.

Leon. Tongue-tied our queen? speak you.
Her. I had thought, sir, to have held my peace until
You had drawn oaths from him not to stay. You, sir,
Charge him too coldly. Tell him, you are sure
All in Bohemia's well; this satisfaction
The by-gone day proclaim'd: say this to him,
He's beat from his best ward.
Leon. Well said, Hermione.
Her. To tell, he longs to see his son, were strong:
But let him say so then, and let him go;
But let him swear so, and he shall not stay,
We'll thwack him hence with distaffs. —
[*To Polixenes*] Yet of your royal presence I'll adventure
The borrow of a week. When at Bohemia
You take my lord, I'll give you my commission
To let him there a month behind the gest
Prefix'd for's parting: — yet, good deed, Leontes,
I love thee not a jar o' the clock behind
What lady should her lord. — You'll stay?
Pol. No, madam.
Her. Nay, but you will?
Pol. I may not, verily.
Her. Verily!
You put me off with limber vows; but I,
Though you would seek t' unsphere the stars with oaths,
Should yet say, "Sir, no going." Verily,
You shall not go: a lady's "verily" 's
As potent as a lord's. Will you go yet?
Force me to keep you as a prisoner,
Not like a guest; so you shall pay your fees
When you depart, and save your thanks. How say you?
My prisoner, or my guest? by your dread "verily,"
One of them you shall be.
Pol. Your guest, then, madam:
To be your prisoner should import offending;
Which is for me less easy to commit
Than you to punish.

Her.   Not your gaoler, then,
But your kind hostess. Come, I'll question you
Of my lord's tricks and yours when you were boys:
You were pretty lordings then?
    Pol.   We were, fair queen,
'Two lads that thought there was no more behind
But such a day to-morrow as to-day,
And to be boy eternal.
    Her. Was not my lord the verier wag o' the two?
    Pol. We were as twinn'd lambs that did frisk i' the sun,
And bleat the one at th' other: what we chang'd
Was innocence for innocence; we knew not
The doctrine of ill-doing, no, nor dream'd
That any did. Had we pursu'd that life,
And our weak spirits ne'er been higher rear'd
With stronger blood, we should have answer'd heaven
Boldly, "Not guilty;" th' imposition clear'd
Hereditary ours.
    Her.   By this we gather
You have tripp'd since.
    Pol.   O my most sacred lady,
Temptations have since then been born to 's; for
In those unfledg'd days was my wife a girl;
Your precious self had then not cross'd the eyes
Of my young playfellow.
    Her.   Grace to boot!
Of this make no conclusion, lest you say
Your queen and I are devils: yet, go on;
Th' offences we have made you do, we'll answer;
If you first sinn'd with us, and that with us
You did continue fault, and that you slipp'd not
With any but with us.
    Leon.   Is he won yet?
    Her. He'll stay, my lord.
    Leon.   At my request he would not.
Hermione, my dear'st, thou never spok'st
To better purpose.

Her. Never?

Leon. Never, but once.

Her. What! have I twice said well? when was 't before?
I prithee tell me; cram's with praise, and make's
As fat as tame things: one good deed dying tongueless
Slaughters a thousand waiting upon that.
Our praises are our wages: you may ride 's
With one soft kiss a thousand furlongs, ere
With spur we heat an acre. But to the goal: —
My last good deed was to entreat his stay:
What was my first? it has an elder sister,
Or I mistake you: O, would her name were Grace!
But once before I spoke to the purpose: when?
Nay, let me have 't; I long.

Leon. Why, that was when
Three crabbèd months had sour'd themselves to death,
Ere I could make thee open thy white hand,
And clap thyself my love: then didst thou utter,
"I am yours for ever."

Her. It is Grace indeed. —
Why, lo you now, I've spoke to the purpose twice:
The one for ever earn'd a royal husband;
Th' other for some while a friend.

[*Giving her hand to Polixenes.*

Leon. [*aside*] Too hot, too hot!
To mingle friendship far, is mingling bloods.
I have *tremor cordis* on me, — my heart dances;
But not for joy, — not joy. — This entertainment
May a free face put on; derive a liberty
From heartiness, from bounty's fertile bosom,
And well become the agent; 't may, I grant:
But to be paddling palms and pinching fingers,
As now they are; and making practis'd smiles,
As in a looking-glass; and then to sigh, as 'twere
The mort o' the deer; O, that is entertainment
My bosom likes not, nor my brows! — Mamillius,
Art thou my boy?

Mam.   Ay, my good lord.
Leon.   I' fecks!
Why, that's my bawcock. What, hast smutch'd thy nose? —
They say, it's a copy out of mine. Come, captain,
We must be neat; — not neat, but cleanly, captain:
And yet the steer, the heifer, and the calf,
Are all call'd neat. — Still virginalling
                    [*Observing Polixenes and Hermione.*
Upon his palm? — How now, you wanton calf!
Art thou my calf?
Mam.   Yes, if you will, my lord.
Leon. Thou want'st a rough pash, and the shoots that I have,
To be full like me: — yet they say we are
Almost as like as eggs; women say so,
That will say any thing: but were they false
As o'er-dy'd blacks, as winds, as waters, — false
As dice are to be wish'd by one that fixes
No bourn 'twixt his and mine; yet were it true
To say this boy were like me. — Come, sir page,
Look on me with your welkin eye: sweet villain!
Most dear'st! my collop! — Can thy dam? — may't be? —
Affection! thy intention stabs the centre:
Thou dost make possible things not so held,
Communicat'st with dreams; — how can this be? —
With what's unreal thou coactive art,
And fellow'st nothing: then 'tis very credent
Thou mayst co-join with something; and thou dost, —
And that beyond commission; and I find it, —
And that to the infection of my brains
And hardening of my brows.
Pol.   What means Sicilia?
Her. He something seems unsettled.
Pol.   Ho, my lord!
What cheer? how is 't with you, best brother?
Her.   You look
As if you held a brow of much distraction:
Are you mov'd, my lord?

Leon. No, in good earnest. —
How sometimes nature will betray its folly,
Its tenderness, and make itself a pastime
To harder bosoms! — Looking on the lines
Of my boy's face, methought I did recoil
Twenty-three years; and saw myself unbreech'd,
In my green velvet coat; my dagger muzzled,
Lest it should bite its master, and so prove,
As ornaments oft do, too dangerous:
How like, methought, I then was to this kernel,
This squash, this gentleman. — Mine honest friend,
Will you take eggs for money?
  Mam. No, my lord, I'll fight.
  Leon. You will? why, happy man be 's dole!—My brother,
Are you so fond of your young prince as we
Do seem to be of ours?
  Pol. If at home, sir,
He's all my exercise, my mirth, my matter:
Now my sworn friend, and then mine enemy;
My parasite, my soldier, statesman, all:
He makes a July's day short as December;
And with his varying childness cures in me
Thoughts that would thick my blood.
  Leon. So stands this squire
Offic'd with me. We two will walk, my lord,
And leave you to your graver steps. — Hermione,
How thou lov'st us, show in our brother's welcome;
Let what is dear in Sicily be cheap:
Next to thyself and my young rover, he's
Apparent to my heart.
  Her. If you would seek us,
We are yours i' the garden: shall 's attend you there?
  Leon. To your own bents dispose you: you'll be found,
Be you beneath the sky. — [*Aside*] I'm angling now,
Though you perceive me not how I give line.
Go to, go to! [*Observing Polixenes and Hermione.*
How she holds up the neb, the bill to him!

And arms her with the boldness of a wife
To her allowing husband! [*Exeunt Pol., Her., and Attend.*
Gone already!
Inch-thick, knee-deep, o'er head and ears a fork'd one! —
Go, play, boy, play: — thy mother plays, and I
Play too; but so disgrac'd a part, whose issue
Will hiss me to my grave: contempt and clamour
Will be my knell. — Go, play, boy, play. — There have been,
Or I am much deceiv'd, cuckolds ere now;
And many a man there is, — even at this present,
Now while I speak this, — holds his wife by th' arm,
That little thinks she has been sluic'd in 's absence,
And his pond fish'd by his next neighbour, by
Sir Smile, his neighbour: nay, there 's comfort in 't,
Whiles other men have gates, and those gates open'd
As mine, against their will: should all despair
That have revolted wives, the tenth of mankind
Would hang themselves. Physic for 't there is none;
It is a bawdy planet, that will strike
Where 'tis predominant; and 'tis powerful, think it,
From east, west, north, and south: be it concluded,
No barricado for a belly; know 't;
It will let in and out the enemy
With bag and baggage: many thousand on 's
Have the disease, and feel 't not. — How now, boy!

 Mam. I am like you, they say.
 Leon.   Why, that's some comfort. —
What, Camillo there?
 Cam.   Ay, my good lord.
 Leon. Go, play, Mamillius; thou 'rt an honest man.
[*Exit Mamillius.*
Camillo, this great sir will yet stay longer.
 Cam. You had much ado to make his anchor hold:
When you cast out, it still came home.
 Leon.   Didst note it?
 Cam. He would not stay at your petitions; made
His business more material.

Leon.   Didst perceive it? —
[*Aside*] They're here with me already; whispering, rounding,
"Sicilia is a — so-forth:" 'tis far gone,
When I shall gust it last. — How came 't, Camillo,
That he did stay?
    Cam.   At the good queen's entreaty.
    Leon. At the queen's be 't: "good" should be pertinent;
But, so it is, it is not. Was this taken
By any understanding pate but thine?
For thy conceit is soaking, will draw in
More than the common blocks: — not noted, is 't,
But of the finer natures? by some severals
Of head-piece extraordinary? lower messes
Perchance are to this business purblind? say.
    Cam. Business, my lord! I think most understand
Bohemia stays here longer.
    Leon.   Ha!
    Cam.   Stays here longer.
    Leon. Ay, but why?
    Cam. To satisfy your highness, and th' entreaties
Of our most gracious mistress.
    Leon.   Satisfy
Th' entreaties of your mistress! — satisfy! —
Let that suffice. I've trusted thee, Camillo,
With all the near'st things to my heart, as well
My chamber-councils; wherein, priest-like, thou
Hast cleans'd my bosom, — I from thee departed
Thy penitent reform'd: but we have been
Deceiv'd in thy integrity, deceiv'd
In that which seems so.
    Cam.   Be 't forbid, my lord!
    Leon. To bide upon 't, — thou art not honest; or,
If thou inclin'st that way, thou art a coward,
Which hoxes honesty behind, restraining
From course requir'd; or else thou must be counted
A servant grafted in my serious trust,
And therein negligent; or else a fool

That seest a game play'd home, the rich stake drawn,
And tak'st it all for jest.
   Cam.   My gracious lord,
I may be negligent, foolish, and fearful;
In every one of these no man is free,
But that his negligence, his folly, fear,
Among the infinite doings of the world,
Sometime puts forth. In your affairs, my lord,
If ever I were wilful-negligent,
It was my folly; if industriously
I play'd the fool, it was my negligence,
Not weighing well the end; if ever fearful
To do a thing, where I the issue doubted,
Whereof the execution did cry out
Against the non-performance, 'twas a fear
Which oft infects the wisest: these, my lord,
Are such allow'd infirmities that honesty
Is never free of. But, beseech your grace,
Be plainer with me; let me know my trespass
By its own visage: if I then deny it,
'Tis none of mine.
   Leon.   Ha' not you seen, Camillo, —
But that's past doubt, you have, or your eye-glass
Is thicker than a cuckold's horn; or heard, —
For, to a vision so apparent, rumour
Cannot be mute; or thought, — for cogitation
Resides not in that man that does not think 't, —
My wife is slippery? If thou wilt confess, —
Or else be impudently negative,
To have nor eyes nor ears nor thought, — then say
My wife 's a hobby-horse; deserves a name
As rank as any flax-wench that puts-to
Before her troth-plight: say 't, and justify 't.
   Cam. I would not be a stander-by to hear
My sovereign mistress clouded so, without
My present vengeance taken: 'shrew my heart,
You never spoke what did become you less

Than this; which to reiterate were sin
As deep as that, though true.
    Leon.   Is whispering nothing?
Is leaning cheek to cheek? is meeting noses?
Kissing with inside lip? stopping the career
Of laughter with a sigh? — a note infallible
Of breaking honesty; — horsing foot on foot?
Skulking in corners? wishing clocks more swift?
Hours, minutes? noon, midnight? and all eyes
Blind with the pin-and-web, but theirs, theirs only,
That would unseen be wicked? is this nothing?
Why, then the world and all that's in 't is nothing;
The covering sky is nothing; Bohemia nothing;
My wife is nothing; nor nothing have these nothings,
If this be nothing.
    Cam.   Good my lord, be cur'd
Of this diseas'd opinion, and betimes;
For 'tis most dangerous.
    Leon.   Say it be, 'tis true.
    Cam. No, no, my lord.
    Leon.   It is; you lie, you lie:
I say thou liest, Camillo, and I hate thee;
Pronounce thee a gross lout, a mindless slave;
Or else a hovering temporizer, that
Canst with thine eyes at once see good and evil,
Inclining to them both: were my wife's liver
Infected as her life, she would not live
The running of one glass.
    Cam.   Who does infect her?
    Leon. Why, he that wears her like a medal, hanging
About his neck, Bohemia: who — if I
Had servants true about me, that bare eyes
To see alike mine honour as their profits,
Their own particular thrifts, — they would do that
Which should undo more doing: ay, and thou,
His cupbearer, — whom I from meaner form
Have bench'd, and rear'd to worship; who mayst see

Plainly, as heaven sees earth, and earth sees heaven,
How I am gall'd, — thou mightst bespice a cup,
To give mine enemy a lasting wink;
Which draught to me were cordial.
 Cam.   Sir, my lord,
I could do this, and that with no rash potion,
But with a lingering dram, that should not work
Maliciously like poison: but I cannot
Believe this crack to be in my dread mistress,
So sovereignly being honourable.
I have lov'd thee, —
 Leon.   Make that thy question, and go rot!
Dost think I am so muddy, so unsettled,
T' appoint myself in this vexation; sully
The purity and whiteness of my sheets, —
Which to preserve is sleep, which being spotted
Is goads, thorns, nettles, tails of wasps;
Give scandal to the blood o' the prince my son, —
Who I do think is mine, and love as mine, —
Without ripe moving to 't? Would I do this?
Could man so blench?
 Cam.   I must believe you, sir:
I do; and will fetch off Bohemia for 't;
Provided that, when he 's remov'd, your highness
Will take again your queen as yours at first,
Even for your son's sake; and thereby for sealing
The injury of tongues in courts and kingdoms
Known and allied to yours.
 Leon.   Thou dost advise me
Even so as I mine own course have set down:
I'll give no blemish to her honour, none.
 Cam. My lord,
Go then; and with a countenance as clear
As friendship wears at feasts, keep with Bohemia
And with your queen. I am his cupbearer:
If from me he have wholesome beverage,
Account me not your servant.

Leon. This is all: —
Do 't, and thou hast the one half of my heart;
Do 't not, thou splitt'st thine own.
Cam. I'll do 't, my lord.
Leon. I will seem friendly, as thou hast advis'd me. [*Exit.*
Cam. O miserable lady! — But, for me,
What case stand I in? I must be the poisoner
Of good Polixenes: and my ground to do 't
Is the obedience to a master; one
Who, in rebellion with himself, will have
All that are his so too. — To do this deed,
Promotion follows: if I could find example
Of thousands that had struck anointed kings,
And flourish'd after, I'd not do 't; but since
Nor brass nor stone nor parchment bears not one,
Let villany itself forswear 't. I must
Forsake the court: to do 't, or no, is certain
To me a break-neck. — Happy star reign now!
Here comes Bohemia.

Re-enter POLIXENES.

Pol. This is strange: methinks
My favour here begins to warp. Not speak? —
Good day, Camillo.
Cam. Hail, most royal sir!
Pol. What is the news i' the court?
Cam. None rare, my lord.
Pol. The king hath on him such a countenance
As he had lost some province, and a region
Lov'd as he loves himself: even now I met him
With customary compliment; when he,
Wafting his eyes to the contrary, and falling
A lip of much contempt, speeds from me; and
So leaves me, to consider what is breeding
That changes thus his manners.
Cam. I dare not know, my lord.
Pol. How! dare not! do not. Do you know, and dare not

Be intelligent to me? 'Tis thereabouts;
For, to yourself, what you do know, you must,
And cannot say you dare not. Good Camillo,
Your chang'd complexions are to me a mirror,
Which shows me mine chang'd too; for I must be
A party in this alteration, finding
Myself thus alter'd with 't.

   Cam.   There is a sickness
Which puts some of us in distemper; but
I cannot name the disease; and it is caught
Of you that yet are well.

   Pol.   How! caught of me!
Make me not sighted like the basilisk:
I've look'd on thousands, who have sped the better
By my regard, but kill'd none so. Camillo, —
As you are certainly a gentleman; thereto
Clerk-like experienc'd, which no less adorns
Our gentry than our parents' noble names,
In whose success we are gentle, — I beseech you,
If you know aught which does behove my knowledge
Thereof to be inform'd, imprison 't not
In ignorant concealment.

   Cam.   I may not answer.

   Pol. A sickness caught of me, and yet I well!
I must be answer'd. — Dost thou hear, Camillo,
I conjure thee, by all the parts of man
Which honour does acknowledge, — whereof the least
Is not this suit of mine, — that thou declare
What incidency thou dost guess of harm
Is creeping toward me; how far off, how near;
Which way to be prevented, if to be;
If not, how best to bear it.

   Cam.   Sir, I'll tell you;
Since I am charg'd in honour, and by him
That I think honourable: therefore mark my counsel,
Which must be even as swiftly follow'd as

I mean to utter 't, or both yourself and me
Cry "lost," and so good night!
  Pol.   On, good Camillo.
  Cam. I am appointed him to murder you.
  Pol. By whom, Camillo?
  Cam.   By the king.
  Pol.   For what?
  Cam. He thinks, nay, with all confidence he swears,
As he had seen 't, or been an instrument
To tice you to 't, that you have touch'd his queen
Forbiddenly.
  Pol.   O, then my best blood turn
To an infected jelly, and my name
Be yok'd with his that did betray the Best!
Turn then my freshest reputation to
A savour that may strike the dullest nostril
Where I arrive, and my approach be shunn'd,
Nay, hated too, worse than the great'st infection
That e'er was heard or read!
  Cam.   Swear his thought over
By each particular star in heaven and
By all their influences, you may as well
Forbid the sea for to obey the moon,
As or by oath remove, or counsel shake
The fabric of his folly, whose foundation
Is pil'd upon his faith, and will continue
The standing of his body.
  Pol.   How should this grow?
  Cam. I know not: but I'm sure 'tis safer to
Avoid what's grown than question how 'tis born.
If, therefore, you dare trust my honesty,
That lies enclosèd in this trunk, which you
Shall bear along impawn'd, — away to-night!
Your followers I will whisper to the business;
And will, by twos and threes, at several posterns,
Clear them o' the city: for myself, I'll put
My fortunes to your service, which are here

By this discovery lost. Be not uncertain;
For, by the honour of my parents, I
Have utter'd truth: which if you seek to prove,
I dare not stand by; nor shall you be safer
Than one condemn'd by the king's own mouth, thereon
His execution sworn.

Pol. I do believe thee:
I saw his heart in 's face. Give me thy hand:
Be pilot to me, and thy places shall
Still neighbour mine. My ships are ready, and
My people did expect my hence-departure
Two days ago. — This jealousy
Is for a precious creature: as she 's rare,
Must it be great; and, as his person 's mighty,
Must it be violent; and as he does conceive
He is dishonour'd by a man which ever
Profess'd to him, why, his revenges must
In that be made more bitter. Fear o'ershades me:
Good expedition be my friend, and comfort
The gracious queen, part of his theme, but nothing
Of his ill-ta'en suspicion! Come, Camillo;
I will respect thee as a father, if
Thou bear'st my life off hence: let us avoid.

Cam. It is in mine authority to command
The keys of all the posterns: please your highness
To take the urgent hour: come, sir, away. [*Exeunt.*

ACT II.

Scene I. *Sicilia. A room in the palace.*

Enter Hermione, Mamillius, *and* Ladies.

Her. Take the boy to you: he so troubles me,
'Tis past enduring.

First Lady. Come, my gracious lord,
Shall I be your playfellow?

Mam. No, I'll none of you.

First Lady. Why, my sweet lord?

Mam.   You'll kiss me hard, and speak to me as if
I were a baby still. — I love you better.
   Sec. Lady.   And why so, my lord?
   Mam.   Not for because
Your brows are blacker; yet black brows, they say,
Become some women best, so that there be not
Too much hair there, but in a semicircle,
Or a half-moon made with a pen.
   Sec. Lady.   Who taught ye this?
   Mam.   I learn'd it out of women's faces. — Pray now
What colour are your eyebrows?
   First Lady.   Blue, my lord.
   Mam.   Nay, that's a mock: I've seen a lady's nose
That has been blue, but not her eyebrows.
   First Lady.   Hark ye;
The queen your mother rounds apace: we shall
Present our services to a fine new prince
One of these days; and then you'd wanton with us,
If we would have you.
   Sec. Lady.   She is spread of late
Into a goodly bulk; good time encounter her!
   Her.   What wisdom stirs amongst you? Come, sir, now
I am for you again: pray you, sit by us,
And tell 's a tale.
   Mam.   Merry or sad shall 't be?
   Her.   As merry as you will.
   Mam.   A sad tale's best for winter: I have one
Of sprites and goblins.
   Her.   Let's have that, good sir.
Come on, sit down: — come on, and do your best
To fright me with your sprites; you're powerful at it.
   Mam.   There was a man, —
   Her.   Nay, come, sit down; then on.
   Mam.   Dwelt by a churchyard: — I will tell it softly;
Yond crickets shall not hear it.
   Her.   Come on, then,
And give't me in mine ear.

Enter LEONTES, ANTIGONUS, *Lords, and* Guards.

Leon. Was he met there? his train? Camillo with him?

First Lord. Behind the tuft of pines I met them; never
Saw I men scour so on their way: I ey'd them
Even to their ships.

Leon. How blest am I
In my just censure, in my true opinion! —
Alack, for lesser knowledge! how accurs'd
In being so blest! — There may be in the cup
A spider steep'd, and one may drink, depart,
And yet partake no venom; for his knowledge
Is not infected: but if one present
Th' abhorr'd ingredient to his eye, make known
How he hath drunk, he cracks his gorge, his sides,
With violent hefts: — I have drunk, and seen the spider.
Camillo was his help in this, his pander: —
There is a plot against my life, my crown;
All's true that is mistrusted: — that false villain,
Whom I employ'd, was pre-employ'd by him:
He has discover'd my design, and I
Remain a pinch'd thing; yea, a very trick
For them to play at will. — How came the posterns
So easily open?

First Lord. By his great authority;
Which often hath no less prevail'd than so,
On your command.

Leon. I know't too well. —
Give me the boy: — I'm glad you did not nurse him:
Though he does bear some signs of me, yet you
Have too much blood in him.

Her. What is this? sport?

Leon. Bear the boy hence; he shall not come about her;
Away with him! — and let her sport herself
[*Exit Mamillius with some of the Guards.*
With that she's big with; — for 'tis Polixenes
Has made thee swell thus.

Her. But I'd say he had not,

And I'll be sworn you would believe my saying,
Howe'er you lean to the nayward.
  Leon.   You, my lords,
Look on her, mark her well; be but about
To say, "She is a goodly lady," and
The justice of your hearts will thereto add,
"'Tis pity she's not honest-honourable:"
Praise her but for this her without-door form, —
Which, on my faith, deserves high speech, — and straight
The shrug, the hum, or ha, — these petty brands
That calumny doth use: — O, I am out,
That mercy does; for calumny will sear
Virtue itself: — these shrugs, these hums and ha's,
When you have said "she's goodly," come between,
Ere you can say "she's honest:" but be 't known,
From him that has most cause to grieve it should be,
She's an adultress.
  Her.   Should a villain say so,
The most replenish'd villain in the world,
He were as much more villain: you, my lord,
Do but mistake.
  Leon.   You have mistook, my lady,
Polixenes for Leontes: O thou thing,
Which I'll not call a creature of thy place,
Lest barbarism, making me the precedent,
Should a like language use to all degrees,
And mannerly distinguishment leave out
Betwixt the prince and beggar! — I have said
She's an adultress; I have said with whom:
More, she's a traitor; and Camillo is
A fedary with her; and one that knows,
What she should shame to know herself
But with her most vile principal, that she
Is a bed-swerver, even as bad as those
That vulgars give bold'st titles; ay, and privy
To this their late escape.
  Her.   No. by my life,

Privy to none of this. How will this grieve you,
When you shall come to clearer knowledge, that
You thus have publish'd me! Gentle my lord,
You scarce can right me throughly then, to say
You did mistake.
    Leon.   No, no; if I mistake
In those foundations which I build upon,
The centre is not big enough to bear
A schoolboy's top. — Away with her to prison!
He who shall speak for her 's afar off guilty
But that he speaks.
    Her.   There's some ill planet reigns:
I must be patient till the heavens look
With an aspéct more favourable. — Good my lords,
I am not prone to weeping, as our sex
Commonly are, — the want of which vain dew
Perchance shall dry your pities; but I have
That honourable grief lodg'd here which burns
Worse than tears drown: beseech you all, my lords,
With thoughts so qualified as your charities
Shall best instruct you, measure me; — and so
The king's will be perform'd!
    Leon. [*to the Guards*]   Shall I be heard?
    Her.   Who is 't that goes with me? — Beseech your high-
        ness,
My women may be with me; for, you see,
My plight requires it. — Do not weep, good fools;
There is no cause: when you shall know your mistress
Has deserv'd prison, then abound in tears
As I come out: this action I now go on
Is for my better grace. — Adieu, my lord:
I never wish'd to see you sorry; now
I trust I shall. — My women, come; you have leave
    Leon.   Go, do our bidding; hence!
                    [*Exeunt Queen and Ladies, with Guards.*
    First Lord.   Beseech your highness, call the queen again.
    Ant.   Be certain what you do, sir, lest your justice

Prove violence; in the which three great ones suffer,
Yourself, your queen, your son.
  First Lord.   For her, my lord,
I dare my life lay down, and will do't, sir,
Please you t' accept it, that the queen is spotless
I' th' eyes of heaven and to you; I mean,
In this which you accuse her.
  Ant.   If it prove
She's otherwise, I'll keep my stables where
I lodge my wife; I'll go in couples with her;
Than when I feel and see her no further trust her;
For every inch of woman in the world,
Ay, every dram of woman's flesh, is false,
If she be.
  Leon. Hold your peaces.
  First Lord.   Good my lord, —
  Ant. It is for you we speak, not for ourselves:
You are abus'd, and by some putter-on,
That will be damn'd for't; would I knew the villain,
I would land-damn him. Be she honour-flaw'd, —
I have three daughters; the eldest is eleven;
The second and the third, nine and some five;
If this prove true, they'll pay for't: by mine honour,
I'll geld 'em all; fourteen they shall not see,
To bring false generations: they are co-heirs;
And I had rather glib myself than they
Should not produce fair issue.
  Leon.   Cease; no more.
You smell this business with a sense as cold
As is a dead man's nose: but I do see't and feel't,
As you feel doing thus, and see withal
          [*Laying hold of his arm.*
The instruments that feel.
  Ant.   If it be so,
We need no grave to bury honesty:
There's not a grain of it the face to sweeten
Of the whole dungy earth.

Leon.   What! lack I credit?
First Lord. I had rather you did lack than I, my lord,
Upon this ground; and more it would content me
To have her honour true than your suspicion,
Be blam'd for't how you might.
   Leon.   Why, what need we
Commune with you of this, but rather follow
Our forceful instigation? Our prerogative
Calls not your counsels; but our natural goodness
Imparts this: which, if you — or stupefied,
Or seeming so in skill — cannot or will not
Relish a truth, like us, inform yourselves
We need no more of your advice: the matter,
The loss, the gain, the ordering on't, is all
Properly ours.
   Ant.   And I wish, my liege,
You had only in your silent judgment tried it,
Without more overture.
   Leon.   How could that be?
Either thou art most ignorant by age,
Or thou wert born a fool. Camillo's flight,
Added to their familiarity, —
Which was as gross as ever touch'd conjecture,
That lack'd sight only, naught for approbation
But only seeing, all other circumstances
Made up to the deed, — doth push on this proceeding:
Yet, for a greater confirmation, —
For, in an act of this importance 'twere
Most piteous to be wild, — I have dispatch'd in post
To sacred Delphos, to Apollo's temple,
Cleomenes and Dion, whom you know
Of stuff'd sufficiency: now, from the oracle
They will bring all; whose spiritual counsel had,
Shall stop or spur me. Have I done well?
   First Lord. Well done, my lord.
   Leon. Though I am satisfied, and need no more
Than what I know, yet shall the oracle

Give rest to the minds of others; such as he
Whose ignorant credulity will not
Come up to the truth. So have we thought it good
From our free person she should be confin'd,
Lest that the treachery of the two fled hence
Be left her to perform. Come, follow us;
We are to speak in public; for this business
Will raise us all.

    Ant. [*aside*] To laughter, as I take it,
If the good truth were known.   [*Exeunt.*

    SCENE II. *The same. The outer room of a prison.*

    Enter PAULINA *and* Attendants.

    Paul. The keeper of the prison, — call to him;
Let him have knowledge who I am.   [*Exit an Attendant.*
                             Good lady!
No court in Europe is too good for thee;
What dost thou, then, in prison?

    Re-enter Attendant, *with the* Gaoler.
                            Now, good sir,
You know me, do you not?
    Gaol.   For a worthy lady,
And one who much I honour.
    Paul.   Pray you, then,
Conduct me to the queen.
    Gaol. I may not, madam: to the contrary
I have express commandment.
    Paul.   Here's ado,
To lock up honesty and honour from
Th' access of gentle visitors! — Is 't lawful,
Pray you, to see her women? any of them?
Emilia?
    Gaol. So please you, madam,
To put apart these your attendants, I
Shall bring Emilia forth.

Paul.   I pray now, call her. —
Withdraw yourselves.   [*Exeunt Attend.*
    Gaol.   And, madam,
I must be present at your conference.
    Paul. Well, be't so, prithee.   [*Exit Gaoler.*
Here's such ado to make no stain a stain,
As passes colouring.

            Re-enter Gaoler, *with* EMILIA.
                Dear gentlewoman,
How fares our gracious lady?
    Emil. As well as one so great and so forlorn
May hold together: on her frights and griefs, —
Which never tender lady hath borne greater, —
She is something before her time deliver'd.
    Paul. A boy?
    Emil.   A daughter; and a goodly babe,
Lusty, and like to live: the queen receives
Much comfort in't; says, "My poor prisoner,
I am innocent as you."
    Paul.   I dare be sworn: —
These dangerous unsafe lunes i' the king, beshrew them!
He must be told on't, and he shall: the office
Becomes a woman best; I'll take't upon me:
If I prove honey-mouth'd, let my tongue blister,
And never to my red-look'd anger be
The trumpet any more. — Pray you, Emilia,
Commend my best obedience to the queen:
If she dares trust me with her little babe,
I'll show't the king, and undertake to be
Her advocate to the loud'st. We do not know
How he may soften at the sight o' the child:
The silence often of pure innocence
Persuades, when speaking fails.
    Emil.   Most worthy madam,
Your honour and your goodness is so evident,
That your free undertaking cannot miss
A thriving issue: there's no lady living

17*

So meet for this great errand. Please your ladyship
To visit the next room, I'll presently
Acquaint the queen of your most noble offer;
Who but to-day hammer'd of this design,
But durst not tempt a minister of honour,
Lest she should be denied.
 Paul.   Tell her, Emilia,
I'll use that tongue I have: if wit flow from 't,
As boldness from my bosom, let 't not be doubted
I shall do good.
 Emil. Now be you bless'd for it!
I'll to the queen: please you, come something nearer.
 Gaol. Madam, if 't please the queen to send the babe,
I know not what I shall incur to pass it,
Having no warrant.
 Paul.   You need not fear it, sir:
The child was prisoner to the womb, and is,
By law and process of great nature, thence
Freed and enfranchis'd; not a party to
The anger of the king, nor guilty of,
If any be, the trespass of the queen.
 Gaol. I do believe it.
 Paul. Do not you fear: upon mine honour, I
Will stand 'twixt you and danger.   [*Exeunt.*

  Scene III. *The same. A room in the palace.*

  Enter Leontes, Antigonus, Lords, *and* Attendants.

 Leon. Nor night nor day no rest: it is but weakness
To bear the matter thus, — mere weakness. If
The cause were not in being, — part o' the cause,
She the adultress; for the harlot king
Is quite beyond mine arm, out of the blank
And level of my brain, plot-proof; but she
I can hook to me: — say that she were gone,
Given to the fire, a moiety of my rest
Might come to me again. — Who's there?

First Atten. [*advancing*] My lord?
Leon. How does the boy?
First Atten. He took good rest to-night;
'Tis hop'd his sickness is discharg'd.
Leon. To see his nobleness!
Conceiving the dishonour of his mother,
He straight declin'd, droop'd, took it deeply,
Fasten'd and fix'd the shame on 't in himself,
Threw off his spirit, his appetite, his sleep,
And downright languish'd. — Leave me solely: — go,
See how he fares. [*Exit First Atten.*] — Fie, fie! no thought
    of him; —
The very thought of my revenges that way
Recoil upon me: in himself too mighty,
And in his parties, his alliance, — let him be,
Until a time may serve: for present vengeance,
Take it on her. Camillo and Polixenes
Laugh at me, make their pastime at my sorrow:
They should not laugh, if I could reach them; nor
Shall she, within my power.

        Enter PAULINA, *with a Child.*
First Lord. You must not enter.
Paul. Nay, rather, good my lords, be second to me:
Fear you his tyrannous passion more, alas,
Than the queen's life? a gracious innocent soul,
More free than he is jealous.
Ant. That's enough.
Sec. Atten. Madam, he hath not slept to-night; com-
    manded
None should come at him.
Paul. Not so hot, good sir:
I come to bring him sleep. 'Tis such as you, —
That creep like shadows by him, and do sigh
At each his needless heavings, — such as you
Nourish the cause of his awaking: I
Do come, with words as med'cinal as true,

Honest as either, to purge him of that humour
That presses him from sleep.

Leon. What noise there, ho?

Paul. No noise, my lord; but needful conference
About some gossips for your highness.

Leon. How! —
Away with that audacious lady! — Antigonus,
I charg'd thee that she should not come about me:
I knew she would.

Ant. I told her so, my lord,
On your displeasure's peril and on mine,
She should not visit you.

Leon. What, canst not rule her?

Paul. From all dishonesty he can: in this, —
Unless he take the course that you have done,
Commit me for committing honour, — trust it,
He shall not rule me.

Ant. La you now, you hear:
When she will take the rein, I let her run;
But she'll not stumble.

Paul. Good my liege, I come, —
And, I beseech you, hear me, who profess
Myself your loyal servant, your physician,
Your most obedient counsellor; yet that dare
Less appear so, in comforting your evils,
Than such as most seem yours: — I say, I come
From your good queen.

Leon. Good queen!

Paul. Good queen, my lord, good queen; I say good
    queen;
And would by combat make her good, so were I
A man, the worst about you.

Leon. Force her hence.

Paul. Let him that makes but trifles of his eyes
First hand me: on mine own accord I'll off;
But first I'll do my errand. — The good queen —

For she is good — hath brought you forth a daughter;
Here 'tis; commends it to your blessing.
                              [*Laying down the Child.*
    Leon.   Out!
A mankind witch! Hence with her, out o' door, —
A most intelligencing bawd!
    Paul.   Not so:
I am as ignorant in that as you
In so entitling me; and no less honest
Than you are mad; which is enough, I'll warrant,
As this world goes, to pass for honest.
    Leon.   Traitors!
Will you not push her out? — Give her the bastard: —
[*To Antigonus*] Thou dotard, thou art woman-tir'd, unroosted
By thy Dame Partlet here: — take up the bastard;
Take 't up, I say; give 't to thy crone.
    Paul.   For ever
Unvenerable be thy hands, if thou
Tak'st up the princess by that forcèd baseness
Which he has put upon 't!
    Leon.   He dreads his wife.
    Paul. So I would you did; then 'twere past all doubt
You 'd call your children yours.
    Leon.   A nest of traitors!
    Ant. I am none, by this good light.
    Paul.   Nor I; nor any,
But one, that 's here, and that 's himself; for he
The sacred honour of himself, his queen's,
His hopeful son's, his babe's, betrays to slander,
Whose sting is sharper than the sword's; and will not —
For, as the case now stands, it is a curse
He cannot be compell'd to 't — once remove
The root of his opinion, which is rotten
As ever oak or stone was sound.
    Leon.   A callet
Of boundless tongue, who late hath beat her husband,
And now baits me! — This brat is none of mine;

It is the issue of Polixenes:
Hence with it; and, together with the dam,
Commit them to the fire!

  Paul.   It is yours;
And, might we lay th' old proverb to your charge,
So like you, 'tis the worse. — Behold, my lords,
Although the print be little, the whole matter
And copy of the father, — eye, nose, lip;
The trick of 's frown; his forehead; nay, the valleys,
The pretty dimples of 's chin and cheek; his smiles;
The very mould and frame of hand, nail, finger: —
And thou, good goddess Nature, which hast made it
So like to him that got it, if thou hast
The ordering of the mind too, 'mongst all colours
No yellow in 't, lest she suspect, as he does,
Her children not her husband's!

  Leon.   A gross hag! —
And, losel, thou art worthy to be hang'd,
That wilt not stay her tongue.

  Ant.   Hang all the husbands
That cannot do that feat, you'll leave yourself
Hardly one subject.

  Leon.   Once more, take her hence.

  Paul. A most unworthy and unnatural lord
Can do no more.

  Leon.   I'll ha' thee burn'd.

  Paul.   I care not:
It is an heretic that makes the fire,
Not she which burns in 't. I'll not call you tyrant;
But this most cruel usage of your queen —
Not able to produce more accusation
Than your own weak-hinge'd fancy — something savours
Of tyranny, and will ignoble make you,
Yea, scandalous to the world.

  Leon.   On your allegiance,
Out of the chamber with her! Were I a tyrant,

Where were her life? she durst not call me so,
If she did know me one. Away with her!

Paul. I pray you, do not push me; I'll be gone. —
Look to your babe, my lord; 'tis yours: Jove send her
A better-guiding spirit! — What need these hands?
You, that are thus so tender o'er his follies,
Will never do him good, not one of you.
So, so: — farewell; we are gone. [*Exit.*

Leon. Thou, traitor, hast set on thy wife to this. —
My child? away with it! — even thou, that hast
A heart so tender o'er it, take it hence,
And see it instantly consum'd with fire;
Even thou, and none but thou. Take it up straight:
Within this hour bring me word 'tis done,
And by good testimony; or I'll seize thy life,
With what thou else call'st thine. If thou refuse,
And wilt encounter with my wrath, say so;
The bastard-brains with these my proper hands
Shall I dash out. Go, take it to the fire;
For thou sett'st on thy wife.

Ant.   I did not, sir:
These lords, my noble fellows, if they please,
Can clear me in't.

First Lord. We can: — my royal liege,
He is not guilty of her coming hither.

Leon. You 're liars all.

First Lord. Beseech your highness, give us better credit:
We 've always truly serv'd you; and beseech you
So to esteem of us: and on our knees we beg, —
As recompense of our dear services
Past and to come, — that you do change this purpose,
Which being so horrible, so bloody, must
Lead on to some foul issue: we all kneel.

Leon. I am a feather for each wind that blows: —
Shall I live on, to see this bastard kneel
And call me father? better burn it now
Than curse it then. But be it; let it live: —

It shall not neither. — You, sir, come you hither;
[*To Antigonus.*

You that have been so tenderly officious
With Lady Margery, your midwife, there,
To save this bastard's life, — for 'tis a bastard,
So sure as thy beard's gray, — what will you adventure
To save this brat's life?

Ant. Any thing, my lord,
That my ability may undergo,
And nobleness impose: at least, thus much, —
I'll pawn the little blood which I have left
To save the innocent: — any thing possible.

Leon. It shall be possible. Swear by this sword
Thou wilt perform my bidding.

Ant. I will, my lord.

Leon. Mark, and perform it, — seest thou? for the fail
Of any point in 't shall not only be
Death to thyself, but to thy lewd-tongu'd wife,
Whom for this time we pardon. We enjoin thee,
As thou art liegeman to us, that thou carry
This female bastard hence; and that thou bear it
To some remote and desert place, quite out
Of our dominions; and that there thou leave it,
Without more mercy, to its own protection
And favour of the climate. As by strange fortune
It came to us, I do in justice charge thee,
On thy soul's peril and thy body's torture,
That thou commend it strangely to some place
Where chance may nurse or end it. Take it up.

Ant. I swear to do this, though a present death
Had been more merciful. — Come on, poor babe:
Some powerful spirit instruct the kites and ravens
To be thy nurses! Wolves and bears, they say,
Casting their savageness aside, have done
Like offices of pity. — Sir, be prosperous
In more than this deed does require! — and blessing,

Against this cruelty, fight on thy side,
Poor thing, condemn'd to loss! [*Exit with the Child.*
  Leon. No, I'll not rear
Another's issue.
  Sec. Atten. Please your highness, posts
From those you sent to th' oracle are come
An hour since: Cleomenes and Dion,
Being well arriv'd from Delphos, are both landed,
Hasting to the court.
  First Lord. So please you, sir, their speed
Hath been beyond account.
  Leon. Twenty-three days
They have been absent: 'tis good speed; foretells
The great Apollo suddenly will have
The truth of this appear. Prepare you, lords;
Summon a session, that we may arraign
Our most disloyal lady; for, as she hath
Been publicly accus'd, so shall she have
A just and open trial. While she lives,
My heart will be a burden to me. Leave me;
And think upon my bidding. [*Exeunt.*

ACT III.

Scene I. *Sicilia. A street in some town.*

Enter Cleomenes, Dion, *and an* Attendant.

  Cleo. The climate's delicate; the air most sweet;
Fertile the isle; the temple much surpassing
The common praise it bears.
  Dion. I shall report,
For most it caught me, the celestial habits —
Methinks I so should term them — and the reverence
Of the grave wearers. O, the sacrifice!
How ceremonious, solemn, and unearthly
It was i' th' offering!
  Cleo. But, of all, the burst
And the ear-deafening voice o' th' oracle,

Kin to Jove's thunder, so surpriz'd my sense,
That I was nothing.
 Dion.   If th' event o' the journey
Prove as successful to the queen, — O, be 't so! —
As it hath been to us rare, pleasant, speedy,
The time is worth the use on't.
 Cleo.   Great Apollo
Turn all to the best! These proclamations,
So forcing faults upon Hermione,
I little like.
 Dion. The violent carriage of it
Will clear or end the business: when the oracle —
Thus by Apollo's great divine seal'd up —
Shall the contents discover, something rare
Even then will rush to knowledge. — [*To Attendant*] Go, —
   fresh horses: —
And gracious be the issue!   [*Exeunt.*

  SCENE II. *The same. A court of justice.*

   LEONTES, Lords, *and* Officers, *discovered.*

 Leon. This session — to our great grief, we pronounce —
Even pushes 'gainst our heart; — the party tried,
The daughter of a king, our wife, and one
Of us too much belov'd. Let us be clear'd
Of being tyrannous, since we so openly
Proceed in justice; which shall have due course,
Even to the guilt or the purgation. —
Produce the prisoner.
 First Off. It is his highness' pleasure that the queen
Appear in person here in court.
 Crier. Silence!

 HERMIONE *is brought in guarded;* PAULINA *and* Ladies
    attending.

 Leon. Read the indictment.
 First Off. [*reads*] "Hermione, queen to the worthy Leontes,
king of Sicilia, thou art here accused and arraigned of high

treason, in committing adultery with Polixenes, king of Bohemia, and conspiring with Camillo to take away the life of our sovereign lord the king, thy royal husband: the pretence whereof being by circumstances partly laid open, thou, Hermione, contrary to the faith and allegiance of a true subject, didst counsel and aid them, for their better safety, to fly away by night."

Her. Since what I am to say must be but that
Which contradicts my accusation, and
The testimony on my part no other
But what comes from myself, it shall scarce boot me
To say, "Not guilty:" mine integrity
Being counted falsehood, shall, as I express it,
Be so receiv'd. But thus: — if powers divine
Behold our human actions, as they do,
I doubt not, then, but innocence shall make
False accusation blush, and tyranny
Tremble at patience. — You, my lord, best know —
Who least will seem to do so — my past life
Hath been as continent, as chaste, as true,
As I am now unhappy: which is more
Than history can pattern, though devis'd
And play'd to take spectators; for, behold me, —
A fellow of the royal bed, which owe
A moiety of the throne, a great king's daughter,
The mother to a hopeful prince, — here standing
To prate and talk for life and honour 'fore
Who please to come and hear. For life, I prize it
As I weigh grief, which I would spare: for honour,
'Tis a derivative from me to mine;
And only that I stand for. I appeal
To your own conscience, sir, before Polixenes
Came to your court, how I was in your grace,
How merited to be so; since he came,
With what encounter so uncurrent I
Have strain'd, t'appear thus: if one jot beyond
The bound of honour, or in act or will

That way inclining, harden'd be the hearts
Of all that hear me, and my near'st of kin
Cry "Fie" upon my grave!

Leon.   I ne'er heard yet
That any of these bolder vices wanted
Less impudence to gainsay what they did
Than to perform it first.

Her.   That's true enough;
Though 'tis a saying, sir, not due to me.

Leon. You will not own it.

Her.   More than mistress of
Which comes to me in name of fault, I must not
At all acknowledge. For Polixenes,—
With whom I am accus'd,—I do confess
I lov'd him, as in honour he requir'd;
With such a kind of love as might become
A lady like me; with a love even such,
So and no other, as yourself commanded:
Which not to have done, I think had been in me
Both disobedience and ingratitude
To you and toward your friend; whose love had spoke,
Even since it could speak, from an infant, freely,
That it was yours. Now, for conspiracy,
I know not how it tastes; though it be dish'd
For me to try how: all I know of it
Is, that Camillo was an honest man;
And why he left your court, the gods themselves,
Wotting no more than I, are ignorant.

Leon. You knew of his departure, as you know what
You've underta'en to do in 's absence.

Her.   Sir,
You speak a language that I understand not:
My life stands in the level of your dreams,
Which I'll lay down.

Leon.   Your actions are my dreams;
You had a bastard by Polixenes,
And I but dream'd it:—as you were past all shame,—

Those of your fact are so, — so past all truth:
Which to deny concerns more than avails;
For as
Thy brat hath been cast out, like to itself,
No father owning it, — which is, indeed,
More criminal in thee than it, — so thou
Shalt feel our justice; in whose easiest passage
Look for no less than death.

  Her.   Sir, spare your threats:
The bug which you would fright me with I seek.
To me can life be no commodity:
The crown and comfort of my life, your favour,
I do give lost; for I do feel it gone,
But know not how it went: my second joy
And first-fruits of my body, from his presence
I'm barr'd, like one infectious: my third comfort,
Starr'd most unluckily, is from my breast,
The innocent milk in its most innocent mouth,
Hal'd out to murder: myself on every post
Proclaim'd a strumpet; with immodest hatred
The child-bed privilege denied, which 'longs
To women of all fashion; lastly, hurried
Here to this place, i' th' open air, before
I have got strength of limit. Now, my liege,
Tell me what blessings I have here alive,
That I should fear to die? Therefore, proceed.
But yet hear this; mistake me not: — for life,
I prize it not a straw; but for mine honour,
Which I would free, if I shall be condemn'd
Upon surmises, all proofs sleeping else,
But what your jealousies awake, — I tell you,
'Tis rigour, and not law. — Your honours all,
I do refer me to the oracle:
Apollo be my judge!

  First Lord. This your request
Is altogether just: — therefore, bring forth,
And in Apollo's name, his oracle. [*Exeunt certain Officers.*

Her. The Emperor of Russia was my father:
O, that he were alive, and here beholding
His daughter's trial! that he did but see
The flatness of my misery, — yet with eyes
Of pity, not revenge!

Re-enter Officers, *with* CLEOMENES *and* DION.

First Off. You here shall swear upon this sword of justice,
That you, Cleomenes and Dion, have
Been both at Delphos; and from thence have brought
This seal'd-up oracle, by the hand deliver'd
Of great Apollo's priest; and that, since then,
You have not dar'd to break the holy seal,
Nor read the secrets in 't.

Cleo. and Dion. All this we swear.

Leon. Break up the seals, and read.

First Off. [*reads*] "Hermione is chaste; Polixenes blameless; Camillo a true subject; Leontes a jealous tyrant; his innocent babe truly begotten; and the king shall live without an heir, if that which is lost be not found."

Lords. Now blessèd be the great Apollo!

Her. Praisèd!

Leon. Hast thou read truth?

First Off. Ay, my lord; even so
As it is here set down.

Leon. There is no truth at all i'' th' oracle:
The session shall proceed: this is mere falsehood.

Enter an Attendant *hastily.*

Atten. My lord the king, the king!

Leon. What is the business?

Atten. O sir, I shall be hated to report it!
The prince your son, with mere conceit and fear
Of the queen's speed, is gone.

Leon. How! gone!

Atten. Is dead.

Leon. Apollo's angry; and the heavens themselves
Do strike at my injustice. [*Hermione faints.*] How now there!

Paul. This news is mortal to the queen: — look down,
And see what death is doing.
 Leon.   Take her hence:
Her heart is but o'ercharg'd; she will recover: —
I have too much believ'd mine own suspicion: —
Beseech you, tenderly apply to her
Some remedies for life. [*Exeunt Paul. and Ladies, with Her.*
      Apollo, pardon
My great profaneness 'gainst thine oracle! —
I'll reconcile me to Polixenes;
New woo my queen; recall the good Camillo,
Whom I proclaim a man of truth, of mercy;
For, being transported by my jealousies
To bloody thoughts and to revenge, I chose
Camillo for the minister, to poison
My friend Polixenes: which had been done,
But that the good mind of Camillo tardied
My swift command, though I with death and with
Reward did threaten and encourage him,
Not doing it and being done: he, most humane,
And fill'd with honour, to my kingly guest
Unclasp'd my practice; quit his fortunes here,
Which you knew great; and to the certain hazard
Of all incertainties himself commended,
No richer than his honour: — how he glisters
Thorough my rust! and how his piety
Does my deeds make the blacker!

     Re-enter PAULINA.

 Paul.   Woe the while!
O, cut my lace, lest my heart, cracking it,
Break too!
 First Lord. What fit is this, good lady?
 Paul. What studied torments, tyrant, hast for me?
What wheels? racks? fires? what flaying? or what boiling
In lead or oil? what old or newer torture
Must I receive, whose every word deserves

To taste of thy most worst? Thy tyranny
Together working with thy jealousies, —
Fancies too weak for boys, too green and idle
For girls of nine, — O, think what they have done,
And then run mad indeed, — stark mad! for all
Thy by-gone fooleries were but spices of it.
That thou betray'dst Polixenes, 'twas nothing, —
That did but show thee, of a fool, inconstant,
And damnable ingrateful; nor was 't much,
Thou wouldst have poison'd good Camillo's honour,
To have him kill a king; — poor trespasses,
More monstrous standing by: whereof I reckon
The casting forth to crows thy baby daughter,
To be or none, or little, — though a devil
Would have shed water out of fire ere done 't;
Nor is 't directly laid to thee, the death
Of the young prince, whose honourable thoughts —
Thoughts high for one so tender — cleft the heart
That could conceive a gross and foolish sire
Blemish'd his gracious dam: this is not, no,
Laid to thy answer: but the last, — O lords,
When I have said, cry, "Woe!" — the queen, the queen,
The sweet'st, dear'st creature's dead; and vengeance for 't
Not dropp'd down yet.

 First Lord. The higher powers forbid!
 Paul. I say she's dead; I'll swear 't. If word nor oath
Prevail not, go and see: if you can bring
Tincture or lustre in her lip, her eye,
Heat outwardly or breath within, I'll serve you
As I would do the gods. — But, O thou tyrant!
Do not repent these things; for they are heavier
Than all thy woes can stir: therefore betake thee
To nothing but despair. A thousand knees
Ten thousand years together, naked, fasting,
Upon a barren mountain, and still winter
In storm perpetual, could not move the gods
To look that way thou wert.

Leon. Go on, go on:
Thou canst not speak too much; I have deserv'd
All tongues to talk their bitterest.
First Lord. Say no more:
Howe'er the business goes, you have made fault
I' the boldness of your speech.
Paul. I'm sorry for 't:
All faults I make, when I shall come to know them,
I do repent. Alas, I've show'd too much
The rashness of a woman! he is touch'd
To the noble heart. — What's gone, and what's past help,
Should be past grief: do not receive affliction
At my petition; I beseech you, rather
Let me be punish'd, that have minded you
Of what you should forget. Now, good my liege,
Sir, royal sir, forgive a foolish woman:
The love I bore your queen, — lo, fool again! —
I'll speak of her no more, nor of your children;
I'll not remember you of my own lord,
Who is lost too: take you your patience to you,
And I'll say nothing.
Leon. Thou didst speak but well,
When most the truth; which I receive much better
Than to be pitied of thee. Prithee, bring me
To the dead bodies of my queen and son:
One grave shall be for both; upon them shall
The causes of their death appear, unto
Our shame perpetual. Once a day I'll visit
The chapel where they lie; and tears shed there
Shall be my recreation: so long as nature
Will bear up with this exercise, so long
I daily vow to use it. Come, and lead me
Unto these sorrows.

[*Exeunt.*

SCENE III. *Bohemia. A desert country near the sea.*

Enter ANTIGONUS *with the Child, and a* Mariner.

Ant. Thou 'rt perfect, then, our ship hath touch'd upon
The deserts of Bohemia?
Mar. Ay, my lord; and fear
We 've landed in ill time: the skies look grimly,
And threaten present blusters. In my conscience,
The heavens with that we have in hand are angry,
And frown upon 's.
Ant. Their sacred wills be done! — Go, get aboard;
Look to thy bark: I'll not be long before
I call upon thee.
Mar. Make your best haste; and go not
Too far i' the land: 'tis like to be loud weather;
Besides, this place is famous for the creatures
Of prey that keep upon 't.
Ant. Go thou away:
I'll follow instantly.
Mar. I 'm glad at heart
To be so rid o' the business.   [*Exit.*
Ant. Come, poor babe: —
I' ve heard, — but not believ'd, — the spirits o' the dead
May walk again: if such thing be, thy mother
Appear'd to me last night; for ne'er was dream
So like a waking. To me comes a creature,
Sometimes her head on one side, some another;
I never saw a vessel of like sorrow,
So fill'd and so becoming: in pure white robes,
Like very sanctity, she did approach
My cabin where I lay; thrice bow'd before me;
And, gasping to begin some speech, her eyes
Became two spouts: the fury spent, anon
Did this break from her: "Good Antigonus,
Since fate, against thy better disposition,
Hath made thy person for the thrower-out
Of my poor babe, according to thine oath, —

Places remote enough are in Bohemia,
There wend, and leave it crying; and, for the babe
Is counted lost for ever, Perdita,
I prithee, call't. For this ungentle business,
Put on thee by my lord, thou ne'er shalt see
Thy wife Paulina more:" — and so, with shrieks,
She melted into air. Affrighted much,
I did in time collect myself; and thought
This was so, and no slumber. Dreams are toys:
Yet, for this once, yea, superstitiously,
I will be squar'd by this. I do believe
Hermione hath suffer'd death; and that
Apollo would, this being indeed the issue
Of king Polixenes, it should here be laid,
Either for life or death, upon the earth
Of its right father. — Blossom, speed thee well!
       [Laying down the Child, with a scroll.
There lie; and there thy character: there these;
          [Laying down a bundle.
Which may, if fortune please, both breed thee, pretty,
And still rest thine. — The storm begins: — poor wretch,
             [Thunder.
That, for thy mother's fault, art thus expos'd
To loss and what may follow! — Weep I cannot,
But my heart bleeds: and most accurs'd am I
To be by oath enjoin'd to this. — Farewell! —
The day frowns more and more: — thou 'rt like to have
A lullaby too rough: — I never saw
The heavens so dim by day. — A savage clamour! —
      [Noise of hunters, dogs, and bears within.
Well may I get aboard! — This is the chase:
I am gone for ever.   *[Exit, pursued by a bear.*

      Enter an old Shepherd.

 Shep. I would there were no age between ten and three-and-twenty, or that youth would sleep out the rest; for there is nothing in the between but getting wenches with child,

wronging the ancientry, stealing, fighting — Hark you now!
— Would any but these boiled brains of nineteen and two-
and-twenty hunt this weather? They have scared away two
of my best sheep, which I fear the wolf will sooner find than
the master: if any where I have them, 'tis by the sea-side,
browzing of ivy. Good luck, an 't be thy will! what have we
here? [*Seeing the Child.*] Mercy on 's, a barn; a very pretty
barn! A boy or a child, I wonder? A pretty one; a very
pretty one: sure, some scape: though I am not bookish, yet
I can read waiting-gentlewoman in the scape. This has been
some stair-work, some trunk-work, some behind-door-work:
they were warmer that got this than the poor thing is here.
I'll take it up for pity: yet I'll tarry till my son come; he
hallooed but even now. — Whoa, ho, hoa!

Clo. [*within*] Hilloa, loa!

Shep. What, art so near? If thou 'lt see a thing to talk
on when thou art dead and rotten, come hither.

Enter Clown.

What ailest thou, man?

Clo. I have seen two such sights, by sea and by land! —
but I am not to say it is a sea, for it is now the sky: betwixt
the firmament and it you cannot thrust a bodkin's point.

Shep. Why, boy, how is it?

Clo. I would you did but see how it chafes, how it rages,
how it takes up the shore! — but that's not to the point. O,
the most piteous cry of the poor souls! sometimes to see 'em,
and not to see 'em; now the ship boring the moon with her
main-mast, and anon swallowed with yest and froth, as you'd
thrust a cork into a hogshead. And then for the land-service,
— to see how the bear tore out his shoulder-bone; how he
cried to me for help, and said his name was Antigonus, a
nobleman: — but to make an end of the ship, — to see how
the sea flap-dragoned it: — but, first, how the poor souls
roared, and the sea mocked them; — and how the poor gentleman roared, and the bear mocked him, both roaring louder
than the sea or weather.

Shep. Name of mercy, when was this, boy?

Clo. Now, now; I have not winked since I saw these sights: the men are not yet cold under water, nor the bear half dined on the gentleman, — he 's at it now.

Shep. Would I had been by, to have helped the old man!

Clo. I would you had been by the ship-side, to have helped her: there your charity would have lacked footing.

Shep. Heavy matters! heavy matters! but look thee here, boy. Now bless thyself: thou mettest with things dying, I with things new-born. Here's a sight for thee; look thee, a bearing-cloth for a squire's child! look thee here; take up, take up, boy; open 't. So, let's see: — it was told me I should be rich by the fairies; this is some changeling: — open 't. What's within, boy?

Clo. You're a made old man: if the sins of your youth are forgiven you, you're well to live. Gold! all gold!

Shep. This is fairy gold, boy, and 'twill prove so; up with 't, keep it close: home, home, the next way. We are lucky, boy; and to be so still, requires nothing but secrecy. — Let my sheep go: — come, good boy, the next way home.

Clo. Go you the next way with your findings. I'll go see if the bear be gone from the gentleman, and how much he hath eaten: they are never curst, but when they are hungry: if there be any of him left, I'll bury it.

Shep. That's a good deed. If thou mayest discern by that which is left of him what he is, fetch me to the sight of him.

Clo. Marry, will I; and you shall help to put him i' the ground.

Shep. 'Tis a lucky day, boy, and we'll do good deeds on't. [*Exeunt.*

ACT IV.

Enter TIME, *as* Chorus.

Time. I, — that please some, try all; both joy and terror
Of good and bad; that make and unfold error, —
Now take upon me, in the name of Time,

To use my wings. Impute it not a crime
To me or my swift passage, that I slide
O'er sixteen years, and leave the growth untried
Of that wide gap; since it is in my power
To o'erthrow law, and in one self-born hour
To plant and o'erwhelm custom. Let me pass
The same I am, ere ancient'st order was,
Or what is now receiv'd: I witness to
The times that brought them in; so shall I do
To the freshest things now reigning, and make stale
The glistering of this present, as my tale
Now seems to it. Your patience this allowing,
I turn my glass, and give my scene such growing
As you had slept between. Leontes leaving,
Th' effects of his fond jealousies so grieving
That he shuts up himself, — imagine me,
Gentle spectators, that I now may be
In fair Bohemia; and remember well,
I mention'd a son o' the king's, which Florizel
I now name to you; and with speed so pace
To speak of Perdita, now grown in grace
Equal with wondering: what of her ensues,
I list not prophesy; but let Time's news
Be known when 'tis brought forth: — a shepherd's daughter,
And what to her adheres, which follows after,
Is th' argument of Time. Of this allow,
If ever you have spent time worse ere now;
If never, yet that Time himself doth say
He wishes earnestly you never may. [*Exit.*

SCENE I. *Bohemia. A room in the palace of* POLIXENES.

Enter POLIXENES *and* CAMILLO.

Pol. I pray thee, good Camillo, be no more importunate:
'tis a sickness denying thee any thing; a death to grant this.

Cam. It is sixteen years since I saw my country: though
I have, for the most part, been aired abroad, I desire to lay

my bones there. Besides, the penitent king, my master, hath
sent for me; to whose feeling sorrows I might be some allay,
or I o'erween to think so, — which is another spur to my departure.

Pol. As thou lovest me, Camillo, wipe not out the rest of
thy services by leaving me now: the need I have of thee, thine
own goodness hath made; better not to have had thee than
thus to want thee: thou, having made me businesses which
none without thee can sufficiently manage, must either stay to
execute them thyself, or take away with thee the very services
thou hast done; which if I have not enough considered, — as
too much I cannot, — to be more thankful to thee shall be my
study; and my profit therein, the heaping friendships. Of that
fatal country Sicilia, prithee speak no more; whose very
naming punishes me with the remembrance of that penitent,
as thou callest him, and reconciled king, my brother; whose
loss of his most precious queen and children are even now to
be afresh lamented. Say to me, when sawest thou the Prince
Florizel, my son? Kings are no less unhappy, their issue not
being gracious, than they are in losing them when they have
approved their virtues.

Cam. Sir, it is three days since I saw the prince. What
his happier affairs may be, are to me unknown: but I have
missingly noted, he is of late much retired from court, and
is less frequent to his princely exercises than formerly he hath
appeared.

Pol. I have considered so much, Camillo, and with some
care; so far, that I have eyes under my service which look
upon his removedness; from whom I have this intelligence: —
that he is seldom from the house of a most homely shepherd; a
man, they say, that from very nothing, and beyond the imagination of his neighbours, is grown into an unspeakable estate.

Cam. I have heard, sir, of such a man, who hath a daughter of most rare note: the report of her is extended more than
can be thought to begin from such a cottage.

Pol. That's likewise part of my intelligence; but I fear
the angle that plucks our son thither. Thou shalt accom-

pany us to the place; where we will, not appearing what we are, have some question with the shepherd; from whose simplicity I think it not uneasy to get the cause of my son's resort thither. Prithee, be my present partner in this business, and lay aside the thoughts of Sicilia.

Cam. I willingly obey your command.

Pol. My best Camillo! — We must disguise ourselves.

[*Exeunt.*

SCENE II. *The same. A road near the Shepherd's cottage.*

Enter AUTOLYCUS, *singing.*

When daffodils begin to peer, —
  With, hey! the doxy over the dale, —
Why, then comes in the sweet o' the year;
  For the red blood reigns in the winter's pale.

The white sheet bleaching on the hedge, —
  With, hey! the sweet birds, O, how they sing! —
Doth set my pugging tooth on edge;
  For a quart of ale is a dish for a king.

The lark, that tirra-lirra chants, —
  With, hey! with, hey! the thrush and the jay, —
Are summer songs for me and my aunts,
  While we lie tumbling in the hay.

I have served Prince Florizel, and, in my time, wore three-pile; but now I am out of service:

But shall I go mourn for that, my dear? [*Singing.*
  The pale moon shines by night:
And when I wander here and there,
  I then do most go right.

If tinkers may have leave to live,
  And bear the sow-skin budget,
Then my account I well may give,
  And in the stocks avouch it.

My traffic is sheets; when the kite builds, look to lesser linen. My father named me Autolycus; who being, as I am, littered

under Mercury, was likewise a snapper-up of unconsidered
trifles. With die and drab I purchased this caparison; and
my revenue is the silly-cheat: gallows and knock are too
powerful on the highway; beating and hanging are terrors to
me; for the life to come, I sleep out the thought of it. — A
prize! a prize!

Enter Clown.

Clo. Let me see: — every 'leven wether tods; every tod
yields pound and odd shilling: fifteen hundred shorn, what
comes the wool to?

Aut. [*aside*] If the spring hold, the cock's mine.

Clo. I cannot do't without counters. — Let me see; what
am I to buy for our sheep-shearing feast? Three pound of
sugar; five pound of currants; rice — what will this sister of
mine do with rice? But my father hath made her mistress of
the feast, and she lays it on. She hath made me four-and-
twenty nosegays for the shearers, — three-man songmen all,
and very good ones; but they are most of them means and
bases; but one puritan amongst them, and he sings psalms to
hornpipes. I must have saffron, to colour the warden-pies;
mace; dates, — none, that's out of my note; nutmegs, seven;
a race or two of ginger, — but that I may beg; four pound of
prunes, and as many of raisins o' the sun.

Aut. O, that ever I was born! [*Grovelling on the ground.*

Clo. I' the name of me, —

Aut. O, help me, help me! pluck but off these rags; and
then, death, death!

Clo. Alack, poor soul! thou hast need of more rags to lay
on thee, rather than have these off.

Aut. O sir, the loathsomeness of them offend me more
than the stripes I have received, which are mighty ones and
millions.

Clo. Alas, poor man! a million of beating may come to a
great matter.

Aut. I am robbed, sir, and beaten; my money and apparel
ta'en from me, and these detestable things put upon me.

Clo. What, by a horseman or a footman?

Aut. A footman, sweet sir, a footman.

Clo. Indeed, he should be a footman by the garments he has left with thee: if this be a horseman's coat, it hath seen very hot service. Lend me thy hand, I'll help thee: come, lend me thy hand. [*Helping him up.*

Aut. O, good sir, tenderly, O!

Clo. Alas, poor soul!

Aut. O, good sir, softly, good sir! I fear, sir, my shoulder-blade is out.

Clo. How now! canst stand?

Aut. Softly, dear sir [*Picks his pocket*]; good sir, softly. You ha' done me a charitable office.

Clo. Dost lack any money? I have a little money for thee.

Aut. No, good sweet sir; no, I beseech you, sir: I have a kinsman not past three quarters of a mile hence, unto whom I was going; I shall there have money, or any thing I want: offer me no money, I pray you, — that kills my heart.

Clo. What manner of fellow was he that robbed you?

Aut. A fellow, sir, that I have known to go about with troll-my-dames: I knew him once a servant of the prince: I cannot tell, good sir, for which of his virtues it was, but he was certainly whipped out of the court.

Clo. His vices, you would say; there's no virtue whipped out of the court: they cherish it, to make it stay there; and yet it will no more but abide.

Aut. Vices, I would say, sir. I know this man well: he hath been since an ape-bearer; then a process-server, — a bailiff; then he compassed a motion of the Prodigal Son, and married a tinker's wife within a mile where my land and living lies; and, having flown over many knavish professions, he settled only in rogue: some call him Autolycus.

Clo. Out upon him! prig, for my life, prig: he haunts wakes, fairs, and bear-baitings.

Aut. Very true, sir; he, sir, he; that's the rogue that put me into this apparel.

Clo. Not a more cowardly rogue in all Bohemia; if you had but looked big and spit at him, he'd have run.

Aut. I must confess to you, sir, I am no fighter; I am false of heart that way; and that he knew, I warrant him.

Clo. How do you now?

Aut. Sweet sir, much better than I was; I can stand and walk: I will even take my leave of you, and pace softly towards my kinsman's.

Clo. Shall I bring thee on the way?

Aut. No, good-faced sir; no, sweet sir.

Clo. Then fare thee well: I must go buy spices for our sheep-shearing.

Aut. Prosper you, sweet sir! [*Exit Clown.*] Your purse is not hot enough to purchase your spice. I'll be with you at your sheep-shearing too: if I make not this cheat bring out another, and the shearers prove sheep, let me be unrolled, and my name put in the book of virtue!

> *Jog on, jog on, the footpath way,* [*Sings.*]
> *And merrily hent the stile-a:*
> *A merry heart goes all the day,*
> *Your sad tires in a mile-a.* [*Exit.*

SCENE III. *The same. A lawn before a* Shepherd's *cottage.*

Enter FLORIZEL *and* PERDITA.

Flo. These your unusual weeds to each part of you
Do give a life: no shepherdess; but Flora
Peering in April's front. This your sheep-shearing
Is as a meeting of the petty gods,
And you the queen on't.

Per.   Sir, my gracious lord,
To chide at your extremes, it not becomes me,—
O, pardon that I name them!—your high self,
The gracious mark o' the land, you have obscur'd
With a swain's wearing; and me, poor lowly maid,
Most goddess-like prank'd up: but that our feasts
In every mess have folly, and the feeders
Digest it with a custom, I should blush

To see you so attirèd; swoon, I think,
To show myself a glass.
    Flo.   I bless the time
When my good falcon made her flight across
Thy father's ground.
    Per.   Now Jove afford you cause!
To me the difference forges dread; your greatness
Hath not been us'd to fear. Even now I tremble
To think, your father, by some accident,
Should pass this way, as you did: O, the Fates!
How would he look, to see his work, so noble,
Vilely bound up? What would he say? Or how
Should I, in these my borrow'd flaunts, behold
The sternness of his presence?
    Flo.   Apprehend
Nothing but jollity. The gods themselves,
Humbling their deities to love, have taken
The shapes of beasts upon them: Jupiter
Became a bull, and bellow'd; the green Neptune
A ram, and bleated; and the fire-rob'd god,
Golden Apollo, a poor humble swain,
As I seem now: — their transformations
Were never for a piece of beauty rarer, —
Nor in a way so chaste, since my desires
Run not before mine honour, nor my lusts
Burn hotter than my faith.
    Per.   O, but, sir,
Your resolution cannot hold, when 'tis
Oppos'd, as it must be, by the power o' the king:
One of these two must be necessities,
Which then will speak, — that you must change this purpose,
Or I my life.
    Flo.   Thou dearest Perdita,
With these forc'd thoughts, I prithee, darken not
The mirth o' the feast: or I'll be thine, my fair,
Or not my father's; for I cannot be
Mine own, nor any thing to any, if

I be not thine: to this I am most constant,
Though destiny say no. Be merry, gentle;
Strangle such thoughts as these with any thing
That you behold the while. Your guests are coming:
Lift up your countenance, as it were the day
Of celebration of that nuptial which
We two have sworn shall come.
  Per.   O Lady Fortune,
Stand you auspicious!
  Flo.   See, your guests approach:
Address yourself to entertain them sprightly,
And let's be red with mirth.

Enter Shepherd, *with* Polixenes *and* Camillo *disguised;* Clown,
 Mopsa, Dorcas, *and other Shepherds and Shepherdesses.*

  Shep. Fie, daughter! when my old wife liv'd, upon
This day she was both pantler, butler, cook;
Both dame and servant; welcom'd all; serv'd all;
Would sing her song and dance her turn; now here,
At upper end o' the table, now i' the middle;
On his shoulder, and his; her face o' fire
With labour, and the thing she took to quench it,
She would to each one sip. You are retir'd,
As if you were a feasted one, and not
The hostess of the meeting: pray you, bid
These unknown friends to 's welcome; for it is
A way to make us better friends, more known.
Come, quench your blushes, and present yourself
That which you are, mistress o' the feast: come on,
And bid us welcome to your sheep-shearing,
As your good flock shall prosper.
  Per. [*to Pol.*]   Sir, welcome: —
It is my father's will I should take on me
The hostess-ship o' the day. — [*To Cam.*] You're welcome,
   sir. —
Give me those flowers there, Dorcas. — Reverend sirs,
For you there's rosemary and rue; these keep

Seeming and savour all the winter long:
Grace and remembrance be to you both,
And welcome to our shearing!
    Pol.   Shepherdess, —
A fair one are you, — well you fit our ages
With flowers of winter.
    Per.   Sir, the year growing ancient, —
Not yet on summer's death, nor on the birth
Of trembling winter, — the fair'st flowers o' the season
Are our carnations, and streak'd gillyvors,
Which some call nature's bastards: of that kind
Our rustic garden's barren; and I care not
To get slips of them.
    Pol.   Wherefore, gentle maiden,
Do you neglect them?
    Per.   For I have heard it said,
There is an art which, in their piedness, shares
With great creating nature.
    Pol.   Say there be;
Yet nature is made better by no mean,
But nature makes that mean: so, o'er that art
Which you say adds to nature, is an art
That nature makes. You see, sweet maid, we marry
A gentler scion to the wildest stock,
And make conceive a bark of baser kind
By bud of nobler race: this is an art
Which does mend nature, — change it rather; but
The art itself is nature.
    Per.   So it is.
    Pol. Then make your garden rich in gillyvors,
And do not call them bastards.
    Per.   I'll not put
The dibble in earth to set one slip of them;
No more than, were I painted, I would wish
This youth should say, 'twere well, and only therefore
Desire to breed by me. — Here's flowers for you;
Hot lavender, mints, savory, marjoram;

The marigold, that goes to bed wi' the sun,
And with him rises weeping: these are flowers
Of middle summer, and, I think, they 're given
To men of middle age. Ye're very welcome.
    Cam. I should leave grazing, were I of your flock,
And only live by gazing.
    Per.   Out, alas!
You'd be so lean, that blasts of January
Would blow you through and through. — Now, my fair'st
        friend,
I would I had some flowers o' the spring that might
Become your time of day; — and yours, and yours,
That wear upon your virgin branches yet
Your maidenheads growing: — O Proserpina,
For the flowers now, that, frighted, thou lett'st fall
From Dis's wagon! daffodils,
That come before the swallow dares, and take
The winds of March with beauty; violets dim,
But sweeter than the lids of Juno's eyes
Or Cytherea's breath; pale primroses,
That die unmarried, ere they can behold
Bright Phœbus in his strength, — a malady
Most incident to maids; bold oxlips and
The crown-imperial; lilies of all kinds,
The flower-de-luce being one! O, these I lack,
To make you garlands of; and my sweet friend,
To strew him o'er and o'er!
    Flo.   What, like a corse?
    Per. No, like a bank for love to lie and play on;
Not like a corse; or if, — not to be buried,
But quick, and in mine arms. — Come, take your flowers:
Methinks I play as I have seen them do
In Whitsun pastorals: sure, this robe of mine
Does change my disposition.
    Flo.   What you do
Still betters what is done. When you speak, sweet,
I'd have you do it ever: when you sing,

I'd have you buy and sell so; so give alms;
Pray so; and, for the ordering your affairs,
To sing them too: when you do dance, I wish you
A wave o' the sea, that you might ever do
Nothing but that; move still, still so,
And own no other function: each your doing,
So singular in each particular,
Crowns what you're doing in the present deeds,
That all your acts are queens.
  Per.   O Doricles,
Your praises are too large: but that your youth,
And the true blood which peeps so fairly through't,
Do plainly give you out an unstain'd shepherd,
With wisdom I might fear, my Doricles,
You woo'd me the false way.
  Flo.   I think you have
As little skill to fear as I have purpose
To put you to 't. — But, come; our dance, I pray:
Your hand, my Perdita: so turtles pair,
That never mean to part.
  Per.   I'll swear for 'em.
  Pol. This is the prettiest low-born lass that ever
Ran on the green-sward: nothing she does or seems
But smacks of something greater than herself,
Too noble for this place.
  Cam.   He tells her something
That makes her blood look out: good sooth, she is
The queen of curds and cream.
  Clo.   Come on, strike up!
  Dor. Mopsa must be your mistress: marry, garlic,
To mend her kissing with!
  Mop.   Now, in good time!
  Clo. Not a word, a word; we stand upon our manners. —
Come, strike up!
   [*Music. Here a dance of Shepherds and Shepherdesses.*
  Pol. Pray, good shepherd, what fair swain is this
Which dances with your daughter?

Shep. They call him Doricles; and boasts himself
To have a worthy feeding: I but have it
Upon his own report, and I believe it;
He looks like sooth. He says he loves my daughter:
I think so too; for never gaz'd the moon
Upon the water, as he'll stand, and read,
As 'twere, my daughter's eyes: and, to be plain,
I think there is not half a kiss to choose
Who loves another best.
   Pol.   She dances featly.
   Shep. So she does any thing; though I report it,
That should be silent: if young Doricles
Do light upon her, she shall bring him that
Which he not dreams of.

Enter a Servant.

   Serv. O master, if you did but hear the pedler at the door, you would never dance again after a tabor and pipe; no, the bagpipe could not move you: he sings several tunes faster than you'll tell money; he utters them as he had eaten ballads, and all men's ears grew to his tunes.

   Clo. He could never come better; he shall come in: I love a ballad but even too well, if it be doleful matter merrily set down, or a very pleasant thing indeed and sung lamentably.

   Serv. He hath songs for man or woman, of all sizes,—no milliner can so fit his customers with gloves: he has the prettiest love-songs for maids; so without bawdry, which is strange; with such delicate burdens of "dildos" and "fadings," "jump her and thump her;" and where some stretch-mouthed rascal would, as it were, mean mischief, and break a foul jape into the matter, he makes the maid to answer, "Whoop, do me no harm, good man;" puts him off, slights him, with "Whoop, do me no harm, good man."

   Pol. This is a brave fellow.

   Clo. Believe me, thou talkest of an admirable-conceited fellow. Has he any unbraided wares?

Serv. He hath ribands of all the colours i' the rainbow; points more than all the lawyers in Bohemia can learnedly handle, though they come to him by the gross; inkles, caddisses, cambrics, lawns: why, he sings 'em over, as they were gods or goddesses; you would think a smock were a she-angel, he so chants to the sleeve-hand, and the work about the square on't.

Clo. Prithee, bring him in; and let him approach singing.

Per. Forewarn him that he use no scurrilous words in's tunes. [*Exit Servant.*

Clo. You have of these pedlers, that have more in them than you'd think, sister.

Per. Ay, good brother, or go about to think.

Enter AUTOLYCUS, *singing.*

Lawn as white as driven snow;
Cyprus black as e'er was crow;
Gloves as sweet as damask roses;
Masks for faces and for noses;
Bugle-bracelet, necklace-amber,
Perfume for a lady's chamber;
Golden quoifs and stomachers,
For my lads to give their dears;
Pins and poking-sticks of steel,
What maids lack from head to heel:
Come buy of me, come; come buy, come buy;
Buy, lads, or else your lasses cry:
Come buy.

Clo. If I were not in love with Mopsa, thou shouldst take no money of me; but being enthralled as I am, it will also be the bondage of certain ribands and gloves.

Mop. I was promised them against the feast; but they come not too late now.

Dor. He hath promised you more than that, or there be liars.

Mop. He hath paid you all he promised you; may be, he has paid you more, — which will shame you to give him again.

Clo. Is there no manners left among maids? will they wear their plackets where they should bear their faces? Is there not milking-time, when you are going to bed, or kiln-hole, to whistle-off these secrets, but you must be tittle-tattling before all our guests? 'tis well they are whispering. Clamour your tongues, and not a word more.

Mop. I have done. Come, you promised me a tawdry-lace and a pair of sweet gloves.

Clo. Have I not told thee how I was cozened by the way, and lost all my money?

Aut. And, indeed, sir, there are cozeners abroad; therefore it behoves men to be wary.

Clo. Fear not thou, man, thou shalt lose nothing here.

Aut. 1 hope so, sir; for I have about me many parcels of charge.

Clo. What hast here? ballads?

Mop. Pray now, buy some: I love a ballad in print a-life, for then we are sure they are true.

Aut. Here's one to a very doleful tune, How a usurer's wife was brought to bed of twenty money-bags at a burden, and how she longed to eat adders' heads and toads carbonadoed.

Mop. Is it true, think you?

Aut. Very true; and but a month old.

Dor. Bless me from marrying a usurer!

Aut. Here's the midwife's name to 't, one Mistress Taleporter, and five or six honest wives' that were present. Why should I carry lies abroad?

Mop. Pray you now, buy it.

Clo. Come on, lay it by: and let's first see more ballads; we'll buy the other things anon.

Aut. Here's another ballad, Of a fish, that appeared upon the coast on Wednesday the fourscore of April, forty thousand fathom above water, and sung this ballad against the hard hearts of maids: it was thought she was a woman, and was turned into a cold fish for she would not exchange flesh with one that loved her: the ballad is very pitiful, and as true.

Dor. Is it true too, think you?

Aut. Five justices' hands at it, and witnesses more than my pack will hold.

Clo. Lay it by too: another.

Aut. This is a merry ballad, but a very pretty one.

Mop. Let's have some merry ones.

Aut. Why, this is a passing merry one, and goes to the tune of, "Two maids wooing a man:" there's scarce a maid westward but she sings it; 'tis in request, I can tell you.

Mop. We can both sing it: if thou 'lt bear a part, thou shalt hear; 'tis in three parts.

Dor. We had the tune on 't a month ago.

Aut. I can bear my part; you must know 'tis my occupation: have at it with you!

Song.

 AUT. *Get you hence, for I must go;*
Where, it fits not you to know.
  DOR. *Whither?* MOP. *O, whither?* DOR. *Whither?*
 MOP. *It becomes thy oath full well,*
Thou to me thy secrets tell:
  DOR. *Me too, let me go thither*

 MOP. *Or thou go'st to the grange or mill:*
 DOR. *If to either, thou dost ill.*
  AUT. *Neither.* DOR. *What, neither?* AUT. *Neither.*
 DOR. *Thou hast sworn my love to be;*
 MOP. *Thou hast sworn it more to me:*
  Then, whither go'st? say, whither?

Clo. We 'll have this song out anon by ourselves: my father and the gentlemen are in sad talk, and we 'll not trouble them. — Come, bring away thy pack after me. — Wenches, I 'll buy for you both. — Pedler, let 's have the first choice. — Follow me, girls. [*Exit with Dorcas and Mopsa.*

Aut. And you shall pay well for 'em. —

   Will you buy any tape,   [*Singing.*
    Or lace for your cape,
   My dainty duck, my dear-a?

Any silk, any thread,
Any toys for your head,
Of the new'st and fin'st, fin'st wear-a?
Come to the pedler ;
Money's a meddler,
That doth utter all men's ware-a.

[*Exit.*

Re-enter Servant.

Serv. Master, there is three carters, three shepherds, three neat-herds, three swine-herds, that have made themselves all men of hair, — they call themselves Saltiers: and they have a dance which the wenches say is a gallimaufry of gambols, because they are not in 't; but they themselves are o' the mind, — if it be not too rough for some that know little but bowling, — it will please plentifully.

Shep. Away! we 'll none on 't: here has been too much homely foolery already. — I know, sir, we weary you.

Pol. You weary those that refresh us: pray, let 's see these four threes of herdsmen.

Serv. One three of them, by their own report, sir, hath danced before the king; and not the worst of the three but jumps twelve foot and a half by the squire.

Shep. Leave your prating: since these good men are pleased, let them come in; but quickly now.

Serv. Why, they stay at door, sir. [*Exit.*

Enter twelve Rustics *habited like Satyrs, who dance, and then exeunt.*

Pol. O, father, you 'll know more of that hereafter. — [*To Cam.*] Is it not too far gone? 'Tis time to part them. He 's simple and tells much. — How now, fair shepherd! Your heart is full of something that does take Your mind from feasting. Sooth, when I was young, And handed love as you do, I was wont To load my she with knacks: I would have ransack'd The pedler's silken treasury, and have pour'd it To her acceptance; you have let him go,

And nothing marted with him. If your lass
Interpretation should abuse, and call this
Your lack of love or bounty, you were straited
For a reply, at least if you make care
Of happy holding her.

 Flo.   Old sir, I know
She prizes not such trifles as these are:
The gifts she looks from me are pack'd and lock'd
Up in my heart; which I have given already,
But not deliver'd. — O, hear me breathe my life
Before this ancient sir, who, it should seem,
Hath sometime lov'd! I take thy hand, — this hand,
As soft as dove's down and as white as it,
Or Ethiop's tooth, or the fann'd snow that's bolted
By the northern blasts twice o'er.

 Pol.   What follows this? —
How prettily the young swain seems to wash
The hand was fair before! — I've put you out: —
But to your protestation; let me hear
What you profess.

 Flo.   Do, and be witness to 't.
 Pol. And this my neighbour too?
 Flo.   And he, and more
Than he, and men, the earth, the heavens, and all: —
That, were I crown'd the most imperial monarch,
Thereof most worthy; were I the fairest youth
That ever made eye swerve; had force and knowledge
More than was ever man's, — I would not prize them
Without her love; for her employ them all;
Commend them, and condemn them, to her service,
Or to their own perdition.

 Pol.   Fairly offer'd.
 Cam. This shows a sound affection.
 Shep.   But, my daughter,
Say you the like to him?

 Per.   I cannot speak
So well, nothing so well; no, nor mean better:

By the pattern of mine own thoughts I cut out
The purity of his.
    Shep.   Take hands, a bargain! —
And, friends unknown, you shall bear witness to 't:
I give my daughter to him, and will make
Her portion equal his.
    Flo.   O, that must be
I' the virtue of your daughter: one being dead,
I shall have more than you can dream of yet;
Enough then for your wonder. But, come on,
Contract us 'fore these witnesses.
    Shep.   Come, your hand; —
And, daughter, yours.
    Pol.   Soft, swain, awhile, beseech you;
Have you a father?
    Flo.   I have: but what of him?
    Pol. Knows he of this?
    Flo.   He neither does nor shall.
    Pol. Methinks a father
Is, at the nuptial of his son, a guest
That best becomes the table. Pray you, once more;
Is not your father grown incapable
Of reasonable affairs? is he not stupid
With age and altering rheums? can he speak? hear?
Know man from man? dispute his own estate?
Lies he not bed-rid? and again does nothing
But what he did being childish?
    Flo.   No, good sir;
He has his health, and ampler strength indeed
Than most have of his age.
    Pol.   By my white beard,
You offer him, if this be so, a wrong
Something unfilial: reason my son
Should choose himself a wife; but as good reason
The father, — all whose joy is nothing else
But fair posterity, — should hold some counsel
In such a business.

Flo.   I yield all this;
But, for some other reasons, my grave sir,
Which 'tis not fit you know, I not acquaint
My father of this business.
   Pol.   Let him know 't.
   Flo. He shall not.
   Pol.   Prithee, let him.
   Flo.   No, he must not.
   Shep. Let him, my son: he shall not need to grieve
At knowing of thy choice.
   Flo.   Come, come, he must not. —
Mark our contráct.
   Pol.   Mark your divorce, young sir,
                       [*Discovering himself.*
Whom son I dare not call; thou art too base
To be acknowledg'd: thou a sceptre's heir,
That thus affect'st a sheep-hook! — Thou old traitor,
I'm sorry that, by hanging thee, I can but
Shorten thy life one week. — And thou, fresh piece
Of excellent witchcraft, who, of force, must know
The royal fool thou cop'st with, —
   Shep.   O, my heart!
   Pol. I'll have thy beauty scratch'd with briers, and made
More homely than thy state. — For thee, fond boy,
If I may ever know thou dost but sigh
That thou no more shalt see this knack, — as never
I mean thou shalt, — we'll bar thee from succession;
Not hold thee of our blood, no, not our kin,
Far' than Deucalion off: — mark thou my words: —
Follow us to the court. — Thou churl, for this time,
Though full of our displeasure, yet we free thee
From the dead blow of it. — And you, enchantment,
Worthy enough a herdsman; yea, him too
That makes himself, but for our honour therein,
Unworthy thee, — if ever henceforth thou
These rural latches to his entrance open,
Or hoop his body more with thy embraces,

I will devise a death as cruel for thee
As thou art tender to 't. [*Exit.*

 Per.   Even here undone!
I was not much afeard; for once or twice
I was about to speak, and tell him plainly,
The selfsame sun that shines upon his court
Hides not his visage from our cottage, but
Looks on alike. — [*To Flo.*] Will't please you, sir, be gone?
I told you what would come of this: beseech you,
Of your own state take care: this dream of mine, —
Being now awake, I'll queen it no inch further,
But milk my ewes and weep.
 Cam.   Why, how now, father!
Speak ere thou diest.
 Shep.   I cannot speak, nor think,
Nor dare to know that which I know. — [*To Florizel*] O sir,
You have undone a man of fourscore three,
That thought to fill his grave in quiet, — yea,
To die upon the bed my father died,
To lie close by his honest bones! but now
Some hangman must put on my shroud, and lay me
Where no priest shovels-in dust. — [*To Perdita*] O cursèd
   wretch,
That knew'st this was the prince, and wouldst adventure
To mingle faith with him! — Undone! undone!
If I might die within this hour, I've liv'd
To die when I desire. [*Exit.*
 Flo.   Why look you so upon me?
I am but sorry, not afeard; delay'd,
But nothing alter'd: what I was, I am;
More straining on for plucking back; not following
My leash unwillingly.
 Cam.   Gracious my lord,
You know your father's temper: at this time
He will allow no speech, — which I do guess
You do not purpose to him; — and as hardly
Will he endure your sight as yet, I fear:

Then, till the fury of his highness settle,
Come not before him.
 Flo.   I not purpose it.
I think Camillo?
 Cam.   Even he, my lord.
 Per. How often have I told you 'twould be thus!
How often said my dignity would last
But till 'twere known!
 Flo.   It cannot fail but by
The violation of my faith; and then
Let nature crush the sides o' th' earth together,
And mar the seeds within! — Lift up thy looks: —
From my succession wipe me, father! I
Am heir to my affection.
 Cam.   Be advis'd.
 Flo. I am, — and by my fancy: if my reason
Will thereto be obedient, I have reason;
If not, my senses, better pleas'd with madness,
Do bid it welcome.
 Cam.   This is desperate, sir.
 Flo. So call it: but it does fulfil my vow;
I needs must think it honesty. Camillo,
Not for Bohemia, nor the pomp that may
Be thereat glean'd; for all the sun sees, or
The close earth wombs, or the profound sea hides
In unknown fathoms, will I break my oath
To this my fair belov'd: therefore, I pray you,
As you've e'er been my father's honour'd friend,
When he shall miss me, — as, in faith, I mean not
To see him any more, — cast your good counsels
Upon his passion: let myself and fortune
Tug for the time to come. This you may know,
And so deliver, — I am put to sea
With her who here I cannot hold on shore;
And, most opportune to our need, I have
A vessel rides fast by, but not prepar'd
For this design. What course I mean to hold

Shall nothing benefit your knowledge, nor
Concern me the reporting.
  Cam.   O my lord,
I would your spirit were easier for advice,
Or stronger for your need!
  Flo.   Hark, Perdita. — [*Taking her aside.*
[*To Camillo*] I'll hear you by and by.
  Cam.   He's irremovable,
Resolv'd for flight. Now were I happy, if
His going I could frame to serve my turn;
Save him from danger, do him love and honour;
Purchase the sight again of dear Sicilia,
And that unhappy king my master, whom
I so much thirst to see.
  Flo.   Now, good Camillo,
I am so fraught with curious business, that
I leave out ceremony.
  Cam.   Sir, I think
You've heard of my poor services, i' the love
That I have borne your father?
  Flo.   Very nobly
Have you deserv'd: it is my father's music
To speak your deeds; not little of his care
To have them recompens'd as thought on.
  Cam.   Well, my lord,
If you may please to think I love the king,
And, through him, what is near'st to him, which is
Your gracious self, embrace but my direction, —
If your more ponderous and settled project
May suffer alteration, — on mine honour
I'll point you where you shall have such receiving
As shall become your highness; where you may
Enjoy your mistress, — from the whom, I see,
There's no disjunction to be made, but by,
As heavens forfend! your ruin; — marry her;
And — with my best endeavours in your absence —

Your discontenting father strive to qualify,
And bring him up to liking.
   Flo.   How, Camillo,
May this, almost a miracle, be done?
That I may call thee something more than man,
And, after that, trust to thee.
   Cam.   Have you thought on
A place whereto you'll go?
   Flo.   Not any yet:
But as th' unthought-on accident is guilty
To what we wildly do, so we profess
Ourselves to be the slaves of chance, and flies
Of every wind that blows.
   Cam.   Then list to me:
This follows, — if you will not change your purpose,
But undergo this flight, — make for Sicilia;
And there present yourself and your fair princess —
For so I see she must be — 'fore Leontes:
She shall be habited as it becomes
The partner of your bed. Methinks I see
Leontes opening his free arms, and weeping
His welcomes forth; asks thee, the son, forgiveness,
As 'twere i' the father's person; kisses the hands
Of your fresh princess; o'er and o'er divides him
'Twixt his unkindness and his kindness, — th' one
He chides to hell, and bids the other grow
Faster than thought or time.
   Flo.   Worthy Camillo,
What colour for my visitation shall I
Hold up before him?
   Cam.   Sent by the king your father
To greet him and to give him comforts. Sir,
The manner of your bearing towards him, with
What you, as from your father, shall deliver,
Things known betwixt us three, I'll write you down:
The which shall point you forth at every sitting
What you must say; that he shall not perceive

But that you have your father's bosom there,
And speak his very heart.
    Flo.   I am bound to you:
There is some sap in this.
    Cam.   A course more promising
Than a wild dedication of yourselves
To unpath'd waters, undream'd shores, most certain
To miseries enough: no hope to help you;
But, as you shake off one, to take another:
Nothing so certain as your anchors; who
Do their best office, if they can but stay you
Where you'll be loth to be: besides, you know
Prosperity's the very bond of love,
Whose fresh complexion and whose heart together
Affliction alters.
    Per.   One of these is true:
I think affliction may subdue the cheek,
But not take in the mind.
    Cam.   Yea, say you so?
There shall not, at your father's house, these seven years
Be born another such.
    Flo.   My good Camillo,
She is as forward of her breeding as
She is i' the rear 'our birth.
    Cam.   I cannot say 'tis pity
She lacks instructions, for she seems a mistress
To most that teach.
    Per.   Your pardon, sir, for this;
I'll blush you thanks.
    Flo.   My prettiest Perdita! —
But, O, the thorns we stand upon! — Camillo, —
Preserver of my father, now of me,
The medicine of our house! — how shall we do?
We are not furnish'd like Bohemia's son,
Nor shall appear in Sicilia.
    Cam.   My lord,
Fear none of this: I think you know my fortunes

Do all lie there: it shall be so my care
To have you royally appointed as if
The scene you play were mine. For instance, sir,
That you may know you shall not want, — one word.

[They talk aside.

Re-enter AUTOLYCUS.

Aut. Ha, ha! what a fool Honesty is! and Trust, his sworn brother, a very simple gentleman! I have sold all my trumpery; not a counterfeit stone, not a riband, glass, pomander, brooch, table-book, ballad, knife, tape, glove, shoetie, bracelet, horn-ring, to keep my pack from fasting: they throng who should buy first, as if my trinkets had been hallowed, and brought a benediction to the buyer: by which means I saw whose purse was best in picture; and what I saw, to my good use I remembered. My clown — who wants but something to be a reasonable man — grew so in love with the wenches' song, that he would not stir his pettitoes till he had both tune and words; which so drew the rest of the herd to me, that all their other senses stuck in ears: you might have pinched a placket, — it was senseless; 'twas nothing to geld a codpiece of a purse, — I would have filed keys off that hung in chains: no hearing, no feeling, but my sir's song, and admiring the nothing of it. So that, in this time of lethargy, I picked and cut most of their festival purses; and had not the old man come in with a whoobub against his daughter and the king's son, and scared my choughs from the chaff, I had not left a purse alive in the whole army.

[*Camillo, Florizel, and Perdita come forward.*

Cam. Nay, but my letters, by this means being there
So soon as you arrive, shall clear that doubt.

Flo. And those that you'll procure from King Leontes, —

Cam. Shall satisfy your father.

Per. Happy be you!
All that you speak shows fair.

Cam. Who have we here?

[*Seeing Autolycus.*

We'll make an instrument of this; omit
Nothing may give us aid.

Aut. [*aside*] If they have overheard me now, — why, hanging.

Cam. How now, good fellow! why shakest thou so? Fear not, man; here's no harm intended to thee.

Aut. I am a poor fellow, sir.

Cam. Why, be so still; here's nobody will steal that from thee: yet, for the outside of thy poverty, we must make an exchange; therefore disease thee instantly,— thou must think there's a necessity in't,— and change garments with this gentleman: though the pennyworth on his side be the worst, yet hold thee, there's some boot. [*Giving money.*

Aut. I am a poor fellow, sir. — [*Aside*] I know ye well enough.

Cam. Nay, prithee, dispatch: the gentleman is half flayed already.

Aut. Are you in earnest, sir? — [*Aside*] I smell the trick on 't.

Flo. Dispatch, I prithee.

Aut. Indeed, I have had earnest; but I cannot with conscience take it.

Cam. Unbuckle, unbuckle. —

[*Florizel and Autolycus exchange garments.*

Fortunate mistress, — let my prophecy
Come home to ye! — you must retire yourself
Into some covert: take your sweetheart's hat,
And pluck it o'er your brows; muffle your face;
Dismantle you; and, as you can, disliken
The truth of your own seeming; that you may —
For I do fear eyes over 's — to shipboard
Get undescried.

Per. I see the play so lies
That I must bear a part.

Cam. No remedy. —
Have you done there?

Flo.   Should I now meet my father,
He would not call me son.
    Cam.   Nay, you shall have no hat. —
                                  [*Giving it to Perdita.*
Come, lady, come. — Farewell, my friend.
    Aut.   Adieu, sir.
    Flo. O Perdita, what have we twain forgot!
Pray you, a word.   . [*They converse apart.*
    Cam. [*aside*] What I do next, shall be to tell the king
Of this escape, and whither they are bound;
Wherein, my hope is, I shall so prevail
To force him after: in whose company
I shall review Sicilia, for whose sight
I have a woman's longing.
    Flo.   Fortune speed us! —
Thus we set on, Camillo, to the sea-side.
    Cam. The swifter speed the better.
                    [*Exeunt Florizel, Perdita, and Camillo.*
    Aut. I understand the business, I hear it: to have an open ear, a quick eye, and a nimble hand, is necessary for a cut-purse; a good nose is requisite also, to smell out work for the other senses. I see this is the time that the unjust man doth thrive. What an exchange had this been without boot! what a boot is here with this exchange! Sure, the gods do this year connive at us, and we may do any thing extempore. The prince himself is about a piece of iniquity, — stealing away from his father with his clog at his heels: if I thought it were not a piece of honesty to acquaint the king withal, I would do 't: I hold it the more knavery to conceal it; and therein am I constant to my profession.

               Re-enter Clown *and* Shepherd.

Aside, aside; — here is more matter for a hot brain: every lane's end, every shop, church, session, hanging, yields a careful man work.
    Clo. See, see; what a man you are now! There is no other way but to tell the king she's a changeling, and none of your flesh and blood.

Shep. Nay, but hear me.

Clo. Nay, but hear me.

Shep. Go to, then.

Clo. She being none of your flesh and blood, your flesh and blood has not offended the king; and so your flesh and blood is not to be punished by him. Show those things you found about her; those secret things, all but what she has with her: this being done, let the law go whistle; I warrant you.

Shep. I will tell the king all, every word, yea, and his son's pranks too, — who, I may say, is no honest man neither to his father nor to me, to go about to make me the king's brother-in-law.

Clo. Indeed, brother-in-law was the furthest off you could have been to him; and then your blood had been the dearer by I know not how much an ounce.

Aut. [*aside*] Very wisely, puppies!

Shep. Well, let us to the king: there is that in this fardel will make him scratch his beard.

Aut. [*aside*] I know not what impediment this complaint may be to the flight of my master.

Clo. Pray heartily he be at the palace.

Aut. [*aside*] Though I am not naturally honest, I am so sometimes by chance: — let me pocket up my pedler's excrement. [*Takes off his false beard.*] — How now, rustics! whither are you bound?

Shep. To the palace, an it like your worship.

Aut. Your affairs there, what, with whom, the condition of that fardel, the place of your dwelling, your names, your ages, of what having, breeding, and any thing that is fitting to be known, discover.

Clo. We are but plain fellows, sir.

Aut. A lie; you are rough and hairy. Let me have no lying: it becomes none but tradesmen, and they often give us soldiers the lie: but we pay them for it with stamped coin, not stabbing steel; therefore they do not give us the lie.

Clo. Your worship had like to have given us one, if you had not taken yourself with the manner.

Shep. Are you a courtier, an't like you, sir?

Aut. Whether it like me or no, I am a courtier. See'st thou not the air of the court in these enfoldings? hath not my gait in it the measure of the court? receives not thy nose court-odour from me? reflect I not on thy baseness court-contempt? Thinkest thou, for that I insinuate, or touse from thee thy business, I am therefore no courtier? I am courtier cap-a-pè; and one that will either push on or pluck back thy business there: whereupon I command thee to open thy affair.

Shep. My business, sir, is to the king.

Aut. What advocate hast thou to him?

Shep. I know not, an't like you.

Clo. [*aside to Shep.*] Advocate 's the court-word for a present: say you have none.

Shep. None, sir; I have no pheasant, cock nor hen.

Aut. How bless'd are we that are not simple men!
Yet nature might have made me as these are,
Therefore I'll not disdain.

Clo. [*aside to Shep.*] This cannot be but a great courtier.

Shep. [*aside to Clo.*] His garments are rich, but he wears them not handsomely.

Clo. [*aside to Shep.*] He seems to be the more noble in being fantastical: a great man, I'll warrant; I know by the picking on 's teeth.

Aut. The fardel there? what 's i' the fardel? Wherefore that box?

Shep. Sir, there lies such secrets in this fardel and box, which none must know but the king; and which he shall know within this hour, if I may come to the speech of him.

Aut. Age, thou hast lost thy labour.

Shep. Why, sir?

Aut. The king is not at the palace; he is gone aboard a new ship to purge melancholy and air himself: for, if thou beest capable of things serious, thou must know the king is full of grief.

Shep. So 'tis said, sir, — about his son, that should have married a shepherd's daughter.

Aut. If that shepherd be not in hand-fast, let him fly: the curses he shall have, the tortures he shall feel, will break the back of man, the heart of monster.

Clo. Think you so, sir?

Aut. Not he alone shall suffer what wit can make heavy and vengeance bitter; but those that are germane to him, though removed fifty times, shall all come under the hangman: which though it be great pity, yet it is necessary. An old sheep-whistling rogue, a ram-tender, to offer to have his daughter come into grace! Some say he shall be stoned; but that death is too soft for him, say I: draw our throne into a sheep-cote! all deaths are too few, the sharpest too easy.

Clo. Has the old man e'er a son, sir, do you hear, an't like you, sir?

Aut. He has a son, — who shall be flayed alive; then, 'nointed over with honey, set on the head of a wasps' nest; there stand till he be three quarters and a dram dead; then recovered again with aqua-vitæ or some other hot infusion; then, raw as he is, and in the hottest day prognostication proclaims, shall he be set against a brick-wall, the sun looking with a southward eye upon him, — where he is to behold him with flies blown to death. But what talk we of these traitorly rascals, whose miseries are to be smiled at, their offences being so capital? Tell me — for you seem to be honest plain men — what you have to the king: being something gently considered, I'll bring you where he is aboard, tender your persons to his presence, whisper him in your behalfs; and if it be in man besides the king to effect your suits, here is man shall do it.

Clo. [*aside to Shep.*] He seems to be of great authority: close with him; give him gold: an though authority be a stubborn bear, yet he is oft led by the nose with gold: show the inside of your purse to the outside of his hand, and no more ado. Remember, — stoned, and flayed alive.

Shep. An't please you, sir, to undertake the business for

us, here is that gold I have: I'll make it as much more, and leave this young man in pawn till I bring it you.

Aut. After I have done what I promised?

Shep. Ay, sir.

Aut. Well, give me the moiety. — Are you a party in this business?

Clo. In some sort, sir: but though my case be a pitiful one, I hope I shall not be flayed out of it.

Aut. O, that's the case of the shepherd's son: — hang him, he'll be made an example.

Clo. [*aside to Shep.*] Comfort, good comfort! We must to the king, and show our strange sights: he must know 'tis none of your daughter nor my sister; we are gone else. — Sir, I will give you as much as this old man does, when the business is performed; and remain, as he says, your pawn till it be brought you.

Aut. I will trust you. Walk before toward the sea-side; go on the right hand: I will but look upon the hedge, and follow you.

Clo. [*aside to Shep.*] We are blessed in this man, as I may say, even blessed.

Shep. [*aside to Clo.*] Let's before, as he bids us: he was provided to do us good. [*Exeunt Shepherd and Clown.*

Aut. If I had a mind to be honest, I see Fortune would not suffer me: she drops booties in my mouth. I am courted now with a double occasion, — gold, and a means to do the prince my master good; which who knows how that may turn back to my advancement? I will bring these two moles, these blind ones, aboard him: if he think it fit to shore them again, and that the complaint they have to the king concerns him nothing, let him call me rogue for being so far officious; for I am proof against that title, and what shame else belongs to 't. To him will I present them: there may be matter in it.
[*Exit.*

ACT V.

SCENE I. *Sicilia. A room in the palace of* LEONTES.

Enter LEONTES, CLEOMENES, DION, PAULINA, *and others.*

Cleo. Sir, you have done enough, and have perform'd
A saint-like sorrow: no fault could you make,
Which you have not redeem'd; indeed, paid down
More penitence than done trespass: at the last,
Do as the heavens have done, forget your evil;
With them, forgive yourself.
 Leon.   Whilst I remember
Her and her virtues, I cannot forget
My blemishes in them; and so still think of
The wrong I did myself: which was so much,
That heirless it hath made my kingdom; and
Destroy'd the sweet'st companion that e'er man
Bred his hopes out of.
 Paul.   True, too true, my lord:
If, one by one, you wedded all the world,
Or from the all that are took something good,
To make a perfect woman, she you kill'd
Would be unparallel'd.
 Leon.   I think so. Kill'd!
Kill'd! — she I kill'd! I did so: but thou strik'st me
Sorely, to say I did; it is as bitter
Upon thy tongue as in my thought: now, good, now,
Say so but seldom.
 Cleo.   Not at all, good lady:
You might have spoke a thousand things that would
Have done the time more benefit, and grac'd
Your kindness better.
 Paul.   You are one of those
Would have him wed again.
 Dion.   If you would not so,
You pity not the state, nor the remembrance
Of his most sovereign name; consider little
What dangers, by his highness' fail of issue,

May drop upon his kingdom, and devour
Incertain lookers-on. What were more holy
Than to rejoice the former queen is well?
What holier than, — for royalty's repair,
For present comfort, and for future good, —
To bless the bed of majesty again
With a sweet-fellow to 't?

  Paul.   There is none worthy,
Respecting her that's gone. Besides, the gods
Will have fulfill'd their secret purposes;
For has not the divine Apollo said,
Is 't not the tenour of his oracle,
That King Leontes shall not have an heir
Till his lost child be found? which that it shall,
Is all as monstrous to our human reason
As my Antigonus to break his grave
And come again to me; who, on my life,
Did perish with the infant. 'Tis your counsel
My lord should to the heavens be contrary,
Oppose against their wills. — [*To Leontes*] Care not for issue;
The crown will find an heir: great Alexander
Left his to the worthiest; so his successor
Was like to be the best.

  Leon.   Good Paulina,
Who hast the memory of Hermione,
I know, in honour, — O, that ever I
Had squar'd me to thy counsel! — then, even now,
I might have look'd upon my queen's full eyes;
Have taken treasure from her lips, —

  Paul.   And left them
More rich for what they yielded.

  Leon.   Thou speak'st truth.
No more such wives; therefore, no wife: one worse,
And better us'd, would make her sainted spirit
Again possess her corpse, and on this stage —
Where we offend her now — appear soul-vex'd,
And begin, "Why to me?"

Paul.   Had she such power,
She had just cause.
    Leon.   She had; and would incense me
To murder her I married.
    Paul.   I should so.
Were I the ghost that walk'd, I'd bid you mark
Her eye, and tell me for what dull part in't
You chose her; then I'd shriek, that even your ears
Should rift to hear me; and the words that follow'd
Should be, "Remember mine."
    Leon.   Stars, stars,
And all eyes else dead coals! — fear thou no wife;
I'll have no wife, Paulina.
    Paul.   Will you swear
Never to marry but by my free leave?
    Leon. Never, Paulina; so be bless'd my spirit!
    Paul. Then, good my lords, bear witness to his oath.
    Cleo. You tempt him over-much.
    Paul.   Unless another,
As like Hermione as is her picture,
Affront his eye.
    Cleo. Good madam, —
    Paul.   I have done.
Yet, if my lord will marry, — if you will, sir,
No remedy, but you will, — give me the office
To choose you a queen: she shall not be so young
As was your former; but she shall be such
As, walk'd your first queen's ghost, it should take joy
To see her in your arms.
    Leon.   My true Paulina,
We shall not marry till thou bidd'st us.
    Paul.   That
Shall be when your first queen's again in breath;
Never till then.

             Enter a Gentleman.

    Gent. One that gives out himself Prince Florizel,
Son of Polixenes, with his princess, — she

The fair'st I've yet beheld, — desires access
To your high presence.
  Leon.   What with him? he comes not
Like to his father's greatness: his approach,
So out of circumstance and sudden, tells us
'Tis not a visitation fram'd, but forc'd
By need and accident. What train?
  Gent.   But few,
And those but mean.
  Leon.   His princess, say you, with him?
  Gent. Ay, the most peerless piece of earth, I think,
That e'er the sun shone bright on.
  Paul.   O Hermione,
As every present time doth boast itself
Above a better gone, so must thy grave
Give way to what's seen now! Sir, you yourself
Have said and writ so; but your writing now
Is colder than that theme, "She had not been,
Nor was not to be equall'd;" — thus your verse
Flow'd with her beauty once: 'tis shrewdly ebb'd,
To say you've seen a better.
  Gent.   Pardon, madam:
The one I have almost forgot, — your pardon;
The other, when she has obtain'd your eye,
Will have your tongue too. This is a creature,
Would she begin a sect, might quench the zeal
Of all professors else; make proselytes
Of who she but bid follow.
  Paul.   How! not women?
  Gent. Women will love her, that she is a woman
More worth than any man; men, that she is
The rarest of all women.
  Leon.   Go, Cleomenes;
Yourself, assisted with your honour'd friends,
Bring them to our embracement. [*Exeunt Cleo. and others.*
        Still, 'tis strange
He thus should steal upon us.

Paul.   Had our prince,
Jewel of children, seen this hour, he had pair'd
Well with this lord: there was not full a month
Between their births.
    Leon.   Prithee, no more; cease; thou know'st
He dies to me again when talk'd of: sure,
When I shall see this gentleman, thy speeches
Will bring me to consider that which may
Unfurnish me of reason. — They are come.

Re-enter CLEOMENES *and others, with* FLORIZEL *and* PERDITA.

Your mother was most true to wedlock, prince;
For she did print your royal father off,
Conceiving you: were I but twenty-one,
Your father's image is so hit in you,
His very air, that I should call you brother,
As I did him, and speak of something wildly
By us perform'd before. Most dearly welcome!
And your fair princess-goddess! — O, alas,
I lost a couple, that 'twixt heaven and earth
Might thus have stood, begetting wonder, as
You, gracious couple, do! and then I lost —
All mine own folly — the society,
Amity too, of your brave father, whom,
Though bearing misery, I desire my life
Once more to look on him.
    Flo.   By his command
Have I here touch'd Sicilia, and from him
Give you all greetings, that a king, at friend,
Can send his brother: and, but infirmity —
Which waits upon worn times — hath something seiz'd
His wish'd ability, he had himself
The lands and waters 'twixt your throne and his
Measur'd to look upon you; whom he loves —
He bade me say so — more than all the sceptres,
And those that bear them, living.
    Leon.   O my brother,

Good gentleman, the wrongs I have done thee stir
Afresh within me; and these thy offices,
So rarely kind, are as interpreters
Of my behindhand slackness! — Welcome hither,
As is the spring to the earth. And hath he too
Expos'd this paragon to the fearful usage —
At least ungentle — of the dreadful Neptune,
To greet a man not worth her pains, much less
Th' adventure of her person?
  Flo.   Good my lord,
She came from Libya.
  Leon.   Where the warlike Smalus,
That noble honour'd lord, is fear'd and lov'd?
  Flo. Most royal sir, from thence; from him, whose daughter
His tears proclaim'd his, parting with her: thence,
A prosperous south-wind friendly, we have cross'd,
To execute the charge my father gave me,
For visiting your highness: my best train
I have from your Sicilian shores dismiss'd;
Who for Bohemia bend, to signify
Not only my success in Libya, sir,
But my arrival, and my wife's, in safety
Here where we are.
  Leon.   The blessèd gods
Purge all infection from our air whilst you
Do climate here! You have a holy father,
A graceful gentleman; against whose person,
So sacred as it is, I have done sin:
For which the heavens, taking angry note,
Have left me issueless; and your father's bless'd,
As he from heaven merits it, with you,
Worthy his goodness. What might I have been,
Might I a son and daughter now have look'd on,
Such goodly things as you!
      Enter a Lord.
  Lord.   Most noble sir,
That which I shall report will bear no credit,

Were not the proof so nigh. Please you, great sir,
Bohemia greets you from himself by me;
Desires you to attach his son, who has —
His dignity and duty both cast off —
Fled from his father, from his hopes, and with
A shepherd's daughter.
 Leon.   Where's Bohemia? speak.
 Lord. Here in your city; I now came from him:
I speak amazedly; and it becomes
My marvel and my message. To your court
Whiles he was hastening, — in the chase, it seems,
Of this fair couple, — meets he on the way
The father of this seeming lady, and
Her brother, having both their country quitted
With this young prince.
 Flo.   Camillo has betray'd me;
Whose honour and whose honesty till now
Endur'd all weathers.
 Lord. Lay't so to his charge:
He's with the king your father.
 Leon.   Who? Camillo?
 Lord. Camillo, sir; I spake with him; who now
Has these poor men in question. Never saw I
Wretches so quake: they kneel, they kiss the earth;
Forswear themselves as often as they speak:
Bohemia stops his ears, and threatens them
With divers deaths in death.
 Per.   O my poor father! —
The heaven sets spies upon us, will not have
Our contract celebrated.
 Leon.   You are married?
 Flo. We are not, sir, nor are we like to be;
The stars, I see, will kiss the valleys first: —
The odds for high and low's alike.
 Leon.   My lord.
Is this the daughter of a king?

Flo.   She is,
When once she is my wife.
    Leon. That "once," I see by your good father's speed,
Will come on very slowly. I am sorry,
Most sorry, you have broken from his liking,
Where you were tied in duty; and as sorry
Your choice is not so rich in worth as beauty,
That you might well enjoy her.
    Flo.   Dear, look up:
Though Fortune, visible an enemy,
Should chase us, with my father, power no jot
Hath she to change our loves. — Beseech you, sir,
Remember since you ow'd no more to time
Than I do now: with thought of such affections,
Step forth mine advocate; at your request
My father will grant precious things as trifles.
    Leon. Would he do so, I'd beg your precious mistress,
Which he counts but a trifle.
    Paul.   Sir, my liege,
Your eye hath too much youth in 't: not a month
'Fore your queen died, she was more worth such gazes
Than what you look on now.
    Leon.   I thought of her,
Even in these looks I made. — [*To Florizel*] But your petition
Is yet unanswer'd. I will to your father:
Your honour not o'erthrown by your desires,
I'm friend to them and you: upon which errand
I now go toward him; therefore follow me,
And mark what way I make: come, good my lord. [*Exeunt.*

    Scene II. *The same. Before the palace of* Leontes.

        Enter Autolycus *and a* Gentleman.

    Aut. Beseech you, sir, were you present at this relation?
    First Gent. I was by at the opening of the fardel, heard the old shepherd deliver the manner how he found it: whereupon, after a little amazedness, we were all commanded out

of the chamber; only this, methought I heard the shepherd say he found the child.

Aut. I would most gladly know the issue of it.

First Gent. I make a broken delivery of the business;— but the changes I perceived in the king and Camillo were very notes of admiration: they seemed almost, with staring on one another, to tear the cases of their eyes; there was speech in their dumbness, language in their very gesture; they looked as they had heard of a world ransomed, or one destroyed: a notable passion of wonder appeared in them; but the wisest beholder, that knew no more but seeing, could not say if the importance, were joy or sorrow,— but in the extremity of the one, it must needs be.— Here comes a gentleman that happily knows more.

Enter another Gentleman.

The news, Rogero?

Sec. Gent. Nothing but bonfires: the oracle is fulfilled; the king's daughter is found: such a deal of wonder is broken out within this hour, that ballad-makers cannot be able to express it.— Here comes the Lady Paulina's steward: he can deliver you more.

Enter a third Gentleman.

How goes it now, sir? this news, which is called true, is so like an old tale, that the verity of it is in strong suspicion: has the king found his heir?

Third Gent. Most true, if ever truth were pregnant by circumstance: that which you hear you'll swear you see, there is such unity in the proofs. The mantle of Queen Hermione's; her jewel about the neck of it; the letters of Antigonus, found with it, which they know to be his character; the majesty of the creature, in resemblance of the mother; the affection of nobleness, which nature shows above her breeding; and many other evidences,— proclaim her with all certainty to be the king's daughter. Did you see the meeting of the two kings?

Sec. Gent. No.

Third Gent. Then have you lost a sight, which was to be

seen, cannot be spoken of. There might you have beheld one joy crown another, so and in such manner, that it seemed sorrow wept to take leave of them, — for their joy waded in tears. There was casting up of eyes, holding up of hands, with countenance of such distraction, that they were to be known by garment, not by favour. Our king, being ready to leap out of himself for joy of his found daughter, as if that joy were now become a loss, cries, "O, thy mother, thy mother!" then asks Bohemia forgiveness; then embraces his son-in-law; then again worries he his daughter with clipping her; now he thanks the old shepherd, which stands by like a weather-bitten conduit of many kings' reigns. I never heard of such another encounter, which lames report to follow it, and undoes description to do it.

Sec. Gent. What, pray you, became of Antigonus, that carried hence the child?

Third Gent. Like an old tale still, which will have matter to rehearse, though credit be asleep, and not an ear open. He was torn to pieces with a bear: this avouches the shepherd's son; who has not only his innocence, which seems much, to justify him, but a handkerchief and rings of his, that Paulina knows.

First Gent. What became of his bark and his followers?

Third Gent. Wrecked the same instant of their master's death, and in the view of the shepherd: so that all the instruments which aided to expose the child were even then lost when it was found. But, O, the noble combat that, 'twixt joy and sorrow, was fought in Paulina! She had one eye declined for the loss of her husband, another elevated that the oracle was fulfilled: she lifted the princess from the earth; and so locks her in embracing, as if she would pin her to her heart, that she might no more be in danger of losing.

First Gent. The dignity of this act was worth the audience of kings and princes, for by such was it acted.

Third Gent. One of the prettiest touches of all, and that which angled for mine eyes — caught the water, though not the fish — was when, at the relation of the queen's death, with the manner how she came to 't, — bravely confessed and lamented by the king, — how attentiveness wounded his daughter; till, from one sign of dolour to another, she did, with an "Alas," I would fain say, bleed tears; for I am sure my heart wept blood. Who was most marble there changed colour; some swooned, all sorrowed: if all the world could have seen 't, the woe had been universal.

First Gent. Are they returned to the court?

Third Gent. No: the princess hearing of her mother's statue, which is in the keeping of Paulina, — a piece many years in doing, and now newly performed by that rare Italian master, Julio Romano, who, had he himself eternity, and could put breath into his work, would beguile Nature of her custom, so perfectly he is her ape: he so near to Hermione hath done Hermione, that they say one would speak to her, and stand in hope of answer: — thither with all greediness of affection are they gone; and there they intend to sup.

Sec. Gent. I thought she had some great matter there in hand; for she hath privately twice or thrice a day, ever since the death of Hermione, visited that removed house. Shall we thither, and with our company piece the rejoicing?

First Gent. Who would be thence that has the benefit of access? every wink of an eye, some new grace will be born: our absence makes us unthrifty to our knowledge. Let's along. [*Exeunt Gentlemen.*

Aut. Now, had I not the dash of my former life in me, would preferment drop on my head. I brought the old man and his son aboard the prince; told him I heard them talk of a fardel, and I know not what: but he at that time, overfond of the shepherd's daughter, — so he then took her to be, — who began to be much sea-sick, and himself little better, extremity of weather continuing, this mystery remained undiscovered. But 'tis all one to me; for had I been the finder-out of this secret, it would not have relished among my other discredits. — Here come those I have done good to against my will, and already appearing in the blossoms of their fortune.

Enter Shepherd *and* Clown, *richly dressed.*

Shep. Come, boy; I am past more children, but thy sons and daughters will be all gentlemen born.

Clo. You are well met, sir. You denied to fight with me this other day, because I was no gentleman born. See you these clothes? say you see them not, and think me still no gentleman born: you were best say these robes are not gentlemen born: give me the lie, do; and try whether I am not now a gentleman born.

Aut. I know you are now, sir, a gentleman born.

Clo. Ay, and have been so any time these four hours.

Shep. And so have I, boy.

Clo. So you have: — but I was a gentleman born before my father; for the king's son took me by the hand, and called me brother; and then the two kings called my father brother; and then the prince my brother and the princess my sister called my father father; and so we wept, — and there was the first gentleman-like tears that ever we shed.

Shep. We may live, son, to shed many more.

Clo. Ay; or else 'twere hard luck, being in so preposterous estate as we are.

Aut. I humbly beseech you, sir, to pardon me all the faults I have committed to your worship, and to give me your good report to the prince my master.

Shep. Prithee, son, do; for we must be gentle, now we are gentlemen.

Clo. Thou wilt amend thy life?

Aut. Ay, an it like your good worship.

Clo. Give me thy hand: I will swear to the prince thou art as honest a true fellow as any is in Bohemia.

Shep. You may say it, but not swear it.

Clo. Not swear it, now I am a gentleman? Let boors and franklins say it, I'll swear it.

Shep. How if it be false, son?

Clo. If it be ne'er so false, a true gentleman may swear it in the behalf of his friend: — and I'll swear to the prince

thou art a tall fellow of thy hands, and that thou wilt not be
drunk; but I know thou art no tall fellow of thy hands, and
that thou wilt be drunk: but I'll swear it; and I would thou
wouldst be a tall fellow of thy hands.

Aut. I will prove so, sir, to my power.

Clo. Ay, by any means prove a tall fellow: if I do not
wonder how thou darest venture to be drunk, not being a tall
fellow, trust me not. — [*Trumpets within.*] Hark! the kings
and the princes, our kindred, are going to see the queen's picture. Come, follow us: we'll be thy good masters. [*Exeunt.*

SCENE III. *The same. A chapel in* PAULINA's *house.*

Enter LEONTES, POLIXENES, FLORIZEL, PERDITA, CAMILLO,
PAULINA, Lords, *and* Attendants.

Leon. O grave and good Paulina, the great comfort
That I have had of thee!

Paul.　　　　　What, sovereign sir,
I did not well, I meant well. All my services
You have paid home: but that you have vouchsaf'd
With your crown'd brother and these your contracted
Heirs of your kingdoms my poor house to visit,
It is a surplus of your grace, which never
My life may last to answer.

Leon.　　　　　O Paulina,
We honour you with trouble: — but we came
To see the statue of our queen: your gallery
Have we pass'd through, not without much content
In many singularities; but we saw not
That which my daughter came to look upon,
The statue of her mother.

Paul.　　　　　As she liv'd peerless,
So her dead likeness, I do well believe,
Excels whatever yet you look'd upon,
Or hand of man hath done; therefore I keep it
Lonely, apart. But here it is: prepare

To see the life as lively mock'd as ever
Still sleep mock'd death: behold, and say 'tis well.
            [*Paulina draws back a curtain, and discovers
                    Hermione standing as a statue.*
I like your silence, — it the more shows off
Your wonder: but yet speak; — first, you, my liege:
Comes it not something near?
    Leon.   Her natural posture! —
Chide me, dear stone, that I may say indeed
Thou art Hermione; or rather, thou art she
In thy not chiding, for she was as tender
As infancy and grace. — But yet, Paulina,
Hermione was not so much wrinkled, nothing
So agèd as this seems.
    Pol.   O, not by much.
    Paul. So much the more our carver's excellence;
Which lets go by some sixteen years, and makes her
As she liv'd now.
    Leon.   As now she might have done,
So much to my good comfort, as it is
Now piercing to my soul. O, thus she stood,
Even with such life of majesty, — warm life,
As now it coldly stands, — when first I woo'd her!
I am asham'd: does not the stone rebuke me
For being more stone than it? — O royal piece,
There's magic in thy majesty; which has
My evils conjur'd to remembrance, and
From thy admiring daughter took the spirits,
Standing like stone with thee!
    Per.   And give me leave,
And do not say 'tis superstition that
I kneel, and then implore her blessing. — Lady,
Dear queen, that ended when I but began,
Give me that hand of yours to kiss.
    Paul.   O, patience!
The statue is but newly fix'd, the colour's
Not dry.

Cam. My lord, your sorrow was too sore laid on,
Which sixteen winters cannot blow away,
So many summers dry: scarce any joy
Did ever so long live; no sorrow
But kill'd itself much sooner.
    Pol.   Dear my brother,
Let him that was the cause of this have power
To take off so much grief from you as he
Will piece up in himself.
    Paul.   Indeed, my lord,
If I had thought the sight of my poor image
Would thus have wrought you, — for the stone is mine, —
I'd not have show'd it.
    Leon.   Do not draw the curtain.
    Paul. No longer shall you gaze on't, lest your fancy
May think anon it moves.
    Leon.   Let be, let be. —
Would I were dead, but that, methinks, already —
What was he that did make it? — See, my lord,
Would you not deem it breath'd? and that those veins
Did verily bear blood?
    Pol.   Masterly done:
The very life seems warm upon her lip.
    Leon. The fixure of her eye has motion in't,
As we are mock'd with art.
    Paul.   I'll draw the curtain:
My lord's almost so far transported, that
He'll think anon it lives.
    Leon.   O sweet Paulina,
Make me to think so twenty years together!
No settled senses of the world can match
The pleasure of that madness. Let 't alone.
    Paul. I'm sorry, sir, I have thus far stirr'd you; but
I could afflict you further.
    Leon.   Do, Paulina;
For this affliction has a taste as sweet
As any cordial comfort. — Still, methinks

There is an air comes from her: what fine chisel
Could ever yet cut breath? Let no man mock me,
For I will kiss her.
  Paul.   Good my lord, forbear:
The ruddiness upon her lip is wet;
You'll mar it, if you kiss it; stain your own
With oily painting. Shall I draw the curtain?
  Leon. No, not these twenty years.
  Per.   So long could I
Stand by, a looker-on.
  Paul.   Either forbear,
Quit presently the chapel, or resolve you
For more amazement. If you can behold it,
I'll make the statue move indeed, descend
And take you by the hand: but then you'll think, —
Which I protest against, — I am assisted
By wicked powers.
  Leon.   What you can make her do,
I am content to look on: what to speak,
I am content to hear; for 'tis as easy
To make her speak as move.
  Paul.   It is requir'd
You do awake your faith. Then all stand still;
Or those that think it is unlawful business
I am about, let them depart.
  Leon.   Proceed:
No foot shall stir.
  Paul.   Music, awake her; strike! — [*Music.*
'Tis time; descend; be stone no more; approach;
Strike all that look upon with marvel. Come;
I'll fill your grave up: stir; nay, come away;
Bequeath to death your numbness, for from him
Dear life redeems you. — You perceive she stirs:
    [*Hermione comes down from the pedestal.*
Start not; her actions shall be holy as
You hear my spell is lawful: do not shun her,
Until you see her die again; for then

You kill her double. Nay, present your hand:
When she was young, you woo'd her; now in age
Is she become the suitor.
    Leon.   O, she's warm!   [*Embracing her.*
If this be magic, let it be an art
Lawful as eating.
    Pol.   She embraces him.
    Cam. She hangs about his neck:
If she pertain to life, let her speak too.
    Pol. Ay, and make 't manifest where she has liv'd,
Or how stol'n from the dead.
    Paul.   That she is living,
Were it but told you, should be hooted at
Like an old tale: but it appears she lives,
Though yet she speak not. Mark a little while. —
Please you to interpose, fair madam; kneel,
And pray your mother's blessing. — Turn, good lady;
Our Perdita is found.
              [*Presenting Perdita, who kneels to Hermione.*
    Her.   You gods, look down,
And from your sacred vials pour your graces
Upon my daughter's head! — Tell me, mine own,
Where hast thou been preserv'd? where liv'd? how found
Thy father's court? for thou shalt hear that I, —
Knowing by Paulina that the oracle
Gave hope thou wast in being, — have preserv'd
Myself to see the issue.
    Paul.   There's time enough for that;
Lest they desire, upon this push, to trouble
Your joys with like relation. — Go together,
You precious winners all; your exultation
Partake to every one. I, an old turtle,
Will wing me to some wither'd bough, and there
My mate, that's never to be found again,
Lament till I am lost.
    Leon.   O, peace, Paulina!
Thou shouldst a husband take by my consent,

As I by thine a wife: this is a match,
And made between's by vows. Thou hast found mine
But how, is to be question'd, — for I saw her,
As I thought, dead; and have, in vain, said many
A prayer upon her grave. I'll not seek far, —
For him, I partly know his mind, — to find thee
An honourable husband. — Come, Camillo,
And take her by the hand; whose worth and honesty
Is richly noted; and here justified
By us, a pair of kings. — Let's from this place. —
What! look upon my brother: — both your pardons,
That e'er I put between your holy looks
My ill suspicion. — This' your son-in-law,
And son unto the king, whom heavens directing,
Is troth-plight to your daughter. — Good Paulina,
Lead us from hence; where we may leisurely
Each one demand, and answer to his part
Perform'd in this wide gap of time, since first
We were dissever'd; hastily lead away. [*Exeunt.*

KING JOHN.

DRAMATIS PERSONÆ.

KING JOHN.
PRINCE HENRY, his son; afterwards King Henry III.
ARTHUR, duke of Bretagne, son to Geffrey, late Duke of Bretagne, the elder brother to King John.
WILLIAM MARESHALL, earl of Pembroke.
GEFFREY FITZ-PETER, earl of Essex, chief-justiciary of England.
WILLIAM LONGSWORD, earl of Salisbury.
ROBERT BIGOT, earl of Norfolk.
HUBERT DE BURGH, chamberlain to the King.
ROBERT FALCONBRIDGE, son to Sir Robert Falconbridge.
PHILIP FALCONBRIDGE, his half-brother, bastard son to King Richard the First.

JAMES GURNEY, servant to Lady Falconbridge.
PETER of Pomfret, a prophet.

PHILIP, king of France.
LOUIS, the Dauphin.
Archduke of Austria.
CARDINAL PANDULPH, the Pope's legate.
MELUN, a French lord.
CHATILLON, ambassador from France to King John.

ELINOR, widow of King Henry II. and mother to King John.
CONSTANCE, mother to Arthur.
BLANCH, daughter to Alphonso, king of Castile, and niece to King John.
LADY FALCONBRIDGE, mother to the Bastard and Robert Falconbridge.

Lords, Citizens of Angiers, Sheriff, Heralds, Officers, Soldiers, Messengers, and other Attendants.

SCENE — *Sometimes in England, and sometimes in France.*

ACT I.

SCENE I. *Northampton. A room of state in the palace.*

Enter King JOHN, Queen ELINOR, PEMBROKE, ESSEX, SALISBURY, *and others, with* CHATILLON.

K. John. Now, say, Chatillon, what would France with us?
Chat. Thus, after greeting, speaks the King of France,
In my behaviour, to the majesty,
The borrow'd majesty of England here.
Eli. A strange beginning; — borrow'd majesty!
K. John. Silence, good mother; hear the embassy.
Chat. Philip of France, in right and true behalf
Of thy deceasèd brother Geffrey's son,
Arthur Plantagenet, lays most lawful claim
To this fair island and the territories, —
To Ireland, Poictiers, Anjou, Touraine, Maine;
Desiring thee to lay aside the sword
Which sways usurpingly these several titles,
And put the same into young Arthur's hand,
Thy nephew and right royal sovereign.
K. John. What follows, if we disallow of this?
Chat. The proud control of fierce and bloody war,
T' enforce these rights so forcibly withheld.
K. John. Here have we war for war, and blood for blood,
Controlment for controlment: so answer France.
Chat. Then take my king's defiance from my mouth,
The furthest limit of my embassy.
K. John. Bear mine to him, and so depart in peace:
Be thou as lightning in the eyes of France;
For ere thou canst report I will be there,
The thunder of my cannon shall be heard:
So, hence! Be thou the trumpet of our wrath,
And sullen presage of your own decay. —
An honourable conduct let him have: —
Pembroke, look to't. — Farewell, Chatillon.
            [*Exeunt Chatillon and Pembroke.*
Eli. What now, my son! have I not ever said

How that ambitious Constance would not cease
Till she had kindled France and all the world
Upon the right and party of her son?
This might have been prevented and made whole
With very easy arguments of love;
Which now the manage of two kingdoms must
With fearful bloody issue arbitrate.

K. John. Our strong possession and our right for us.

Eli. [*aside to K. John*] Your strong possession much more
     than your right,
Or else it must go wrong with you and me:
So much my conscience whispers in your ear,
Which none but heaven and you and I shall hear.

Enter the Sheriff *of Northamptonshire, who whispers* Essex.

Essex. My liege, here is the strangest controversy,
Come from the country to be judg'd by you,
That e'er I heard: shall I produce the men?

K. John. Let them approach. —   [*Exit Sheriff.*
Our abbeys and our priories shall pay
This expedition's charge.

Re-enter Sheriff, *with* Robert Falconbridge, *and* Philip
   his bastard brother.

      What men are you?

Bast. Your faithful subject I, a gentleman
Born in Northamptonshire, and eldest son,
As I suppose, to Robert Falconbridge, —
A soldier, by the honour-giving hand
Of Cœur-de-lion knighted in the field.

K. John. What art thou?

Rob. The son and heir to that same Falconbridge.

K. John. Is that the elder, and art thou the heir?
You came not of one mother, then, it seems.

Bast. Most certain of one mother, mighty king, —
That is well known; and, as I think, one father:
But for the certain knowledge of that truth,

I put you o'er to heaven and to my mother: —
Of that I doubt, as all men's children may.

 Eli. Out on thee, rude man! thou dost shame thy mother
And wound her honour with this diffidence.

 Bast. I, madam? no, I have no reason for it, —
That is my brother's plea, and none of mine;
The which if he can prove, 'a pops me out
At least from fair five hundred pound a year:
Heaven guard my mother's honour and my land!

 K. John. A good blunt fellow. — Why, being younger born,
Doth he lay claim to thine inheritance?

 Bast. I know not why, except to get the land.
But once he slander'd me with bastardy:
But whêr I be as true begot or no,
That still I lay upon my mother's head;
But, that I am as well begot, my liege, —
Fair fall the bones that took the pains for me! —
Compare our faces, and be judge yourself.
If old Sir Robert did beget us both,
And were our father, and this son like him, —
O old Sir Robert, father, on my knee
I give heaven thanks I was not like to thee!

 K. John. Why, what a madcap hath heaven lent us here!

 Eli. He hath a trick of Cœur-de-lion's face;
The accent of his tongue affecteth him:
Do you not read some tokens of my son
In the large composition of this man?

 K. John. Mine eye hath well examinèd his parts,
And finds them perfect Richard. — Sirrah, speak,
What doth move you to claim your brother's land?

 Bast. Because he hath a half-face, like my father,
With that half-face would he have all my land:
A half-fac'd groat five hundred pound a year!

 Rob. My gracious liege, when that my father liv'd,
Your brother did employ my father much, —

 Bast. Well, sir, by this you cannot get my land:
Your tale must be, how he employ'd my mother.

Rob. And once dispatch'd him in an embassy
To Germany, there with the emperor
To treat of high affairs touching that time.
'Th' advantage of his absence took the king,
And in the mean time sojourn'd at my father's;
Where how he did prevail, I shame to speak, —
But truth is truth: large lengths of seas and shores
Between my father and my mother lay, —
As I have heard my father speak himself, —
When this same lusty gentleman was got.
Upon his death-bed he by will bequeath'd
His lands to me; and took it, on his death,
That this, my mother's son, was none of his;
And if he were, he came into the world
Full fourteen weeks before the course of time.
Then, good my liege, let me have what is mine,
My father's land, as was my father's will.

K. John. Sirrah, your brother is legitimate, —
Your father's wife did after wedlock bear him;
And if she did play false, the fault was hers;
Which fault lies on the hazards of all husbands
That marry wives. Tell me, how if my brother,
Who, as you say, took pains to get this son,
Had of your father claim'd this son for his?
In sooth, good friend, your father might have kept
This calf, bred from his cow, from all the world;
In sooth, he might: then, if he were my brother's,
My brother might not claim him; nor your father,
Being none of his, refuse him: this concludes, —
My mother's son did get your father's heir;
Your father's heir must have your father's land.

Rob. Shall, then, my father's will be of no force
To dispossess that child which is not his?

Bast. Of no more force to dispossess me, sir,
Than was his will to get me, as I think.

Eli. Whether hadst thou rather be a Falconbridge,
And like thy brother, to enjoy thy land,

Or the reputed son of Cœur-de-lion,
Lord of thy presence, and no land beside?

Bast. Madam, an if my brother had my shape,
And I had his, Sir Robert his, like him;
And if my legs were two such riding-rods,
My arms such eel-skins stuff'd; my face so thin,
That in mine ear I durst not stick a rose,
Lest men should say, "Look, where three-farthings goes!"
And, to his shape, were heir to all this land, —
Would I might never stir from off this place,
I'd give it every foot to have this face;
I would not be Sir Nob in any case.

Eli. I like thee well: wilt thou forsake thy fortune,
Bequeath thy land to him, and follow me?
I am a soldier, and now bound to France.

Bast. Brother, take you my land, I'll take my chance:
Your face hath got five hundred pound a year;
Yet sell your face for five pence, and 'tis dear. —
Madam, I'll follow you unto the death.

Eli. Nay, I would have you go before me thither.

Bast. Our country manners give our betters way.

K. John. What is thy name?

Bast. Philip, my liege, — so is my name begun, —
Philip, good old Sir Robert's wife's eld'st son.

K. John. From henceforth bear his name whose form thou bear'st:
Kneel thou down Philip, but arise more great, —
Arise Sir Richard and Plantagenet.

Bast. Brother by the mother's side, give me your hand:
My father gave me honour, yours gave land. —
Now blessèd be the hour, by night or day,
When I was got, Sir Robert was away!

Eli. The very spirit of Plantagenet! —
I am thy grandam, Richard; call me so.

Bast. Madam, by chance, but not by truth: what though?
Something about, a little from the right,

In at the window, or else o'er the hatch;
Who dares not stir by day must walk by night;
And have is have, however men do catch;
Near or far off, well won is still well shot;
And I am I, howe'er I was begot.

K. John. Go, Falconbridge: now hast thou thy desire;
A landless knight makes thee a landed squire. —
Come, madam, — and come, Richard; we must speed
For France, for France; for it is more than need.

Bast. Brother, adieu: good fortune come to thee!
For thou wast got i' the way of honesty.
        [*Exeunt all except the Bastard.*
A foot of honour better than I was;
But many a many foot of land the worse.
Well, now can I make any Joan a lady: —
"Good den, Sir Richard:" — "God-a-mercy, fellow;" —
And if his name be George, I'll call him Peter;
For new-made honour doth forget men's names, —
'Tis too respective and too sociable
For your conversion. Now your traveller, —
He and his toothpick at my worship's mess;
And when my knightly stomach is suffic'd,
Why then I suck my teeth, and catechize
My pickèd man of countries: — "My dear sir,"
Thus, leaning on mine elbow, I begin,
"I shall beseech you" — that is question now;
And then comes answer like an Abcee-book: —
"O sir," says answer, "at your best command;
At your employment; at your service, sir:"
"No, sir," says question, "I, sweet sir, at yours:"
And so, ere answer knows what question would, —
Saving in dialogue of compliment,
And talking of the Alps and Apennines,
The Pyrenean and the river Po, —
It draws toward supper in conclusion so.
But this is worshipful society,
And fits the mounting spirit like myself;

For he is but a bastard to the time,
That doth not smack of observation, —
And so am I, whether I smack or no;
And not alone in habit and device,
Exterior form, outward accoutrement,
But from the inward motion to deliver
Sweet, sweet, sweet poison for the age's tooth:
Which, though I will not practise to deceive,
Yet, to avoid deceit, I mean to learn;
For it shall strew the footsteps of my rising. —
But who comes in such haste in riding-robes?
What woman-post is this? hath she no husband,
That will take pains to blow a horn before her?

    Enter Lady FALCONBRIDGE *and* JAMES GURNEY.

O me! it is my mother. — How now, good lady!
What brings you here to court so hastily?
    Lady F. Where is that slave, thy brother?- where is he,
That holds in chase mine honour up and down?
    Bast. My brother Robert? old Sir Robert's son?
Colbrand the giant, that same mighty man?
Is it Sir Robert's son that you seek so?
    Lady F. Sir Robert's son! Ay, thou unreverend boy,
Sir Robert's son: why scorn'st thou at Sir Robert?
He is Sir Robert's son; and so art thou.
    Bast. James Gurney, wilt thou give us leave awhile?
    Gur. Good leave, good Philip.
    Bast.   Philip? — sparrow! — James,
There's toys abroad: anon I'll tell thee more. [*Exit Gurney.*
Madam, I was not old Sir Robert's son;
Sir Robert might have eat his part in me
Upon Good-Friday, and ne'er broke his fast:
Sir Robert could do well: marry, to confess,
Could he get me? Sir Robert could not do it, —
We know his handiwork: — therefore, good mother,
To whom am I beholding for these limbs?
Sir Robert never holp to make this leg.

Lady F. Hast thou conspirèd with thy brother too,
That for thine own gain shouldst defend mine honour?
What means this scorn, thou most untoward knave?

Bast. Knight, knight, good mother, — Basilisco-like:
What! I am dubb'd; I have it on my shoulder.
But, mother, I am not Sir Robert's son;
I have disclaim'd Sir Robert; and my land,
Legitimation, name, and all is gone:
Then, good my mother, let me know my father, —
Some proper man, I hope: who was it, mother?

Lady F. Hast thou denied thyself a Falconbridge?

Bast. As faithfully as I deny the devil.

Lady F. King Richard Cœur-de-lion was thy father:
By long and vehement suit I was seduc'd
To make room for him in my husband's bed: —
Heaven lay not my transgression to my charge! —
Thou art the issue of my dear offence,
Which was so strongly urg'd, past my defence.

Bast. Now, by this light, were I to get again,
Madam, I would not wish a better father.
Some sins do bear their privilege on earth,
And so doth yours; your fault was not your folly:
Needs must you lay your heart at his dispose,
Subjécted tribute to commanding love,
Against whose fury and unmatchèd force
The awless lion could not wage the fight,
Nor keep his princely heart from Richard's hand:
He that perforce robs lions of their hearts
May easily win a woman's. Ay, my mother,
With all my heart I thank thee for my father.
Who lives and dares but say, thou didst not well
When I was got, I'll send his soul to hell.
Come, lady, I will show thee to my kin;
And they shall say, when Richard me begot,
If thou hadst said him nay, it had been sin:
Who says it was, he lies; I say 'twas not. [*Exeunt.*

ACT II.

SCENE I. *France. Before the walls of Angiers.*

Enter, on one side, PHILIP, *king of France,* LOUIS, CONSTANCE, ARTHUR, *and Forces; on the other, the* Archduke of Austria *and Forces.*

K. Phi. Before Angiers well met, brave Austria. —
Arthur, that great forerunner of thy blood,
Richard, that robb'd the lion of his heart,
And fought the holy wars in Palestine,
By this brave duke came early to his grave:
And, for amends to his posterity,
At our importance hither is he come,
To spread his colours, boy, in thy behalf;
And to rebuke the usurpation
Of thy unnatural uncle, English John:
Embrace him, love him, give him welcome hither.

Arth. God shall forgive you Cœur-de-lion's death
The rather that you give his offspring life,
Shadowing their right under your wings of war:
I give you welcome with a powerless hand,
But with a heart full of unstained love:
Welcome before the gates of Angiers, duke.

K. Phi. A noble boy! Who would not do thee right?

Aust. Upon thy cheek lay I this zealous kiss,
As seal to this indenture of my love; —
That to my home I will no more return,
Till Angiers, and the right thou hast in France,
Together with that pale, that white-fac'd shore,
Whose foot spurns back the ocean's roaring tides,
And coops from other lands her islanders, —
Even till that England, hedg'd in with the main,
That water-walled bulwark, still secure
And confident from foreign purposes, —
Even till that utmost corner of the west
Salute thee for her king: till then, fair boy,
Will I not think of home, but follow arms.

Const. O, take his mother's thanks, a widow's thanks,
Till your strong hand shall help to give him strength
To make a more requital to your love!

Aust. The peace of heaven is theirs that lift their swords
In such a just and charitable war.

K. Phi. Well, then, to work: our cannon shall be bent
Against the brows of this resisting town. —
Call for our chiefest men of discipline,
To cull the plots of best advantages:
We'll lay before this town our royal bones,
Wade to the market-place in Frenchmen's blood,
But we will make it subject to this boy.

Const. Stay for an answer to your embassy,
Lest unadvis'd you stain your swords with blood;
My Lord Chatillon may from England bring
That right in peace, which here we urge in war;
And then we shall repent each drop of blood
That hot rash haste so indirectly shed.

K. Phi. A wonder, lady, — lo, upon thy wish,
Our messenger Chatillon is arriv'd!

Enter CHATILLON.

What England says, say briefly, gentle lord;
We coldly pause for thee; Chatillon, speak.

Chat. Then turn your forces from this paltry siege,
And stir them up against a mightier task.
England, impatient of your just demands,
Hath put himself in arms: the adverse winds,
Whose leisure I have stay'd, have given him time
To land his legions all as soon as I;
His marches are expedient to this town,
His forces strong, his soldiers confident.
With him along is come the mother-queen,
An Até, stirring him to blood and strife;
With her her niece, the Lady Blanch of Spain;
With them a bastard of the king's deceas'd:
And all th' unsettled humours of the land, —

Rash, inconsiderate, fiery voluntaries,
With ladies' faces and fierce dragons' spleens, —
Have sold their fortunes at their native homes,
Bearing their birthrights proudly on their backs,
To make a hazard of new fortunes here:
In brief, a braver choice of dauntless spirits,
Than now the English bottoms have waft o'er,
Did never float upon the swelling tide,
To do offence and scathe in Christendom.
The interruption of their churlish drums   [*Drums within.*
Cuts off more circumstance: they are at hand,
To parley or to fight; therefore prepare.

    K. Phi. How much unlook'd for is this expedition!

    Aust. By how much unexpected, by so much
We must awake endeavour for defence;
For courage mounteth with occasion:
Let them be welcome, then; we are prepar'd.

    Enter King John, Elinor, Blanch, *the* Bastard, Lords,
              and Forces.

    K. John. Peace be to France, if France in peace permit
Our just and lineal entrance to our own!
If not, bleed France, and peace ascend to heaven!
Whiles we, God's wrathful agent, do correct
Their proud contempt that beat his peace to heaven.

    K. Phi. Peace be to England, if that war return
From France to England, there to live in peace!
England we love; and for that England's sake
With burden of our armour here we sweat.
This toil of ours should be a work of thine;
But thou from loving England art so far,
That thou hast under-wrought his lawful king,
Cut off the sequence of posterity,
Out-facèd infant state, and done a rape
Upon the maiden virtue of the crown.
Look here upon thy brother Geffrey's face; —
These eyes, these brows, were moulded out of his:

This little abstract doth contain that large
Which died in Geffrey; and the hand of time
Shall draw this brief into as huge a volume.
That Geffrey was thy elder brother born,
And this his son; England was Geffrey's right,
And his is Geffrey's: in the name of God,
How comes it, then, that thou art call'd a king,
When living blood doth in these temples beat,
Which owe the crown that thou o'ermasterest?
    K. John. From whom hast thou this great commission,
              France,
To draw my answer from thy articles?
    K. Phi. From that supernal judge, that stirs good thoughts
In any breast of strong authority,
To look into the blots and stains of right.
That judge hath made me guardian to this boy:
Under whose warrant I impeach thy wrong;
And by whose help I mean to chástise it.
    K. John. Alack, thou dost usurp authority.
    K. Phi. Excuse, — it is to beat usurping down.
    Eli. Who is it thou dost call usurper, France?
    Const. Let me make answer; — thy usurping son.
    Eli. Out, insolent! thy bastard shall be king,
That thou mayst be a queen, and check the world!
    Const. My bed was ever to thy son as true
As thine was to thy husband; and this boy
Liker in feature to his father Geffrey
Than thou and John in manners, — being as like
As rain to water, or devil to his dam.
My boy a bastard! By my soul, I think
His father never was so true begot:
It cannot be, an if thou wert his mother.
    Eli. There's a good mother, boy, that blots thy father.
    Const. There's a good grandam, boy, that would blot thee.
    Aust. Peace!
    Bast.   Hear the crier.
    Aust.   What the devil art thou?

Bast. One that will play the devil, sir, with you,
And 'a may catch your hide and you alone:
You are the hare of whom the proverb goes,
Whose valour plucks dead lions by the beard:
I'll smoke your skin-coat, an I catch you right;
Sirrah, look to't; i' faith, I will, i' faith.
 Blanch. O, well did he become that lion's robe
That did disrobe the lion of that robe!
 Bast. It lies as sightly on the back of him
As great Alcides' shows upon an ass: —
But, ass, I'll take that burden from your back,
Or lay on that shall make your shoulders crack.
 Aust. What cracker is this same that deafs our ears
With this abundance of superfluous breath? —
King Philip, determine what we shall do straight.
 K. Phi. Women and fools, break off your conference. —
King John, this is the very sum of all, —
England and Ireland, Anjou, Touraine, Maine,
In right of Arthur do I claim of thee:
Wilt thou resign them, and lay down thy arms?
 K. John. My life as soon: — I do defy thee, France. —
Arthur of Bretagne, yield thee to my hand;
And, out of my dear love, I'll give thee more
Than e'er the coward hand of France can win:
Submit thee, boy.
 Eli.   Come to thy grandam, child.
 Const. Do, child, go to it' grandam, child;
Give grandam kingdom, and it' grandam will
Give it a plum, a cherry, and a fig:
There's a good grandam.
 Arth.   Good my mother, peace!
I would that I were low laid in my grave:
I am not worth this coil that's made for me.
 Eli. His mother shames him so, poor boy, he weeps.
 Const. Now shame upon you, whêr she does or no!
His grandam's wrongs, and not his mother's shames,
Draw those heaven-moving pearls from his poor eyes,

Which heaven shall take in nature of a fee;
Ay, with these crystal beads heaven shall be brib'd
To do him justice, and revenge on you.

   Eli. Thou monstrous slanderer of heaven and earth!

   Const. Thou monstrous injurer of heaven and earth!
Call not me slanderer; thou and thine usurp
The dominations, royalties, and rights
Of this oppressèd boy: this is thy eld'st son's son,
Infortunate in nothing but in thee:
Thy sins are visited in this poor child;
The canon of the law is laid on him,
Being but the second generation
Removèd from thy sin-conceiving womb.

   K. John. Bedlam, have done.

   Const.   I have but this to say,—
That he's not only plaguèd for her sin,
But God hath made her sin and her the plague
On this removèd issue, plagu'd for her,
And with her plagu'd; her sin his injury,
Her injury the beadle to her sin;
All punish'd in the person of this child,
And all for her; a plague upon her!

   Eli. Thou unadvisèd scold, I can produce
A will that bars the title of thy son.

   Const. Ay, who doubts that? a will! a wicked will;
A woman's will; a canker'd grandam's will!

   K. Phi. Peace, lady! pause, or be more temperate:
It ill beseems this presence to cry aim
To these ill-tunèd repetitions.—
Some trumpet summon hither to the walls
These men of Angiers: let us hear them speak,
Whose title they admit, Arthur's or John's.

      Trumpet sounds. Enter Citizens *upon the walls.*

   First Cit. Who is it that hath warn'd us to the walls?

   K. Phi. 'Tis France, for England.

K. John. England, for itself: —
You men of Angiers, and my loving subjects, —
 K. Phi. You loving men of Angiers, Arthur's subjects,
Our trumpet call'd you to this gentle parle, —
 K. John. For our advantage; therefore hear us first.
These flags of France, that are advancèd here
Before the eye and prospect of your town,
Have hither march'd to your endamagement:
The cannons have their bowels full of wrath,
And ready mounted are they to spit forth
Their iron indignation 'gainst your walls:
All preparation for a bloody siege
And merciless proceeding by these French
Confront your city's eyes, your winking gates;
And, but for our approach, those sleeping stones,
That as a waist do girdle you about,
By the compulsion of their ordnance
By this time from their fixèd beds of lime
Had been dishabited, and wide havoc made
For bloody power to rush upon your peace.
But, on the sight of us, your lawful king, —
Who painfully, with much expedient march,
Have brought a countercheck before your gates,
To save unscratch'd your city's threaten'd cheeks, —
Behold, the French, amaz'd, vouchsafe a parle;
And now, instead of bullets wrapp'd in fire,
To make a shaking fever in your walls,
They shoot but calm words, folded up in smoke,
To make a faithless error in your ears:
Which trust accordingly, kind citizens,
And let us in, your king; whose labour'd spirits,
Forwearied in this action of swift speed,
Crave harbourage within your city-walls.
 K. Phi. When I have said, make answer to us both.
Lo, in this right hand, whose protection
Is most divinely vow'd upon the right
Of him it holds, stands young Plantagenet,

Son to the elder brother of this man,
And king o'er him, and all that he enjoys:
For this down-trodden equity, we tread
In warlike march these greens before your town;
Being no further enemy to you
Than the constraint of hospitable zeal
In the relief of this oppressèd child
Religiously provokes. Be pleasèd, then,
To pay that duty which you truly owe
To him that owes it, namely, this young prince:
And then our arms, like to a muzzled bear,
Save in aspéct, have all offence seal'd up;
Our cannons' malice vainly shall be spent
Against th' invulnerable clouds of heaven;
And with a blessèd and unvex'd retire,
With unhack'd swords and helmets all unbruis'd,
We will bear home that lusty blood again,
Which here we came to spout against your town,
And leave your children, wives, and you in peace.
But if you fondly pass our proffer'd offer,
'Tis not the rondure of your old-fac'd walls
Can hide you from our messengers of war,
Though all these English, and their discipline,
Were harbour'd in their rude circumference.
Then, tell us, shall your city call us lord,
In that behalf which we have challeng'd it?
Or shall we give the signal to our rage,
And stalk in blood to our possession?

First Cit. In brief, we are the king of England's subjects:
For him, and in his right, we hold this town.

K. John. Acknowledge, then, the king, and let me in.

First Cit. That can we not; but he that proves the king,
To him will we prove loyal: till that time
Have we ramm'd up our gates against the world.

K. John. Doth not the crown of England prove the king?
And if not that, I bring you witnesses,
Twice fifteen thousand hearts of England's breed, —

Bast. Bastards, and else.

K. John. To verify our title with their lives.

K. Phi. As many and as well-born bloods as those,—

Bast. Some bastards too.

K. Phi. Stand in his face, to contradict his claim.

First Cit. Till you compound whose right is worthiest,
We for the worthiest hold the right from both.

K. John. Then God forgive the sin of all those souls
That to their everlasting residence,
Before the dew of evening fall, shall fleet,
In dreadful trial of our kingdom's king!

K. Phi. Amen, amen!— Mount, chevaliers! to arms!

Bast. Saint George, that swinge'd the dragon, and e'er since
Sits on his horse' back at mine hostess' door,
Teach us some fence!— [*To Austria*] Sirrah, were I at home,
At your den, sirrah, with your lioness,
I'd set an ox-head to your lion's hide,
And make a monster of you.

Aust. Peace! no more.

Bast. O, tremble, for you hear the lion roar!

K. John. Up higher to the plain; where we'll set forth
In best appointment all our regiments.

Bast. Speed, then, to take advantage of the field.

K. Phi. It shall be so;— [*To Louis*] and at the other hill
Command the rest to stand.— God and our right!

[*Exeunt, severally, the English and French Kings, &c.*

After excursions, enter a French Herald, *with trumpets, to the gates.*

F. Her. You men of Angiers, open wide your gates,
And let young Arthur, Duke of Bretagne, in,
Who, by the hand of France, this day hath made
Much work for tears in many an English mother,
Whose sons lie scatter'd on the bleeding ground:
Many a widow's husband grovelling lies,
Coldly embracing the discolour'd earth;

And victory, with little loss, doth play
Upon the dancing banners of the French,
Who are at hand, triumphantly display'd,
To enter conquerors, and to proclaim
Arthur of Bretagne England's king and yours.

Enter an English Herald, *with trumpets.*

E. Her. Rejoice, you men of Angiers, ring your bells;
King John, your king and England's, doth approach,
Commander of this hot malicious day:
Their armours, that march'd hence so silver-bright,
Hither return all gilt with Frenchmen's blood;
There stuck no plume in any English crest
That is removèd by a staff of France;
Our colours do return in those same hands
That did display them when we first march'd forth;
And, like a jolly troop of huntsmen, come
Our lusty English, all with purpled hands,
Dy'd in the dying slaughter of their foes:
Open your gates, and give the victors way.

First Cit. Heralds, from off our towers we might behold,
From first to last, the onset and retire
Of both your armies; whose equality
By our best eyes cannot be censurèd:
Blood hath bought blood, and blows have answer'd blows;
Strength match'd with strength, and power confronted
   power:
Both are alike; and both alike we like.
One must prove greatest: while they weigh so even,
We hold our town for neither; yet for both.

Re-enter, on one side, King John, Elinor, Blanch, *the* Bastard,
Lords, *and Forces; on the other,* King Philip, Louis, Austria,
   and Forces.

K. John. France, hast thou yet more blood to cast away?
Say, shall the current of our right run on?
Whose passage, vex'd with thy impediment,
Shall leave his native channel, and o'erswell

With course disturb'd even thy confining shores,
Unless thou let his silver waters keep
A peaceful progress to the ocean.

 K. Phi. England, thou hast not sav'd one drop of blood,
In this hot trial, more than we of France;
Rather, lost more: and by this hand I swear,
That sways the earth this climate overlooks,
Before we will lay down our just-borne arms,
We'll put thee down, 'gainst whom these arms we bear,
Or add a royal number to the dead,
Gracing the scroll that tells of this war's loss
With slaughter coupled to the name of kings.

 Bast. Ha, majesty! how high thy glory towers,
When the rich blood of kings is set on fire!
O, now doth Death line his dead chaps with steel;
The swords of soldiers are his teeth, his fangs;
And now he feasts, mousing the flesh of men,
In undetermin'd differences of kings. —
Why stand these royal fronts amazèd thus?
Cry "havoc," kings! back to the stainèd field,
You equal-potent, fiery-kindled spirits!
Then let confusion of one part confirm
The other's peace; till then, blows, blood, and death!

 K. John. Whose party do the townsmen yet admit?

 K. Phi. Speak, citizens, for England; who's your king?

 First Cit. The king of England, when we know the king.

 K. Phi. Know him in us, that here hold up his right.

 K. John. In us, that are our own great deputy,
And bear possession of our person here;
Lord of our presence, Angiers, and of you.

 First Cit. A greater power than we denies all this;
And till it be undoubted, we do lock
Our former scruple in our strong-barr'd gates;
King'd of our fears, until our fears, resolv'd,
Be by some certain king purg'd and depos'd.

 Bast. By heaven, these scroyles of Angiers flout you,
    kings,

And stand securely on their battlements,
As in a theatre, whence they gape and point
At your industrious scenes and acts of death.
Your royal presences be rul'd by me: —
Do like the mutines of Jerusalem,
Be friends awhile, and both conjointly bend
Your sharpest deeds of malice on this town:
By east and west let France and England mount
Their battering cannon, chargèd to the mouths,
Till their soul-fearing clamours have brawl'd down
The flinty ribs of this contemptuous city:
I'd play incessantly upon these jades,
Even till unfencèd desolation
Leave them as naked as the vulgar air.
That done, dissever your united strengths,
And part your mingled colours once again;
Turn face to face, and bloody point to point;
Then, in a moment, Fortune shall cull forth
Out of one side her happy minion,
To whom in favour she shall give the day,
And kiss him with a glorious victory.
How like you this wild counsel, mighty states?
Smacks it not something of the policy?

   K. John. Now, by the sky that hangs above our heads,
I like it well. — France, shall we knit our powers,
And lay this Angiers even with the ground;
Then, after, fight who shall be king of it?

   Bast. An if thou hast the mettle of a king, —
Being wrong'd, as we are, by this peevish town, —
Turn thou the mouth of thy artillery,
As we will ours, against these saucy walls;
And when that we have dash'd them to the ground,
Why, then defy each other, and, pell-mell,
Make work upon ourselves, for heaven or hell.

   K. Phi. Let it be so. — Say, where will you assault?

   K. John. We from the west will send destruction
Into this city's bosom.

Aust. I from the north.
K. Phi. Our thunders from the south
Shall rain their drift of bullets on this town.
Bast. [*aside*] O prudent discipline! From north to south,—
Austria and France shoot in each other's mouth:
I'll stir them to it. — Come, away, away!
First Cit. Hear us, great kings: vouchsafe awhile to stay,
And I shall show you peace and fair-fac'd league;
Win you this city without stroke or wound;
Rescue those breathing lives to die in beds,
That here come sacrifices for the field:
Persever not, but hear me, mighty kings.
K. John. Speak on, with favour; we are bent to hear.
First Cit. That daughter there of Spain, the Lady Blanch,
Is niece to England: — look upon the years
Of Louis the Dauphin and that lovely maid:
If lusty love should go in quest of beauty,
Where should he find it fairer than in Blanch?
If zealous love should go in search of virtue,
Where should he find it purer than in Blanch?
If love ambitious sought a match of birth,
Whose veins bound richer blood than Lady Blanch?
Such as she is, in beauty, virtue, birth,
Is the young Dauphin every way complete,—
If not complete, O, say he is not she;
And she again wants nothing, to name want,
If want it be not, that she is not he:
He is the half part of a blessèd man,
Left to be finishèd by such a she;
And she a fair divided excellence,
Whose fulness of perfection lies in him.
O, two such silver currents, when they join,
Do glorify the banks that bound them in;
And two such shores to two such streams made one,
Two such controlling bounds shall you be, kings,
To these two princes, if you marry them.
This union shall do more than battery can

To our fast-closèd gates; for, at this match,
With swifter spleen than powder can enforce,
The mouth of passage shall we fling wide ope.
And give you entrance: but without this match,
The sea enragèd is not half so deaf,
Lions more confident, mountains and rocks
More free from motion; no, not Death himself
In mortal fury half so peremptory,
As we to keep this city.
    Bast.   Here's a stay,
That shakes the rotten carcass of old Death
Out of his rags! Here's a large mouth, indeed,
That spits forth death and mountains, rocks and seas;
Talks as familiarly of roaring lions
As maids of thirteen do of puppy-dogs!
What cannoneer begot this lusty blood?
He speaks plain cannon, — fire and smoke and bounce;
He gives the bastinado with his tongue:
Our ears are cudgell'd; not a word of his
But buffets better than a fist of France:
Zounds, I was never so bethump'd with words
Since I first call'd my brother's father dad.
    Eli. [*aside to K. John*] Son, list to this conjunction, make
           this match;
Give with our niece a dowry large enough:
For by this knot thou shalt so surely tie
Thy now-unsur'd assurance to the crown,
That yon green boy shall have no sun to ripe
The bloom that promiseth a mighty fruit.
I see a yielding in the looks of France;
Mark, how they whisper: urge them while their souls
Are capable of this ambition,
Lest zeal, now melted by the windy breath
Of soft petitions, pity, and remorse,
Cool and congeal again to what it was.
    First Cit. Why answer not the double majesties
This friendly treaty of our threaten'd town?

K. Phi. Speak England first, that hath been forward first
To speak unto this city: what say you?
   K. John. If that the Dauphin there, thy princely son,
Can in this book of beauty read "I love,"
Her dowry shall weigh equal with a queen:
For Anjou, and fair Touraine, Maine, Poictiers,
And all that we upon this side the sea —
Except this city now by us besieg'd —
Find liable to our crown and dignity,
Shall gild her bridal bed; and make her rich
In titles, honours, and promotions,
As she in beauty, education, blood,
Holds hand with any princess of the world.
   K. Phi. What say'st thou, boy? look in the lady's face.
   Lou. I do, my lord; and in her eye I find
A wonder, or a wondrous miracle,
The shadow of myself form'd in her eye;
Which, being but the shadow of your son,
Becomes a sun, and makes your son a shadow:
I do protest I never lov'd myself,
Till now infixèd I beheld myself
Drawn in the flattering table of her eye.
                                           [*Whispers with Blanch.*
   Bast. [*aside*] Drawn in the flattering table of her eye! —
Hang'd in the frowning wrinkle of her brow! —
And quarter'd in her heart! — he doth espy
Himself love's traitor: — this is pity now,
That, hang'd and drawn and quarter'd, there should be
In such a love so vile a lout as he.
   Blanch. My uncle's will in this respect is mine:
If he see aught in you that makes him like,
That any thing he sees, which moves his liking,
I can with ease translate it to my will;
Or if you will, to speak more properly,
I will enforce it easily to my love.
Further I will not flatter you, my lord,
That all I see in you is worthy love,

Than this,— that nothing do I see in you,
Though churlish thoughts themselves should be your judge,
That I can find should merit any hate.

 K. John. What say these young ones? — What say you,
     my niece?

 Blanch. That she is bound in honour still to do
What you in wisdom still vouchsafe to say.

 K. John. Speak then, Prince Dauphin; can you love this
     lady?

 Lou. Nay, ask me if I can refrain from love;
For I do love her most unfeignedly.

 K. John. Then do I give Volquessen, Touraine, Maine,
Poictiers, and Anjou, these five provinces,
With her to thee; and this addition more,
Full thirty thousand marks of English coin. —
Philip of France, if thou be pleas'd withal,
Command thy son and daughter to join hands.

 K. Phi. It likes us well. — Young princes, close your
    hands.

 Aust. And your lips too; for I am well assur'd
That I did so when I was first assur'd.

 K. Phi. Now, citizens of Angiers, ope your gates,
Let in that amity which you have made;
For at Saint Mary's chapel presently
The rites of marriage shall be solemniz'd. —
Is not the Lady Constance in this troop?
I know she is not; for this match made up
Her presence would have interrupted much:
Where is she and her son? tell me, who knows.

 Lou. She's sad and passionate at your highness' tent.

 K. Phi. And, by my faith, this league that we have made
Will give her sadness very little cure. —
Brother of England, how may we content
This widow lady? In her right we came;
Which we, God knows, have turn'd another way,
To our own vantage.

 K. John.   We will heal up all;

For we'll create young Arthur Duke of Bretagne
And Earl of Richmond; and this rich fair town
We make him lord of. — Call the Lady Constance;
Some speedy messenger bid her repair
To our solemnity: — I trust we shall,
If not fill up the measure of her will,
Yet in some measure satisfy her so
That we shall stop her exclamation.
Go we, as well as haste will suffer us,
To this unlook'd-for, unprepar`ed pomp.

[*Exeunt all except the Bastard. The Citizens retire from the walls.*]

Bast. Mad world! mad kings! mad composition!
John, to stop Arthur's title in the whole,
Hath willingly departed with a part;
And France, — whose armour conscience buckled on,
Whom zeal and charity brought to the field
As God's own soldier, — rounded in the ear
With that same purpose-changer, that sly devil;
That broker, that still breaks the pate of faith;
That daily break-vow; he that wins of all,
Of kings, of beggars, old men, young men, maids, —
Who having no external thing to lose
But the word "maid," cheats the poor maid of that;
That smooth-fac'd gentleman, tickling commodity, —
Commodity, the bias of the world;
The world, who of itself is peis`ed well,
Made to run even upon even ground,
Till this advantage, this vile-drawing bias,
This sway of motion, this commodity,
Makes it take head from all indifferency,
From all direction, purpose, course, intent:
And this same bias, this commodity,
This bawd, this broker, this all-changing word,
Clapp'd on the outward eye of fickle France,
Hath drawn him from his own determin'd aim,
From a resolv'd and honourable war,

To a most base and vile-concluded peace. —
And why rail I on this commodity?
But for because he hath not woo'd me yet:
Not that I have the power to clutch my hand,
When his fair angels would salute my palm;
But for my hand, as unattempted yet,
Like a poor beggar, raileth on the rich.
Well, whiles I am a beggar, I will rail,
And say, There is no sin but to be rich:
And being rich, my virtue then shall be
To say, There is no vice but beggary:
Since kings break faith upon commodity,
Gain, be my lord, — for I will worship thee! [*Exit.*

ACT III.

Scene I. *France. The French King's tent.*

Enter Constance, Arthur, *and* Salisbury.

Const. Gone to be married! gone to swear a peace!
False blood to false blood join'd! gone to be friends!
Shall Louis have Blanch? and Blanch those provinces?
It is not so; thou hast misspoke, misheard;
Be well advis'd, tell o'er thy tale again:
It cannot be; thou dost but say 'tis so:
I trust I may not trust thee; for thy word
Is but the vain breath of a common man:
Believe me, I do not believe thee, man;
I have a king's oath to the contrary.
Thou shalt be punish'd for thus frighting me,
For I am sick, and capable of fears;
Oppress'd with wrongs, and therefore full of fears;
A widow, husbandless, subject to fears;
A woman, naturally born to fears;
And though thou now confess thou didst but jest,
With my vex'd spirits I cannot take a truce,
But they will quake and tremble all this day.

What dost thou mean by shaking of thy head?
Why dost thou look so sadly on my son?
What means that hand upon that breast of thine?
Why holds thine eye that lamentable rheum,
Like a proud river peering o'er his bounds?
Be these sad signs confirmers of thy words?
Then speak again, — not all thy former tale,
But this one word, whether thy tale be true.

Sal. As true as I believe you think them false
That give you cause to prove my saying true.

Const. O, if thou teach me to believe this sorrow,
Teach thou this sorrow how to make me die;
And let belief and life encounter so
As doth the fury of two desperate men,
Which in the very meeting fall and die! —
Louis marry Blanch! O boy, then where art thou?
France friend with England! what becomes of me? —
Fellow, be gone: I cannot brook thy sight;
This news hath made thee a most ugly man.

Sal. What other harm have I, good lady, done,
But spoke the harm that is by others done?

Const. Which harm within itself so heinous is,
As it makes harmful all that speak of it.

Arth. I do beseech you, madam, be content.

Const. If thou, that bidd'st me be content, wert grim,
Ugly, and slanderous to thy mother's womb,
Full of unpleasing blots and sightless stains,
Lame, foolish, crookèd, swart, prodigious,
Patch'd with foul moles and eye-offending marks,
I would not care, I then would be content;
For then I should not love thee; no, nor thou
Become thy great birth, nor deserve a crown.
But thou art fair; and at thy birth, dear boy,
Nature and Fortune join'd to make thee great:
Of Nature's gifts thou mayst with lilies boast
And with the half-blown rose: but Fortune, O!
She is corrupted, chang'd, and won from thee;

She adulterates hourly with thine uncle John;
And with her golden hand hath pluck'd on France
To tread down fair respect of sovereignty,
And made his majesty the bawd to theirs.
France is a bawd to Fortune and King John, —
That strumpet Fortune, that usurping John! —
Tell me, thou fellow, is not France forsworn?
Envenom him with words; or get thee gone,
And leave those woes alone which I alone
Am bound to under-bear.

   Sal.   Pardon me, madam,
I may not go without you to the kings.

   Const. Thou mayst, thou shalt; I will not go with thee:
I will instruct my sorrows to be proud;
For grief is proud, and makes his owner stout.
To me, and to the state of my great grief,
Let kings assemble; for my grief's so great,
That no supporter but the huge firm earth
Can hold it up: here I and sorrow sit;
Here is my throne, bid kings come bow to it.
                       [*Seats herself on the ground.*

Enter King John, King Philip, Louis, Blanch, Elinor,
      the Bastard, Austria, *and* Attendants.

   K. Phi. 'Tis true, fair daughter; and this blessèd day
Ever in France shall be kept festival:
To solemnize this day the glorious sun
Stays in his course, and plays the alchemist,
Turning with splendour of his precious eye
The meagre cloddy earth to glittering gold:
The yearly course that brings this day about
Shall never see it but a holiday.

   Const. A wicked day, and not a holy day! —   [*Rising.*
What hath this day deserv'd? what hath it done,
That it in golden letters should be set
Among the high tides in the calendar?
Nay, rather turn this day out of the week,

This day of shame, oppression, perjury:
Or, if it must stand still, let wives with child
Pray that their burdens may not fall this day,
Lest that their hopes prodigiously be cross'd:
But on this day let seamen fear no wreck;
No bargains break that are not this day made:
This day, all things begun come to ill end, —
Yea, faith itself to hollow falsehood change!

 K. Phi. By heaven, lady, you shall have no cause
To curse the fair proceedings of this day:
Have I not pawn'd to you my majesty?

 Const. You have beguil'd me with a counterfeit
Resembling majesty; which, being touch'd and tried,
Proves valueless: you are forsworn, forsworn;
You came in arms to spill mine enemies' blood,
But now in arms you strengthen it with yours:
The grappling vigour and rough frown of war
Is cold in amity and painted peace,
And our oppression hath made up this league. —
Arm, arm, you heavens, against these perjur'd kings!
A widow cries; be husband to me, heavens!
Let not the hours of this ungodly day
Wear out the day in peace; but, ere sunset,
Set armèd discord 'twixt these perjur'd kings!
Hear me, O, hear me!

 Aust.   Lady Constance, peace!

 Const. War! war! no peace! peace is to me a war.
O Limoges! O Austria! thou dost shame
That bloody spoil: thou slave, thou wretch, thou coward!
Thou little valiant, great in villany!
Thou ever strong upon the stronger side!
Thou Fortune's champion that dost never fight
But when her humorous ladyship is by
To teach thee safety! thou art perjur'd too,
And sooth'st up greatness. What a fool art thou,
A ramping fool, to brag, and stamp, and swear,
Upon my party! Thou cold-blooded slave,

Hast thou not spoke like thunder on my side?
Been sworn my soldier? bidding me depend
Upon thy stars, thy fortune, and thy strength?
And dost thou now fall over to my foes?
Thou wear a lion's hide! doff it for shame,
And hang a calf's-skin on those recreant limbs.
 Aust. O, that a man should speak those words to me!
 Bast. And hang a calf's-skin on those recreant limbs.
 Aust. Thou dar'st not say so, villain, for thy life.
 Bast. And hang a calf's-skin on those recreant limbs.
 K. John. We like not this; thou dost forget thyself.
 K. Phi. Here comes the holy legate of the Pope.

Enter PANDULPH, *attended.*

 Pand. Hail, you anointed deputies of heaven!
To thee, King John, my holy errand is.
I Pandulph, of fair Milan cardinal,
And from Pope Innocent the legate here,
Do in his name religiously demand,
Why thou against the church, our holy mother,
So wilfully dost spurn, and, force perforce,
Keep Stephen Langton, chosen archbishop
Of Canterbury, from that holy see?
This, in our foresaid holy father's name,
Pope Innocent, I do demand of thee.
 K. John. What earthly name to interrogatories
Can task the free breath of a sacred king?
Thou canst not, cardinal, devise a name
So slight, unworthy, and ridiculous,
To charge me to an answer, as the Pope.
Tell him this tale; and from the mouth of England
Add thus much more, — That no Italian priest
Shall tithe or toll in our dominions;
But as we, under heaven, are supreme head,
So, under Him, that great supremacy,
Where we do reign, we will alone uphold,
Without th' assistance of a mortal hand:

So tell the Pope; all reverence set apart
To him and his usurp'd authority.

 K. Phi. Brother of England, you blaspheme in this.

 K. John. Though you, and all the kings of Christendom,
Are led so grossly by this meddling priest,
Dreading the curse that money may buy out;
And by the merit of vile gold, dross, dust,
Purchase corrupted pardon of a man,
Who in that sale sells pardon from himself;
Though you and all the rest, so grossly led,
This juggling witchcraft with revenue cherish;
Yet I, alone, alone do me oppose
Against the Pope, and count his friends my foes.

 Pand. Then, by the lawful power that I have,
Thou shalt stand curs'd and excommunicate:
And blessèd shall he be that doth revolt
From his allegiance to an heretic;
And meritorious shall that hand be call'd,
Canónizèd, and worshipp'd as a saint,
That takes away by any secret course
Thy hateful life.

 Const. O, lawful let it be
That I have room with Rome to curse awhile!
Good father cardinal, cry thou amen
To my keen curses; for without my wrong
There is no tongue hath power to curse him right.

 Pand. There's law and warrant, lady, for my curse.

 Const. And for mine too: when law can do no right,
Let it be lawful that law bar no wrong:
Law cannot give my child his kingdom here;
For he that holds his kingdom holds the law:
Therefore, since law itself is perfect wrong,
How can the law forbid my tongue to curse?

 Pand. Philip of France, on peril of a curse,
Let go the hand of that arch-heretic;
And raise the power of France upon his head,
Unless he do submit himself to Rome.

Eli. Look'st thou pale, France? do not let go thy hand.
Const. Look to that, devil; lest that France repent,
And by disjoining hands, hell lose a soul.
Aust. King Philip, listen to the cardinal.
Bast. And hang a calf's-skin on his recreant limbs.
Aust. Well, ruffian, I must pocket up these wrongs,
Because —
Bast. Your breeches best may carry them.
K. John. Philip, what say'st thou to the cardinal?
Const. What should he say, but as the cardinal?
Lou. Bethink you, father; for the difference
Is, purchase of a heavy curse from Rome,
Or the light loss of England for a friend:
Forgo the easier.
Blanch. That's the curse of Rome.
Const. O Louis, stand fast! the devil tempts thee here
In likeness of a new-uptrimmèd bride.
Blanch. The Lady Constance speaks not from her faith,
But from her need.
Const. O, if thou grant my need,
Which only lives but by the death of faith,
That need must needs infer this principle, —
That faith would live again by death of need!
O, then, tread down my need, and faith mounts up;
Keep my need up, and faith is trodden down!
K. John. The king is mov'd, and answers not to this.
Const. O, be remov'd from him, and answer well!
Aust. Do so, King Philip; hang no more in doubt.
Bast. Hang nothing but a calf's-skin, most sweet lout.
K. Phi. I am perplex'd, and know not what to say.
Pand. What canst thou say but will perplex thee more,
If thou stand excommunicate and curs'd?
K. Phi. Good reverend father, make my person yours,
And tell me how you would bestow yourself.
This royal hand and mine are newly knit,
And the conjunction of our inward souls
Married in league, coupled and link'd together

With all religious strength of sacred vows;
The latest breath that gave the sound of words
Was deep-sworn faith, peace, amity, true love
Between our kingdoms and our royal selves;
And even before this truce, but new before, —
No longer than we well could wash our hands,
To clap this royal bargain up of peace, —
Heaven knows, they were besmear'd and overstain'd
With slaughter's pencil, where revenge did paint
The fearful difference of incensèd kings:
And shall these hands, so lately purg'd of blood,
So newly join'd in love, so strong in both,
Unyoke this seizure and this kind regreet?
Play fast and loose with faith? so jest with heaven,
Make such unconstant children of ourselves,
As now again to snatch our palm from palm;
Unswear faith sworn; and on the marriage-bed
Of smiling peace to march a bloody host,
And make a riot on the gentle brow
Of true sincerity? O, holy sir,
My reverend father, let it not be so!
Out of your grace, devise, ordain, impose
Some gentle order; and then we shall be blest
To do your pleasure, and continue friends.

Pand. All form is formless, order orderless,
Save what is opposite to England's love.
Therefore, to arms! be champion of our church!
Or let the church, our mother, breathe her curse, —
A mother's curse, — on her revolting son.
France, thou mayst hold a serpent by the tongue,
A chafèd lion by the mortal paw,
A fasting tiger safer by the tooth,
Than keep in peace that hand which thou dost hold.

K. Phi. I may disjoin my hand, but not my faith.

Pand. So mak'st thou faith an enemy to faith;
And, like a civil war, sett'st oath to oath,
Thy tongue against thy tongue   O, let thy vow

First made to heaven, first be to heaven perform'd, —
That is, to be the champion of our church!
What since thou swor'st is sworn against thyself,
And may not be performèd by thyself:
For that which thou hast sworn to do amiss
Is not amiss when it is truly done;
And being not done, where doing tends to ill,
The truth is then most done, not doing it:
The better act of purposes mistook
Is to mistake again; though indirect,
Yet indirection thereby grows direct,
And falsehood falsehood cures; as fire cools fire
Within the scorchèd veins of one new-burn'd.
It is religion that doth make vows kept;
But thou hast sworn against religion:
By which thou swear'st against the thing thou swear'st;
And mak'st an oath the surety for thy truth
Against an oath: the truth thou art unsure
To swear, swears only not to be forsworn;
Else what a mockery should it be to swear!
But thou dost swear only to be forsworn;
And most forsworn, to keep what thou dost swear.
Therefore thy later vow against thy first
Is in thyself rebellion to thyself;
And better conquest never canst thou make
Than arm thy constant and thy nobler parts
Against these giddy-loose suggestions:
Upon which better part our prayers come in,
If thou vouchsafe them; but if not, then know
The peril of our curses light on thee,
So heavy as thou shalt not shake them off,
But in despair die under their black weight.

 Aust. Rebellion, flat rebellion!
 Bast.   Will't not be?
Will not a calf's-skin stop that mouth of thine?
 Lou. Father, to arms!
 Blanch.   Upon thy wedding-day?

Against the blood that thou hast married?
What, shall our feast be kept with slaughter'd men?
Shall braying trumpets and loud churlish drums, —
Clamours of hell, — be measures to our pomp?
O husband, hear me! — ay, alack, how new
Is husband in my mouth! — even for that name,
Which till this time my tongue did ne'er pronounce,
Upon my knee I beg, go not to arms
Against mine uncle.
 Const.   O, upon my knee,
Made hard with kneeling, I do pray to thee,
Thou virtuous Dauphin, alter not the doom
Forethought by heaven!
 Blanch. Now shall I see thy love: what motive may
Be stronger with thee than the name of wife?
 Const. That which upholdeth him that thee upholds,
His honour: — O, thine honour, Louis, thine honour!
 Lou. I muse your majesty doth seem so cold,
When such profound respects do pull you on.
 Pand. I will denounce a curse upon his head.
 K. Phi. Thou shalt not need. — England, I'll fall from thee.
 Const. O fair return of banish'd majesty!
 Eli. O foul revolt of French inconstancy!
 K. John. France, thou shalt rue this hour within this hour.
 Bast. Old Time the clock-setter, that bald sexton Time,
Is it as he will? well, then, France shall rue.
 Blanch. The sun's o'ercast with blood: fair day, adieu!
Which is the side that I must go withal?
I am with both: each army hath a hand;
And in their rage, I having hold of both,
They whirl asunder and dismember me.
Husband, I cannot pray that thou mayst win;
Uncle, I needs must pray that thou mayst lose;
Father, I may not wish the fortune thine;
Grandam, I will not wish thy wishes thrive:
Whoever wins, on that side shall I lose;
Assurèd loss before the match be play'd.

Lou. Lady, with me; with me thy fortune lies.
Blanch. There where my fortune lives, there my life dies.
K. John. Cousin, go draw our puissance together.
[*Exit Bastard.*
France, I am burn'd up with inflaming wrath;
A rage whose heat hath this condition,
That nothing can allay't, nothing but blood, —
The blood, and dearest-valu'd blood of France.
K. Phi. Thy rage shall burn thee up, and thou shalt turn
To ashes, ere our blood shall quench that fire:
Look to thyself, thou art in jeopardy.
K. John. No more than he that threats. — To arms let's hie!
[*Exeunt, severally, the English and French Kings, &c.*

Scene II. *The same. Plains near Angiers.*

Alarums: excursions. Enter the Bastard, *with* Austria's *head.*

Bast. Now, by my life, this day grows wondrous hot;
Some airy devil hovers in the sky,
And pours down mischief. — Austria's head lie there,
While Philip breathes.

Enter King John, Arthur, *and* Hubert.

K. John. Hubert, keep thou this boy. — Philip, make up:
My mother is assailèd in our tent,
And ta'en, I fear.
Bast. My lord, I rescu'd her;
Her highness is in safety, fear you not:
But on, my liege; for very little pains
Will bring this labour to an happy end. [*Exeunt.*

Scene III. *The same. Another part of the plains.*

Alarums: excursions; retreat. Enter King John, Elinor, Arthur,
the Bastard, Hubert, *and* Lords.

K. John. [*to Elinor*] So shall it be; your grace shall stay
behind,
So strongly guarded. — [*To Arthur*] Cousin, look not sad:

Thy grandam loves thee; and thy uncle will
As dear be to thee as thy father was.
    Arth. O, this will make my mother die with grief!
    K. John. [*to the Bastard*] Cousin, away for England; haste
       before:
And, ere our coming, see thou shake the bags
Of hoarding abbots; set at liberty
Imprison'd angels: the fat ribs of peace
Must by the hungry now be fed upon:
Use our commission in his utmost force.
    Bast. Bell, book, and candle shall not drive me back,
When gold and silver becks me to come on.
I leave your highness. — Grandam, I will pray —
If ever I remember to be holy —
For your fair safety; so, I kiss your hand.
    Eli. Farewell, gentle cousin.
    K. John.   . Coz, farewell.
                                        [*Exit Bastard.*
    Eli. Come hither, little kinsman; hark, a word.
                                    [*Takes Arthur aside.*
    K. John. Come hither, Hubert. O my gentle Hubert,
We owe thee much! within this wall of flesh
There is a soul counts thee her creditor,
And with advantage means to pay thy love:
And, my good friend, thy voluntary oath
Lives in this bosom, dearly cherishèd.
Give me thy hand. I had a thing to say, —
But I will fit it with some better time.
By heaven, Hubert, I'm almost asham'd
To say what good respect I have of thee.
    Hub. I am much bounden to your majesty.
    K. John. Good friend, thou hast no cause to say so yet:
But thou shalt have; and creep time ne'er so slow,
Yet it shall come for me to do thee good.
I had a thing to say, — but let it go:
The sun is in the heaven, and the proud day,
Attended with the pleasures of the world,

Is all too wanton and too full of gauds
To give me audience: — if the midnight bell
Did, with his iron tongue and brazen mouth,
Sound one into the drowsy ear of night;
If this same were a churchyard where we stand,
And thou possessèd with a thousand wrongs;
Or if that surly spirit, melancholy,
Had bak'd thy blood, and made it heavy-thick,
Which else runs tickling up and down the veins,
Making that idiot, laughter, keep men's eyes,
And strain their cheeks to idle merriment, —
A passion hateful to my purposes;
Or if that thou couldst see me without eyes,
Hear me without thine ears, and make reply
Without a tongue, using conceit alone,
Without eyes, ears, and harmful sound of words;
Then, in despite of brooded watchful day,
I would into thy bosom pour my thoughts:
But, ah, I will not! — yet I love thee well;
And, by my troth, I think thou lov'st me well.

Hub. So well, that what you bid me undertake,
Though that my death were adjunct to my act,
By heaven, I'd do't.

K. John. Do not I know thou wouldst?
Good Hubert, Hubert, Hubert, throw thine eye
On yon young boy: I'll tell thee what, my friend,
He is a very serpent in my way;
And wheresoe'er this foot of mine doth tread,
He lies before me: — dost thou understand me?
Thou art his keeper.

Hub. And I'll keep him so,
That he shall not offend your majesty.

K. John. Death.

Hub. My lord?

K. John. 'A grave.

Hub. He shall not live.

K. John. Enough.

I could be merry now. Hubert, I love thee;
Well, I'll not say what I intend for thee:
Remember. — Madam, fare you well:
I'll send those powers o'er to your majesty.

 Eli. My blessing go with thee!

 K. John.   For England, cousin, go:
Hubert shall be your man, t' attend on you
With all true duty. — On toward Calais, ho! *[Exeunt.*

  Scene IV. *The same. The* French King's *tent.*

 Enter King Philip, Louis, Pandulph, *and* Attendants.

 K. Phi. So, by a roaring tempest on the flood,
A whole armado of convented sail
Is scatter'd and disjoin'd from fellowship.

 Pand. Courage and comfort! all shall yet go well.

 K. Phi. What can go well, when we have run so ill?
Are we not beaten? Is not Angiers lost?
Arthur ta'en prisoner? divers dear friends slain?
And bloody England into England gone,
O'erbearing interruption, spite of France?

 Lou. What he hath won, that hath he fortified:
So hot a speed with such advice dispos'd,
Such temperate order in so fierce a course,
Doth want example: who hath read or heard
Of any kindred action like to this?

 K. Phi. Well could I bear that England had this praise,
So we could find some pattern of our shame. —
Look, who comes here! a grave unto a soul;
Holding th' eternal spirit, against her will,
In the vile prison of afflicted breath.

     Enter Constance.

I prithee, lady, go away with me.

 Const. Lo, now! now see the issue of your peace!

 K. Phi. Patience, good lady! comfort, gentle Constance!

Const. No, I defy all counsel, all redress,
But that which ends all counsel, true redress,
Death, death: — O amiable lovely death!
Thou odoriferous stench! sound rottenness!
Arise forth from the couch of lasting night,
Thou hate and terror to prosperity,
And I will kiss thy detestable bones;
And put my eyeballs in thy vaulty brows;
And ring these fingers with thy household worms;
And stop this gap of breath with fulsome dust;
And be a carrion monster like thyself:
Come, grin on me; and I will think thou smil'st,
And buss thee as thy wife! Misery's love,
O, come to me!

K. Phi. O fair affliction, peace!

Const. No, no, I will not, having breath to cry: —
O, that my tongue were in the thunder's mouth!
Then with a passion would I shake the world;
And rouse from sleep that fell anatomy
Which cannot hear a lady's feeble voice,
Which scorns a modern invocation.

Pand. Lady, you utter madness, and not sorrow.

Const. Thou art not holy to belie me so;
I am not mad: this hair I tear is mine;
My name is Constance; I was Geffrey's wife;
Young Arthur is my son, and he is lost:
I am not mad; — I would to heaven I were!
For then 'tis like I should forget myself:
O, if I could, what grief should I forget! —
Preach some philosophy to make me mad,
And thou shalt be canóniz'd, cardinal;
For, being not mad, but sensible of grief,
My reasonable part produces reason
How I may be deliver'd of these woes,
And teaches me to kill or hang myself:
If I were mad, I should forget my son,
Or madly think a babe of clouts were he:

I am not mad; too well, too well I feel
The different plague of each calamity.
    K. Phi. Bind up those tresses. — O, what love I note
In the fair multitude of those her hairs!
Where but by chance a silver drop hath fall'n,
Even to that drop ten thousand wiry friends
Do glue themselves in sociable grief;
Like true, inseparable, faithful loves,
Sticking together in calamity.
    Const. To England, if you will.
    K. Phi.   Bind up your hairs.
    Const. Yes, that I will; and wherefore will I do it?
I tore them from their bonds, and cried aloud,
"O, that these hands could so redeem my son,
As they have given these hairs their liberty!"
But now I envy at their liberty,
And will again commit them to their bonds,
Because my poor child is a prisoner. —
And, father cardinal, I have heard you say
That we shall see and know our friends in heaven:
If that be true, I shall see my boy again;
For since the birth of Cain, the first male child,
To him that did but yesterday suspire,
There was not such a gracious creature born.
But now will canker-sorrow eat my bud,
And chase the native beauty from his cheek,
And he will look as hollow as a ghost,
As dim and meagre as an ague-fit;
And so he'll die; and, rising so again,
When I shall meet him in the court of heaven
I shall not know him: therefore never, never
Must I behold my pretty Arthur more.
    Pand. You hold too heinous a respect of grief.
    Const. He talks to me that never had a son.
    K. Phi. You are as fond of grief as of your child.
    Const. Grief fills the room up of my absent child,
Lies in his bed, walks up and down with me,

Puts on his pretty looks, repeats his words,
Remembers me of all his gracious parts,
Stuffs out his vacant garments with his form;
Then have I reason to be fond of grief.
Fare you well: had you such a loss as I,
I could give better comfort than you do. —
I will not keep this form upon my head,
[Dishevelling her hair.
When there is such disorder in my wit.
O Lord! my boy, my Arthur, my fair son!
My life, my joy, my food, my all the world!
My widow-comfort, and my sorrows' cure! *[Exit.*
   K. Phi. I fear some outrage, and I'll follow her. *[Exit.*
   Lou. There's nothing in this world can make me joy:
Life is as tedious as a twice-told tale
Vexing the dull ear of a drowsy man;
And bitter shame hath spoil'd the sweet world's taste,
That it yields naught but shame and bitterness.
   Pand. Before the curing of a strong disease,
Even in the instant of repair and health,
The fit is strongest; evils that take leave,
On their departure most of all show evil:
What have you lost by losing of this day?
   Lou. All days of glory, joy, and happiness.
   Pand. If you had won it, certainly you had.
No, no; when Fortune means to men most good,
She looks upon them with a threatening eye.
'Tis strange to think how much King John hath lost
In this which he accounts so clearly won:
Are not you griev'd that Arthur is his prisoner?
   Lou. As heartily as he is glad he hath him.
   Pand. Your mind is all as youthful as your blood.
Now hear me speak with a prophetic spirit;
For even the breath of what I mean to speak
Shall blow each dust, each straw, each little rub,
Out of the path which shall directly lead
Thy foot to England's throne; and therefore mark.

24*

John hath seiz'd Arthur; and it cannot be,
That, whiles warm life plays in that infant's veins,
The misplac'd John should entertain one hour,
One minute, nay, one quiet breath of rest:
A sceptre snatch'd with an unruly hand
Must be as boisterously maintain'd as gain'd;
And he that stands upon a slippery place
Makes nice of no vile hold to stay him up:
That John may stand, then Arthur needs must fall;
So be it, for it cannot be but so.

Lou. But what shall I gain by young Arthur's fall?

Pand. You, in the right of Lady Blanch your wife,
May then make all the claim that Arthur did.

Lou. And lose it, life and all, as Arthur did.

Pand. How green you are, and fresh in this old world!
John lays you plots; the times conspire with you;
For he that steeps his safety in true blood
Shall find but bloody safety and untrue.
This act, so evilly borne, shall cool the hearts
Of all his people, and freeze up their zeal,
That none so small advantage shall step forth
To check his reign, but they will cherish it;
No natural exhalation in the sky,
No scape of nature, no distemper'd day,
No common wind, no customèd event,
But they will pluck away his natural cause,
And call them meteors, prodigies, and signs,
Abortives, présages, and tongues of heaven,
Plainly denouncing vengeance upon John.

Lou. May be he will not touch young Arthur's life,
But hold himself safe in his prisonment.

Pand. O, sir, when he shall hear of your approach,
If that young Arthur be not gone already,
Even at that news he dies; and then the hearts
Of all his people shall revolt from him,
And kiss the lips of unacquainted change;
And pick strong matter of revolt and wrath

Out of the bloody fingers' ends of John.
Methinks I see this hurly all on foot:
And, O, what better matter breeds for you
Than I have nam'd! — The bastard Falconbridge
Is now in England, ransacking the church,
Offending charity: if but a dozen French
Were there in arms, they would be as a call
To train ten thousand English to their side;
Or, as a little snow, tumbled about,
Anon becomes a mountain. O noble Dauphin,
Go with me to the king: — 'tis wonderful
What may be wrought out of their discontent,
Now that their souls are topful of offence:
For England go: — I will whet on the king.

   Lou. Strong reasons make strong actions: let us go:
If you say ay, the king will not say no.   [*Exeunt.*

ACT IV.

Scene I. *Northampton. A room in the castle.*

Enter Hubert *and two* Attendants.

   Hub. Heat me these irons hot; and look you stand
Within the arras: when I strike my foot
Upon the bosom of the ground, rush forth,
And bind the boy which you shall find with me
Fast to the chair: be heedful: hence, and watch.
   First Attend. I hope your warrant will bear out the deed.
   Hub. Uncleanly scruples! fear not you: look to't.
                                          [*Exeunt Attendants.*
Young lad, come forth; I have to say with you.

Enter Arthur.

   Arth. Good morrow, Hubert.
   Hub.   Good morrow, little prince.
   Arth. As little prince, having so great a title
To be more prince, as may be. — You are sad.
   Hub. Indeed, I have been merrier.

Arth. Mercy on me!
Methinks no body should be sad but I:
Yet, I remember, when I was in France,
Young gentlemen would be as sad as night
Only for wantonness. By my christendom,
So I were out of prison, and kept sheep,
I should be merry as the day is long;
And so I would be here, but that I doubt
My uncle practises more harm to me:
He is afraid of me, and I of him:
Is it my fault that I was Geffrey's son?
No, indeed, is't not; and I would to heaven
I were your son, so you would love me, Hubert.

Hub. [*aside*] If I talk to him, with his innocent prate
He will awake my mercy, which lies dead:
Therefore I will be sudden and dispatch.

Arth. Are you sick, Hubert? you look pale to-day:
In sooth, I would you were a little sick,
That I might sit all night and watch with you:
I warrant I love you more than you do me.

Hub. [*aside*] His words do take possession of my bosom. —
Read here, young Arthur. [*Showing a paper.*
[*Aside*] How now, foolish rheum!
Turning dispiteous torture out of door!
I must be brief, lest resolution drop
Out at mine eyes in tender womanish tears. —
Can you not read it? is it not fair writ?

Arth. Too fairly, Hubert, for so foul effect:
Must you with hot irons burn out both mine eyes?

Hub. Young boy, I must.

Arth. And will you?

Hub. And I will.

Arth. Have you the heart? When your head did but ache,
I knit my handkercher about your brows, —
The best I had, a princess wrought it me, —
And I did never ask it you again;
And with my hand at midnight held your head;

And like the watchful minutes to the hour,
Still and anon cheer'd up the heavy time,
Saying, "What lack you?" and, "Where lies your grief?"
Or, "What good love may I perform for you?"
Many a poor man's son would have lien still,
And ne'er have spoke a loving word to you;
But you at your sick service had a prince.
Nay, you may think my love was crafty love,
And call it cunning: — do, an if you will:
If heaven be pleas'd that you must use me ill,
Why, then you must. — Will you put out mine eyes?
These eyes that never did nor never shall
So much as frown on you?

 Hub.   I've sworn to do it;
And with hot irons must I burn them out.

 Arth. Ah, none but in this iron age would do it!
The iron of itself, though heat red-hot,
Approaching near these eyes, would drink my tears,
And quench his fiery indignation
Even in the water of mine innocence;
Nay, after that, consume away in rust,
But for containing fire to harm mine eyes.
Are you more stubborn-hard than hammer'd iron?
An if an angel should have come to me,
And told me Hubert should put out mine eyes,
I would not have believ'd him, — no tongue but Hubert's.

 Hub. Come forth!   [*Stamps.*

   Re-enter Attendants, *with cord, irons, &c.*

Do as I bid you do.

 Arth. O, save me, Hubert, save me! my eyes are out
Even with the fierce looks of these bloody men.

 Hub. Give me the iron, I say, and bind him here.

 Arth. Alas, what need you be so boisterous-rough?
I will not struggle, I will stand stone-still.
For heaven-sake, Hubert, let me not be bound!
Nay, hear me, Hubert! — drive these men away,

And I will sit as quiet as a lamb;
I will not stir, nor wince, nor speak a word,
Nor look upon the iron angerly:
Thrust but these men away, and I'll forgive you,
Whatever torment you do put me to.
  Hub. Go, stand within; let me alone with him.
  First Attend. I am best pleas'd to be from such a deed.
  [*Exeunt Attendants.*
  Arth. Alas, I then have chid away my friend!
He hath a stern look, but a gentle heart: —
Let him come back, that his compassion may
Give life to yours.
  Hub.   Come, boy, prepare yourself.
  Arth. Is there no remedy?
  Hub.   None, but to lose your eyes.
  Arth. O heaven! — that there were but a mote in yours,
A grain, a dust, a gnat, a wandering hair,
Any annoyance in that precious sense!
Then, feeling what small things are boisterous there,
Your vile intent must needs seem horrible.
  Hub. Is this your promise? go to, hold your tongue.
  Arth. Hubert, the utterance of a brace of tongues
Must needs want pleading for a pair of eyes:
Let me not hold my tongue, — let me not, Hubert;
O, Hubert, if you will, cut out my tongue,
So I may keep mine eyes: O, spare mine eyes,
Though to no use but still to look on you! —
Lo, by my troth, the instrument is cold,
And would not harm me.
  Hub.   I can heat it, boy.
  Arth. No, in good sooth; the fire is dead with grief,
Being create for comfort, to be us'd
In undeserv'd extremes: see else yourself;
There is no malice in this burning coal;
The breath of heaven hath blown his spirit out,
And strew'd repentant ashes on his head.
  Hub. But with my breath I can revive it, boy.

Arth. And if you do, you will but make it blush,
And glow with shame of your proceedings, Hubert:
Nay, it perchance will sparkle in your eyes;
And, like a dog that is compell'd to fight,
Snatch at his master that doth tarre him on.
All things that you should use to do me wrong
Deny their office: only you do lack
That mercy which fierce fire and iron extend,
Creatures of note for mercy-lacking uses.
 Hub. Well, see to live; I will not touch thine eyes
For all the treasure that thine uncle owes:
Yet am I sworn, and I did purpose, boy,
With this same very iron to burn them out.
 Arth. O, now you look like Hubert! all this while
You were disguisèd.
 Hub. Peace; no more. Adieu.
Your uncle must not know but you are dead;
I'll fill these doggèd spies with false reports:
And, pretty child, sleep doubtless and secure
That Hubert, for the wealth of all the world,
Will not offend thee.
 Arth. O heaven! I thank you, Hubert.
 Hub. Silence; no more: go closely in with me:
Much danger do I undergo for thee. [*Exeunt.*

SCENE II. *The same. A room of state in the palace.*

Enter King JOHN, *crowned;* PEMBROKE, SALISBURY, *and other Lords. The King takes his state.*

K. John. Here once again we sit, once again crown'd,
And look'd upon, I hope, with cheerful eyes.
 Pem. This once again, but that your highness pleas'd,
Was once superfluous: you were crown'd before,
And that high royalty was ne'er pluck'd off;
The faiths of men ne'er stainèd with revolt;
Fresh expectation troubled not the land
With any long'd-for change or better state.

Sal.   Therefore, to be possess'd with double pomp,
To guard a title that was rich before,
To gild refinèd gold, to paint the lily,
To throw a perfume on the violet,
To smooth the ice, or add another hue
Unto the rainbow, or with taper-light
To seek the beauteous eye of heaven to garnish,
Is wasteful and ridiculous excess.

Pem.   But that your royal pleasure must be done,
This act is as an ancient tale new-told;
And in the last repeating troublesome,
Being urgèd at a time unseasonable.

Sal.   In this, the antique and well-noted face
Of plain old form is much disfigurèd;
And, like a shifted wind unto a sail,
It makes the course of thoughts to fetch about;
Startles and frights consideration;
Makes sound opinion sick, and truth suspected,
For putting on so new a fashion'd robe.

Pem.   When workmen strive to do better than well,
They do confound their skill in covetousness;
And oftentimes excusing of a fault
Doth make the fault the worse by the excuse, —
As patches set upon a little breach
Discredit more in hiding of the fault
Than did the fault before it was so patch'd.

Sal.   To this effect, before you were new-crown'd,
We breath'd our counsel: but it pleas'd your highness
To overbear 't; and we are all well pleas'd,
Since all and every part of what we would
Doth make a stand at what your highness will.

K. John.   Some reasons of this double coronation
I have possess'd you with, and think them strong;
And more, more strong, when lesser is my fear,
I shall indue you with: meantime but ask
What you would have reform'd that is not well,

And well shall you perceive how willingly
I will both hear and grant you your requests.

Pem. Then I — as one that am the tongue of these,
To sound the purposes of all their hearts,
Both for myself and them, but, chief of all,
Your safety, for the which myself and them
Bend their best studies — heartily request
Th' enfranchisement of Arthur; whose restraint
Doth move the murmuring lips of discontent
To break into this dangerous argument, —
If what in rest you have in right you hold,
Why should your fears — which, as they say, attend
The steps of wrong — then move you to mew up
Your tender kinsman, and to choke his days
With barbarous ignorance, and deny his youth
The rich advantage of good exercise?
That the time's enemies may not have this
To grace occasions, let it be our suit,
That you have bid us ask, his liberty;
Which for our goods we do no further ask
Than whereupon our weal, on you depending,
Counts it your weal he have his liberty.

K. John. Let it be so: I do commit his youth
To your direction.

Enter Hubert; *whom King John takes aside.*

Hubert, what news with you?

Pem. This is the man should do the bloody deed;
He show'd his warrant to a friend of mine:
The image of a wicked heinous fault
Lives in his eye; that close aspéct of his
Does show the mood of a much-troubled breast;
And I do fearfully believe 'tis done,
What we so fear'd he had a charge to do.

Sal. The colour of the king doth come and go
Between his purpose and his conscience,

Like heralds 'twixt two dreadful battles set:
His passion is so ripe, it needs must break.

Pem. And when it breaks, I fear will issue thence
The foul corruption of a sweet child's death.

K. John. We cannot hold mortality's strong hand:—
Good lords, although my will to give is living,
The suit which you demand is gone and dead:
He tells us Arthur is deceas'd to-night.

Sal. Indeed, we fear'd his sickness was past cure.

Pem. Indeed, we heard how near his death he was
Before the child himself felt he was sick:
This must be answer'd either here or hence.

K. John. Why do you bend such solemn brows on me?
Think you I bear the shears of destiny?
Have I commandment on the pulse of life?

Sal. It is apparent foul-play; and 'tis shame
That greatness should so grossly offer it:
So thrive it in your game! and so, farewell.

Pem. Stay yet, Lord Salisbury; I'll go with thee,
And find th' inheritance of this poor child,
His little kingdom of a forcèd grave.
That blood which ow'd the breadth of all this isle,
Three foot of it doth hold:— bad world the while!
This must not be thus borne: this will break out
To all our sorrows, and ere long I doubt. [*Exeunt Lords.*

K. John. They burn in indignation. I repent:
There is no sure foundation set on blood,
No certain life achiev'd by others' death.—

Enter a Messenger.

A fearful eye thou hast: where is that blood
That I have seen inhabit in those cheeks?
So foul a sky clears not without a storm:
Pour down thy weather:— how goes all in France?

Mess. From France to England.— Never such a power
For any foreign preparation
Was levied in the body of a land.

The copy of your speed is learn'd by them;
For when you should be told they do prepare,
The tidings come that they are all arriv'd.
    K. John. O, where hath our intelligence been drunk?
Where hath it slept? Where is my mother's ear,
That such an army could be drawn in France,
And she not hear of it?
    Mess.   My liege, her ear
Is stopp'd with dust; the first of April died
Your noble mother: and, as I hear, my lord,
The Lady Constance in a frenzy died
Three days before; but this from rumour's tongue
I idly heard, — if true or false I know not.
    K. John. Withhold thy speed, dreadful occasion!
O, make a league with me, till I have pleas'd
My discontented peers! — What! mother dead!
How wildly, then, walks my estate in France! —
Under whose conduct come those powers of France
That thou for truth giv'st out are landed here?
    Mess. Under the Dauphin.
    K. John.   Thou hast made me giddy
With these ill tidings.

        Enter the Bastard *and* Peter *of Pomfret.*
                Now, what says the world
To your proceedings? do not seek to stuff
My head with more ill news, for it is full.
    Bast. But if you be afeard to hear the worst,
Then let the worst, unheard, fall on your head.
    K. John. Bear with me, cousin; for I was amaz'd
Under the tide: but now I breathe again
Aloft the flood; and can give audience
To any tongue, speak it of what it will.
    Bast. How I have sped among the clergymen,
The sums I have collected shall express.
But as I travell'd hither through the land,
I find the people strangely fantasied;

Possess'd with rumours, full of idle dreams,
Not knowing what they fear, but full of fear:
And here's a prophet, that I brought with me
From forth the streets of Pomfret, whom I found
With many hundreds treading on his heels;
To whom he sung, in rude harsh-sounding rhymes,
That, ere the next Ascension-day at noon,
Your highness should deliver up your crown.

 K. John. Thou idle dreamer, wherefore didst thou so?
 Peter. Foreknowing that the truth will fall out so.
 K. John. Hubert, away with him; imprison him;
And on that day at noon, whereon he says
I shall yield up my crown, let him be hang'd.
Deliver him to safety; and return,
For I must use thee.   [*Exit Hubert with Peter.*
     O my gentle cousin,
Hear'st thou the news abroad, who are arriv'd?
 Bast. The French, my lord; men's mouths are full of it:
Besides, I met Lord Bigot and Lord Salisbury
With eyes as red as new-enkindled fire,
And others more, going to seek the grave
Of Arthur, who, they say, is kill'd to-night
On your suggestion.
 K. John.   Gentle kinsman, go,
And thrust thyself into their companies:
I have a way to win their loves again;
Bring them before me.
 Bast.   I will seek them out.
 K. John. Nay, but make haste; the better foot before.
O, let me have no subject enemies,
When adverse foreigners affright my towns
With dreadful pomp of stout invasion!
Be Mercury, set feathers to thy heels,
And fly like thought from them to me again.
 Bast. The spirit of the time shall teach me speed.
 K. John. Spoke like a sprightful noble gentleman.
          [*Exit Bastard.*

Go after him; for he perhaps shall need
Some messenger betwixt me and the peers;
And be thou he.
    Mess.   With all my heart, my liege.   [*Exit.*
    K. John. My mother dead!

    Re-enter HUBERT.

    Hub. My lord, they say five moons were seen to-night;
Four fixèd; and the fifth did whirl about
The other four in wondrous motion.
    K. John. Five moons!
    Hub.   Old men and beldams in the streets
Do prophesy upon it dangerously:
Young Arthur's death is common in their mouths:
And when they talk of him, they shake their heads,
And whisper one another in the ear;
And he that speaks doth gripe the hearer's wrist;
Whilst he that hears makes fearful action,
With wrinkled brows, with nods, with rolling eyes.
I saw a smith stand with his hammer, thus,
The whilst his iron did on the anvil cool,
With open mouth swallowing a tailor's news;
Who, with his shears and measure in his hand,
Standing on slippers,—which his nimble haste
Had falsely thrust upon contrary feet,—
Told of a many thousand warlike French
That were embattailèd and rank'd in Kent:
Another lean unwash'd artificer
Cuts off his tale, and talks of Arthur's death.
    K. John. Why seek'st thou to possess me with these fears?
Why urgest thou so oft young Arthur's death?
Thy hand hath murder'd him: I had mighty cause
To wish him dead, but thou hadst none to kill him.
    Hub. No had, my lord! why, did you not provoke me?
    K. John. It is the curse of kings to be attended
By slaves that take their humours for a warrant
To break within the bloody house of life;

And, on the winking of authority,
To understand a law; to know the meaning
Of dangerous majesty, when perchance it frowns
More upon humour than advis'd respect.

    Hub. Here is your hand and seal for what I did.

    K. John. O, when the last account 'twixt heaven and earth
Is to be made, then shall this hand and seal
Witness against us to damnation!
How oft the sight of means to do ill deeds
Make ill deeds done! Hadst not thou been by,
A fellow by the hand of nature mark'd,
Quoted, and sign'd, to do a deed of shame,
This murder had not come into my mind:
But, taking note of thy abhorr'd aspéct,
Finding thee fit for bloody villany,
Apt, liable to be employ'd in danger,
I faintly broke with thee of Arthur's death;
And thou, to be endearèd to a king,
Made it no conscience to destroy a prince.

    Hub. My lord, —

    K. John. Hadst thou but shook thy head, or made a pause,
When I spake darkly what I purposèd,
Or turn'd an eye of doubt upon my face,
And bid me tell my tale in express words,
Deep shame had struck me dumb, made me break off,
And those thy fears might have wrought fears in me:
But thou didst understand me by my signs,
And didst in signs again parley with sin;
Yea, without stop, didst let thy heart consent,
And consequently thy rude hand to act
The deed, which both our tongues held vile to name. —
Out of my sight, and never see me more!
My nobles leave me; and my state is brav'd,
Even at my gates, with ranks of foreign powers:
Nay, in the body of this fleshly land,
This kingdom, this confine of blood and breath,

Hostility and civil tumult reign
Between my conscience and my cousin's death.
 Hub. Arm you against your other enemies,
I'll make a peace between your soul and you.
Young Arthur is alive: this hand of mine
Is yet a maiden and an innocent hand,
Not painted with the crimson spots of blood.
Within this bosom never enter'd yet
The dreadful motion of a murderous thought;
And you have slander'd nature in my form, —
Which, howsoever rude exteriorly,
Is yet the cover of a fairer mind
Than to be butcher of an innocent child.
 K. John. Doth Arthur live? O, haste thee to the peers,
Throw this report on their incensèd rage,
And make them tame to their obedience!
Forgive the comment that my passion made
Upon thy feature; for my rage was blind,
And foul-imaginary eyes of blood
Presented thee more hideous than thou art.
O, answer not; but to my closet bring
The angry lords with all expedient haste!
I cónjure thee but slowly; run more fast. [*Exeunt.*

SCENE III. *The same. Before the castle.*

Enter, on the walls, ARTHUR, *disguised as a ship-boy.*
 Arth. The wall is high, and yet will I leap down: —
Good ground, be pitiful, and hurt me not! —
There's few or none do know me: if they did,
This ship-boy's semblance hath disguis'd me quite.
I am afraid; and yet I'll venture it.
If I get down, and do not break my limbs,
I'll find a thousand shifts to get away:
As good to die and go, as die and stay. [*Leaps down.*
O me! my uncle's spirit is in these stones: —
Heaven take my soul, and England keep my bones! [*Dies.*

Enter PEMBROKE, SALISBURY, *and* BIGOT.

Sal. Lords, I will meet him at Saint Edmund's-Bury:
It is our safety, and we must embrace
This gentle offer of the perilous time.
Pem. Who brought that letter from the cardinal?
Sal. The Count Melun, a noble lord of France;
Whose private with me of the Dauphin's love
Is much more general than these lines import.
Big. To-morrow morning let us meet him, then.
Sal. Or rather then set forward; for 'twill be
Two long days' journey, lords, or e'er we meet.

Enter the Bastard.

Bast. Once more to-day well met, distemper'd lords!
The king by me requests your presence straight.
Sal. The king hath dispossess'd himself of us:
We will not line his thin bestainèd cloak
With our pure honours, nor attend the foot
That leaves the print of blood where'er it walks.
Return and tell him so: we know the worst.
Bast. Whate'er you think, good words, I think, were best.
Sal. Our griefs, and not our manners, reason now.
Bast. But there is little reason in your grief;
Therefore 'twere reason you had manners now.
Pem. Sir, sir, impatience hath his privilege.
Bast. 'Tis true, — to hurt his master, no man else.
Sal. This is the prison: — what is he lies here?

[*Seeing Arthur.*

Pem. O death, made proud with pure and princely beauty!
The earth had not a hole to hide this deed.
Sal. Murder, as hating what himself hath done,
Doth lay it open to urge on revenge.
Big. Or, when he doom'd this beauty to a grave,
Found it too precious-princely for a grave.
Sal. Sir Richard, what think you? Have you beheld,
Or have you read or heard? or could you think?
Or do you almost think, although you see,

That you do see? could thought, without this object,
Form such another? This is the very top,
The height, the crest, or crest unto the crest,
Of murder's arms: this is the bloodiest shame,
The wildest savagery, the vilest stroke,
That ever wall-ey'd wrath or staring rage
Presented to the tears of soft remorse.

Pem. All murders past do stand excus'd in this:
And this, so sole and so unmatchable,
Shall give a holiness, a purity,
To the yet-unbegotten sins of time;
And prove a deadly bloodshed but a jest,
Exampled by this heinous spectacle.

Bast. It is a damnèd and a bloody work;
The graceless action of a heavy hand,—
If that it be the work of any hand.

Sal. If that it be the work of any hand!—
We had a kind of light what would ensue:
It is the shameful work of Hubert's hand;
The practice and the purpose of the king:—
From whose obedience I forbid my soul,
Kneeling before this ruin of sweet life,
And breathing to his breathless excellence
The incense of a vow, a holy vow,
Never to taste the pleasures of the world,
Never to be infected with delight,
Nor conversant with ease and idleness,
Till I have set a glory to this head,
By giving it the worship of revenge.

Pem.
Big. } Our souls religiously confirm thy words.

Enter HUBERT.

Hub. Lords, I am hot with haste in seeking you:
Arthur doth live; the king hath sent for you.

Sal. O, he is bold, and blushes not at death:—
Avaunt, thou hateful villain, get thee gone!

Hub. I am no villain.
Sal.   Must I rob the law?
                                     [*Drawing his sword.*
Bast. Your sword is bright, sir; put it up again.
Sal. Not till I sheathe it in a murderer's skin.
Hub. Stand back, Lord Salisbury, — stand back, I say;
By heaven, I think my sword's as sharp as yours:
I would not have you, lord, forget yourself,
Nor tempt the danger of my true defence;
Lest I, by marking of your rage, forget
Your worth, your greatness, and nobility.
Big. Out, dunghill! dar'st thou brave a nobleman?
Hub. Not for my life: but yet I dare defend
My innocent self against an emperor.
Sal. Thou art a murderer.
Hub.   Do not prove me so;
Yet I am none: whose tongue soe'er speaks false,
Not truly speaks; who speaks not truly, lies.
Pem. Cut him to pieces.
Bast.   Keep the peace, I say.
Sal. Stand by, or I shall gall you, Falconbridge.
Bast. Thou wert better gall the devil, Salisbury:
If thou but frown on me, or stir thy foot,
Or teach thy hasty spleen to do me shame,
I'll strike thee dead. Put up thy sword betime;
Or I'll so maul you and your toasting-iron,
That you shall think the devil is come from hell.
Big. What wilt thou do, renownèd Falconbridge?
Second a villain and a murderer?
Hub. Lord Bigot, I am none.
Big.   Who kill'd this prince?
Hub. 'Tis not an hour since I left him well:
I honour'd him, I lov'd him; and will weep
My date of life out for his sweet life's loss.
Sal. Trust not those cunning waters of his eyes,
For villany is not without such rheum;
And he, long traded in it, makes it seem

Like rivers of remorse and innocency.
Away with me, all you whose souls abhor
Th' uncleanly savours of a slaughter-house;
For I am stifled with this smell of sin.
   Big. Away toward Bury, to the Dauphin there!
   Pem. There, tell the king, he may inquire us out.
                                           [*Exeunt Lords.*
   Bast. Here's a good world! — Knew you of this fair work?
Beyond the infinite and boundless reach
Of mercy, if thou didst this deed of death,
Art thou damn'd, Hubert.
   Hub.   Do but hear me, sir: —
   Bast. Ha! I'll tell thee what;
Thou'rt damn'd as black — nay, nothing is so black;
Thou art more deep damn'd than Prince Lucifer:
There is not yet so ugly a fiend of hell
As thou shalt be, if thou didst kill this child.
   Hub. Upon my soul, —
   Bast.   If thou didst but consent
To this most cruel act, do but despair;
And if thou want'st a cord, the smallest thread
That ever spider twisted from her womb
Will serve to strangle thee; a rush will be a beam
To hang thee on; or wouldst thou drown thyself,
Put but a little water in a spoon,
And it shall be as all the ocean,
Enough to stifle such a villain up.
I do suspect thee very grievously.
   Hub. If I in act, consent, or sin of thought,
Be guilty of the stealing that sweet breath
Which was embounded in this beauteous clay,
Let hell want pains enough to torture me!
I left him well.
   Bast.   Go, bear him in thine arms. —
I am amaz'd, methinks; and lose my way
Among the thorns and dangers of this world. —
How easy dost thou take all England up!

From forth this morsel of dead royalty,
The life, the right, and truth of all this realm
Is fled to heaven; and England now is left
To tug and scamble, and to part by the teeth
Th' unowèd interest of proud-swelling state.
Now for the bare-pick'd bone of majesty
Doth doggèd war bristle his angry crest,
And snarleth in the gentle eyes of peace:
Now powers from home and discontents at home
Meet in one line; and vast confusion waits,
As doth a raven on a sick-fall'n beast,
The imminent decay of wrested pomp.
Now happy he whose cloak and cincture can
Hold out this tempest. — Bear away that child,
And follow me with speed: I'll to the king:
A thousand businesses are brief in hand,
And heaven itself doth frown upon the land.   [*Exeunt.*

ACT V.

Scene I. *Northampton. A room in the palace.*

Enter King John, Pandulph *with the crown, and* Attendants.

K. John. Thus have I yielded up into your hand
The circle of my glory.
    Pand.   Take 't again
                  [*Giving King John the crown.*
From this my hand, as holding of the Pope
Your sovereign greatness and authority.
    K. John. Now keep your holy word: go meet the French;
And from his holiness use all your power
To stop their marches 'fore we are inflam'd.
Our discontented counties do revolt;
Our people quarrel with obedience;
Swearing allegiance and the love of soul
To stranger blood, to foreign royalty.
This inundation of mistemper'd humour

Rests by you only to be qualified:
Then pause not; for the present time's so sick,
That present medicine must be minister'd,
Or overthrow incurable ensues.

 Pand. It was my breath that blew this tempest up,
Upon your stubborn usage of the Pope:
But since you are a gentle convertite,
My tongue shall hush again this storm of war,
And make fair weather in your blustering land.
On this Ascension-day, remember well,
Upon your oath of service to the Pope,
Go I to make the French lay down their arms.   [*Exit.*

 K. John. Is this Ascension-day? Did not the prophet
Say, that before Ascension-day at noon
My crown I should give off? Even so I have:
I did suppose it should be on constraint;
But, heaven be thank'd, it is but voluntary.

Enter the Bastard.

 Bast. All Kent hath yielded; nothing there holds out
But Dover Castle: London hath receiv'd,
Like a kind host, the Dauphin and his powers:
Your nobles will not hear you, but are gone
To offer service to your enemy;
And wild amazement hurries up and down
The little number of your doubtful friends.

 K. John. Would not my lords return to me again,
After they heard young Arthur was alive?

 Bast. They found him dead, and cast into the streets;
An empty casket, where the jewel of life
By some damn'd hand was robb'd and ta'en away.

 K. John. That villain Hubert told me he did live.

 Bast. So, on my soul, he did, for aught he knew.
But wherefore do you droop? why look you sad?
Be great in act, as you have been in thought;
Let not the world see fear and sad distrust
Govern the motion of a kingly eye:

Be stirring as the time; be fire with fire;
Threaten the threatener, and outface the brow
Of bragging horror: so shall inferior eyes,
That borrow their behaviours from the great,
Grow great by your example, and put on
The dauntless spirit of resolution.
Away, and glister like the god of war,
When he intendeth to become the field:
Show boldness and aspiring confidence.
What, shall they seek the lion in his den,
And fright him there? and make him tremble there?
O, let it not be said! — Forage, and run
To meet displeasure further from the doors,
And grapple with him ere he come so nigh.

 K. John. The legate of the Pope hath been with me,
And I have made a happy peace with him;
And he hath promis'd to dismiss the powers
Led by the Dauphin.

 Bast.   O inglorious league!
Shall we, upon the footing of our land,
Send fair-play offers, and make compromise,
Insinuation, parley, and base truce,
To arms invasive? shall a beardless boy,
A cocker'd silken wanton, brave our fields,
And flesh his spirit in a warlike soil,
Mocking the air with colours idly spread,
And find no check? Let us, my liege, to arms:
Perchance the cardinal cannot make your peace;
Or if he do, let it at least be said
They saw we had a purpose of defence.

 K. John. Have thou the ordering of this present time.

 Bast. Away, then, with good courage! yet, I know,
Our party may well meet a prouder foe.

            [Exeunt.

SCENE II. *Near St. Edmund's-Bury. The French camp.*

Enter, in arms, LOUIS, SALISBURY, MELUN, PEMBROKE, BIGOT, *and* Soldiers.

Lou. My Lord Melun, let this be copied out,
And keep it safe for our remembrance:
Return the precedent to these lords again;
That, having our fair order written down,
Both they and we, perusing o'er these notes,
May know wheréfore we took the sacrament,
And keep our faiths firm and inviolable.

Sal. Upon our sides it never shall be broken.
And, noble Dauphin, albeit we swear
A voluntary zeal and unurg'd faith
To your proceedings; yet, believe me, prince,
I am not glad that such a sore of time
Should seek a plaster by contemn'd revolt,
And heal th' inveterate canker of one wound
By making many. O, it grieves my soul,
That I must draw this metal from my side
To be a widow-maker! O, and there
Where honourable rescue and defence
Cries out upon the name of Salisbury!
But such is the infection of the time,
That, for the health and physic of our right,
We cannot deal but with the very hand
Of stern injustice and confusèd wrong. —
And is 't not pity, O my grievèd friends,
That we, the sons and children of this isle,
Were born to see so sad an hour as this;
Wherein we step after a stranger-march
Upon her gentle bosom, and fill up
Her enemies' ranks, — I must withdraw and weep
Upon the spur of this enforcèd cause, —
To grace the gentry of a land remote,
And follow unacquainted colours here?
What, here? — O nation, that thou couldst remove!

That Neptune's arms, who clippeth thee about,
Would bear thee from the knowledge of thyself,
And grapple thee unto a pagan shore;
Where these two Christian armies might combine
The blood of malice in a vein of league,
And not to spend it so unneighbourly!

 Lou. A noble temper dost thou show in this;
And great affections wrestling in thy bosom
Do make an earthquake of nobility.
O, what a noble combat hast thou fought
Between compulsion and a brave respect!
Let me wipe off this honourable dew
That silverly doth progress on thy cheeks:
My heart hath melted at a lady's tears,
Being an ordinary inundation;
But this effusion of such manly drops,
This shower, blown up by tempest of the soul,
Startles mine eyes, and makes me more amaz'd
Than had I seen the vaulty top of heaven
Figur'd quite o'er with burning meteors.
Lift up thy brow, renownèd Salisbury,
And with a great heart heave away this storm:
Commend these waters to those baby eyes
That never saw the giant world enrag'd;
Nor met with fortune other than at feasts,
Full of warm blood, of mirth, of gossipping.
Come, come; for thou shalt thrust thy hand as deep
Into the purse of rich prosperity
As Louis himself: — so, nobles, shall you all,
That knit your sinews to the strength of mine. —
And even there, methinks, an angel spake:
Look, where the holy legate comes apace,
To give us warrant from the hand of heaven,
And on our actions set the name of right
With holy breath.

     Enter PANDULPH, *attended.*

 Pand. Hail, noble Prince of France!

The next is this, — King John hath reconcil'd
Himself to Rome; his spirit is come in,
That so stood out against the holy church,
The great metropolis and see of Rome :
Therefore thy threatening colours now wind up;
And tame the savage spirit of wild war,
That, like a lion foster'd-up at hand,
It may lie gently at the foot of peace,
And be no further harmful than in show.
 Lou. Your grace shall pardon me, I will not back:
I am too high-born to be propertied,
To be a secondary at control,
Or useful serving-man, and instrument,
To any sovereign state throughout the world.
Your breath first kindled the dead coal of wars
Between this chástis'd kingdom and myself,
And brought in matter that should feed this fire;
And now 'tis far too huge to be blown out
With that same weak wind which enkindled it.
You taught me how to know the face of right,
Acquainted me with interest to this land,
Yea, thrust this enterprise into my heart;
And come ye now to tell me John hath made
His peace with Rome? What is that peace to me?
I, by the honour of my marriage-bed,
After young Arthur, claim this land for mine;
And, now it is half-conquer'd, must I back
Because that John hath made his peace with Rome?
Am I Rome's slave? What penny hath Rome borne,
What men provided, what munition sent,
To underprop this action? Is 't not I
That undergo this charge? who else but I,
And such as to my claim are liable,
Sweat in this business and maintain this war?
Have I not heard these islanders shout out,
Vive le roi! as I have bank'd their towns?
Have I not here the best cards for the game,

To win this easy match play'd for a crown?
And shall I now give o'er the yielded set?
No, on my soul, it never shall be said.

   Pand. You look but on the outside of this work.

   Lou. Outside or inside, I will not return
Till my attempt so much be glorified
As to my ample hope was promisèd
Before I drew this gallant head of war,
And cull'd these fiery spirits from the world,
To outlook conquest, and to win renown
Even in the jaws of danger and of death. — [*Trumpet sounds.*
What lusty trumpet thus doth summon us?

         Enter the Bastard, *attended.*

   Bast. According to the fair-play of the world,
Let me have audience; I am sent to speak: —
My holy lord of Milan, from the king
I come, to learn how you have dealt for him;
And, as you answer, I do know the scope
And warrant limited unto my tongue.

   Pand. The Dauphin is too wilful-opposite,
And will not temporize with my entreaties;
He flatly says he'll not lay down his arms.

   Bast. By all the blood that ever fury breath'd,
The youth says well. — Now hear our English king;
For thus his royalty doth speak in me.
He is prepar'd; and reason too he should:
This apish and unmannerly approach,
This harness'd masque and unadvisèd revel,
This unhair'd sauciness and boyish troop,
The king doth smile at; and is well prepar'd
To whip this dwarfish war, these pigmy arms,
From out the circle of his territories.
That hand which had the strength, even at your door,
To cudgel you, and make you take the hatch;
To dive, like buckets, in concealèd wells;
To crouch in litter of your stable planks;

To lie, like pawns, lock'd up in chests and trunks;
To hug with swine; to seek sweet safety out
In vaults and prisons; and to thrill and shake
Even at the crying of your nation's crow,
Thinking his voice an armèd Englishman; —
Shall that victorious hand be feebled here,
That in your chambers gave you chastisement?
No: know the gallant monarch is in arms;
And, like an eagle o'er his aery, towers,
To souse annoyance that comes near his nest. —
And you degenerate, you ingrate revolts,
You bloody Neroes, ripping up the womb
Of your dear mother England, blush for shame;
For your own ladies and pale-visag'd maids,
Like Amazons, come tripping after drums, —
Their thimbles into armèd gauntlets chang'd,
Their neelds to lances, and their gentle hearts
To fierce and bloody inclination.

Lou. There end thy brave, and turn thy face in peace;
We grant thou canst outscold us: fare thee well;
We hold our time too precious to be spent
With such a brabbler.

Pand. Give me leave to speak.

Bast. No, I will speak.

Lou. We will attend to neither. —
Strike up the drums; and let the tongue of war
Plead for our interest and our being here.

Bast. Indeed, your drums, being beaten, will cry out;
And so shall you, being beaten: do but start
An echo with the clamour of thy drum,
And even at hand a drum is ready brac'd
That shall reverberate all as loud as thine;
Sound but another, and another shall,
As loud as thine, rattle the welkin's ear,
And mock the deep-mouth'd thunder: for at hand —
Not trusting to this halting legate here,
Whom he hath us'd rather for sport than need —

Is warlike John; and in his forehead sits
A bare-ribb'd death, whose office is this day
To feast upon whole thousands of the French.

Lou. Strike up our drums, to find this danger out.
Bast. And thou shalt find it, Dauphin, do not doubt.
[*Exeunt.*

Scene III. *The same. A field of battle.*

Alarums. Enter King John *and* Hubert.

K. John. How goes the day with us? O, tell me, Hubert.
Hub. Badly, I fear. How fares your majesty?
K. John. This fever, that hath troubled me so long,
Lies heavy on me; — O, my heart is sick!

Enter a Messenger.

Mess. My lord, your valiant kinsman, Falconbridge,
Desires your majesty to leave the field,
And send him word by me which way you go.
K. John. Tell him, toward Swinstead, to the abbey there.
Mess. Be of good comfort; for the great supply,
That was expected by the Dauphin here,
Are wreck'd three nights ago on Goodwin Sands.
This news was brought to Richard but even now:
The French fight coldly, and retire themselves.
K. John. Ay me, this tyrant fever burns me up,
And will not let me welcome this good news! —
Set on toward Swinstead: to my litter straight;
Weakness possesseth me, and I am faint. [*Exeunt.*

Scene IV. *The same. Another part of the same.*

Enter Salisbury, Pembroke, *and* Bigot.

Sal. I did not think the king so stor'd with friends.
Pem. Up once again; put spirit in the French:
If they miscarry, we miscarry too.
Sal. That misbegotten devil, Falconbridge,
In spite of spite, alone upholds the day.
Pem. They say King John sore-sick hath left the field.

Enter MELUN *wounded, and led by* Soldiers.

Mel. Lead me to the revolts of England here.
Sal. When we were happy we had other names.
Pem. It is the Count Melun.
Sal.   Wounded to death.
Mel. Fly, noble English, you are bought and sold;
Unthread the rude eye of rebellion,
And welcome home again discarded faith.
Seek out King John, and fall before his feet;
For if the French be lords of this loud day,
He means to recompense the pains you take
By cutting off your heads: thus hath he sworn,
And I with him, and many more with me,
Upon the altar at Saint Edmund's-Bury;
Even on that altar where we swore to you
Dear amity and everlasting love.
   Sal. May this be possible? may this be true?
   Mel. Have I not hideous death within my view,
Retaining but a quantity of life,
Which bleeds away, even as a form of wax
Resolveth from his figure 'gainst the fire?
What in the world should make me now deceive,
Since I must lose the use of all deceit?
Why should I, then, be false, since it is true
That I must die here, and live hence by truth?
I say again, if Louis do win the day,
He is forsworn, if e'er those eyes of yours
Behold another day break in the east:
But even this night, — whose black contagious breath
Already smokes about the burning crest
Of the old, feeble, and day-wearied sun, —
Even this ill night, your breathing shall expire,
Paying the fine of rated treachery,
Even with a treacherous fine of all your lives,
If Louis by your assistance win the day.
Commend me to one Hubert, with your king:
The love of him, — and this respect besides,

For that my grandsire was an Englishman, —
Awakes my conscience to confess all this.
In lieu whereof, I pray you, bear me hence
From forth the noise and rumour of the field;
Where I may think the remnant of my thoughts
In peace, and part this body and my soul
With contemplation and devout desires.

Sal. We do believe thee: — and beshrew my soul
But I do love the favour and the form
Of this most fair occasion, by the which
We will untread the steps of damnèd flight;
And, like a bated and retirèd flood,
Leaving our rankness and irregular course,
Stoop low within those bounds we have o'erlook'd,
And calmly run on in obedience,
Even to our ocean, to our great King John. —
My arm shall give thee help to bear thee hence;
For I do see the cruel pangs of death
Right in thine eye. — Away, my friends! New flight;
And happy newness, that intends old right.

[*Exeunt, leading off Melun.*

Scene V. *The same. The French camp.*

Enter Louis and his Train.

Lou. The sun of heaven methought was loth to set,
But stay'd, and made the western welkin blush,
When th' English measur'd backward their own ground
In faint retire. O, bravely came we off,
When with a volley of our needless shot,
After such bloody toil, we bid good night;
And wound our tattering colours clearly up,
Last in the field, and almost lords of it!

Enter a Messenger.

Mess. Where is my prince, the Dauphin?
Lou. Here: — what news?

Mess. The Count Melun is slain; the English lords,
By his persuasion, are again fall'n off;
And your supply, which you have wish'd so long,
Are cast away and sunk on Goodwin Sands.
 Lou. Ah, foul shrewd news! — beshrew thy very heart! —
I did not think to be so sad to-night
As this hath made me. — Who was he that said
King John did fly an hour or two before
The stumbling night did part our weary powers?
 Mess. Whoever spoke it, it is true, my lord.
 Lou. Well; keep good quarter and good care to-night:
The day shall not be up so soon as I,
To try the fair adventure of to-morrow.   [*Exeunt.*

  Scene VI. *An open place near Swinstead Abbey.*

   Enter, severally, the Bastard *and* Hubert.

 Hub. Who's there? speak, ho! speak quickly, or I shoot.
 Bast. A friend. — What art thou?
 Hub.   Of the part of England.
 Bast. Whither dost thou go?
 Hub. What's that to thee?
 Bast.   Why may not I demand
Of thine affairs, as well as thou of mine?
Hubert I think?
 Hub.   Thou hast a perfect thought:
I will, upon all hazards, well believe
Thou art my friend, that know'st my tongue so well.
Who art thou?
 Bast.   Who thou wilt: an if thou please,
Thou mayst befriend me so much as to think
I come one way of the Plantagenets.
 Hub. Unkind remembrance! thou and eyeless night
Have done me shame: — brave soldier, pardon me,
That any accent breaking from thy tongue
Should scape the true acquaintance of mine ear.
 Bast. Come, come; sans compliment, what news abroad?

Hub. Why, here walk I, in the black brow of night,
To find you out.

Bast. Brief, then; and what's the news?

Hub. O, my sweet sir, news fitting to the night, —
Black, fearful, comfortless, and horrible.

Bast. Show me the very wound of this ill news:
I am no woman, I'll not swoon at it.

Hub. The king, I fear, is poison'd by a monk:
I left him almost speechless; and broke out
T' acquaint you with this evil, that you might
The better arm you to the sudden time,
Than if you had at leisure known of this.

Bast. How did he take it? who did taste to him?

Hub. A monk, I tell you; a resolvèd villain,
Whose bowels suddenly burst out: the king
Yet speaks, and peradventure may recover.

Bast. Who didst thou leave to tend his majesty?

Hub. Why, know you not the lords are all come back,
And brought Prince Henry in their company?
At whose request the king hath pardon'd them,
And they are all about his majesty.

Bast. Withhold thine indignation, mighty heaven,
And tempt us not to bear above our power! —
I'll tell thee, Hubert, half my power this night,
Passing these flats, are taken by the tide, —
These Lincoln washes have devourèd them;
Myself, well-mounted, hardly have escap'd.
Away, before! conduct me to the king;
I doubt he will be dead or e'er I come. [*Exeunt.*

SCENE VII. *The orchard of Swinstead Abbey.*

Enter Prince HENRY, SALISBURY, *and* BIGOT.

P. Hen. It is too late: the life of all his blood
Is touch'd corruptibly; and his pure brain —
Which some suppose the soul's frail dwelling-house —

Doth, by the idle comments that it makes,
Foretell the ending of mortality.

Enter PEMBROKE.

Pem. His highness yet doth speak; and holds belief
That, being brought into the open air,
It would allay the burning quality
Of that fell poison which assaileth him.

P. Hen. Let him be brought into the orchard here. —
Doth he still rage? [*Exit Bigot.*

Pem. He is more patient
Than when you left him; even now he sung.

P. Hen. O vanity of sickness! fierce extremes
In their continuance will not feel themselves.
Death, having prey'd upon the outward parts,
Leaves them insensible; and's siege is now
Against the mind, the which he pricks and wounds
With many legions of strange fantasies,
Which, in their throng and press to that last hold,
Confound themselves. "Tis strange that death should sing. —
I am the cygnet to this pale faint swan,
Who chants a doleful hymn to his own death,
And from the organ-pipe of frailty sings
His soul and body to their lasting rest.

Sal. Be of good comfort, prince; for you are born
To set a form upon that indigest
Which he hath left so shapeless and so rude.

Re-enter BIGOT, *with* Attendants *carrying* King JOHN *in a chair.*

K. John. Ay, marry, now my soul hath elbow-room;
It would not out at windows nor at doors.
There is so hot a summer in my bosom,
That all my bowels crumble up to dust:
I am a scribbled form, drawn with a pen
Upon a parchment; and against this fire
Do I shrink up.

26*

P. Hen. How fares your majesty?

K. John. Poison'd, — ill fare; — dead, forsook, cast off:
And none of you will bid the winter come,
To thrust his icy fingers in my maw;
Nor let my kingdom's rivers take their course
Through my burn'd bosom; nor entreat the north
To make his bleak winds kiss my parchèd lips,
And comfort me with cold: — I do not ask you much,
I beg cold comfort; and you are so strait,
And so ingrateful, you deny me that.

P. Hen. O, that there were some virtue in my tears,
That might relieve you!

K. John. The salt in them is hot. —
Within me is a hell; and there the poison
Is, as a fiend, confin'd to tyrannize
On unreprievable condemnèd blood.

Enter the Bastard.

Bast. O, I am scalded with my violent motion,
And spleen of speed to see your majesty!

K. John. O cousin, thou art come to set mine eye:
The tackle of my heart is crack'd and burn'd;
And all the shrouds, wherewith my life should sail,
Are turnèd to one thread, one little hair:
My heart hath one poor string to stay it by,
Which holds but till thy news be utterèd;
And then all this thou see'st is but a clod,
And model of confounded royalty.

Bast. The Dauphin is preparing hitherward,
Where heaven he knows how we shall answer him;
For in a night the best part of my power,
As I upon advantage did remove,
Were in the washes all unwarily
Devourèd by the unexpected flood.   [*King John dies.*

Sal. You breathe these dead news in as dead an ear. —
My liege! my lord! — but now a king, — now thus.

P. Hen. Even so must I run on, and even so stop.

What surety of the world, what hope, what stay,
When this was now a king, and now is clay?
   Bast. Art thou gone so? I do but stay behind
To do the office for thee of revenge,
And then my soul shall wait on thee to heaven,
As it on earth hath been thy servant still. —
Now, now, you stars that move in your right spheres,
Where be your powers? show now your mended faiths;
And instantly return with me again,
To push destruction and perpetual shame
Out of the weak door of our fainting land.
Straight let us seek, or straight we shall be sought;
The Dauphin rages at our very heels.
   Sal. It seems you know not, then, so much as we:
The Cardinal Pandulph is within at rest,
Who half an hour since came from the Dauphin,
And brings from him such offers of our peace
As we with honour and respect may take,
With purpose presently to leave this war.
   Bast. He will the rather do it when he sees
Ourselves well sinewèd to our defence.
   Sal. Nay, it is in a manner done already;
For many carriages he hath dispatch'd
To the sea-side, and put his cause and quarrel
To the disposing of the cardinal:
With whom yourself, myself, and other lords,
If you think meet, this afternoon will post
To consummate this business happily.
   Bast. Let it be so: — and you, my noble prince,
With other princes that may best be spar'd,
Shall wait upon your father's funeral.
   P. Hen. At Worcester must his body be interr'd;
For so he will'd it.
   Bast.   Thither shall it, then:
And happily may your sweet self put on
The lineal state and glory of the land!
To whom, with all submission, on my knee,

I do bequeath my faithful services
And true subjection everlastingly.
    Sal. And the like tender of our love we make,
To rest without a spot for evermore.
    P. Hen. I have a kind soul that would give you thanks,
And knows not how to do it but with tears.
    Bast. O, let us pay the time but needful woe,
Since it hath been beforehand with our griefs. —
This England never did, nor never shall,
Lie at the proud foot of a conqueror,
But when it first did help to wound itself.
Now these her princes are come home again,
Come the three corners of the world in arms,
And we shall shock them: naught shall make us rue,
If England to itself do rest but true.   [*Exeunt.*

KING RICHARD II.

DRAMATIS PERSONÆ.

KING RICHARD the Second.
JOHN OF GAUNT, duke of Lancaster, \
EDMUND OF LANGLEY, duke of York, / uncles to the King.
HENRY, surnamed Bolingbroke, duke of Hereford, son to John of Gaunt; afterwards King Henry IV.
DUKE OF AUMERLE, son to the Duke of York.
THOMAS MOWBRAY, duke of Norfolk.
DUKE OF SURREY.
EARL OF SALISBURY.
LORD BERKLEY.
BUSHY, \
BAGOT, } creatures to King Richard.
GREEN, /
EARL OF NORTHUMBERLAND.
HENRY PERCY, his son.
LORD ROSS.
LORD WILLOUGHBY.
LORD FITZWATER.
Bishop of Carlisle.
Abbot of Westminster.
Lord Marshal.
SIR STEPHEN SCROOP.
SIR PIERCE of Exton.
Captain of a band of Welshmen.

Queen to King Richard.
DUCHESS OF YORK.
DUCHESS OF GLOSTER.
Ladies attending on the Queen.

Lords, Heralds, Officers, Soldiers, two Gardeners, Keeper, Messenger, Groom, and other Attendants.

SCENE — *dispersedly in England and Wales.*

ACT I.

SCENE I. *London. A room in the palace.*

Enter King RICHARD, *attended;* GAUNT, *and other* Nobles.

K. Rich. Old John of Gaunt, time-honour'd Lancaster,
Hast thou, according to thy oath and band,

Brought hither Henry Hereford thy bold son,
Here to make good the boisterous late appeal,
Which then our leisure would not let us hear,
Against the duke of Norfolk, Thomas Mowbray?

Gaunt. I have, my liege.

K. Rich. Tell me, moreover, hast thou sounded him,
If he appeal the duke on ancient malice;
Or worthily, as a good subject should,
On some known ground of treachery in him?

Gaunt. As near as I could sift him on that argument, —
On some apparent danger seen in him
Aim'd at your highness, — no inveterate malice.

K. Rich. Then call them to our presence: face to face,
And frowning brow to brow, ourselves will hear
Th' accuser and th' accused freely speak: —

[*Exeunt some Attendants.*

High-stomach'd are they both, and full of ire,
In rage deaf as the sea, hasty as fire.

Re-enter Attendants, *with* BOLINGBROKE *and* NORFOLK.

Boling. May many years of happy days befal
My gracious sovereign, my most loving liege!

Nor. Each day still better other's happiness;
Until the heavens, envying earth's good hap,
Add an immortal title to your crown!

K. Rich. We thank you both: yet one but flatters us,
As well appeareth by the cause you come;
Namely, t' appeal each other of high treason. —
Cousin of Hereford, what dost thou object
Against the duke of Norfolk, Thomas Mowbray?

Boling. First, — heaven be the record to my speech! —
In the devotion of a subject's love,
Tendering the precious safety of my prince,
And free from other misbegotten hate,
Come I appellant to this princely presence. —
Now, Thomas Mowbray, do I turn to thee,
And mark my greeting well; for what I speak

My body shall make good upon this earth,
Or my divine soul answer it in heaven.
Thou art a traitor and a miscreant,
Too good to be so, and too bad to live, —
Since the more fair and crystal is the sky,
The uglier seem the clouds that in it fly.
Once more, the more to aggravate the note,
With a foul traitor's name stuff I thy throat;
And wish, — so please my sovereign, — ere 1 move,
What my tongue speaks, my right-drawn sword may prove.

    Nor. Let not my cold words here accuse my zeal:
'Tis not the trial of a woman's war,
The bitter clamour of two eager tongues,
Can arbitrate this cause betwixt us twain;
The blood is hot that must be cool'd for this:
Yet can I not of such tame patience boast
As to be hush'd, and naught at all to say:
First, the fair reverence of your highness curbs me
From giving reins and spurs to my free speech;
Which else would post until it had return'd
These terms of treason doubled down his throat.
Setting aside his high blood's royalty,
And let him be no kinsman to my liege,
I do defy him, and I spit at him;
Call him a slanderous coward and a villain:
Which to maintain, I would allow him odds;
And meet him, were I tied to run a-foot
Even to the frozen ridges of the Alps,
Or any other ground inhabitable,
Wherever Englishman durst set his foot.
Meantime let this defend my loyalty, —
By all my hopes, most falsely doth he lie.

    Boling. Pale trembling coward, there I throw my gage,
Disclaiming here the kindred of the king;
And lay aside my high blood's royalty,
Which fear, not reverence, makes thee to except.
If guilty dread have left thee so much strength

As to take up mine honour's pawn, then stoop:
By that and all the rites of knighthood else,
Will I make good against thee, arm to arm,
What I have spoke, or thou canst worse devise.

Nor. I take it up; and by that sword I swear,
Which gently laid my knighthood on my shoulder,
I'll answer thee in any fair degree,
Or chivalrous design of knightly trial:
And when I mount, alive may I not light,
If I be traitor or unjustly fight!

K. Rich. What doth our cousin lay to Mowbray's charge?
It must be great that can inherit us
So much as of a thought of ill in him.

Boling. Look, what I speak, my life shall prove it true;—
That Mowbray hath receiv'd eight thousand nobles
In name of lendings for your highness' soldiers,
The which he hath detain'd for lewd employments,
Like a false traitor and injurious villain.
Besides, I say, and will in battle prove,—
Or here, or elsewhere to the furthest verge
That ever was survey'd by English eye,—
That all the treasons for these eighteen years
Complotted and contrivèd in this land
Fetch from false Mowbray their first head and spring.
Further, I say,— and further will maintain
Upon his bad life to make all this good,—
That he did plot the Duke of Gloster's death,
Suggest his soon-believing adversaries,
And consequently, like a traitor-coward,
Sluic'd out his innocent soul through streams of blood:
Which blood, like sacrificing Abel's, cries,
Even from the tongueless caverns of the earth,
To me for justice and rough chastisement;
And, by the glorious worth of my descent,
This arm shall do it, or this life be spent.

K. Rich. How high a pitch his resolution soars!—
Thomas of Norfolk, what say'st thou to this?

Nor. O, let my sovereign turn away his face,
And bid his ears a little while be deaf,
Till I have told this slander of his blood,
How God and good men hate so foul a liar!

K. Rich. Mowbray, impartial are our eyes and ears:
Were he my brother, nay, my kingdom's heir,—
As he is but my father's brother's son,—
Now, by my sceptre's awe, I make a vow,
Such neighbour-nearness to our sacred blood
Should nothing privilege him, nor partialise
Th' unstooping firmness of my upright soul:
He is our subject, Mowbray, so art thou;
Free speech and fearless I to thee allow.

Nor. Then, Bolingbroke, as low as to thy heart,
Through the false passage of thy throat, thou liest!
Three parts of that receipt I had for Calais
Disburs'd I duly to his highness' soldiers;
The other part reserv'd I by consent,
For that my sovereign liege was in my debt
Upon remainder of a dear account,
Since last I went to France to fetch his queen:
Now swallow down that lie. — For Gloster's death,—
I slew him not; but, to my own disgrace,
Neglected my sworn duty in that case. —
For you, my noble Lord of Lancaster,
The honourable father to my foe,
Once did I lay an ambush for your life,—
A trespass that doth vex my grievèd soul:
But, ere I last receiv'd the sacrament,
I did confess it; and exactly begg'd
Your grace's pardon, and I hope I had it.
This is my fault: as for the rest appeal'd,
It issues from the rancour of a villain,
A recreant and most degenerate traitor:
Which in myself I boldly will defend;
And interchangeably hurl down my gage
Upon this overweening traitor's foot,

To prove myself a loyal gentleman
Even in the best blood chamber'd in his bosom.
In haste whereof, most heartily I pray
Your highness to assign our trial-day.

K. Rich. Wrath-kindled gentlemen, be rul'd by me;
Let's purge this choler without letting blood:
This we prescribe, though no physician;
Deep malice makes too deep incision:
Forget, forgive; conclude and be agreed;
Our doctors say this is no month to bleed. —
Good uncle, let this end where it begun;
We'll calm the Duke of Norfolk, you your son.

Gaunt. To be a make-peace shall become my age: —
Throw down, my son, the Duke of Norfolk's gage.

K. Rich. And, Norfolk, throw down his.

Gaunt. When, Harry? when?
Obedience bids I should not bid agen.

K. Rich. Norfolk, throw down; we bid; there is no boot.

Nor. Myself I throw, dread sovereign, at thy foot.
My life thou shalt command, but not my shame:
The one my duty owes; but my fair name —
Despite of death — that lives upon my grave,
To dark dishonour's use thou shalt not have.
I am disgrac'd, impeach'd, and baffled here;
Pierc'd to the soul with slander's venom'd spear,
The which no balm can cure but his heart-blood
Which breath'd this poison.

K. Rich. Rage must be withstood: —
Give me his gage: — lions make leopards tame.

Nor. Yea, but not change his spots: take but my shame,
And I resign my gage. My dear dear lord,
The purest treasure mortal times afford
Is spotless reputation; that away,
Men are but gilded loam or painted clay.
A jewel in a ten-times-barr'd-up chest
Is a bold spirit in a loyal breast.
Mine honour is my life; both grow in one;

Take honour from me, and my life is done:
Then, dear my liege, mine honour let me try;
In that I live, and for that will I die.

K. Rich. Cousin, throw down your gage; do you begin.

Boling. O, God defend my soul from such foul sin!
Shall I seem crest-fall'n in my father's sight?
Or with pale beggar-fear impeach my height
Before this outdar'd dastard? Ere my tongue
Shall wound my honour with such feeble wrong,
Or sound so base a parle, my teeth shall tear
The slavish motive of recanting fear,
And spit it bleeding in his high disgrace,
Where shame doth harbour, even in Mowbray's face.
[*Exit Gaunt.*

K. Rich. We were not born to sue, but to command; —
Which since we cannot do to make you friends,
Be ready, as your lives shall answer it,
At Coventry, upon Saint Lambert's day:
There shall your swords and lances arbitrate
The swelling difference of your settled hate:
Since we can not atone you, we shall see
Justice design the victor's chivalry. —
Marshal, command our officers-at-arms
Be ready to direct these home-alarms. [*Exeunt.*

Scene II. *The same. A room in the* Duke of Lancaster's *palace.*

Enter Gaunt *and* Duchess of Gloster.

Gaunt. Alas, the part I had in Woodstock's blood
Doth more solicit me than your exclaims,
To stir against the butchers of his life!
But since correction lieth in those hands
Which made the fault that we cannot correct,
Put we our quarrel to the will of heaven;
Who, when they see the hours ripe on earth,
Will rain hot vengeance on offenders' heads.

Duch. Finds brotherhood in thee no sharper spur?
Hath love in thy old blood no living fire?
Edward's seven sons, whereof thyself art one,
Were as seven vials of his sacred blood,
Or seven fair branches springing from one root:
Some of those seven are dried by nature's course,
Some of those branches by the Destinies cut;
But Thomas, my dear lord, my life, my Gloster,
One vial full of Edward's sacred blood,
One flourishing branch of his most royal root,
Is crack'd, and all the precious liquor spilt,
Is hack'd down, and his summer-leaves all faded,
By envy's hand and murder's bloody axe.
Ah, Gaunt, his blood was thine! that bed, that womb,
That mettle, that self-mould, that fashion'd thee,
Made him a man; and though thou liv'st and breath'st,
Yet art thou slain in him: thou dost consent
In some large measure to thy father's death,
In that thou seest thy wretched brother die,
Who was the model of thy father's life.
Call it not patience, Gaunt, — it is despair:
In suffering thus thy brother to be slaughter'd,
Thou show'st the naked pathway to thy life,
Teaching stern murder how to butcher thee:
That which in mean men we entitle patience,
Is pale cold cowardice in noble breasts.
What shall I say? to safeguard thine own life,
The best way is to venge my Gloster's death.

Gaunt. God's is the quarrel; for God's substitute,
His deputy anointed in his sight,
Hath caus'd his death: the which if wrongfully,
Let heaven revenge; for I may never lift
An angry arm against his minister.

Duch. Where, then, alas, may I complain myself?

Gaunt. To God, the widow's champion and defence.

Duch. Why, then, I will. Farewell, old Gaunt:
Thou go'st to Coventry, there to behold

Our cousin Hereford and fell Mowbray fight:
O, sit my husband's wrongs on Hereford's spear,
That it may enter butcher Mowbray's breast!
Or, if misfortune miss the first career,
Be Mowbray's sins so heavy in his bosom,
That they may break his foaming courser's back,
And throw the rider headlong in the lists,
A caitiff recreant to my cousin Hereford!
Farewell, old Gaunt: thy sometimes brother's wife
With her companion grief must end her life.

Gaunt. Sister, farewell; I must to Coventry:
As much good stay with thee as go with me!

Duch. Yet one word more: — grief boundeth where it falls,
Not with the empty hollowness, but weight:
I take my leave before I have begun;
For sorrow ends not when it seemeth done.
Commend me to my brother, Edmund York.
Lo, this is all: — nay, yet depart not so;
Though this be all, do not so quickly go;
I shall remember more. Bid him — ah, what? —
With all good speed at Plashy visit me.
Alack, and what shall good old York there see,
But empty lodgings and unfurnish'd walls,
Unpeopled offices, untrodden stones?
And what hear there for welcome, but my groans?
Therefore commend me; let him not come there,
To seek out sorrow that dwells every where.
Desolate, desolate, will I hence and die:
The last leave of thee takes my weeping eye. [*Exeunt.*

SCENE III. *Gosford Green, near Coventry.*

Lists *set out, and a throne; with Attendants. Enter the* Lord Marshal *and* AUMERLE.

Mar. My Lord Aumerle, is Harry Hereford arm'd?
Aum. Yea, at all points; and longs to enter in.

Mar. The Duke of Norfolk, sprightfully and bold,
Stays but the summons of th' appellant's trumpet.
Aum. Why, then, the champions are prepar'd, and stay
For nothing but his majesty's approach.

Flourish of trumpets. Enter King Richard, *who takes his seat on his throne;* Gaunt, Bushy, Bagot, Green, *and others, who take their places. A trumpet is sounded, and answered by another trumpet within. Then enter* Norfolk *in armour, preceded by a Herald.*

K. Rich. Marshal, demand of yonder champion
The cause of his arrival here in arms:
Ask him his name; and orderly proceed
To swear him in the justice of his cause.
Mar. In God's name and the king's, say who thou art,
And why thou com'st thus knightly clad in arms;
Against what man thou com'st, and what thy quarrel:
Speak truly, on thy knighthood and thy oath;
As so defend thee heaven and thy valour!
Nor. My name is Thomas Mowbray, duke of Norfolk;
Who hither come engagèd by my oath, —
Which God defend a knight should violate! —
Both to defend my loyalty and truth
To God, my king, and his succeeding issue,
Against the Duke of Hereford that appeals me;
And, by the grace of God and this mine arm,
To prove him, in defending of myself,
A traitor to my God, my king, and me:
And as I truly fight, defend me heaven!

Trumpet sounds. Enter Bolingbroke *in armour, preceded by a Herald.*

K. Rich. Marshal, ask yonder knight in arms,
Both who he is, and why he cometh hither
Thus plated in habiliments of war;
And formally, according to our law,
Depose him in the justice of his cause.

Mar. What is thy name? and wherefore com'st thou hither,
Before King Richard in his royal lists?
Against whom comest thou? and what's thy quarrel?
Speak like a true knight, so defend thee heaven!

Boling. Harry of Hereford, Lancaster, and Derby,
Am I; who ready here do stand in arms,
To prove, by God's grace and my body's valour,
In lists, on Thomas Mowbray, duke of Norfolk,
That he's a traitor, foul and dangerous,
To God of heaven, King Richard, and to me:
And as I truly fight, defend me heaven!

Mar. On pain of death, no person be so bold
Or daring-hardy as to touch the lists,
Except the marshal and such officers
Appointed to direct these fair designs.

Boling. Lord marshal, let me kiss my sovereign's hand,
And bow my knee before his majesty:
For Mowbray and myself are like two men
That vow a long and weary pilgrimage;
Then let us take a ceremonious leave
And loving farewell of our several friends.

Mar. Th' appellant in all duty greets your highness,
And craves to kiss your hand and take his leave.

K. Rich. We will descend and fold him in our arms. —
Cousin of Hereford, as thy cause is right,
So be thy fortune in this royal fight!
Farewell, my blood; which if to-day thou shed,
Lament we may, but not revenge thee dead.

Boling. O, let no noble eye profane a tear
For me, if I be gor'd with Mowbray's spear:
As confident as is the falcon's flight
Against a bird, do I with Mowbray fight. —
[*To Lord Marshal*] My loving lord, I take my leave of you; —
Of you, my noble cousin, Lord Aumerle;
Not sick, although I have to do with death,
But lusty, young, and cheerly drawing breath. —
Lo, as at English feasts, so I regreet

The daintiest last, to make the end most sweet:
[*To Gaunt*] O thou, the earthly author of my blood, —
Whose youthful spirit, in me regenerate,
Doth with a twofold vigour lift me up
To reach at victory above my head, —
Add proof unto mine armour with thy prayers;
And with thy blessings steel my lance's point,
That it may enter Mowbray's waxen coat,
And furbish new the name of John o' Gaunt,
Even in the lusty haviour of his son.

   Gaunt. God in thy good cause make thee prosperous!
Be swift like lightning in the execution;
And let thy blows, doubly redoubled,
Fall like amazing thunder on the casque
Of thy adverse pernicious enemy:
Rouse up thy youthful blood, be valiant and live.

   Boling. Mine innocency and Saint George to thrive!

   Nor. However God or fortune cast my lot,
There lives or dies, true to King Richard's throne,
A loyal, just, and upright gentleman:
Never did captive with a freer heart
Cast off his chains of bondage, and embrace
His golden uncontroll'd enfranchisement,
More than my dancing soul doth celebrate
This feast of battle with mine adversary. —
Most mighty liege, — and my companion peers, —
Take from my mouth the wish of happy years:
As gentle and as jocund as to jest
Go I to fight: truth hath a quiet breast.

   K. Rich. Farewell, my lord: securely I espy
Virtue with valour couchèd in thine eye. —
Order the trial, marshal, and begin.

   Mar. Harry of Hereford, Lancaster, and Derby,
Receive thy lance; and God defend the right!

   Boling. Strong as a tower in hope, I cry amen.

   Mar. [*to an Officer*] Go bear this lance to Thomas, duke
        of Norfolk.

First Her. Harry of Hereford, Lancaster, and Derby,
Stands here for God, his sovereign, and himself,
On pain to be found false and recreant,
To prove the duke of Norfolk, Thomas Mowbray,
A traitor to his God, his king, and him;
And dares him to set forward to the fight.

Sec. Her. Here standeth Thomas Mowbray, duke of Norfolk,
On pain to be found false and recreant,
Both to defend himself, and to approve
Henry of Hereford, Lancaster, and Derby,
To God, his sovereign, and to him disloyal;
Courageously, and with a free desire,
Attending but the signal to begin.

Mar. Sound, trumpets; and set forward, combatants.
[*A charge sounded.*
Stay, stay, the king hath thrown his warder down.

K. Rich. Let them lay by their helmets and their spears,
And both return back to their chairs again: —
Withdraw with us: — and let the trumpets sound
While we return these dukes what we decree. —
[*A long flourish.*
Draw near, [*To the Combatants.*
And list what with our council we have done.
For that our kingdom's earth should not be soil'd
With that dear blood which it hath fosterèd;
And for our eyes do hate the dire aspéct
Of cruel wounds plough'd up with neighbours' swords;
And for we think the eagle-wingèd pride
Of sky-aspiring and ambitious thoughts,
With rival-hating envy, set on you
To wake our peace, which in our country's cradle
Draws the sweet infant breath of gentle sleep;
Which so rous'd up with boisterous untun'd drums,
With harsh-resounding trumpets' dreadful bray,
And grating shock of wrathful iron arms,
Might from our quiet confines fright fair peace,
And make us wade even in our kindred's blood; —

Therefore we banish you our territories: —
You, cousin Hereford, upon pain of life,
Till twice five summers have enrich'd our fields
Shall not regreet our fair dominions,
But tread the stranger paths of banishment.

   Boling. Your will be done: this must my comfort be, —
That sun that warms you here shall shine on me;
And those his golden beams to you here lent
Shall point on me and gild my banishment.

   K. Rich. Norfolk, for thee remains a heavier doom,
Which I with some unwillingness pronounce:
The fly-slow hours shall not determinate
The dateless limit of thy dear exile; —
The hopeless word of "never to return"·
Breathe I against thee, upon pain of life.

   Nor. A heavy sentence, my most sovereign liege,
And all unlook'd-for from your highness' mouth:
A dearer merit, not so deep a maim
As to be cast forth in the common air,
Have I deservèd at your highness' hands.
The language I have learn'd these forty years,
My native English, now I must forgo:
And now my tongue's use is to me no more
Than an unstringèd viol or a harp;
Or like a cunning instrument cas'd up,
Or, being open, put into his hands
That knows no touch to tune the harmony:
Within my mouth you have engaol'd my tongue,
Doubly portcullis'd with my teeth and lips;
And dull, unfeeling, barren ignorance
Is made my gaoler to attend on me.
I am too old to fawn upon a nurse,
Too far in years to be a pupil now:
What is thy sentence, then, but speechless death,
Which robs my tongue from breathing native breath?

   K. Rich. It boots thee not to be compassionate:
After our sentence plaining comes too late.

Nor. Then thus I turn me from my country's light,
To dwell in solemn shades of endless night.
　K. Rich. Return again, and take an oath with ye.
Lay on our royal sword your banish'd hands;
Swear by the duty that you owe to God, —
Our part therein we banish with yourselves, —
To keep the oath that we administer: —
You never shall — so help you truth and God! —
Embrace each other's love in banishment;
Nor never look upon each other's face;
Nor never write, regreet, nor reconcile
This louring tempest of your home-bred hate;
Nor never by advisèd purpose meet
To plot, contrive, or complot any ill
'Gainst us, our state, our subjects, or our land.
　Boling. I swear.
　Nor. And I, to keep all this.
　Boling. Norfolk, so far as to mine enemy; —
By this time, had the king permitted us,
One of our souls had wander'd in the air,
Banish'd this frail sepulchre of our flesh,
As now our flesh is banish'd from this land:
Confess thy treasons, ere thou fly the realm;
Since thou hast far to go, bear not along
The clogging burden of a guilty soul.
　Nor. No, Bolingbroke: if ever I were traitor,
My name be blotted from the book of life,
And I from heaven banish'd, as from hence!
But what thou art, God, thou, and I do know;
And all too soon, I fear, the king shall rue. —
Farewell, my liege. — Now no way can I stray:
Save back to England, all the world's my way.　　　[*Exit.*
　K. Rich. Uncle, even in the glasses of thine eyes
I see thy grievèd heart: thy sad aspéct
Hath from the number of his banish'd years
Pluck'd four away. — [*To Boling.*] Six frozen winters spent,
Return with welcome home from banishment.

Boling. How long a time lies in one little word!
Four lagging winters and four wanton springs
End in a word: such is the breath of kings.
  Gaunt. I thank my liege, that in regard of me
He shortens four years of my son's exile:
But little vantage shall I reap thereby;
For, ere the six years that he hath to spend
Can change their moons and bring their times about,
My oil-dried lamp and time-bewasted light
Shall be extinct with age and endless night;
My inch of taper will be burnt and done,
And blindfold death not let me see my son.
  K. Rich. Why, uncle, thou hast many years to live.
  Gaunt. But not a minute, king, that thou canst give:
Shorten my days thou canst with sullen sorrow,
And pluck nights from me, but not lend a morrow;
Thou canst help time to furrow me with age,
But stop no wrinkle in his pilgrimage;
Thy word is current with him for my death,
But dead, thy kingdom cannot buy my breath.
  K. Rich. Thy son is banish'd upon good advice,
Whereto thy tongue a party-verdict gave:
Why at our justice seem'st thou, then, to lour?
  Gaunt. Things sweet to taste prove in digestion sour.
You urg'd me as a judge; but I had rather
You would have bid me argue like a father.
O, had it been a stranger, not my child,
To smooth his fault I should have been more mild:
A partial slander sought I to avoid,
And in the sentence my own life destroy'd.
Alas, I look'd when some of you should say,
I was too strict to make mine own away;
But you gave leave to my unwilling tongue
Against my will to do myself this wrong.
  K. Rich. Cousin, farewell;—and, uncle, bid him so:
Six years we banish him, and he shall go.
  [*Flourish. Exeunt King Richard and Train.*

Aum. Cousin, farewell: what presence must not know,
From where you do remain let paper show.
　Mar. My lord, no leave take I; for I will ride,
As far as land will let me, by your side.
　Gaunt. O, to what purpose dost thou hoard thy words,
That thou return'st no greeting to thy friends?
　Boling. I have too few to take my leave of you,
When the tongue's office should be prodigal
To breathe th' abundant dolour of the heart.
　Gaunt. Thy grief is but thy absence for a time.
　Boling. Joy absent, grief is present for that time.
　Gaunt. What is six winters? they are quickly gone.
　Boling. To men in joy; but grief makes one hour ten.
　Gaunt. Call it a travel that thou tak'st for pleasure.
　Boling. My heart will sigh when I miscall it so,
Which finds it an enforcèd pilgrimage.
　Gaunt. The sullen passage of thy weary steps
Esteem as foil, wherein thou art to set
The precious jewel of thy home-return.
　Boling. Nay, rather, every tedious stride I make
Will but remember me what deal of world
I wander from the jewels that I love.
Must I not serve a long apprenticehood
To foreign passages; and in the end,
Having my freedom, boast of nothing else
But that I was a journeyman to grief?
　Gaunt. All places that the eye of heaven visits
Are to a wise man ports and happy havens.
Teach thy necessity to reason thus;
There is no virtue like necessity.
Think not the king did banish thee,
But thou the king: woe doth the heavier sit,
Where it perceives it is but faintly borne.
Go say, I sent thee forth to purchase honour,
And not, the king exil'd thee; or suppose
Devouring pestilence hangs in our air,
And thou art flying to a fresher clime:

Look, what thy soul holds dear, imagine it
To lie that way thou go'st, not whence thou com'st:
Suppose the singing-birds musicians,
The grass whereon thou tread'st the presence strew'd,
The flowers fair ladies, and thy steps no more
Than a delightful measure or a dance;
For gnarling sorrow hath less power to bite
The man that mocks at it and sets it light.

   Boling. O, who can hold a fire in his hand
By thinking on the frosty Caucasus?
Or cloy the hungry edge of appetite
By bare imagination of a feast?
Or wallow naked in December snow
By thinking on fantastic summer's heat?
O, no! the apprehension of the good
Gives but the greater feeling to the worse:
Fell sorrow's tooth doth never rankle more
Than when it bites, but lanceth not the sore.

   Gaunt. Come, come, my son, I'll bring thee on thy way:
Had I thy youth and cause, I would not stay.

   Boling. Then, England's ground, farewell; sweet soil,
       adieu;
My mother, and my nurse, that bears me yet!
Where'er I wander, boast of this I can, —
Though banish'd, yet a true-born Englishman.   [*Exeunt.*

Scene IV. *The court.*

Enter, from one side, King Richard, Bagot, *and* Green;
    from the other, Aumerle.

   K. Rich. We did observe. — Cousin Aumerle,
How far brought you high Hereford on his way?

   Aum. I brought high Hereford, if you call him so,
But to the next highway, and there I left him.

   K. Rich. And say, what store of parting tears were shed?

   Aum. Faith, none for me; except the north-east wind,
Which then blew bitterly against our faces,

Awak'd the sleeping rheum, and so by chance
Did grace our hollow parting with a tear.
  K. Rich. What said our cousin when you parted with him?
  Aum. "Farewell:"
And, for my heart disdainèd that my tongue
Should so profane the word, that taught me craft
To counterfeit oppression of such grief,
That words seem'd buried in my sorrow's grave.
Marry, would the word "farewell" have lengthen'd hours,
And added years to his short banishment,
He should have had a volume of "farewells;"
But since it would not, he had none of me.
  K. Rich. He is our cousin, cousin; but 'tis doubt,
When time shall call him home from banishment,
Whether our kinsman come to see his friends.
Ourself, and Bushy, Bagot here, and Green,
Observ'd his courtship to the common people;
How he did seem to dive into their hearts
With humble and familiar courtesy;
What reverence he did throw away on slaves;
Wooing poor craftsmen with the craft of smiles,
And patient underbearing of his fortune,
As 'twere to banish their affects with him.
Off goes his bonnet to an oyster-wench;
A brace of draymen bid God speed him well,
And had the tribute of his supple knee;
With "Thanks, my countrymen, my loving friends;"
As were our England in reversion his,
And he our subjects' next degree in hope.
  Green. Well, he is gone; and with him go these thoughts.
Now for the rebels which stand out in Ireland, —
Expedient manage must be made, my liege,
Ere further leisure yield them further means
For their advantage and your highness' loss.
  K. Rich. We will ourself in person to this war:
And, for our coffers, with too great a court
And liberal largess, are grown somewhat light,

We are enforc'd to farm our royal realm;
The revenue whereof shall furnish us
For our affairs in hand. If that come short,
Our substitutes at home shall have blank charters;
Whereto, when they shall know what men are rich,
They shall subscribe them for large sums of gold,
And send them after to supply our wants;
For we will make for Ireland presently.

Enter BUSHY.

Bushy, what news?
   Bushy. Old John of Gaunt is grievous sick, my lord,
Suddenly taken; and hath sent post-haste
'I" entreat your majesty to visit him.
   K. Rich. Where lies he?
   Bushy. At Ely-house.
   K. Rich. Now put it, God, in his physician's mind
To help him to his grave immediately!
The lining of his coffers shall make coats
To deck our soldiers for these Irish wars. —
Come, gentlemen, let's all go visit him:
Pray God we may make haste, and come too late! [*Exeunt.*

ACT II.

SCENE I. *London. A room in Ely-house.*

GAUNT *on a couch; the* Duke of York *and others standing by him.*

   Gaunt. Will the king come, that I may breathe my last
In wholesome counsel to his unstaid youth?
   York. Vex not yourself, nor strive not with your breath;
For all in vain comes counsel to his ear.
   Gaunt. O, but they say the tongues of dying men
Enforce attention like deep harmony:
Where words are scarce, they're seldom spent in vain;
For they breathe truth that breathe their words in pain.
He that no more must say is listen'd more

Than they whom youth and ease have taught to gloze;
More are men's ends mark'd than their lives before:
  The setting sun, and music at the close,
As the last taste of sweets, is sweetest last,
Writ in remembrance more than things long past:
Though Richard my life's counsel would not hear,
My death's sad tale may yet undeaf his ear.
  York. No; it is stopp'd with other flattering sounds,
As, praises of his state: then there are found
Lascivious metres, to whose venom-sound
The open ear of youth doth always listen;
Report of fashions in proud Italy,
Whose manners still our tardy-apish nation
Limps after in base imitation.
Where doth the world thrust forth a vanity, —
So it be new, there's no respect how vile, —
That is not quickly buzz'd into his ears?
Then all too late comes counsel to be heard,
Where will doth mutiny with wit's regard.
Direct not him, whose way himself will choose:
'Tis breath thou lack'st, and that breath wilt thou lose.
  Gaunt. Methinks I am a prophet new-inspir'd,
And thus, expiring, do foretell of him:
His rash fierce blaze of riot cannot last,
For violent fires soon burn out themselves;
Small showers last long, but sudden storms are short;
He tires betimes that spurs too fast betimes;
With eager feeding food doth choke the feeder:
Light vanity, insatiate cormorant,
Consuming means, soon preys upon itself.
This royal throne of kings, this scepter'd isle,
This earth of majesty, this seat of Mars,
This other Eden, demi-paradise;
This fortress built by Nature for herself
Against infection and the hand of war;
This happy breed of men, this little world;
This precious stone set in the silver sea,

Which serves it in the office of a wall,
Or as a moat defensive to a house,
Against the envy of less happier lands;
This blessèd plot, this earth, this realm, this England,
This nurse, this teeming womb of royal kings,
Fear'd by their breed, and famous by their birth,
Renownèd for their deeds as far from home, —
For Christian service and true chivalry, —
As is the sepulchre, in stubborn Jewry,
Of the world's ransom, blessèd Mary's Son; —
This land of such dear souls, this dear dear land,
Dear for her reputation through the world,
Is now leas'd out — I die pronouncing it —
Like to a tenement or pelting farm:
England, bound in with the triumphant sea,
Whose rocky shore beats back the envious siege
Of watery Neptune, 's now bound in with shame,
With inky blots, and rotten parchment bonds:
That England, that was wont to conquer others,
Hath made a shameful conquest of itself.
Ah, would the scandal vanish with my life,
How happy then were my ensuing death!

Enter King RICHARD *and* Queen, AUMERLE, BUSHY, GREEN,
BAGOT, ROSS, *and* WILLOUGHBY.

York. The king is come: deal mildly with his youth;
For young hot colts being rag'd do rage the more.
Queen. How fares our noble uncle, Lancaster?
K. Rich. What comfort, man? how is't with agèd Gaunt?
Gaunt. O, how that name befits my composition!
Old Gaunt, indeed; and gaunt in being old:
Within me grief hath kept a tedious fast;
And who abstains from meat, that is not gaunt?
For sleeping England long time have I watch'd;
Watching breeds leanness, leanness is all gaunt:
The pleasure that some fathers feed upon,
Is my strict fast, — I mean, my children's looks;

And therein fasting, hast thou made me gaunt:
Gaunt am I for the grave, gaunt as a grave,
Whose hollow womb inherits naught but bones.

   K. Rich. Can sick men play so nicely with their names?
   Gaunt. No, misery makes sport to mock itself:
Since thou dost seek to kill my name in me,
I mock my name, great king, to flatter thee.
   K. Rich. Should dying men flatter with those that live?
   Gaunt. No, no, men living flatter those that die.
   K. Rich. Thou, now a-dying, say'st thou flatter'st me.
   Gaunt. O, no! thou diest, though I the sicker be.
   K. Rich. I am in health, I breathe, and see thee ill.
   Gaunt. Now, He that made me knows I see thee ill;
Ill in myself to see, and in thee seeing ill.
Thy death-bed is no lesser than thy land,
Wherein thou liest in reputation sick;
And thou, too careless patient as thou art,
Committ'st thy 'nointed body to the cure
Of those physicians that first wounded thee:
A thousand flatterers sit within thy crown,
Whose compass is no bigger than thy head;
And yet, incagèd in so small a verge,
The waste is no whit lesser than thy land.
O, had thy grandsire, with a prophet's eye,
Seen how his son's son should destroy his sons,
From forth thy reach he would have laid thy shame,
Deposing thee before thou wert possess'd,
Which art possess'd now to depose thyself.
Why, cousin, wert thou regent of the world,
It were a shame to let this land by lease;
But for thy world enjoying but this land,
Is it not more than shame to shame it so?
Landlord of England art thou now, not king:
Thy state of law is bond-slave to the law;
And —
   K. Rich. And thou a lunatic lean-witted fool,
Presuming on an ague's privilege,

Dar'st with thy frozen admonition
Make pale our cheek, chasing the royal blood
With fury from his native residence.
Now, by my seat's right royal majesty,
Wert thou not brother to great Edward's son,
This tongue that runs so roundly in thy head
Should run thy head from thy unreverent shoulders.

 Gaunt. O, spare me not, my brother Edward's son,
For that I was his father Edward's son; —
That blood already, like the pelican,
Hast thou tapp'd out, and drunkenly carous'd:
My brother Gloster, plain well-meaning soul, —
Whom fair befal in heaven 'mongst happy souls! —
May be a precedent and witness good
That thou respect'st not spilling Edward's blood:
Join with the present sickness that I have;
And thy unkindness be like crookèd age,
To crop at once a too-long wither'd flower.
Live in thy shame, but die not shame with thee! —
These words hereafter thy tormentors be! —
Convey me to my bed, then to my grave:
Love they to live that love and honour have.
      [*Exit, borne out by his Attendants.*

 K. Rich. And let them die that age and sullens have;
For both hast thou, and both become the grave.

 York. Beseech your majesty, impute his words
To wayward sickliness and age in him:
He loves you, on my life, and holds you dear
As Harry duke of Hereford, were he here.

 K. Rich. Right, you say true: as Hereford's love, so his;
As theirs, so mine; and all be as it is.

     Enter NORTHUMBERLAND.

 North. My liege, old Gaunt commends him to your majesty.
 K. Rich. What says he?
 North.   Nay, nothing; all is said:

His tongue is now a stringless instrument;
Words, life, and all, old Lancaster hath spent.
 York. Be York the next that must be bankrupt so!
Though death be poor, it ends a mortal woe.
 K. Rich. The ripest fruit first falls, and so doth he;
His time is spent, our pilgrimage must be:
So much for that. — Now for our Irish wars:
We must supplant those rough rug-headed kerns,
Which live like venom, where no venom else,
But only they, hath privilege to live.
And for these great affairs do ask some charge,
Towards our assistance we do seize to us
The plate, coin, revenues, and movables,
Whereof our uncle Gaunt did stand possess'd.
 York. How long shall I be patient? ah, how long
Shall tender duty make me suffer wrong?
Not Gloster's death, nor Hereford's banishment,
Not Gaunt's rebukes, nor England's private wrongs,
Nor the prevention of poor Bolingbroke
About his marriage, nor my own disgrace,
Have ever made me sour my patient cheek,
Or bend one wrinkle on my sovereign's face.
I am the last of noble Edward's sons,
Of whom thy father, Prince of Wales, was first:
In war was never lion rag'd more fierce,
In peace was never gentle lamb more mild,
Than was that young and princely gentleman.
His face thou hast, for even so look'd he,
Accomplish'd with the number of thy hours;
But when he frown'd, it was against the French,
And not against his friends: his noble hand
Did win what he did spend, and spent not that
Which his triumphant father's hand had won:
His hands were guilty of no kindred's blood,
But bloody with the enemies of his kin.
O Richard! York is too far gone with grief,
Or else he never would compare between.

K. Rich. Why, uncle, what's the matter?
York. O my liege,
Pardon me, if you please; if not, I, pleas'd
Not to be pardon'd, am content withal.
Seek you to seize, and gripe into your hands,
The royalties and rights of banish'd Hereford?
Is not Gaunt dead? and doth not Hereford live?
Was not Gaunt just? and is not Harry true?
Did not the one deserve to have an heir?
Is not his heir a well-deserving son?
Take Hereford's rights away, and take from time
His charters and his customary rights;
Let not to-morrow, then, ensue to-day;
Be not thyself, — for how art thou a king
But by fair sequence and succession?
Now, afore God, — God forbid I say true! —
If you do wrongfully seize Hereford's rights,
Call in the letters-patents that he hath
By his attorneys-general to sue
His livery, and deny his offer'd homage,
You pluck a thousand dangers on your head,
You lose a thousand well-disposèd hearts,
And prick my tender patience to those thoughts
Which honour and allegiance cannot think.
K. Rich. Think what you will, we seize into our hands
His plate, his goods, his money, and his lands.
York. I'll not be by the while: my liege, farewell:
What will ensue hereof, there's none can tell;
But by bad courses may be understood
That their events can never fall out good. [*Exit.*
K. Rich. Go, Bushy, to the Earl of Wiltshire straight:
Bid him repair to us to Ely-house
To see this business. To-morrow next
We will for Ireland; and 'tis time, I trow:
And we create, in absence of ourself,
Our uncle York lord governor of England;
For he is just, and always lov'd us well. —

Come on, our queen: to-morrow must we part;
Be merry, for our time of stay is short. [*Flourish. Exeunt King,
   Queen, Aumerle, Bushy, Green, and Bagot.*
   North. Well, lords, the Duke of Lancaster is dead.
   Ross. And living too; for now his son is duke.
   Willo. Barely in title, not in revenue.
   North. Richly in both, if justice had her right.
   Ross. My heart is great; but it must break with silence,
Ere 't be disburden'd with a liberal tongue.
   North. Nay, speak thy mind; and let him ne'er speak more
That speaks thy words again to do thee harm!
   Willo. Tends that thou wouldst speak to the Duke of
      Hereford?
If it be so, out with it boldly, man;
Quick is mine ear to hear of good towards him.
   Ross. No good at all, that I can do for him;
Unless you call it good to pity him,
Bereft and gelded of his patrimony.
   North. Now, afore God, 'tis shame such wrongs are borne
In him a royal prince and many more
Of noble blood in this declining land.
The king is not himself, but basely led
By flatterers; and what they will inform,
Merely in hate, 'gainst any of us all,
That will the king severely prosecute
'Gainst us, our lives, our children, and our heirs.
   Ross. The commons hath he pill'd with grievous taxes,
And lost their hearts: the nobles hath he fin'd
For ancient quarrels, and quite lost their hearts.
   Willo. And daily new exactions are devis'd, —
As blanks, benevolences, and I wot not what:
But what, o' God's name, doth become of this?
   North. Wars have not wasted it, for warr'd he hath not,
But basely yielded upon compromise
That which his ancestors achiev'd with blows:
More hath he spent in peace than they in wars.
   Ross. The Earl of Wiltshire hath the realm in farm.

Willo. The king's grown bankrupt, like a broken man.
North. Reproach and dissolution hangeth over him.
Ross. He hath not money for these Irish wars,
His burdenous taxations notwithstanding,
ut by the robbing of the banish'd duke.
North. His noble kinsman: — most degenerate king!
But, lords, we hear this fearful tempest sing,
Yet seek no shelter to avoid the storm;
We see the wind sit sore upon our sails,
And yet we strike not, but securely perish.
Ross. We see the very wreck that we must suffer;
And unavoided is the danger now,
For suffering so the causes of our wreck.
North. Not so; even through the hollow eyes of death
I spy life peering; but I dare not say
How near the tidings of our comfort is.
Willo. Nay, let us share thy thoughts, as thou dost ours.
Ross. Be confident to speak, Northumberland:
We three are but thyself; and, speaking so,
Thy words are but as thoughts; therefore, be bold.
North. Then thus: — I have from Port le Blanc, a bay
In Brittany, receiv'd intelligence
That Harry Duke of Hereford, Renald Lord Cobham,
†. . . . .
That late broke from the Duke of Exeter,
His brother, Archbishop late of Canterbury,
Sir Thomas Erpingham, Sir John Ramston,
Sir John Norbery, Sir Robert Waterton, and Francis Quoint, —
All these well furnish'd by the Duke of Bretagne,
With eight tall ships, three thousand men of war,
Are making hither with all due expedience,
And shortly mean to touch our northern shore:
Perhaps they had ere this, but that they stay
The first departing of the king for Ireland.
If, then, we shall shake off our slavish yoke,

† Here a line has evidently dropt out; and Malone introduced within brackets "The son of Richard Earl of Arundel." —

Imp out our drooping country's broken wing,
Redeem from broking pawn the blemish'd crown,
Wipe off the dust that hides our sceptre's gilt,
And make high majesty look like itself,
Away with me in post to Ravenspurg;
But if you faint, as fearing to do so,
Stay and be secret, and myself will go.
 Ross. To horse, to horse! urge doubts to them that fear.
 Willo. Hold out my horse, and I will first be there.
 [*Exeunt.*

SCENE II. *The same. A room in the palace.*

Enter Queen, Busby, *and* Bagot.

 Bushy. Madam, your majesty is too much sad:
You promis'd, when you parted with the king,
To lay aside life-harming heaviness,
And entertain a cheerful disposition.
 Queen. To please the king, I did; to please myself,
I cannot do it; yet I know no cause
Why I should welcome such a guest as grief,
Save bidding farewell to so sweet a guest
As my sweet Richard: yet, again, methinks
Some unborn sorrow, ripe in fortune's womb,
Is coming towards me; and my inward soul
With nothing trembles: at something it grieves,
More than with parting from my lord the king.
 Bushy. Each substance of a grief hath twenty shadows,
Which show like grief itself, but are not so;
For sorrow's eye, glazèd with blinding tears,
Divides one thing entire to many objects;
Like perspectives, which rightly gaz'd upon,
Show nothing but confusion, — ey'd awry,
Distinguish form: so your sweet majesty,
Looking awry upon your lord's departure,
Finds shapes of grief, more than himself, to wail;
Which, look'd on as it is, is naught but shadows
Of what it is not. Then, thrice-gracious queen,

28*

More than your lord's departure weep not, — more's not seen;
Or if it be, 'tis with false sorrow's eye,
Which for things true weeps things imaginary.

    Queen. It may be so; but yet my inward soul
Persuades me it is otherwise: howe'er it be,
I cannot but be sad; so heavy sad,
As, — though, in thinking, on no thought I think, —
Makes me with heavy nothing faint and shrink.

    Bushy. 'Tis nothing but conceit, my gracious lady.

    Queen. 'Tis nothing less: conceit is still deriv'd
From some forefather grief; mine is not so,
For nothing hath begot my something grief;
Or something hath the nothing that I grieve:
'Tis in reversion that I do possess;
But what it is, that is not yet known; what
I cannot name; 'tis nameless woe, I wot.

              Enter GREEN.

    Green. God save your majesty! — and well met, gentle-
        men: —
I hope the king is not yet shipp'd for Ireland.

    Queen. Why hop'st thou so? 'tis better hope he is;
For his designs crave haste, his haste good hope:
Then wherefore dost thou hope he is not shipp'd?

    Green. That he, our hope, might have retir'd his power,
And driven into despair an enemy's hope,
Who strongly hath set footing in this land:
The banish'd Bolingbroke repeals himself,
And with uplifted arms is safe arriv'd
At Ravenspurg.

    Queen.   Now God in heaven forbid!

    Green. Ah madam, 'tis too true: and that is worse,
The Lord Northumberland, his son young Henry Percy,
The Lords of Ross, Beaumond, and Willoughby,
With all their powerful friends, are fled to him.

    Bushy. Why have you not proclaim'd Northumberland,
And all the rest of the revolted faction,
Traitors?

Green. We have: whereupon the Earl of Worcester
Hath broke his staff, resign'd his stewardship,
And all the household servants fled with him
To Bolingbroke.
 Queen. So, Green, thou art the midwife to my woe,
And Bolingbroke my sorrow's dismal heir:
Now hath my soul brought forth her prodigy;
And I, a gasping new-deliver'd mother,
Have woe to woe, sorrow to sorrow join'd.
 Bushy. Despair not, madam.
 Queen. Who shall hinder me?
I will despair, and be at enmity
With cozening hope, — he is a flatterer,
A parasite, a keeper-back of death,
Who gently would dissolve the bands of life,
Which false hope lingers in extremity.
 Green. Here comes the Duke of York.
 Queen. With signs of war about his agèd neck:
O, full of careful business are his looks!

Enter YORK.

Uncle, for God's sake, speak comfortable words.
 York. Should I do so, I should belie my thoughts:
Comfort's in heaven; and we are on the earth,
Where nothing lives but crosses, care, and grief.
Your husband, he is gone to save far off,
Whilst others come to make him lose at home:
Here am I left to underprop his land,
Who, weak with age, cannot support myself:
Now comes the sick hour that his surfeit made;
Now shall he try his friends that flatter'd him.

Enter a Servant.

 Serv. My lord, your son was gone before I came.
 York. He was? — Why, so! — go all which way it will! —
The nobles they are fled, the commons cold,
And will, I fear, revolt on Hereford's side. —
Sirrah,

Get thee to Plashy, to my sister Gloster;
Bid her send me presently a thousand pound: —
Hold, take my ring.
    Serv. My lord, I had forgot to tell your lordship,
To-day, as I came by, I callèd there; —
But I shall grieve you to report the rest.
    York. What is it, knave?
    Serv. An hour before I came, the duchess died.
    York. God for his mercy! what a tide of woes
Comes rushing on this woful land at once!
I know not what to do: — I would to God, —
So my untruth had not provok'd him to it, —
The king had cut off my head with my brother's. —
What, are there posts dispatch'd for Ireland? —
How shall we do for money for these wars? —
Come, sister, — cousin, I'd say, — pray, pardon me. —
[*To the Servant*] Go, fellow, get thee home, provide some carts,
And bring away the armour that is there.   [*Exit Servant.*
Gentlemen, will you go muster men? If I
Know how or which way t' order these affairs,
Thus thrust disorderly into my hands,
Never believe me. Both are my kinsmen: —
Th' one is my sovereign, whom both my oath
And duty bids defend; th' other, again,
Is my near kinsman, whom the king hath wrong'd,
Whom conscience and my kindred bids to right.
Well, somewhat we must do. — Come, cousin, I'll
Dispose of you. — Gentlemen, go muster up your men,
And meet me presently at Berkley-castle.
I should to Plashy too; —
But time will not permit: — all is uneven,
And every thing is left at six and seven.
                                [*Exeunt York and Queen.*
    Bushy. The wind sits fair for news to go to Ireland,
But none returns. For us to levy power
Proportionable to the enemy
Is all unpossible.

Green. Besides, our nearness to the king in love
Is near the hate of those love not the king.
Bagot. And that's the wavering commons: for their love
Lies in their purses; and whoso empties them,
By so much fills their hearts with deadly hate.
Bushy. Wherein the king stands generally condemn'd.
Bagot. If judgment lie in them, then so do we,
Because we ever have been near the king.
Green. Well,
I will for refuge straight to Bristol-castle:
The Earl of Wiltshire is already there.
Bushy. Thither will I with you; for little office
The hateful commons will perform for us,
Except like curs to tear us all to pieces. —
Will you go along with us?
Bagot. No;
I will to Ireland to his majesty.
Farewell: if heart's presages be not vain,
We three here part that ne'er shall meet again.
Bushy. That's as York thrives to beat back Bolingbroke.
Green. Alas, poor duke! the task he undertakes
Is numbering sands, and drinking oceans dry:
Where one on his side fights, thousands will fly.
Bagot. Farewell at once, — for once, for all, and ever.
Bushy. Well, we may meet again.
Bagot.   I fear me, never.
                                        [*Exeunt.*

SCENE III. *The wilds in Glostershire.*

Enter BOLINGBROKE *and* NORTHUMBERLAND, *with Forces.*

Boling. How far is it, my lord, to Berkley now?
North. Believe me, noble lord,
I am a stranger here in Glostershire:
These high wild hills and rough uneven ways
Draw out our miles, and make them wearisome;
And yet your fair discourse hath been as sugar,
Making the hard way sweet and délectable.

But I bethink me what a weary way
From Ravenspurg to Cotswold will be found
In Ross and Willoughby, wanting your company,
Which, I protest, hath very much beguil'd
The tediousness and process of my travel:
But theirs is sweeten'd with the hope to have
The present benefit which I possess;
And hope to joy is little less in joy
Than hope enjoy'd: by this the weary lords
Shall make their way seem short; as mine hath done
By sight of what I have, your noble company.
  Boling. Of much less value is my company
Than your good words. — But who comes here?
  North. It is my son, young Harry Percy,
Sent from my brother Worcester, whencesoever.

Enter PERCY.

Harry, how fares your uncle?
  Percy. I had thought, my lord, t' have learn'd his health
      of you.
  North. Why, is he not with the queen?
  Percy. No, my good lord; he hath forsook the court,
Broken his staff of office, and dispers'd
The household of the king.
  North.   What was his reason?
He was not so resolv'd when last we spake together.
  Percy. Because your lordship was proclaimèd traitor.
But he, my lord, is gone to Ravenspurg,
To offer service to the Duke of Hereford;
And sent me o'er by Berkley, to discover
What power the Duke of York had levied there;
Then with direction to repair to Ravenspurg.
  North. Have you forgot the Duke of Hereford, boy?
  Percy. No, my good lord; for that is not forgot
Which ne'er I did remember: to my knowledge,
I never in my life did look on him.
  North. Then learn to know him now; this is the duke

Percy. My gracious lord, I tender you my service,
Such as it is, being tender, raw, and young;
Which elder days shall ripen, and confirm
To more approvèd service and desert.
  Boling. I thank thee, gentle Percy; and be sure
I count myself in nothing else so happy
As in a soul remembering my good friends;
And, as my fortune ripens with thy love,
It shall be still thy true love's recompense:
My heart this covenant makes, my hand thus seals it.
  North. How far is it to Berkley? and what stir
Keeps good old York there with his men of war?
  Percy. There stands the castle, by yond tuft of trees,
Mann'd with three hundred men, as I have heard;
And in it are the Lords of York, Berkley, and Seymour, —
None else of name and noble estimate.
  North. Here come the Lords of Ross and Willoughby,
Bloody with spurring, fiery-red with haste.

Enter Ross *and* Willoughby.

  Boling. Welcome, my lords. I wot your love pursues
A banish'd traitor: all my treasury
Is yet but unfelt thanks, which, more enrich'd,
Shall be your love and labour's recompense.
  Ross. Your presence makes us rich, most noble lord.
  Willo. And far surmounts our labour to attain it.
  Boling. Evermore thanks, th' exchequer of the poor;
Which, till my infant fortune comes to years,
Stands for my bounty. — But who is't comes here?
  North. It is my Lord of Berkley, as I guess.

Enter Berkley.

  Berk. My Lord of Hereford, my message is to you.
  Boling. My lord, my answer is — "to Lancaster;"
And I am come to seek that name in England;
And I must find that title in your tongue,
Before I make reply to aught you say.
  Berk. Mistake me not, my lord; 'tis not my meaning

To raze one title of your honour out: —
To you, my lord, I come, — what lord you will, —
From the most gracious regent of this land,
The Duke of York, to know what pricks you on
To take advantage of the absent time,
And fright our native peace with self-born arms.

   Boling. I shall not need transport my words by you;
Here comes his grace in person.

                Enter YORK *attended.*

                        My noble uncle!   [*Kneels.*
   York. Show me thy humble heart, and not thy knee,
Whose duty is deceivable and false.
   Boling. My gracious uncle! —
   York. Tut, tut!
Grace me no grace, nor uncle me no uncle:
I am no traitor's uncle; and that word "grace"
In an ungracious mouth is but profane.
Why have those banish'd and forbidden legs
Dar'd once to touch a dust of England's ground?
But, then, more why, — why have they dar'd to march
So many miles upon her peaceful bosom,
Frighting her pale-fac'd villages with war
And ostentation of despisèd arms?
Com'st thou because th' anointed king is hence?
Why, foolish boy, the king is left behind,
And in my loyal bosom lies his power.
Were I but now the lord of such hot youth
As when brave Gaunt thy father, and myself,
Rescu'd the Black Prince, that young Mars of men,
From forth the ranks of many thousand French,
O, then, how quickly should this arm of mine,
Now prisoner to the palsy, chastise thee,
And minister correction to thy fault!
   Boling. My gracious uncle, let me know my fault;
In what condition stands it and wherein?
   York. Even in condition of the worst degree, —

In gross rebellion and detested treason:
Thou art a banish'd man; and here art come
Before the expiration of thy time,
In braving arms against thy sovereign.

 Boling. As I was banish'd, I was banish'd Hereford;
But as I come, I come for Lancaster.
And, noble uncle, I beseech your grace
Look on my wrongs with an indifferent eye:
You are my father, for methinks in you
I see old Gaunt alive; O, then, my father,
Will you permit that I shall stand condemn'd
A wandering vagabond; my rights and royalties
Pluck'd from my arms perforce, and given away
To upstart unthrifts? Wherefore was I born?
If that my cousin king be King of England,
It must be granted I am Duke of Lancaster.
You have a son, Aumerle, my noble kinsman;
Had you first died, and he been thus trod down,
He should have found his uncle Gaunt a father,
To rouse his wrongs, and chase them to the bay.
I am denied to sue my livery here,
And yet my letters-patents give me leave:
My father's goods are all distrain'd and sold;
And these and all are all amiss employ'd.
What would you have me do? I am a subject,
And challenge law: attorneys are denied me;
And therefore personally I lay my claim
To my inheritance of free descent.

 North. The noble duke hath been too much abus'd.
 Ross. It stands your grace upon to do him right.
 Willo. Base men by his endowments are made great.
 York. My lords of England, let me tell you this: —
I have had feeling of my cousin's wrongs,
And labour'd all I could to do him right;
But in this kind to come, in braving arms,
Be his own carver, and cut out his way,
To find out right with wrong, — it may not be;

And you that do abet him in this kind
Cherish rebellion and are rebels all.
  North. The noble duke hath sworn his coming is
But for his own; and for the right of that
We all have strongly sworn to give him aid;
And let him ne'er see joy that breaks that oath!
  York. Well, well, I see the issue of these arms; —
I cannot mend it, I must needs confess,
Because my power is weak and all ill left:
But if I could, by him that gave me life,
I would attach you all, and make you stoop
Unto the sovereign mercy of the king;
But since I cannot, be it known to you
I do remain as neuter. So, fare you well; —
Unless you please to enter in the castle,
And there repose you for this night.
  Boling. An offer, uncle, that we will accept:
But we must win your grace to go with us
To Bristol-castle, which they say is held
By Bushy, Bagot, and their complices,
The caterpillars of the commonwealth,
Which I have sworn to weed and pluck away.
  York. 'T may be I'll go with you: — but yet I'll pause;
For I am loth to break our country's laws.
Nor friends nor foes, to me welcóme you are:
Things past redress are now with me past care.   [*Exeunt.*

SCENE IV. *A camp in Wales.*

Enter SALISBURY *and a* Captain.

  Cap. My Lord of Salisbury, we have stay'd ten days,
And hardly kept our countrymen together,
And yet we hear no tidings from the king;
Therefore we will disperse ourselves: farewell.
  Sal. Stay yet another day, thou trusty Welshman:
The king reposeth all his confidence in thee.
  Cap 'Tis thought the king is dead; we will not stay.

The bay-trees in our country all are wither'd,
And meteors fright the fixèd stars of heaven;
The pale-fac'd moon looks bloody on the earth,
And lean-look'd prophets whisper fearful change;
Rich men look sad, and ruffians dance and leap, —
The one in fear to lose what they enjoy,
The other to enjoy by rage and war:
These signs forerun the death or fall of kings. —
Farewell: our countrymen are gone and fled,
As well assur'd Richard their king is dead. [*Exit.*

Sal. Ah, Richard, with the eyes of heavy mind,
I see thy glory, like a shooting star,
Fall to the base earth from the firmament!
Thy sun sets weeping in the lowly west,
Witnessing storms to come, woe, and unrest:
Thy friends are fled, to wait upon thy foes
And crossly to thy good all fortune goes. [*Exit.*

ACT III.

SCENE I. BOLINGBROKE'S *camp at Bristol.*

Enter BOLINGBROKE, YORK, NORTHUMBERLAND, PERCY, WILLOUGHBY, ROSS: Officers *behind, with* BUSHY *and* GREEN, *prisoners.*

Boling. Bring forth these men. —
Bushy and Green, I will not vex your souls —
Since presently your souls must part your bodies —
With too much urging your pernicious lives,
For 'twere no charity; yet, to wash your blood
From off my hands, here, in the view of men,
I will unfold some causes of your deaths.
You have misled a prince, a royal king,
A happy gentleman in blood and lineaments,
By you unhappied and disfigur'd clean:
You have in manner with your sinful hours
Made a divorce betwixt his queen and him;

Broke the possession of a royal bed,
And stain'd the beauty of a fair queen's cheeks
With tears drawn from her eyes by your foul wrongs.
Myself, — a prince by fortune of my birth,
Near to the king in blood, and near in love
Till you did make him misinterpret me, —
Have stoop'd my neck under your injuries,
And sigh'd my English breath in foreign clouds,
Eating the bitter bread of banishment;
Whilst you have fed upon my signories,
Dispark'd my parks, and fell'd my forest-woods,
From my own windows torn my household coat,
Raz'd out my imprese, leaving me no sign,
Save men's opinions and my living blood,
To show the world I am a gentleman.
This and much more, much more than twice all this,
Condemns you to the death. — See them deliver'd over
To execution and the hand of death.

 Bushy. More welcome is the stroke of death to me
Than Bolingbroke to England. — Lords, farewell.

 Green. My comfort is, that heaven will take our souls,
And plague injustice with the pains of hell.

 Boling. My Lord Northumberland, see them dispatch'd.
    [*Exeunt Northumberland and others, with the
     prisoners.*
Uncle, you say the queen is at your house;
For God's sake, fairly let her be entreated:
Tell her I send to her my kind commends;
Take special care my greetings be deliver'd.

 York. A gentleman of mine I have dispatch'd
With letters of your love to her at large.

 Boling. Thanks, gentle uncle. — Come, my lords, away,
To fight with Glendower and his complices:
Awhile to work, and after holiday.
            [*Exeunt.*

Scene II. *The coast of Wales. A castle is in view.*

Flourish; drums and trumpets. Enter King Richard, *the* Bishop of Carlisle, Aumerle, *and Soldiers, with colours.*

K. Rich. Barkloughly-castle call they this at hand?

Aum. Yea, my good lord. How brooks your grace the air, After late tossing on the breaking seas?

K. Rich. Needs must I like it well: I weep for joy
To stand upon my kingdom once again. —
Dear earth, I do salute thee with my hand,
Though rebels wound thee with their horses' hoofs:
As a long-parted mother with her child
Plays fondly with her tears and smiles in meeting,
So, weeping-smiling, greet I thee, my earth,
And do thee favour with my royal hands.
Feed not thy sovereign's foe, my gentle earth,
Nor with thy sweets comfort his ravenous sense;
But let thy spiders, that suck up thy venom,
And heavy-gaited toads, lie in their way,
Doing annoyance to the treacherous feet
Which with usurping steps do trample thee:
Yield stinging-nettles to mine enemies;
And when they from thy bosom pluck a flower,
Guard it, I pray thee, with a lurking adder,
Whose double tongue may with a mortal touch
Throw death upon thy sovereign's enemies. —
Mock not my senseless conjuration, lords:
This earth shall have a feeling, and these stones
Prove armèd soldiers, ere her native king
Shall falter under foul rebellion's arms.

Car. Fear not, my lord: that Power that made you king
Hath power to keep you king in spite of all.
The means that heaven yields must be embrac'd,
And not neglected; else, if heaven would,
And we will not, heaven's offer we refuse,
The proffer'd means of succour and redress.

Aum. He means, my lord, that we are too remiss;

Whilst Bolingbroke, through our security,
Grows strong and great in substance and in friends.
 K. Rich. Discomfortable cousin! know'st thou not
That when the searching eye of heaven is hid
Behind the globe, that lights the lower world,
Then thieves and robbers range abroad unseen,
In murders and in outrage, boldly here;
But when, from under this terrestrial ball,
He fires the proud tops of the eastern pines,
And darts his light through every guilty hole,
Then murders, treasons, and detested sins,
The cloak of night being pluck'd from off their backs,
Stand bare and naked, trembling at themselves?
So when this thief, this traitor, Bolingbroke, —
Who all this while hath revell'd in the night,
Whilst we were wandering with th' Antipodes, —
Shall see us rising in our throne, the east,
His treasons will sit blushing in his face,
Not able to endure the sight of day,
But self-affrighted tremble at his sin.
Not all the water in the rough-rude sea
Can wash the balm from an anointed king;
The breath of worldly men cannot depose
The deputy elected by the Lord:
For every man that Bolingbroke hath press'd
To lift shrewd steel against our golden crown,
God for his Richard hath in heavenly pay
A glorious angel: then, if angels fight,
Weak men must fall; for heaven still guards the right.

     Enter SALISBURY.
Welcome, my lord: how far off lies your power?
 Sal. Nor near nor further off, my gracious lord,
Than this weak arm: discomfort guides my tongue,
And bids me speak of nothing but despair.
One day too late, I fear, my noble lord,
Hath clouded all thy happy days on earth:

O, call back yesterday, bid time return,
And thou shalt have twelve thousand fighting men!
To-day, to-day, unhappy day, too late,
O'erthrows thy joys, friends, fortune, and thy state;
For all the Welshmen, hearing thou wert dead,
Are gone to Bolingbroke, dispers'd, and fled.
   Aum. Comfort, my liege: why looks your grace so pale?
   K. Rich. But now the blood of twenty thousand men
Did triumph in my face, and they are fled;
And, till so much blood thither come agen,
Have I not reason to look pale and dead?
All souls that will be safe, fly from my side;
For time hath set a blot upon my pride.
   Aum. Comfort, my liege; remember who you are.
   K. Rich. I had forgot myself: am I not king?
Awake, thou sluggard majesty! thou sleepest.
Is not the king's name forty thousand names?
Arm, arm, my name! a puny subject strikes
At thy great glory. — Look not to the ground,
Ye favourites of a king: are we not high?
High be our thoughts: I know my uncle York
Hath power enough to serve our turn. — But who comes here?

Enter SCROOP.

   Scroop. More health and happiness betide my liege
Than can my care-tun'd tongue deliver him!
   K. Rich. Mine ear is open and my heart prepar'd:
The worst is worldly loss thou canst unfold.
Say, is my kingdom lost? why, 'twas my care;
And what loss is it to be rid of care?
Strives Bolingbroke to be as great as we?
Greater he shall not be; if he serve God,
We'll serve Him too, and be his fellow so:
Revolt our subjects? that we cannot mend;
They break their faith to God as well as us:
Cry woe, destruction, ruin, loss, decay;
The worst is death, and death will have his day.

Scroop. Glad am I that your highness is so arm'd
To bear the tidings of calamity.
Like an unseasonable stormy day,
Which makes the silver rivers drown their shores,
As if the world were all dissolv'd to tears;
So high above his limits swells the rage
Of Bolingbroke, covering your fearful land
With hard bright steel, and hearts harder than steel.
White-beards have arm'd their thin and hairless scalps
Against thy majesty; boys with women's voices
Strive to speak big, and clap their female joints
In stiff unwieldy arms against thy crown;
Thy very beadsmen learn to bend their bows
Of double-fatal yew against thy state;
Yea, distaff-women manage rusty bills
Against thy seat: both young and old rebel,
And all goes worse than I have power to tell.

K. Rich. Too well, too well thou tell'st a tale so ill.
Where is the Earl of Wiltshire? where is Bagot?
What is become of Bushy? where is Green?
That they have let the dangerous enemy
Measure our confines with such peaceful steps?
If we prevail, their heads shall pay for it:
I warrant they've made peace with Bolingbroke.

Scroop. Peace have they made with him, indeed, my lord.

K. Rich. O villains, vipers, damn'd without redemption!
Dogs, easily won to fawn on any man!
Snakes, in my heart-blood warm'd, that sting my heart!
Three Judases, each one thrice worse than Judas!
Would they make peace? terrible hell make war
Upon their spotted souls for this offence!

Scroop. Sweet love, I see, changing his property,
Turns to the sourest and most deadly hate: —
Again uncurse their souls; their peace is made
With heads, and not with hands: those whom you curse
Have felt the worst of death's destroying wound,
And lie full low, grav'd in the hollow ground.

Aum. Is Bushy, Green, and th' Earl of Wiltshire dead?
Scroop. Yea, all of them at Bristol lost their heads.
Aum. Where is the duke my father with his power?
K. Rich. No matter where; — of comfort no man speak:
Let's talk of graves, of worms, and epitaphs;
Make dust our paper, and with rainy eyes
Write sorrow on the bosom of the earth.
Let's choose executors, and talk of wills:
And yet not so, — for what can we bequeath,
Save our deposèd bodies to the ground?
Our lands, our lives, and all are Bolingbroke's,
And nothing can we call our own but death,
And that small model of the barren earth
Which serves as paste and cover to our bones.
For God's sake, let us sit upon the ground,
And tell sad stories of the death of kings: —
How some have been depos'd; some slain in war;
Some haunted by the ghosts they have depos'd;
Some poison'd by their wives; some sleeping kill'd;
All murder'd: — for within the hollow crown
That rounds the mortal temples of a king
Keeps Death his court; and there the antic sits,
Scoffing his state, and grinning at his pomp;
Allowing him a breath, a little scene,
To monarchize, be fear'd, and kill with looks;
Infusing him with self and vain conceit, —
As if this flesh, which walls-about our life,
Were brass impregnable; and humour'd thus,
Comes at the last, and with a little pin
Bores through his castle-wall, and — farewell king!
Cover your heads, and mock not flesh and blood
With solemn reverence; throw away respect,
Tradition, form, and ceremonious duty;
For you have but mistook me all this while:
I live with bread like you, feel want, taste grief,
Need friends: — subjécted thus,
How can you say to me, I am a king?

Car. My lord, wise men ne'er wail their present woes,
But presently prevent the ways to wail.
To fear the foe, since fear oppresseth strength,
Gives, in your weakness, strength unto your foe,
And so your follies fight against yourself.
Fear, and be slain; no worse can come to fight:
And fight and die is death destroying death;
Where fearing dying pays death servile breath.
　　Aum. My father hath a power; inquire of him;
And learn to make a body of a limb.
　　K. Rich. Thou chid'st me well: — proud Bolingbroke,
　　　　I come
To change blows with thee for our day of doom.
This ague-fit of fear is over-blown;
An easy task it is to win our own. —
Say, Scroop, where lies our uncle with his power?
Speak sweetly, man, although thy looks be sour.
　　Scroop. Men judge by the complexion of the sky
　　The state and inclination of the day;
So may you by my dull and heavy eye
　　My tongue hath but a heavier tale to say.
I play the torturer, by small and small
To lengthen out the worst that must be spoken: —
Your uncle York is join'd with Bolingbroke;
And all your northern castles yielded up,
And all your southern gentlemen in arms
Upon his party.
　　K. Rich.　　Thou hast said enough. —
[*To Aumerle*] Beshrew thee, cousin, which didst lead me forth
Of that sweet way I was in to despair!
What say you now? what comfort have we now?
By heaven, I'll hate him everlastingly
That bids me be of comfort any more.
Go to Flint-castle: there I'll pine away;
A king, woe's slave, shall kingly woe obey.
That power I have, discharge; and let them go
To ear the land that hath some hope to grow,

For I have none: — let no man speak again
To alter this, for counsel is but vain.
    Aum. My liege, one word.
    K. Rich.   He does me double wrong
That wounds me with the flatteries of his tongue.
Discharge my followers: let them hence away,
From Richard's night to Bolingbroke's fair day.   [*Exeunt.*

          SCENE III. *Wales. Before Flint-castle.*

Enter, with drum and colours, BOLINGBROKE *and forces;* YORK,
          NORTHUMBERLAND, *and others.*

    Boling. So that by this intelligence we learn
The Welshmen are dispers'd; and Salisbury
Is gone to meet the king, who lately landed
With some few private friends upon this coast.
    North. The news is very fair and good, my lord:
Richard not far from hence hath hid his head.
    York. It would beseem the Lord Northumberland
To say "King Richard:" — alack the heavy day
When such a sacred king should hide his head!
    North. Your grace mistakes me; only to be brief,
Left I his title out.
    York.   The time hath been,
Would you have been so brief with him, he would
Have been so brief with you, to shorten you,
For taking so the head, your whole head's length.
    Boling. Mistake not, uncle, further than you should.
    York. Take not, good cousin, further than you should,
Lest you mistake: the heavens are o'er our heads.
    Boling. I know it, uncle; and I not oppose
Myself against their will. — But who comes here?

              Enter PERCY.

Welcome, Harry: what, will not this castle yield?
    Percy. The castle royally is mann'd, my lord,
Against thy entrance.

Boling. Royally!
Why, it contains no king?
    Percy.   Yes, my good lord,
It doth contain a king; King Richard lies
Within the limits of yond lime and stone:
And with him are the Lord Aumerle, Lord Salisbury,
Sir Stephen Scroop; besides a clergyman
Of holy reverence, who I cannot learn.
    North. O, belike it is the Bishop of Carlisle.
    Boling. [*to North.*] Noble lord,
Go to the rude ribs of that ancient castle;
Through brazen trumpet send the breath of parle
Into his ruin'd ears, and thus deliver: —
Henry Bolingbroke
On both his knees doth kiss King Richard's hand,
And sends allegiance and true faith of heart
To his most royal person; hither come
Even at his feet to lay my arms and power,
Provided that, my banishment repeal'd,
And lands restor'd again, be freely granted:
If not, I'll use th' advantage of my power,
And lay the summer's dust with showers of blood
Rain'd from the wounds of slaughter'd Englishmen:
The which, how far off from the mind of Bolingbroke
It is, such crimson tempest should bedrench
The fresh green lap of fair King Richard's land,
My stooping duty tenderly shall show.
Go, signify as much, while here we march
Upon the grassy carpet of this plain. —
          [*Northumberland advances to the castle with a trumpet.*
Let's march without the noise of threatening drum,
That from this castle's tatter'd battlements
Our fair appointments may be well perus'd.
Methinks King Richard and myself should meet
With no less terror than the elements
Of fire and water, when their thundering shock
At meeting tears the cloudy cheeks of heaven.

Be he the fire, I'll be the yielding water:
The rage be his, while on the earth I rain
My waters, — on the earth, and not on him.
March on, and mark King Richard how he looks.

*A parle sounded, and answered by another trumpet within.
Flourish. Enter, on the walls,* King RICHARD, *the* Bishop of
Carlisle, AUMERLE, SCROOP, *and* SALISBURY.

Percy. See, see, King Richard doth himself appear,
As doth the blushing discontented sun
From out the fiery portal of the east,
When he perceives the envious clouds are bent
To dim his glory, and to stain the track
Of his bright passage to the occident.

York. Yet looks he like a king: behold, his eye,
As bright as is the eagle's, lightens forth
Controlling majesty: — alack, alack, for woe,
That any storm should stain so fair a show!

K. Rich. [*to Northumberland*] We are amaz'd; and thus
 long have we stood
To watch the fearful bending of thy knee,
Because we thought ourself thy lawful king:
And if we be, how dare thy joints forget
To pay their awful duty to our presence?
If we be not, show us the hand of God
That hath dismiss'd us from our stewardship;
For well we know, no hand of blood and bone
Can gripe the sacred handle of our sceptre,
Unless he do profane, steal, or usurp.
And though you think that all, as you have done,
Have torn their souls by turning them from us,
And we are barren and bereft of friends;
Yet know, — my master, God omnipotent,
Is mustering in his clouds, on our behalf,
Armies of pestilence; and they shall strike
Your children yet unborn and unbegot,
That lift your vassal hands against my head,

And threat the glory of my precious crown.
Tell Bolingbroke, — for yond methinks he stands, —
That every stride he makes upon my land
Is dangerous treason: he is come to ope
The purple testament of bleeding war;
But ere the crown he looks for live in peace,
Ten thousand bloody crowns of mothers' sons
Shall ill become the flower of England's face,
Change the complexion of her maid-pale peace
To scarlet indignation, and bedew
Her pastures' grass with faithful English blood.
    North. The king of heaven forbid our lord the king
Should so with civil and uncivil arms
Be rush'd upon! Thy thrice-noble cousin
Harry Bolingbroke doth humbly kiss thy hand;
And by the honourable tomb he swears
That stands upon your royal grandsire's bones,
And by the royalties of both your bloods, —
Currents that spring from one most gracious head, —
And by the buried hand of warlike Gaunt,
And by the worth and honour of himself,
Comprising all that may be sworn or said, —
His coming hither hath no further scope
Than for his lineal royalties, and to beg
Enfranchisement immediate on his knees:
Which on thy royal party granted once,
His glittering arms he will commend to rust,
His barbèd steeds to stables, and his heart
To faithful service of your majesty.
This swears he, as he is a prince, is just;
And, as I am a gentleman, I credit him.
    K. Rich. Northumberland, say thus the king returns: —
His noble cousin is right welcome hither;
And all the number of his fair demands
Shall be accomplish'd without contradiction:
With all the gracious utterance thou hast
Speak to his gentle hearing kind commends. —

[To Aumerle] We do debase ourself, cousin, do we not,
To look so poorly, and to speak so fair?
Shall we call back Northumberland, and send
Defiance to the traitor, and so die?

Aum. No, good my lord; let's fight with gentle words
Till time lend friends, and friends their helpful swords.

K. Rich. O God, O God! that e'er this tongue of mine,
That laid the sentence of dread banishment
On yond proud man, should take it off again
With words of sooth! O, that I were as great
As is my grief, or lesser than my name!
Or that I could forget what I have been!
Or not remember what I must be now!
Swell'st thou, proud heart? I'll give thee scope to beat,
Since foes have scope to beat both thee and me.

Aum. Northumberland comes back from Bolingbroke.

K. Rich. What must the king do now? must he submit?
The king shall do it: must he be depos'd?
The king shall be contented: must he lose
The name of king? o' God's name, let it go:
I'll give my jewels for a set of beads,
My gorgeous palace for a hermitage,
My gay apparel for an alms-man's gown,
My figur'd goblets for a dish of wood,
My sceptre for a palmer's walking-staff,
My subjects for a pair of carvèd saints,
And my large kingdom for a little grave,
A little little grave, an obscure grave; —
Or I'll be buried in the king's highway,
Some way of common trade, where subjects' feet
May hourly trample on their sovereign's head;
For on my heart they tread now whilst I live;
And buried once, why not upon my head? —
Aumerle, thou weep'st, — my tender-hearted cousin! —
We'll make foul weather with despisèd tears;
Our sighs and they shall lodge the summer corn,
And make a dearth in this revolting land.

Or shall we play the wantons with our woes,
And make some pretty match with shedding tears?
As thus; — to drop them still upon one place,
Till they have fretted us a pair of graves
Within the earth; and, therein laid, — "There lies
Two kinsmen digg'd their graves with weeping eyes."
Would not this ill do well? — Well, well, I see
I talk but idly, and you mock at me. —
Most mighty prince, my Lord Northumberland,
What says King Bolingbroke? will his majesty
Give Richard leave to live till Richard die?
You make a leg, and Bolingbroke says ay.

 North. My lord, in the base court he doth attend
To speak with you; — may 't please you to come down.
 K. Rich. Down, down I come; like glistering Phaëthon,
Wanting the manage of unruly jades.
In the base court? Base court, where kings grow base,
To come at traitors' calls, and do them grace.
In the base court? Come down? Down, court! down, king!
For night-owls shriek where mounting larks should sing.
            [Exeunt above.

 Boling. What says his majesty?
 North.   Sorrow and grief of heart
Makes him speak fondly, like a frantic man:
Yet he is come.

    Enter King Richard *attended, below.*

 Boling. Stand all apart,
And show fair duty to his majesty. —
My gracious lord, —   *[Kneeling.*
 K. Rich. Fair cousin, you debase your princely knee
To make the base earth proud with kissing it:
Me rather had my heart might feel your love
Than my unpleas'd eye see your courtesy.
Up, cousin, up; — your heart is up, I know,
Thus high at least [*Touching his own head*], although your
    knee be low.

Boling. My gracious lord, I come but for mine own.
K. Rich. Your own is yours, and I am yours, and all.
Boling. So far be mine, my most redoubted lord,
As my true service shall deserve your love.
K. Rich. Well you deserve: — they well deserve to have,
That know the strong'st and surest way to get. —
Uncle, give me your hand: nay, dry your eyes;
Tears show their love, but want their remedies. —
Cousin, I am too young to be your father,
Though you are old enough to be my heir.
What you will have, I'll give, and willing too;
For do we must what force will have us do. —
Set on towards London: — cousin, is it so?
Boling. Yea, my good lord.
K. Rich.   Then I must not say no.
                                  [*Flourish. Exeunt.*

SCENE IV. *Langley. The* Duke of York's *garden.*

Enter the Queen *and two* Ladies.

Queen. What sport shall we devise here in this garden,
To drive away the heavy thought of care?
First Lady. Madam, we'll play at bowls.
Queen. 'Twill make me think the world is full of rubs,
And that my fortune runs against the bias.
First Lady. Madam, we'll dance.
Queen. My legs can keep no measure in delight,
When my poor heart no measure keeps in grief:
Therefore, no dancing, girl; some other sport.
First Lady. Madam, we'll tell tales.
Queen. Of sorrow or of joy?
First Lady.   Of either, madam.
Queen. Of neither, girl:
For if of joy, being altogether wanting,
It doth remember me the more of sorrow;
Or if of grief, being altogether had,
It adds more sorrow to my want of joy:

For what I have, I need not to repeat;
And what I want, it boots not to complain.
    First Lady. Madam, I'll sing.
    Queen.   'Tis well that thou hast cause;
But thou shouldst please me better, wouldst thou weep.
    First Lady. I could weep, madam, would it do you good.
    Queen. And I could weep, would weeping do me good,
And never borrow any tear of thee. —
But stay, here come the gardeners:
Let's step into the shadow of these trees.
My wretchedness unto a row of pins,
They'll talk of state; for every one doth so
Against a change: woe is forerun with woe.
                            [*Queen and Ladies retire.*
    Enter a Gardener *and two* Servants.
    Gard. Go, bind thou up yond dangling apricocks,
Which, like unruly children, make their sire
Stoop with oppression of their prodigal weight:
Give some supportance to the bending twigs. —
Go thou, and, like an executioner,
Cut off the heads of too-fast-growing sprays,
That look too lofty in our commonwealth:
All must be even in our government. —
You thus employ'd, I will go root away
The noisome weeds, that without profit suck
The soil's fertility from wholesome flowers.
    First Serv. Why should we, in the compass of a pale,
Keep law and form and due proportion,
Showing, as in a model, a firm state,
When our sea-wallèd garden, the whole land,
Is full of weeds; her fairest flowers chok'd up,
Her fruit-trees all unprun'd, her hedges ruin'd,
Her knots disorder'd, and her wholesome herbs
Swarming with caterpillars?
    Gard.   Hold thy peace: —
He that hath suffer'd this disorder'd spring
Hath now himself met with the fall of leaf:

The weeds that his broad-spreading leaves did shelter,
That seem'd in eating him to hold him up,
Are pluck'd up root and all by Bolingbroke,—
I mean the Earl of Wiltshire, Bushy, Green.
 First Serv. What, are they dead?
 Gard.   They are; and Bolingbroke
Hath seiz'd the wasteful king.— O, what pity is it
That he had not so trimm'd and dress'd his land
As we this garden! We at time of year
Do wound the bark, the skin of our fruit-trees,
Lest, being over-proud in sap and blood,
With too much riches it confound itself:
Had he done so to great and growing men,
They might have liv'd to bear, and he to taste
Their fruits of duty. All superfluous branches
We lop away, that bearing boughs may live:
Had he done so, himself had borne the crown,
Which waste of idle hours hath quite thrown down.
 First Serv. What, think you, then, the king shall be
     depos'd?
 Gard. Depress'd he is already; and depos'd
'Tis doubt he will be: letters came last night
To a dear friend of the good Duke of York's,
That tell black tidings.
 Queen. O, I am press'd to death through want of speak-
     ing!—   [*Comes forward with Ladies.*
Thou, old Adam's likeness, set to dress this garden,
How dares
Thy harsh-rude tongue sound this unpleasing news?
What Eve, what serpent, hath suggested thee
To make a second fall of cursèd man?
Why dost thou say King Richard is depos'd?
Dar'st thou, thou little better thing than earth,
Divine his downfal? Say, where, when, and how,
Cam'st thou by this ill tidings? speak, thou wretch.
 Gard. Pardon me, madam: little joy have I
To breathe this news: yet what I say is true.

King Richard, he is in the mighty hold
Of Bolingbroke: their fortunes both are weigh'd:
In your lord's scale is nothing but himself,
And some few vanities that make him light;
But in the balance of great Bolingbroke,
Besides himself, are all the English peers,
And with that odds he weighs King Richard down.
Post you to London, and you'll find it so;
I speak no more than every one doth know.

Queen. Nimble mischance, that art so light of foot,
Doth not thy embassage belong to me,
And am I last that knows it? O, thou think'st
To serve me last, that I may longest keep
Thy sorrow in my breast. — Come, ladies, go,
To meet at London London's king in woe. —
What, was I born to this, that my sad look
Should grace the triumph of great Bolingbroke?
Gardener, for telling me this news of woe,
Pray God the plants thou graft'st may never grow.
[Exeunt Queen and Ladies.

Gard. Poor queen! so that thy state might be no worse,
I would my skill were subject to thy curse. —
Here did she fall a tear; here, in this place,
I'll set a bank of rue, sour herb of grace:
Rue, even for ruth, here shortly shall be seen,
In the remembrance of a weeping queen. *[Exeunt.*

ACT IV.

Scene I. *London. Westminster Hall.*

The Lords spiritual on the right side of the throne; the Lords temporal on the left; the Commons below. Enter BOLINGBROKE, AUMERLE, SURREY, NORTHUMBERLAND, PERCY, FITZWATER, *another Lord, the* Bishop of Carlisle, *the* Abbot of Westminster, *and* Attendants. Officers *behind, with* BAGOT.

Boling. Call forth Bagot. *[Officers bring Bagot to the bar.*
Now, Bagot, freely speak thy mind;

What thou dost know of noble Gloster's death;
Who wrought it with the king, and who perform'd
The bloody office of his timeless end.
    Bagot. Then set before my face the Lord Aumerle.
    Boling. Cousin, stand forth, and look upon that man.
    Bagot. My Lord Aumerle, I know your daring tongue
Scorns to unsay what once it hath deliver'd.
In that dead time when Gloster's death was plotted,
I heard you say, — "Is not my arm of length,
That reacheth from the restful English court
As far as Calais, to my uncle's head?"
Amongst much other talk, that very time,
I heard you say that you had rather refuse
The offer of an hundred thousand crowns
Than Bolingbroke's return to England;
Adding withal, how blest this land would be
In this your cousin's death.
    Aum.   Princes, and noble lords,
What answer shall I make to this base man?
Shall I so much dishonour my fair stars,
On equal terms to give him chastisement?
Either I must, or have mine honour soil'd
With the attainder of his slanderous lips. —
There is my gage, the manual seal of death,
That marks thee out for hell: I say, thou liest,
And will maintain what thou hast said is false
In thy heart-blood, though being all too base
To stain the temper of my knightly sword.
    Boling. Bagot, forbear; thou shalt not take it up.
    Aum. Excepting one, I would he were the best
In all this presence that hath mov'd me so.
    Fitz. If that thy valour stand on sympathy,
There is my gage, Aumerle, in gage to thine:
By that fair sun which shows me where thou stand'st,
I heard thee say, and vauntingly thou spak'st it,
That thou wert cause of noble Gloster's death.
If thou deny'st it twenty times, thou liest;

And I will turn thy falsehood to thy heart,
Where it was forgèd, with my rapier's point.
    Aum. Thou dar'st not, coward, live to see that day.
    Fitz. Now, by my soul, I would it were this hour.
    Aum. Fitzwater, thou art damn'd to hell for this.
    Percy. Aumerle, thou liest; his honour is as true
In this appeal as thou art all unjust;
And that thou art so, there I throw my gage,
To prove it on thee to th' extremest point
Of mortal breathing: seize it, if thou dar'st.
    Aum. And if I do not, may my hands rot off,
And never brandish more revengeful steel
Over the glittering helmet of my foe!
    Lord. I task thee to the like, forsworn Aumerle;
And spur thee on with full as many lies
As may be holla'd in thy treacherous ear
From sun to sun: there is my honour's pawn;
Engage it to the trial, if thou dar'st.
    Aum. Who sets me else? by heaven, I'll throw at all:
I have a thousand spirits in one breast,
To answer twenty thousand such as you.
    Surrey. My Lord Fitzwater, I do remember well
The very time Aumerle and you did talk.
    Fitz. 'Tis very true: you were in presence then;
And you can witness with me this is true.
    Surrey. As false, by heaven, as heaven itself is true.
    Fitz. Surrey, thou liest.
    Surrey.   Dishonourable boy!
That lie shall lie so heavy on my sword,
That it shall render vengeance and revenge
Till thou the lie-giver and that lie do lie
In earth as quiet as thy father's skull:
In proof whereof, there is my honour's pawn;
Engage it to the trial, if thou dar'st.
    Fitz. How fondly dost thou spur a forward horse!
If I dare eat, or drink, or breathe, or live,
I dare meet Surrey in a wilderness,

And spit upon him, whilst I say he lies,
And lies, and lies: there is my bond of faith,
To tie thee to my strong correction. —
As I intend to thrive in this new world,
Aumerle is guilty of my true appeal:
Besides, I heard the banish'd Norfolk say,
That thou, Aumerle, didst send two of thy men
To execute the noble duke at Calais.

Aum. Some honest Christian trust me with a gage,
That Norfolk lies: here do I throw down this,
If he may be repeal'd, to try his honour.

Boling. These differences shall all rest under gage,
Till Norfolk be repeal'd: repeal'd he shall be,
And, though mine enemy, restor'd again
To all his lands and signories: when he's return'd,
Against Aumerle we will enforce his trial.

Car. That honourable day shall ne'er be seen.
Many a time hath banish'd Norfolk fought
For Jesu Christ in glorious Christian field,
Streaming the ensign of the Christian cross
Against black pagans, Turks, and Saracens;
And toil'd with works of war, retir'd himself
To Italy; and there, at Venice, gave
His body to that pleasant country's earth,
And his pure soul unto his captain Christ,
Under whose colours he had fought so long.

Boling. Why, bishop, is Norfolk dead?

Car. As surely as I live, my lord.

Boling. Sweet peace conduct his sweet soul to the bosom
Of good old Abraham! — My lords appellants,
Your differences shall all rest under gage
Till we assign you to your days of trial.

Enter YORK, *attended.*

York. Great Duke of Lancaster, I come to thee
From plume-pluck'd Richard; who with willing soul
Adopts thee heir, and his high sceptre yields

To the possession of thy royal hand:
Ascend his throne, descending now from him, —
And long live Henry, of that name the fourth!
    Boling. In God's name, I'll ascend the regal throne.
    Car. Marry, God forbid! —
Worst in this royal presence may I speak,
Yet best beseeming me to speak the truth.
Would God that any in this noble presence
Were enough noble to be upright judge
Of noble Richard! then true nobless would
Learn him forbearance from so foul a wrong.
What subject can give sentence on his king?
And who sits here that is not Richard's subject?
Thieves are not judg'd but they are by to hear,
Although apparent guilt be seen in them;
And shall the figure of God's majesty,
His captain, steward, deputy elect,
Anointed, crownèd, planted many years,
Be judg'd by subject and inferior breath,
And he himself not present? O, forfend it, God,
That, in a Christian climate, souls refin'd
Should show so heinous, black, obscene a deed!
I speak to subjects, and a subject speaks,
Stirr'd up by God, thus boldly for his king.
My Lord of Hereford here, whom you call king,
Is a foul traitor to proud Hereford's king;
And if you crown him, let me prophesy, —
The blood of English shall manure the ground,
And future ages groan for this foul act;
Peace shall go sleep with Turks and infidels,
And in this seat of peace tumultuous wars
Shall kin with kin and kind with kind confound;
Disorder, horror, fear, and mutiny,
Shall here inhabit, and this land be call'd
The field of Golgotha and dead men's skulls.
O, if you raise this house against this house,
It will the wofullest division prove

That ever fell upon this cursèd earth.
Prevent, resist it, let it not be so,
Lest children's children cry against you "woe!"

North. Well have you argu'd, sir; and, for your pains,
Of capital treason we arrest you here. —
My Lord of Westminster, be it your charge
To keep him safely till his day of trial. —
May't please you, lords, to grant the commons' suit.

Boling. Fetch hither Richard, that in common view
He may surrender; so we shall proceed
Without suspicion.

York. I will be his conduct. [*Exit.*

Boling. Lords, you that here are under our arrest,
Procure your sureties for your days of answer. —
Little are we beholding to your love, [*To Carlisle.*
And little look'd for at your helping hands.

Re-enter YORK, *with* King RICHARD, *and* Officers *bearing the crown, &c.*

K. Rich. Alack, why am I sent for to a king,
Before I have shook off the regal thoughts
Wherewith I reign'd? I hardly yet have learn'd
T" insinuate, flatter, bow, and bend my knee:
Give sorrow leave awhile to tutor me
To this submission. Yet I well remember
The favours of these men: were they not mine?
Did they not sometime cry, "All hail!" to me?
So Judas did to Christ: but he, in twelve,
Found truth in all but one; I, in twelve thousand, none.
God save the king! — Will no man say amen?
Am I both priest and clerk? well then, amen.
God save the king! although I be not he;
And yet, amen, if heaven do think him me. —
To do what service am I sent for hither?

York. To do that office of thine own good will
Which tirèd majesty did make thee offer, —

The resignation of thy state and crown
To Henry Bolingbroke.

K. Rich. Give me the crown. [*The crown is brought to Richard, who seizes it.*] — Here, cousin,
On this side my hand, and on that side yours.
Now is this golden crown like a deep well
That owes two buckets, filling one another;
The emptier ever dancing in the air,
The other down, unseen, and full of water:
That bucket down and full of tears am I,
Drinking my griefs, whilst you mount up on high.

Boling. I thought you had been willing to resign.

K. Rich. My crown I am; but still my griefs are mine:
You may my glories and my state depose,
But not my griefs; still am I king of those.

Boling. Part of your cares you give me with your crown.

K. Rich. Your cares set up do not pluck my cares down.
My care is, loss of care, by old care done;
Your care is, gain of care, by new care won:
The cares I give, I have, though given away;
They tend the crown, yet still with me they stay.

Boling. Are you contented to resign the crown?

K. Rich. Ay, no; — no, ay; for I must nothing be;
Therefore no no, for I resign to thee.
Now mark me, how I will undo myself: —
I give this heavy weight from off my head,
And this unwieldy sceptre from my hand,
The pride of kingly sway from out my heart;
With mine own tears I wash away my balm,
With mine own hands I give away my crown,
With mine own tongue deny my sacred state,
With mine own breath release all duty's rites:
All pomp and majesty I do forswear;
My manors, rents, revenues I forgo;
My acts, decrees, and statutes I deny:
God pardon all oaths that are broke to me!
God keep all vows unbroke that swear to thee!

Make me, that nothing have, with nothing griev'd,
And thou with all pleas'd, that hast all achiev'd!
Long mayst thou live in Richard's seat to sit,
And soon lie Richard in an earthy pit!
God save King Henry, unking'd Richard says,
And send him many years of sunshine days! —
What more remains?

   North.   No more, but that you read
                                        [*Offering a paper.*
These accusations, and these grievous crimes
Committed by your person and your followers
Against the state and profit of this land;
That, by confessing them, the souls of men
May deem that you are worthily depos'd.

   K. Rich. Must I do so? and must I ravel out
My weav'd-up follies? Gentle Northumberland,
If thy offences were upon record,
Would it not shame thee in so fair a troop
To read a lecture of them? If thou wouldst,
There shouldst thou find one heinous article, —
Containing the deposing of a king,
And cracking the strong warrant of an oath, —
Mark'd with a blot, damn'd in the book of heaven: —
Nay, all of you that stand and look upon,
Whilst that my wretchedness doth bait myself, —
Though some of you, with Pilate, wash your hands,
Showing an outward pity; yet you Pilates
Have here deliver'd me to my sour cross,
And water cannot wash away your sin.

   North. My lord, dispatch; read o'er these articles.

   K. Rich. Mine eyes are full of tears, I cannot see:
And yet salt water blinds them not so much
But they can see a sort of traitors here.
Nay, if I turn mine eyes upon myself,
I find myself a traitor with the rest;
For I have given here my soul's consent
T' undeck the pompous body of a king;

Made glory base, and sovereignty a slave,
Proud majesty a subject, state a peasant.
   North. My lord, —
   K. Rich. No lord of thine, thou haught-insulting man,
Nor no man's lord; I have no name, no title, —
No, not that name was given me at the font, —
But 'tis usurp'd: — alack the heavy day,
That I have worn so many winters out,
And know not now what name to call myself!
O, that I were a mockery-king of snow,
Standing before the sun of Bolingbroke,
To melt myself away in water-drops! —
Good king, — great king, — and yet not greatly good, —
An if my word be sterling yet in England,
Let it command a mirror hither straight,
That it may show me what a face I have,
Since it is bankrupt of his majesty.
   Boling. Go, some of you and fetch a looking-glass.
                            [*Exit an Attendant.*
   North. Read o'er this paper while the glass doth come.
   K. Rich. Fiend, thou torment'st me ere I come to hell!
   Boling. Urge it no more, my Lord Northumberland.
   North. The commons will not, then, be satisfied.
   K. Rich. They shall be satisfied: I'll read enough,
When I do see the very book indeed
Where all my sins are writ, and that's myself.
        Re-enter Attendant *with a glass.*
Give me the glass, and therein will I read. —
No deeper wrinkles yet? hath sorrow struck
So many blows upon this face of mine,
And made no deeper wounds? — O flattering glass,
Like to my followers in prosperity,
Thou dost beguile me! Was this face the face
That every day under his household roof
Did keep ten thousand men? was this the face
That, like the sun, did make beholders wink?
Was this the face that fac'd so many follies,

And was at last out-fac'd by Bolingbroke?
A brittle glory shineth in this face:
As brittle as the glory is the face;
     [*Dashes the glass against the ground.*
For there it is, crack'd in a hundred shivers. —
Mark, silent king, the moral of this sport, —
How soon my sorrow hath destroy'd my face.
 Boling. The shadow of your sorrow hath destroy'd
The shadow of your face.
 K. Rich.   Say that again.
The shadow of my sorrow? ha! let's see: —
'Tis very true, my grief lies all within;
And these external manners of lament
Are merely shadows to the unseen grief
That swells with silence in the tortur'd soul;
There lies the substance: and I thank thee, king,
For thy great bounty, that not only giv'st
Me cause to wail, but teachest me the way
How to lament the cause. I'll beg one boon,
And then be gone and trouble you no more.
Shall I obtain it?
 Boling. Name it, my fair cousin.
 K. Rich. Fair cousin! I am greater than a king:
For when I was a king, my flatterers
Were then but subjects; being now a subject,
I have a king here to my flatterer.
Being so great, I have no need to beg.
 Boling. Yet ask.
 K. Rich. And shall I have?
 Boling. You shall.
 K. Rich. Then give me leave to go.
 Boling. Whither?
 K. Rich. Whither you will, so I were from your sights.
 Boling. Go, some of you convey him to the Tower.
 K. Rich. O, good! convey? — conveyers are you all,
That rise thus nimbly by a true king's fall.
   [*Exeunt King Richard, some Lords, and a Guard.*

Boling. On Wednesday next we solemnly set down
Our coronation: lords, prepare yourselves.
                    [*Exeunt all except the Bishop of Carlisle, the
                        Abbot of Westminster, and Aumerle.*

Abbot. A woful pageant have we here beheld.
Car. The woe's to come; the children yet unborn
Shall feel this day as sharp to them as thorn.
Aum. You holy clergymen, is there no plot
To rid the realm of this pernicious blot?
Abbot. Before I freely speak my mind herein,
You shall not only take the sacrament
To bury mine intents, but to effect
Whatever I shall happen to devise. —
I see your brows are full of discontent,
Your hearts of sorrow, and your eyes of tears:
Come home with me to supper: I will lay
A plot shall show us all a merry day.   [*Exeunt.*

ACT V.

SCENE I. *London. A street leading to the Tower.*

Enter Queen *and* Ladies.

Queen. This way the king will come; this is the way
To Julius Cæsar's ill-erected tower,
To whose flint bosom my condemnèd lord
Is doom'd a prisoner by proud Bolingbroke:
Here let us rest, if this rebellious earth
Have any resting for her true king's queen. —
But soft, but see, or rather do not see,
My fair rose wither: yet look up, behold,
That you in pity may dissolve to dew,
And wash him fresh again with true-love tears.

Enter King RICHARD *and* Guards.

Ah, thou, the model where old Troy did stand,
Thou map of honour, thou King Richard's tomb,
And not King Richard; thou most beauteous inn,

Why should hard-favour'd grief be lodg'd in thee,
When triumph is become an alehouse guest?

K. Rich. Join not with grief, fair woman, do not so,
To make my end too sudden: learn, good soul,
To think our former state a happy dream;
From which awak'd, the truth of what we are
Shows us but this: I am sworn brother, sweet,
To grim Necessity; and he and I
Will keep a league till death. Hie thee to France,
And cloister thee in some religious house:
Our holy lives must win a new world's crown,
Which our profane hours here have stricken down.

Queen. What, is my Richard both in shape and mind
Transform'd and weaken'd? hath Bolingbroke depos'd
Thine intellect? hath he been in thy heart?
The lion dying thrusteth forth his paw,
And wounds the earth, if nothing else, with rage
To be o'erpower'd; and wilt thou, pupil-like,
Take thy correction mildly, kiss the rod,
And fawn on rage with base humility,
Which art a lion and a king of beasts?

K. Rich. A king of beasts, indeed; if aught but beasts,
I had been still a happy king of men.
Good sometime queen, prepare thee hence for France:
Think I am dead; and that even here thou tak'st,
As from my death-bed, thy last living leave.
In winter's tedious nights sit by the fire
With good old folks, and let them tell thee tales
Of woful ages long ago betid;
And ere thou bid good night, to quit their griefs
Tell thou the lamentable tale of me,
And send the hearers weeping to their beds:
For why the senseless brands will sympathize
The heavy accent of thy moving tongue,
And in compassion weep the fire out;
And some will mourn in ashes, some coal-black,
For the deposing of a rightful king.

Enter NORTHUMBERLAND *attended.*

North. My lord, the mind of Bolingbroke is chang'd;
You must to Pomfret, not unto the Tower. —
And, madam, there is order ta'en for you;
With all swift speed you must away to France.

K. Rich. Northumberland, thou ladder wherewithal
The mounting Bolingbroke ascends my throne,
The time shall not be many hours of age
More than it is, ere foul sin gathering head
Shall break into corruption: thou shalt think,
Though he divide the realm, and give thee half,
It is too little, helping him to all;
And he shall think, that thou, which know'st the way
To plant unrightful kings, wilt know again,
Being ne'er so little urg'd, another way
To pluck him headlong from th' usurpèd throne.
The love of wicked friends converts to fear;
That fear to hate; and hate turns one or both
To worthy danger and deservèd death.

North. My guilt be on my head, and there an end.
Take leave, and part; for you must part forthwith.

K. Rich. Doubly divorc'd! — Bad men, ye violate
A twofold marriage, — 'twixt my crown and me,
And then betwixt me and my married wife. —
Let me unkiss the oath 'twixt thee and me;
And yet not so, for with a kiss 'twas made. —
Part us, Northumberland; I towards the north,
Where shivering cold and sickness pine the clime;
My wife to France, — from whence, set forth in pomp,
She came adornèd hither like sweet May,
Sent back like Hallowmas or short'st of day.

Queen. And must we be divided? must we part?
K. Rich. Ay, hand from hand, my love, and heart from heart.
Queen. Banish us both, and send the king with me.
North. That were some love, but little policy.
Queen. Then whither he goes, thither let me go.
K. Rich. So two, together weeping, make one woe.

Weep thou for me in France, I for thee here;
Better far off than, near, be ne'er the near.
Go, count thy way with sighs; I, mine with groans.

Queen. So longest way shall have the longest moans.

K. Rich. Twice for one step I'll groan, the way being short,
And piece the way out with a heavy heart.
Come, come, in wooing sorrow let's be brief,
Since, wedding it, there is such length in grief:
One kiss shall stop our mouths, and dumbly part;
Thus give I mine, and thus take I thy heart. [*They kiss.*

Queen. Give me mine own again; 'twere no good part
To take on me to keep and kill thy heart. [*They kiss again.*
So, now I have mine own again, be gone,
That I may strive to kill it with a groan.

K. Rich. We make woe wanton with this fond delay:
Once more, adieu; the rest let sorrow say. [*Exeunt.*

SCENE II. *The same. A room in the* Duke of York's *palace.*

Enter YORK *and his* Duchess.

Duch. My lord, you told me you would tell the rest,
When weeping made you break the story off
Of our two cousins coming into London.

York. Where did I leave?

Duch. At that sad stop, my lord,
Where rude misgovern'd hands from window-tops
Threw dust and rubbish on King Richard's head.

York. Then, as I said, the duke, great Bolingbroke,—
Mounted upon a hot and fiery steed,
Which his aspiring rider seem'd to know,—
With slow but stately pace kept on his course,
While all tongues cried "God save thee, Bolingbroke!"
You would have thought the very windows spake,
So many greedy looks of young and old
Through casements darted their desiring eyes
Upon his visage; and that all the walls
With painted imagery had said at once,

"Jesu preserve thee! welcome, Bolingbroke!"
Whilst he, from one side to the other turning,
Bareheaded, lower than his proud steed's neck,
Bespake them thus, — "I thank you, countrymen:"
And thus still doing, thus he pass'd along.

    Duch. Alas, poor Richard! where rode he the whilst?
    York. As in a theatre, the eyes of men,
After a well-grac'd actor leaves the stage,
Are idly bent on him that enters next,
Thinking his prattle to be tedious;
Even so, or with much more contempt, men's eyes
Did scowl on Richard; no man cried, "God save him!"
No joyful tongue gave him his welcome home:
But dust was thrown upon his sacred head;
Which with such gentle sorrow he shook off, —
His face still combating with tears and smiles,
The badges of his grief and patience, —
That had not God, for some strong purpose, steel'd
The hearts of men, they must perforce have melted,
And barbarism itself have pitied him.
But heaven hath a hand in these events,
To whose high will we bow our calm contents.
To Bolingbroke are we sworn subjects now,
Whose state and honour I for aye allow.

    Duch. Here comes my son Aumerle.
    York.   Aumerle that was;
But that is lost for being Richard's friend,
And, madam, you must call him Rutland now:
I am in parliament pledge for his truth
And lasting fealty to the new-made king.

                Enter AUMERLE.

    Duch. Welcome, my son: who are the violets now
That strew the green lap of the new-come spring?
    Aum. Madam, I know not, nor I greatly care not:
God knows I had as lief be none as one.
    York. Well, bear you well in this new spring of time,

Lest you be cropp'd before you come to prime.
What news from Oxford? hold those justs and triumphs?
  Aum. For aught I know, my lord, they do.
  York. You will be there, I know.
  Aum. If God prevent it not, I purpose so.
  York. What seal is that that hangs without thy bosom?
Yea, look'st thou pale, sir? let me see the writing.
  Aum. My lord, 'tis nothing.
  York.   No matter, then, who sees it:
I will be satisfied; let me see the writing.
  Aum. I do beseech your grace to pardon me:
It is a matter of small consequence,
Which for some reasons I would not have seen.
  York. Which for some reasons, sir, I mean to see.
I fear, I fear,—
  Duch.   What should you fear? It is
Nothing but some bond that he's enter'd into
For gay apparel 'gainst the triumph-day.
  York. Bound to himself! what doth he with a bond
That he is bound to? Wife, thou art a fool.—
Boy, let me see the writing.
  Aum. Beseech you, pardon me; I may not show it.
  York. I will be satisfied: let me see 't, I say.
                              [*Snatches it, and reads.*
Treason! foul treason!— Villain! traitor! slave!
  Duch. What's the matter, my lord?
  York. Ho! who's within there? ho!

Enter a Servant.

                              Saddle my horse.—
God for his mercy, what treachery is here!
  Duch. Why, what is't, my lord?
  York. Give me my boots, I say; saddle my horse.—
Now, by mine honour, by my life, my troth, [*Exit Servant.*
I will appeach the villain.
  Duch.   What's the matter?
  York. Peace, foolish woman.

Duch. I will not peace. — What is the matter, son?
Aum. Good mother, be content; it is no more
Than my poor life must answer.
Duch.   Thy life answer!
York. Bring me my boots: — I will unto the king.

Re-enter Servant *with boots.*

Duch. Strike him, Aumerle. — Poor boy, thou art amaz'd. —
[*To the Servant*] Hence, villain! never more come in my sight.
York. Give me my boots, I say.   [*Exit Servant.*
Duch. Why, York, what wilt thou do?
Wilt thou not hide the trespass of thine own?
Have we more sons? or are we like to have?
Is not my teeming date drunk up with time?
And wilt thou pluck my fair son from mine age,
And rob me of a happy mother's name?
Is he not like thee? is he not thine own?
York. Thou fond mad woman,
Wilt thou conceal this dark conspiracy?
A dozen of them here have ta'en the sacrament,
And interchangeably set down their hands,
To kill the king at Oxford.
Duch.   He shall be none;
We'll keep him here: then what is that to him?
York. Away, fond woman! were he twenty times
My son, I would appeach him.
Duch.   Hadst thou groan'd for him
As I have done, thou'dst be more pitiful.
But now I know thy mind; thou dost suspect
That I have been disloyal to thy bed,
And that he is a bastard, not thy son:
Sweet York, sweet husband, be not of that mind:
He is as like thee as a man may be,
Not like to me, nor any of my kin,
And yet I love him.
York.   Make way, unruly woman!   [*Exit.*
Duch. After, Aumerle! mount thee upon his horse;

Spur post, and get before him to the king,
And beg thy pardon ere he do accuse thee.
I'll not be long behind; though I be old,
I doubt not but to ride as fast as York;
And never will I rise up from the ground
Till Bolingbroke have pardon'd thee. Away, be gone! [*Exeunt.*

Scene III. *Windsor. A room in the castle.*

Enter Bolingbroke *as King*, Percy, *and other* Lords.

Boling. Can no man tell of my unthrifty son?
'Tis full three months since I did see him last: —
If any plague hang over us, 'tis he.
I would to God, my lords, he might be found:
Inquire at London, 'mongst the taverns there,
For there, they say, he daily doth frequent,
With unrestrained loose companions, —
Even such, they say, as stand in narrow lanes,
And beat our watch, and rob our passengers;
While he, young wanton and effeminate boy,
Takes on the point of honour to support
So dissolute a crew.

Percy. My lord, some two days since I saw the prince
And told him of those triumphs held at Oxford.

Boling. And what said the gallant?

Percy. His answer was, — he would unto the stews,
And from the common'st creature pluck a glove,
And wear it as a favour; and with that
He would unhorse the lustiest challenger.

Boling. As dissolute as desperate; yet through both
I see some sparkles of a better hope,
Which elder days may happily bring forth. —
But who comes here?

Enter Aumerle, *hastily.*

Aum. Where is the king?
Boling. What means
Our cousin, that he stares and looks so wildly?

Aum. God save your grace! I do beseech your majesty.
To have some conference with your grace alone.
   Boling. Withdraw yourselves, and leave us here alone.
                                        [*Exeunt Percy and Lords.*
What is the matter with our cousin now?
   Aum. For ever may my knees grow to the earth, [*Kneels.*
My tongue cleave to the roof within my mouth,
Unless a pardon ere I'rise or speak.
   Boling. Intended or committed was this fault?
If on the first, how heinous e'er it be,
To win thy after-love I pardon thee.
   Aum. Then give me leave that I may turn the key,
That no man enter till my tale be done.
   Boling. Have thy desire.   [*Aumerle locks the door.*
   York. [*within*] My liege, beware; look to thyself;
Thou hast a traitor in thy presence there.
   Boling. Villain, I'll make thee safe.   [*Drawing.*
   Aum. Stay thy revengeful hand;
Thou hast no cause to fear.
   York. [*within*] Open the door, secure, foolhardy king:
Shall I, for love, speak treason to thy face?
Open the door, or I will break it open.
               [*Bolingbroke unlocks the door, and afterwards
                          locks it again.*

                     Enter YORK.

   Boling. What is the matter, uncle? speak;
Recover breath; tell us how near is danger,
That we may arm us to encounter it.
   York. Peruse this writing here, and thou shalt know
The treason that my haste forbids me show.
   Aum. Remember, as thou read'st, thy promise pass'd:
I do repent me; read not my name there;
My heart is not confederate with my hand.
   York. 'Twas, villain, ere thy hand did set it down. —
I tore it from the traitor's bosom, king;
Fear, and not love, begets his penitence:

Forget to pity him, lest thy pity prove
A serpent that will sting thee to the heart.
　Boling. O heinous, strong, and bold conspiracy! —
O loyal father of a treacherous son!
Thou sheer, immaculate, and silver fountain,
From whence this stream through muddy passages
Hath held his current, and defil'd himself!
Thy overflow of good converts to bad;
And thy abundant goodness shall excuse
This deadly blot in thy digressing son.
　York. So shall my virtue be his vice's bawd;
And he shall spend mine honour with his shame,
As thriftless sons their scraping fathers' gold.
Mine honour lives when his dishonour dies,
Or my sham'd life in his dishonour lies:
Thou kill'st me in his life; giving him breath,
The traitor lives, the true man's put to death.
　Duch. [*within*] What ho, my liege! for God's sake, let me in.
　Boling. What shrill-voic'd suppliant makes this eager cry?
　Duch. [*within*] A woman, and thy aunt, great king; 'tis I.
Speak with me, pity me, open the door:
A beggar begs that never begg'd before.
　Boling. Our scene is alter'd from a serious thing,
And now chang'd to "The Beggar and the King." —
My dangerous cousin, let your mother in:
I know she's come to pray for your foul sin.
　　　　　　　　　　[*Aumerle unlocks the door.*
　York. If thou do pardon, whosoever pray,
More sins, for this forgiveness, prosper may.
This fester'd joint cut off, the rest rest sound;
This let alone will all the rest confound.

　　　　　　Enter Duchess.

　Duch. O king, believe not this hard-hearted man!
Love loving not itself, none other can.
　York. Thou frantic woman, what dost thou make here?
Shall thy old dugs once more a traitor rear?

Duch. Sweet York, be patient. — Hear me, gentle liege.
[*Kneels.*

Boling. Rise up, good aunt.
Duch. Not yet, I thee beseech:
For ever will I walk upon my knees,
And never see day that the happy sees,
Till thou give joy; until thou bid me joy,
By pardoning Rutland, my transgressing boy.
 Aum. Unto my mother's prayers I bend my knee. [*Kneels.*
 York. Against them both my true joints bended be.
[*Kneels.*
Ill mayst thou thrive, if thou grant any grace!
 Duch. Pleads he in earnest? look upon his face;
His eyes do drop no tears, his prayers are jest;
His words come from his mouth, ours from our breast:
He prays but faintly, and would be denied;
We pray with heart and soul, and all beside:
His weary joints would gladly rise, I know;
Our knees shall kneel till to the ground they grow:
His prayers are full of false hypocrisy;
Ours of true zeal and deep integrity.
Our prayers do out-pray his; then let them have
That mercy which true prayers ought to have.
 Boling. Good aunt, stand up.
 Duch. Nay, do not say "stand up;"
But "pardon" first, and afterwards "stand up."
An if I were thy nurse, thy tongue to teach,
"Pardon" should be the first word of thy speech.
I never long'd to hear a word till now;
Say "pardon," king; let pity teach thee how:
The word is short, but not so short as sweet;
No word like "pardon" for kings' mouths so meet.
 York. Speak it in French, king; say, *pardonnez-moi.*
 Duch. Dost thou teach pardon pardon to destroy?
Ah, my sour husband, my hard-hearted lord,
That sett'st the word itself against the word! —
Speak "pardon" as 'tis current in our land;

The chopping French we do not understand.
Thine eye begins to speak, set thy tongue there:
Or in thy piteous heart plant thou thine ear;
That hearing how our plaints and prayers do pierce,
Pity may move thee "pardon" to rehearse.

   Boling. Good aunt, stand up.
   Duch.   I do not sue to stand;
Pardon is all the suit I have in hand.
   Boling. I pardon him, as God shall pardon me.
   Duch. O happy vantage of a kneeling knee!
Yet am I sick for fear: speak it again;
Twice saying "pardon" doth not pardon twain,
But makes one pardon strong.
   Boling.   With all my heart
I pardon him.
   Duch.   A god on earth thou art.
   Boling. But for our trusty brother-in-law, and th' abbot,
With all the rest of that consorted crew,
Destruction straight shall dog them at the heels. —
Good uncle, help to order several powers
To Oxford, or where'er these traitors are:
They shall not live within this world, I swear
But I will have them, if I once know where.
Uncle, farewell: — and, cousin mine, adieu:
Your mother well hath pray'd, and prove you true.
   Duch. Come, my old son: — I pray God make thee new.
                                                   [*Exeunt.*

      SCENE IV. *Another room in the same.*

     Enter Sir PIERCE of EXTON *and a Servant.*
   Exton. Didst thou not mark the king, what words he
            spake, —
"Have I no friend will rid me of this living fear?"
Was it not so?
   Serv.   Those were his very words.
   Exton. "Have I no friend?" quoth he: he spake it twice,
And urg'd it twice together, — did he not?

Serv. He did.

Exton. And speaking it, he wistly look'd on me;
As who should say, — I would thou wert the man
That would divorce this terror from my heart, —
Meaning the king at Pomfret. Come, let's go:
I am the king's friend, and will rid his foe. [*Exeunt.*

Scene V. *Pomfret. The dungeon of the castle.*

Enter King Richard.

K. Rich. I have been studying how I may compare
This prison where I live unto the world:
And, for because the world is populous,
And here is not a creature but myself,
I cannot do it; — yet I'll hammer 't out.
My brain I'll prove the female to my soul,
My soul the father: and these two beget
A generation of still-breeding thoughts,
And these same thoughts people this little world;
In humours like the people of this world,
For no thought is contented. The better sort, —
As thoughts of things divine, — are intermix'd
With scruples, and do set the word itself
Against the word:
As thus, "Come, little ones;" and then again,
"It is as hard to come as for a camel
To thread the postern of a small needl's eye."
Thoughts tending to ambition, they do plot
Unlikely wonders; how these vain weak nails
May tear a passage through the flinty ribs
Of this hard world, my ragged prison-walls;
And, for they cannot, die in their own pride.
Thoughts tending to content flatter themselves
That they are not the first of fortune's slaves,
Nor shall not be the last; like silly beggars,
Who, sitting in the stocks, refuge their shame,
That many have, and others must sit there;

And in this thought they find a kind of ease,
Bearing their own misfortune on the back
Of such as have before endur'd the like.
Thus play I, in one person, many people,
And none contented: sometimes am I king;
Then treason makes me wish myself a beggar,
And so I am: then crushing penury
Persuades me I was better when a king;
Then am I king'd again: and by and by
Think that I am unking'd by Bolingbroke,
And straight am nothing: — but whate'er I am,
Nor I, nor any man that but man is,
With nothing shall be pleas'd, till he be eas'd
With being nothing. — Music do I hear? [*Music.*
Ha, ha! keep time: — how sour sweet music is,
When time is broke and no proportion kept!
So is it in the music of men's lives.
And here have I the daintiness of ear
To check time broke in a disorder'd string;
But, for the concord of my state and time,
Had not an ear to hear my true time broke.
I wasted time, and now doth time waste me;
For now hath time made me his numbering clock:
My thoughts are minutes; and with sighs they jar
Their watches to mine eyes, the outward watch,
Whereto my finger, like a dial's point,
Is pointing still, in cleansing them from tears:
Now, sir, the sounds that tell what hour it is,
Are clamorous groans, that strike upon my heart,
Which is the bell: so sighs and tears and groans
Show minutes, times, and hours: — but my time
Runs posting on in Bolingbroke's proud joy,
While I stand fooling here, his Jack o' the clock.
This music mads me; let it sound no more;
For though it have holp madmen to their wits,
In me it seems it will make wise men mad.
Yet, blessing on his heart that gives it me!

For 'tis a sign of love; and love to Richard
Is a strange brooch in this all-hating world.

Enter Groom.

Groom. Hail, royal prince!
K. Rich. Thanks, noble peer;
The cheapest of us is ten groats too dear.
What art thou? and how com'st thou hither now,
Where no man ever comes, but that sad dog
That brings me food to make misfortune live?

Groom. I was a poor groom of thy stable, king,
When thou wert king; who, travelling towards York,
With much ado at length have gotten leave
To look upon my sometimes master's face.
O, how it yearn'd my heart, when I beheld,
In London streets, that coronation-day,
When Bolingbroke rode on roan Barbary, —
That horse that thou so often hast bestrid,
That horse that I so carefully have dress'd!

K. Rich. Rode he on Barbary? Tell me, gentle friend,
How went he under him?

Groom. So proud as if he had disdain'd the ground.

K. Rich. So proud that Bolingbroke was on his back!
That jade hath eat bread from my royal hand;
This hand hath made him proud with clapping him.
Would he not stumble? would he not fall down, —
Since pride must have a fall, — and break the neck
Of that proud man that did usurp his back?
Forgiveness, horse! why do I rail on thee,
Since thou, created to be aw'd by man,
Wast born to bear? I was not made a horse;
And yet I bear a burden like an ass,
Spur-gall'd and tir'd by jauncing Bolingbroke.

Enter Keeper, *with a dish.*

Keep. [*to the Groom*] Fellow, give place; here is no longer
   stay.
K. Rich. If thou love me, 'tis time thou wert away.

Groom. What my tongue dares not, that my heart shall
    say.   *[Exit.*
Keep. My lord, will't please you to fall to?
K. Rich. Taste of it first, as thou art wont to do.
Keep. My lord, I dare not. Sir Pierce of Exton,
Who late came from the king, commands the contrary.
  K. Rich. The devil take Henry of Lancaster and thee!
Patience is stale, and I am weary of it.   *[Beats the Keeper.*
  Keep. Help, help, help!

Enter Sir Pierce *of* Exton *and Servants, armed.*

  K. Rich. How now! what means death in this rude assault?
Villain, thy own hand yields thy death's instrument.
        [Snatching a weapon, and killing a Servant.
Go thou, and fill another room in hell.
        [He kills another Servant. Then Exton
        strikes him down.
That hand shall burn in never-quenching fire
That staggers thus my person. — Exton, thy fierce hand
Hath with the king's blood stain'd the king's own land.
Mount, mount, my soul! thy seat is up on high;
Whilst my gross flesh sinks downward, here to die.   *[Dies.*
  Exton. As full of valour as of royal blood:
Both have I spilt; — O, would the deed were good!
For now the devil, that told me I did well,
Says that this deed is chronicled in hell.
This dead king to the living king I'll bear: —
Take hence the rest, and give them burial here.   *[Exeunt.*

    Scene VI. *Windsor. A room in the castle.*

Flourish. Enter Bolingbroke *as King,* York, *Lords, and*
        Attendants.

  Boling. Kind uncle York, the latest news we hear
Is that the rebels have consum'd with fire
Our town of Ciceter in Glostershire;
But whether they be ta'en or slain we hear not.

Enter NORTHUMBERLAND.

Welcome, my lord: what is the news?
 North.   First, to
Thy sacred state wish I all happiness.
The next news is, I have to London sent
The heads of Salisbury, Spencer, Blunt, and Kent:
The manner of their taking may appear
At large discoursed in this paper here. [*Presenting a paper.*
 Boling. We thank thee, gentle Percy, for thy pains;
And to thy worth will add right worthy gains.

Enter FITZWATER.

 Fitz. My lord, I have from Oxford sent to London
The heads of Brocas and Sir Bennet Seely,
Two of the dangerous consorted traitors
That sought at Oxford thy dire overthrow.
 Boling. Thy pains, Fitzwater, shall not be forgot;
Right noble is thy merit, well I wot.

Enter PERCY, *with the* Bishop of Carlisle.

 Percy. The grand conspirator, Abbot of Westminster,
With clog of conscience and sour melancholy,
Hath yielded up his body to the grave;
But here is Carlisle living, to abide
Thy kingly doom and sentence of his pride.
 Boling. Carlisle, this is your doom: —
Choose out some secret place, some reverend room,
More than thou hast, and with it joy thy life;
So, as thou liv'st in peace, die free from strife:
For though mine enemy thou hast ever been,
High sparks of honour in thee have I seen

Enter Sir PIERCE of EXTON, *with* Attendants *bearing a coffin.*

 Exton. Great king, within this coffin I present
Thy buried fear: herein all breathless lies
The mightiest of thy greatest enemies,
Richard of Bourdeaux, by me hither brought.
 Boling. Exton, I thank thee not; for thou hast wrought

A deed of slander, with thy fatal hand,
Upon my head and all this famous land.
    Exton. From your own mouth, my lord, did I this deed.
    Boling. They love not poison that do poison need,
Nor do I thee: though I did wish him dead,
I hate the murderer, love him murderèd.
The guilt of conscience take thou for thy labour,
But neither my good word nor princely favour:
With Cain go wander through the shades of night,
And never show thy head by day nor light. —
Lords, I protest, my soul is full of woe
That blood should sprinkle me to make me grow:
Come, mourn with me for that I do lament,
And put on sullen black incontinent:
I'll make a voyage to the Holy Land,
To wash this blood off from my guilty hand: —
March sadly after; grace my mournings here,
In weeping after this untimely bier.   [*Exeunt.*

PRINTING OFFICE OF THE PUBLISHER.

www.ingramcontent.com/pod-product-compliance
Lightning Source LLC
Chambersburg PA
CBHW021416300426
44114CB00010B/520